SAVING THE WORLD?

From the 1950s, tens of thousands of well-meaning Westerners left their homes to volunteer in distant corners of the globe. Aflame with optimism, they set out to save the world, but their actions were invariably intertwined with decolonization, globalization and the Cold War. Closely exploring British, American and Australian programs, Agnieszka Sobocinska situates Western volunteers at the heart of the "humanitarian-development complex." This nexus of governments, NGOs, private corporations and public opinion encouraged continuous and accelerating intervention in the Global South from the 1950s. Volunteers attracted a great deal of support in their home countries. But critics across the Global South protested that volunteers put an attractive face on neocolonial power and extended the logic of intervention embedded in the global system of international development. *Saving the World?* brings together a wide range of sources to construct a rich narrative of the meeting between Global North and Global South.

AGNIESZKA SOBOCINSKA is Senior Lecturer in the School of Philosophical, Historical and International Studies at Monash University, Australia.

Global and International History

Series Editors

Erez Manela, *Harvard University*
Heather Streets-Salter, *Northeastern University*

The Global and International History series seeks to highlight and explore the convergences between the new International History and the new World History. Its editors are interested in approaches that mix traditional units of analysis such as civilizations, nations and states with other concepts such as transnationalism, diasporas and international institutions.

Titles in the Series

Agnieszka Sobocinska, *Saving the World? Western Volunteers and the Rise of the Humanitarian-Development Complex*

Kirwin R. Shaffer, *Anarchists of the Caribbean: Countercultural Politics and Transnational Networks in the Age of US Expansion*

Stephen J. Macekura and Erez Manela, *The Development Century: A Global History*

Amanda Kay McVety, *The Rinderpest Campaigns: A Virus, Its Vaccines, and Global Development in the Twentieth Century*

Michele L. Louro, *Comrades against Imperialism*

Antoine Acker, *Volkswagen in the Amazon: The Tragedy of Global Development in Modern Brazil*

Christopher R. W. Dietrich, *Oil Revolution: Anti-Colonial Elites, Sovereign Rights, and the Economic Culture of Decolonization*

Nathan J. Citino, *Envisioning the Arab Future: Modernization in U.S.-Arab Relations, 1945–1967*

Stefan Rinke, *Latin America and the First World War*

Timothy Nunan, *Humanitarian Invasion: Global Development in Cold War Afghanistan*

Michael Goebel, *Anti-Imperial Metropolis: Interwar Paris and the Seeds of Third World Nationalism*

Stephen J. Macekura, *Of Limits and Growth: The Rise of Global Sustainable Development in the Twentieth Century*

SAVING THE WORLD?

Western Volunteers and the Rise of the Humanitarian-Development Complex

AGNIESZKA SOBOCINSKA
Monash University, Victoria

Shaftesbury Road, Cambridge CB2 8EA, United Kingdom

One Liberty Plaza, 20th Floor, New York, NY 10006, USA

477 Williamstown Road, Port Melbourne, VIC 3207, Australia

314–321, 3rd Floor, Plot 3, Splendor Forum, Jasola District Centre, New Delhi – 110025, India

103 Penang Road, #05–06/07, Visioncrest Commercial, Singapore 238467

Cambridge University Press is part of Cambridge University Press & Assessment, a department of the University of Cambridge.

We share the University's mission to contribute to society through the pursuit of education, learning and research at the highest international levels of excellence.

www.cambridge.org
Information on this title: www.cambridge.org/9781108746885

DOI: 10.1017/9781108784320

First published 2021
First paperback edition 2022

A catalogue record for this publication is available from the British Library

ISBN 978-1-108-47813-7 Hardback
ISBN 978-1-108-74688-5 Paperback

CONTENTS

FIGURES

ACKNOWLEDGMENTS

This book grew out of a project funded by a Discovery Early Career Research Award (DE160100076) awarded by the Australian Research Council. My first thanks therefore go to the ARC: a large project like this, demanding research on multiple continents, would simply not have been possible without the time and funding offered by a DECRA. Christina Twomey and Clare Corbould helped me conceptualize this project for a DECRA application; for this I am eternally grateful.

I became interested in the history of development volunteering while writing my first book on Australian travel to Asia, but the idea for a global history came during a period of sabbatical leave taken at the Center for Australian, New Zealand & Pacific Studies within the Walsh School of Foreign Service at Georgetown University. My thanks to Alan Tidwell for illuminating discussions at an early stage of this research. A good proportion of the Australian research was conducted during a National Library Fellowship at the National Library of Australia. I would like to acknowledge the staff of this wonderful institution for their enthusiasm and patience as I worked my way through several extensive collections. Much of the final manuscript was written during a fellowship at the Whitney and Betty MacMillan Center for International and Area Studies at Yale University. I am forever grateful to Dani Botsman and Crystal Feimster for making my stay in New Haven both possible and exceedingly comfortable.

Many librarians and archivists helped make research for this book possible. Special thanks, however, must go to Gerry McAleney, who among other things looks after VSO's records at the headquarters in outer London. He knows where the boxes are buried and he was kind enough to dig them out for me. I am also grateful to the former volunteers and others who made their time and records available to me, including Ailsa Zainu'ddin, Don Anderson, Jeff Miles, Lindsey Cleland and Sylvia Cleland.

Series editors Erez Manela and Heather Streets-Salter have been unflagging sources of support and generous feedback as I prepared this manuscript. At Cambridge University Press, I was lucky to work with two legendary commissioning editors, Debbie Gershenowitz and Lucy Rhymer. Both were expert and supportive; I am very grateful for their faith in this project. I am also grateful to editorial assistants Rachel Blaifeder and Emily Sharp, and copy editor Judith Harvey, for their diligent and generous assistance. Feedback provided by two anonymous reviewers was exceedingly helpful in the final stages of writing. The book's index was expertly compiled by Geraldine Suter, whose seemingly limitless patience I greatly admire.

Many of my wonderful colleagues at Monash read various drafts and provided thoughtful feedback. I am particularly grateful to Adam Clulow, Daniella Doron, Pierre Fuller, Guy Geltner, Charlotte Greenhalgh, Michael Hau, Dan Heller, Julie Kalman, Paula Michaels, Kate Murphy, Seamus O'Hanlon, Susie Protschky, Noah Shenker, David Slucki, Joshua Specht and Christina Twomey for comments and ideas that markedly improved this book. Special thanks must go to Ruth Morgan, who almost managed to keep me to an intricate set of writing deadlines spanning the best part of two years, and Nick Ferns for, among other things, making sense of material viewed in negative on a superannuated microfiche machine.

In the course of researching and writing this book I've had two children, Maja and Feliks. They have made life much more joyful, but the logistics more complicated. Completing this book would simply not have been possible without the love and daily practical support of my partner, Jonathan Stoddart. Jonathan has taken multiple setbacks to his career so that I could pursue mine, not to mention the months he spent looking after an unruly and/or jetlagged toddler as I worked in one archive or another. I wish every working woman had a partner as supportive, but I realize that this is not the case and I am very lucky indeed.

ABBREVIATIONS

ABC – American Broadcasting Company
ACFID – Australian Council for International Development
AVA – Australian Volunteers Abroad
BA – Bachelor of Arts
CIA – Central Intelligence Agency (US)
CMS – Church Mission Society
CPP – Convention People's Party (Ghana)
CUSO – Canadian University Service Overseas
ECOSOC – United Nations Economic and Social Council
FFHC – Freedom from Hunger Campaign
GANEFO – Games of the New Emerging Forces
GMKI – *Gerakan Mahasiswa Kristen Indonesia* (Indonesian Student Christian Movement)
GVSO – Graduate Voluntary Service Overseas
JFKL – John F. Kennedy Presidential Library and Museum
LSE – London School of Economics Women's Library
NAA – National Archives of Australia
NACP – National Archives at College Park (US)
NATO – North Atlantic Treaty Organization
NCNC – National Council of Nigeria and the Cameroons (political party)
NGO – Non-Governmental Organization
NIEO – New International Economic Order
NLA – National Library of Australia
NLF – National Liberation Front (Vietnam)
PCV – Peace Corps Volunteer
PGP – *Peraturan Gaji Pegawai Negeri Republik Indonesia 1948* (Civil Service Salary Scale)
PKI – *Partai Komunis Indonesia* (Indonesian Communist Party)
RPCV – Returned Peace Corps Volunteer
RVA – Returned Volunteer Action
SCM – Student Christian Movement
SEATO – Southeast Asia Treaty Organization
TNA – The National Archives (UK)

UMNO – United Malays National Organisation (political party)
UN – United Nations
UNCTAD – United Nations Conference on Trade and Development
UNESCO – United Nations Educational, Scientific and Cultural Organization
UNHCR – United Nations High Commissioner for Refugees
UNICEF – United Nations Children's Fund
UNTAA – United Nations Technical Assistance Administration
UNV – United Nations Volunteers
USAID – United States Agency for International Development
USIA – United States Information Agency
VGS – Volunteer Graduate Scheme
VISTA – Volunteers in Service to America
VSO – Voluntary Service Overseas
WBC – Westinghouse Broadcasting Company
YDL – Yale University Divinity School Library

INTRODUCTION

Western Volunteers and the Rise of the Humanitarian-Development Complex

In September 1964, eighteen-year-old Helen Rosenberg departed the English seaside town of Worthing to take up a volunteer posting in the township of Abeokuta, some fifty miles north of Lagos in Nigeria. Helen had joined Voluntary Service Overseas (commonly known by its abbreviation, VSO) immediately after high school; now she was to be Senior Science Teacher at Abeokuta Girls' Grammar School. Helen's acceptance into VSO had caused great excitement at home. Not only was volunteering abroad "obviously glamorous and exotic," the London *Daily Mail* enthused, but "few ... can fail to be inspired by what our young men and women are doing in all parts of the world."[1]

Although she had high hopes, Helen found the reality of working in Nigeria disheartening. Her students were habitually unresponsive and occasionally defiant; after her first term, Helen admitted she was "not quite sure what I have achieved."[2] She had applied for "the opportunity to spend a year abroad helping the people and so obtaining an understanding of the people, their ways and their problems."[3] But, on arrival, Helen's relations with the broader community quickly became strained. "I feel somewhat misjudged," she wrote. "'They' don't understand I mutter but inwardly I admit that 'they' possibly do!"[4] Some of the tension related to her lifestyle and relationships. Volunteer stipends went a long way in Nigeria. Helen shared a large, comfortable bungalow with a Peace Corps volunteer, and the pair hired an Igbo housekeeper to cook and clean for them, so that "we live like kings."[5] Although surrounded by Nigerians, Helen socialized almost exclusively with other Westerners. Even a relatively small town like Abeokuta was home to a significant volunteer population: in 1964 there were eight volunteers from Britain's VSO, nine from the United States Peace Corps and a further handful from Australia, Canada and several European nations. Altogether, Helen was

[1] Peter Lewis, "Features: Youth in Action," *Daily Mail*, October 30, 1963, p. 6; "Wasted Youth," *Daily Mail*, November 1, 1963.

[2] Helen Rosenberg to Mr. Haig, October 14, 1964, VSO Archive, microfiche files.

[3] Application: Helen Rosenberg, February 28, 1964, VSO Archive, microfiche files.

[4] Helen Rosenberg to Mr. Haig, July 19, 1965, VSO Archive, microfiche files.

[5] Helen Rosenberg to Mr. Haig, September 22, 1964, VSO Archive, microfiche files.

one of some 800 Western volunteers in Nigeria, and this posed what she called the "Expatriate Dilemma."[6] Rather than building friendships with Nigerians, her weekends and holidays were taken up by visits and parties with other volunteers. Many Nigerians were bemused by the day-to-day behavior of volunteers in their midst. Some thought they were benign, but others bristled at the "smugness and mediocrity" of volunteers who were untrained, inexperienced and yet somehow overconfident.[7] As we shall see, at a highpoint of decolonization, Nigerian critics joined others across the Third World to declare the influx of Western volunteers a virulent form of neocolonialism.

During the 1950s and 1960s, tens of thousands of well-meaning Westerners just like Helen Rosenberg left their homes to volunteer in distant corners of the globe. Aflame with optimism, they set out to save the world, but their actions were invariably intertwined with the overlapping contexts of decolonization, globalization and the Cold War. This book examines three of the earliest and most influential development volunteering programs from their origins until the late 1970s: Australia's Volunteer Graduate Scheme, founded in 1950; Britain's VSO, established in 1958; and the United States Peace Corps, launched by President Kennedy in 1961. These programs had different origins and there were institutional differences. But they all aimed to contribute to the economic and social modernization of "underdeveloped" nations across Asia, Africa and Latin America, they were all underwritten by national governments and their volunteers did similar work, often in the same places. Rather than viewing development volunteer programs as manifestations of national characteristics or domestic political trends, this book explores development volunteering as a phenomenon that played out on a global scale.

A wider scope brings overarching patterns into view. In this book I situate Western volunteers at the heart of a "humanitarian-development complex," defined here as a nexus of governments, NGOs, private corporations and public opinion that encouraged continuous and accelerating intervention in the Global South from the 1950s. Medical anthropologist Vinh-Kim Nguyen identified a "humanitarian/development complex" in relation to the AIDS industry of the early twenty-first century.[8] I extend the term's usage beyond public health and situate its origins in an earlier period – the "development age" of the 1950s, 1960s and 1970s.[9] The deployment of volunteers like Helen Rosenberg was enabled by an extraordinary assemblage of moral and financial support across the West. Development volunteering agencies were backed by

6 Helen Rosenberg to Mr. Haig, December 15, 1964, VSO Archive, microfiche files.

7 "Opinion: American Champions," *Daily Express* (Lagos), October 14, 1961, p. 4.

8 Vinh-Kim Nguyen, "Antiretroviral Globalism, Biopolitics and Therapeutic Citizenship," in *Global Assemblages: Technology, Politics and Ethics as Anthropological Problems*, ed. Aihwa Ong and Stephen Collier, pp. 124–44 (Oxford: Blackwell, 2005).

9 Gilbert Rist, *The History of Development: From Western Origins to Global Faith* (New York: Zed Books, 2002), p. 71.

governments, NGOs and private corporations. They also evoked the support of civic and religious groups as well as vast swathes of public support. No international development program involved more people than development volunteering, and few humanitarian campaigns reached an audience as wide. I argue that the unusually broad base of material and moral support for development volunteering played a significant role in forging the near-consensus that "underdeveloped" nations required Western intervention including the provision of funds and technical expertise, and extending to broad and ill-defined social, cultural and psychological assistance. The humanitarian-development complex extended beyond development volunteering. In subsequent decades it grew to encompass many aspects of national, multilateral and non-governmental development agencies as well as public-facing humanitarian campaigns. But development volunteering was central to its rise.

Volunteering organizations played a key role in the rise of the humanitarian-development complex by blurring the boundaries between state and non-state action in international relations. The Volunteer Graduate Scheme, VSO and the Peace Corps were all dependent on state funding, but they also relied on civic and public support for further donations, political leverage and, most importantly, as the source of volunteers. Development volunteering demanded ordinary people leave the comforts of home to spend one, two or more years in previously unfamiliar reaches of the Global South. By the end of the 1960s, hundreds of thousands of Australians, Britons and Americans had enthusiastically responded to this call. Individual motivations were multiple and often overlapping, but, as we shall see, idealism and a genuine desire to help others were prominent among them. Through development volunteering, the desire to assist distant Others became enmeshed with the expanding structures of State, and the line between interpersonal and international relations became blurred.

Volunteers collapsed the distinction between international development and humanitarianism, and employed an emotional and moral lexicon in support of projects enmeshed in state, economic and cultural power. In increasingly sophisticated public relations and media campaigns, volunteering agencies portrayed volunteers as altruistic humanitarians and as citizen diplomats building bridges across boundaries of race and culture. Western audiences loved it. One 1961 Gallup Poll found that more Americans knew about the Peace Corps than about the Twist, the dance craze then at the height of its popularity.[10] New programs sprang up across Europe and as far afield as Japan. As one observer noted, by the mid-1960s, "Volunteers were indisputably In."[11]

[10] George Gallup, "American 'Peace Corps' proposal wins broad approval from public," *The Washington Post*, February 1, 1961.

[11] Glyn Roberts, *Volunteers and Neo-Colonialism: An Inquiry into the Role of Foreign Volunteers in the Third World* (Manchester, UK: A. J. Wright & Sons, 1968), p. 20.

This publicity contributed to the rise of a popular humanitarian sensibility, focused on long-term development rather than emergency reconstruction, which grew in size and influence over coming decades.[12] Images of altruistic development produced in the West supported a logic of intervention, but took little account of – or even displaced – local politics in hundreds of cities and towns across Asia, Africa, Latin America, the Middle East and the Caribbean.[13]

Volunteers were typically well-intentioned, but good intentions can be misguided if recipients' wishes aren't taken into consideration. Development was a key priority for postcolonial states, and Western development assistance was actively desired and requested by governments of all political hues.[14] But development volunteering agencies were not always attentive to the desires and specific requests of recipient communities. Some volunteers were placed in jobs that urgently needed filling, especially in the immediate postcolonial period. But others were sent to expatriate-run, elite institutions, where colonial cultures and mores were perpetuated, both within and beyond formal colonialism. Still others were assigned vague roles in "community development," where they used their (Western-informed) initiative to determine locals' needs.[15] The largest number worked as teachers in schools across dozens of nations. In the immediate postcolonial period, it was hoped they would plug an acute shortage of teachers, but like Helen Rosenberg, many volunteers were inexperienced graduates fresh from high school or college. The benefits brought by untrained and underqualified volunteer teachers were often unclear, but effectiveness was rarely measured by organizations too busy finding new placements to properly monitor or evaluate the success of volunteers already in the field. Senior executives at the Volunteer Graduate Scheme, VSO and the Peace Corps routinely dismissed critical responses from recipient nations as Communist propaganda, or the grumblings of anti-colonial zealots. And so development volunteering continued apace, helping normalize a culture of foreign aid in which good intentions were considered sufficient to justify Western intervention across vast swathes of the globe.

[12] Kevin O'Sullivan, "Humanitarian Encounters: Biafra, NGOs and Imaginings of the Third World in Britain and Ireland, 1967–1970," *Journal of Genocide Research* 16, no. 2–3 (2014): 299–315; Andrew Jones, "Band Aid Revisited: Humanitarianism, Consumption and Philanthropy in the 1980s," *Contemporary British History* 31, no. 2 (2017): 189–209; Tehila Sasson, "In the Name of Humanity: Britain and the Rise of Global Humanitarianism" (PhD thesis, University of California, Berkeley, 2015); Tehila Sasson, "Milking the Third World? Humanitarianism, Capitalism, and the Moral Economy of the Nestle Boycott," *American Historical Review* 121, no. 4 (2016): 1196–224.

[13] James Ferguson, *The Anti-Politics Machine: 'Development', Depoliticization, and Bureaucratic Power in Lesotho* (Cambridge: Cambridge University Press, 1990).

[14] Sara Lorenzini, *Global Development: A Cold War History* (Princeton, NJ: Princeton University Press, 2019), esp. pp. 40–3.

[15] Daniel Immerwahr, *Thinking Small: The United States and the Lure of Community Development* (Cambridge, MA: Harvard University Press, 2015).

Where volunteers' good intentions drew enthusiastic praise at home, people in countries with recent colonial histories were just as likely to regard Western volunteers with caution, if not outright suspicion. Although some volunteers liked to imagine they were the first foreigners to arrive in untouched lands, the reality was that most African, Asian and Latin American nations had long histories of Western intervention. Abeokuta – to take just one example – had been founded in 1830 as a place of refuge from slave-hunters feeding the American market for bonded labor. British Baptist and Anglican missionaries had arrived in the 1840s, introducing the local Egba peoples to Western rhetoric of altruism and good intentions over a century before VSO and the Peace Corps.[16] The military arrived soon after. By the 1860s the Egba had had enough of British influence; over the following decades they tried to expel missionaries and traders, and organized protests against creeping taxes levied by the expanding British colonial state in Nigeria. The resistance continued into the 1940s, when the Abeokuta Women's Union staged a strike opposing further taxes imposed by the colonial government.[17] When she arrived in 1964, Helen Rosenberg was largely unaware of Abeokuta's long history of resistance against Western intervention. She regarded her students' impassivity as stubbornness, or worse, stupidity. But in reality, the Egba and other residents of Abeokuta were deploying strategies of resistance honed over decades.

Helen Rosenberg was disappointed by the underwhelming response of her Nigerian students and colleagues, but in fact she was lucky; other volunteers were directly accused of espionage or of trying to smuggle neocolonialism in the Trojan Horse of development assistance. Critics across the Global South protested that volunteers simply put an attractive face on neocolonial power and extended the logic of intervention embedded in the global system of international development. Simmering suspicions and a wealth of what we would now term micro-aggressions occasionally flared into anti-volunteer violence or protests. By the 1970s, some of these criticisms made their way back home, and radical anti-volunteering movements sprang up in Britain and the United States. And yet, every year brought more young volunteers eager to save the world, whether it wanted saving or not.

The problem of volunteers who were eager to help, but whose assistance was not necessarily desired, is revealing of broader failings within the humanitarian-development complex. Development volunteering was powered by Western ideals and intentions, and it operated at a remove from on-the-ground realities,

[16] Temilola Alanamu, "Church Missionary Society Evangelists and Women's Labour in Nineteenth-Century Abẹ́òkúta," *Africa* 88, no. 2 (2018): 291–311.

[17] Judith A. Byfield, "Taxation, Women and the Colonial State: Egba Women's Tax Revolt," *Meridians: Feminism, Race, Transnationalism* 3, no. 2 (2003): 250–77; Samuel Fury Childs Daly, "From Crime to Coercion: Policing Dissent in Abeokuta, Nigeria, 1900–1940," *Journal of Imperial and Commonwealth History* 47, no. 3 (2019): 474–89.

or what we might call "actually existing development." The institutional culture of development volunteering agencies in Washington, London and Melbourne took little notice of the day-to-day experiences of volunteers, or of what they actually achieved. Once we look, a vast gulf emerges between good intentions and on-the-ground realities; Helen Rosenberg's example is echoed in countless similar stories. This is significant not only for development volunteering but also for foreign aid more broadly. It gives us an insight into the workings of the humanitarian-development complex, which frequently paid more attention to Western priorities than the stated needs of recipient nations, despite rhetoric proclaiming the contrary. Foreign aid interventions took their cue from discourses branding the Global South as "underdeveloped," "developing" or "Least Developed" and therefore creating a demand for development intervention.[18] On the contrary, this study uncovers Western actors with a strong desire to help, but with no clear sense of object. Where, or whom, volunteers would assist was of secondary importance to their goodwill. In Australia, Britain and the United States, volunteer agencies emphasized the rhetoric of service and sacrifice. Western volunteers' desire to help – that is to change the lives of distant others – was widely celebrated and considered justification enough for development volunteering programs to expand across the globe. It was also considered a sufficient reason for support from governments, private corporations, civic groups and large swathes of the general public. Critical questions of whom they would help and where, and most importantly how they would render assistance and towards what end, were rarely asked, either within development volunteering organizations or by the long lists of supporters and donors amassed by the Volunteer Graduate Scheme, VSO and Peace Corps. Neither were sufficient questions asked about what volunteer-receiving communities wanted, or how volunteers were regarded by those at the receiving end of their goodwill. Those avenues were shut off by generalizing rhetoric that spoke of "host country nationals" in "those countries" – sweeping terms that were routinely deployed though rarely defined. In the absence of precision, this space was filled by casual assumptions about where was "developed" and where was not; assumptions often carried over from the colonial era and imprinted with racial and cultural chauvinism. Imprecise, totalizing language, and policies that prioritized expansion rather than evaluation of existing projects, suggested that vast swathes of the globe required development intervention by volunteers.

Although it was often contested by recipient communities, development volunteering had significant effects on Western cultures of humanitarianism. By drawing in the public, development volunteering helped shape an emerging popular culture of foreign aid that channeled a moral sense of duty to

[18] The classic study remains Ferguson, *The Anti-Politics Machine*. See also Arturo Escobar, *Encountering Development: The Making and Unmaking of the Third World* (Princeton, NJ: Princeton University Press, 1995).

humanity into individual action, whether by volunteering or by donating to humanitarian campaigns. In so doing, development volunteering personalized and depoliticized the question of global inequality, nudging Westerners away from proposals for structural change such as a New International Economic Order or, more radically, for the redistribution of wealth on a global scale. Along with the human rights paradigm emerging around the same time, the humanitarian-development complex helped funnel a revolutionary expansion of global concern into limited and manageable channels, thus rendering it safe for neoliberal times.[19]

Situating the Humanitarian-Development Complex

The past three decades have seen a surge of historical interest in international development and humanitarianism. Historians have now situated international development at the heart of twentieth-century international relations; a recent collection dubbed it *The Development Century*.[20] A major wave of historiography focused on the United States, situating modernization theory and development assistance as weapons within the state's Cold War arsenal.[21] This was complicated by studies of British, Dutch and French development programs, all of which originated in colonial development regimes and so demanded that decolonization be considered as an explanatory factor alongside the "Cold War lens."[22] More recently, historians have begun to trace the

[19] Samuel Moyn, *Not Enough: Human Rights in an Unequal World* (Cambridge, MA: Harvard University Press, 2018).

[20] Stephen Macekura and Erez Manela, eds., *The Development Century: A Global History* (Cambridge: Cambridge University Press, 2018).

[21] Michael E. Latham, *Modernization as Ideology: American Social Science and 'Nation Building' in the Kennedy Era* (Chapel Hill, NC: University of North Carolina Press, 2000); Michael E. Latham, *The Right Kind of Revolution: Modernization, Development and US Foreign Policy from the Cold War to the Present* (Ithaca, NY: Cornell University Press, 2010); Nils Gilman, *Mandarins of the Future: Modernization Theory in Cold War America* (Baltimore, MD: Johns Hopkins University Press, 2003); David Ekbladh, *The Great American Mission: Modernization and the Construction of an American World Order* (Princeton, NJ: Princeton University Press, 2011). For an excellent two-part review essay see Joseph Morgan Hodge, "Writing the History of Development (Part 1: The First Wave)," *Humanity* 6, no. 3 (2015): 429–63; Joseph Morgan Hodge, "Writing the History of Development (Part 2: Longer, Deeper, Wider)," *Humanity* 7, no. 1 (2016): 125–74.

[22] Joseph Morgan Hodge, *Triumph of the Expert: Agrarian Doctrines of Development and the Legacies of British Colonialism* (Athens, OH: Ohio University Press, 2007); Charlotte Lydia Riley, "Monstrous Predatory Vampires and Beneficent Fairy-Godmothers: British Post-War Colonial Development in Africa" (PhD thesis, University College London, 2013); Marc Frey, "Control, Legitimacy, and the Securing of Interests: European Development Policy in South-East Asia from the Late Colonial Period to the Early 1960s," *Contemporary European History* 12, no. 4 (2003): 395–412; Veronique Dimier, *The Invention of a European Development Aid Bureaucracy: Recycling Empire* (London: Palgrave Macmillan, 2014); Suzanne Moon, *Technology and Ethical Idealism: A History of*

circulations and transfers of development expertise between multiple actors across the First, Second and Third Worlds. A small number have cultivated a dual focus on donor and recipient nations, revealing the complex negotiations and interactions that took place within the contexts of decolonization and the Cold War.[23] Their work has expanded beyond the limits of the nation, revealing international development as a global space in which political, ideological, racial and cultural motives and allegiances intersected and interacted.

Histories of humanitarianism have also surged. The historiography of humanitarianism reaches further back than that of international development, with substantial work focusing on abolition movements of the eighteenth and nineteenth centuries, and on colonial humanitarianism and the "protection" of Indigenous populations in settler colonies.[24] Historians of twentieth-century humanitarianism have largely drawn on the recently opened archives of non-governmental organizations to track their increasing professionalization, and the tense interplay between altruism and realpolitik that attended their expansion from grassroots to the global sphere.[25] Where histories of development

Development in the Netherlands East Indies (Leiden: CNWS Publications, 2007); Matthew Connelly, "Taking Off the Cold War Lens: Visions of North–South Conflict During the Algerian War for Independence," *American Historical Review* 105, no. 3 (2000): 739–69.

23 David C. Engerman, *The Price of Aid: The Economic Cold War in India* (Cambridge, MA: Harvard University Press, 2018); Vijay Prashad, *The Darker Nations: A People's History of the Third World* (New York: W. W. Norton, 2007); Priya Lal, *African Socialism in Postcolonial Tanzania: Between the Village and the World* (Cambridge: Cambridge University Press, 2015); Alden Young, *Transforming Sudan* (Cambridge: Cambridge University Press, 2017).

24 Ian Tyrrell, *Reforming the World: The Creation of America's Moral Empire* (Princeton, NJ: Princeton University Press, 2010); Michael Barnett, *Empire of Humanity: A History of Humanitarianism* (Ithaca, NY: Cornell University Press, 2011); Didier Fassin, *Humanitarian Reason: A Moral History of the Present* (Berkeley, CA: University of California Press, 2012); Rob Skinner and Alan Lester, "Humanitarianism and Empire: New Research Agendas," *Journal of Imperial and Commonwealth History* 40, no. 5 (2012): 729–47; Margaret Abruzzo, *Polemical Pain: Slavery, Cruelty and the Rise of Humanitarianism* (Baltimore, MD: Johns Hopkins University Press, 2011); Claire McLisky, "'Due Observance of Justice, and the Protection of Their Rights': Philanthropy, Humanitarianism and Moral Purpose in the Aborigines Protection Society Circa 1837 and Its Portrayal in Australian Historiography, 1883–2003," *Limina* 11 (2005): 57–66; Anne O'Brien, "Humanitarianism and Reparation in Colonial Australia," *Journal of Colonialism and Colonial History* 12, no. 2 (2011).

25 Julia F. Irwin, *Making the World Safe: The American Red Cross and a Nation's Humanitarian Awakening* (New York: Oxford University Press, 2013); Emily Baugham, "'Every Citizen of Empire Implored to Save the Children!': Empire, Internationalism and the Save the Children Fund in Inter-War Britain," *Historical Research* 86, no. 231 (2013): 116–37; Matthew Hilton, "International Aid and Development NGOs in Britain and Human Rights since 1945," *Humanity* 3, no. 3 (2012): 449–72; Matthew Hilton, "Charity and the End of Empire: British Non-Governmental Organizations, Africa, and

emerged from diplomatic history and continue to focus largely on state actors, histories of humanitarianism have been more open to the influence of civic society, the role of women and the significance of affect and emotion in spurring and mediating humanitarian action.[26]

These historiographies have remained surprisingly separate. Only in the past few years have historians attempted to bridge the chasm, to show that humanitarianism and international development met at the intersection of the Cold War and decolonization.[27] Timothy Nunan has demonstrated that humanitarianism and development were inextricable from state and military power as it manifested in late twentieth-century Afghanistan.[28] Young-Sun Hong has coined the term "global humanitarian regime" to describe interactions between nations from the First, Second and Third Worlds conducted amidst profound inequalities between Global North and the Global South.[29] Taken together, their work suggests that by the mid-twentieth century, humanitarianism and international development were mutually dependent. Development actors used the altruistic rhetoric of humanitarianism to make their intervention palatable. Humanitarian organizations, in the meantime, actively assisted state- and bloc-based power through the provision of supplies and legitimacy to deeply politicized – and sometimes weaponized – power contests.

International Development in the 1960s," *American Historical Review* 123, no. 2 (2018): 493–517; Matthew Hilton et al., *The Politics of Expertise: How NGOs Shaped Modern Britain* (Oxford: Oxford University Press, 2013); Kevin O'Sullivan, "A 'Global Nervous System': The Rise and Rise of European Humanitarian NGOs, 1945–1985," in *International Organizations and Development, 1945–1990*, edited by Sonke Kunkel, Marc Frey and Corinna R. Unger, pp. 196–219 (Basingstoke, UK: Palgrave Macmillan, 2014); James Crossland, Melanie Oppenheimer and Neville Wylie, eds., *The Red Cross Movement: Re-Evaluating and Re-Imagining the History of Humanitarianism* (Manchester, UK: Manchester University Press, 2020).

26 Heide Fehrenbach and Davide Rodogno, eds., *Humanitarian Photography: A History* (Cambridge: Cambridge University Press, 2016); Jane Lydon, *Imperial Emotions: The Politics of Empathy Across the British Empire* (Cambridge: Cambridge University Press, 2019); Bertrand Taithe, "Compassion Fatigue: The Changing Nature of Humanitarian Emotions," in *Emotional Bodies: The Historical Performativity of Emotions*, edited by Delores Martin-Moruno and Beatriz Pichel, pp. 242–62 (Champaign, IL: University of Illinois Press, 2019).

27 Andrew Thompson has also drawn attention to the place of human rights in the knotted histories of humanitarianism and decolonization. See Andrew S. Thompson, "Unravelling the Relationships Between Humanitarianism, Human Rights and Decolonization: Time for a Radical Rethink?" In *The Oxford Handbook of the Ends of Empire* edited by Martin Thomas and Andrew S. Thompson, pp. 453–74 (Oxford: Oxford University Press, 2018).

28 Timothy Nunan, *Humanitarian Invasion: Global Development in Cold War Afghanistan* (Cambridge: Cambridge University Press, 2016).

29 Young-Sun Hong, *Cold War Germany, the Third World, and the Global Humanitarian Regime* (Cambridge: Cambridge University Press, 2015).

The history of development volunteering further blurs the line between humanitarianism and international development; between non-state altruism and official foreign relations. The Volunteer Graduate Scheme and VSO were nominally non-governmental organizations, but they depended on their national governments for the vast majority of their funding; the Peace Corps was a US government agency from the start. Backing for development volunteering cut across the social fabric of mid-century Australia, Britain and the United States. Support came from the political left and right in all three nations; it also came from established sources of civic power including churches, clubs and societies as well as from the private sector. In return, development volunteering bolstered many corporations transitioning from colonial to globalized markets. Volunteering boosted the tourism industry, for example, through bulk purchases of airfares and hotel accommodation for volunteers in transit, but also by spurring a desire for leisure travel amongst volunteers and broader audiences at a time when mass tourism to "developing" destinations was rapidly expanding. Development volunteering was also bolstered by the enthusiastic support of members of the general public, including aspiring volunteers. The overlapping of the state, the private sector, non-government organizations and the public in support of development volunteering reveals that humanitarian motivations, corporate interests and state-based power were bedfellows from the very creation of the postwar international order. And all these disparate groups came together in support of Western intervention in the so-called underdeveloped world, even when the benefits of these interventions were not clear or even precisely defined. This vague but nonetheless enthusiastic support for foreign intervention lies at the heart of the humanitarian-development complex.

National, Transnational, International and Global

Westerners had travelled abroad citing altruistic motives for hundreds of years. But development volunteering differed from previous manifestations in four key ways. First, the Volunteer Graduate Scheme, VSO and the Peace Corps explicitly framed their contribution in the language of international development that emerged in the postwar period, as well as speaking to the established rhetoric of humanitarianism. Second, development volunteering organizations benefited from a significant level of government funding in addition to various kinds of non-state support. Third, development volunteering agencies were nominally secular; regardless of their personal beliefs, volunteers were not encouraged to regard theirs as a missionary endeavor. Finally, volunteers were placed for a relatively long period of time – typically one or two years – rather than the weeks or months of work camps, which had become popular in the interwar period.[30]

Development volunteering programs were firmly tied to national contexts. Australia's Volunteer Graduate Scheme, Britain's VSO and the United States Peace Corps were claimed as exemplars of all that was good about their respective nations. By the 1950s, many Australians had begun to worry about their nation's reputation amid growing Asian opposition to the restrictive White Australia Policy.[31] Britons began to express considerable disquiet about Britain's declining status in the wake of decolonization.[32] Many Americans, too, became concerned about their nation's image amid widespread critiques of American mass culture. As founding Director of the Peace Corps R. Sargent Shriver put it, there was a "widespread belief that many Americans have gone soft," and a concomitant doubt "whether America is qualified to lead the free world."[33] The 1958 publication of *The Ugly American*, an influential novel that situated development assistance at the heart of the Cold War battle for hearts and minds, had focused anxieties on the figures cut by Americans abroad.[34] Development volunteers were posited as an answer to all these challenges to national image. Volunteers would be willing to build genuine relationships across the boundaries of race and culture, and to accept a less ostentatious lifestyle than counterparts in the diplomatic corps or private sector. Their goodwill would capture the hearts and minds of ordinary people across the decolonizing world and so help shift negative opinion about their home nations.

Development volunteering programs were also related to debates about race and citizenship at home. The 1950s and 1960s saw new heat enter domestic discussions about immigration and Indigenous issues in Australia. Britain saw fierce contests, and even race riots, amid Commonwealth immigration and the growing racism of far-right groups. The United States, too, experienced unrest as the civil rights movement

[30] Arthur Gillette, *One Million Volunteers: The Story of Volunteer Youth Service* (Harmondsworth, UK: Penguin, 1968); William Peters, *Passport to Friendship: The Story of the Experiment in International Living* (New York: J. B. Lippincott Company, 1957).

[31] David Walker, *Stranded Nation: White Australia in an Asian Region* (Crawley, Western Australia: UWA Publishing, 2019); David Walker, "General Cariappa Encounters 'White Australia': Australia, India and the Commonwealth in the 1950s," *The Journal of Imperial and Commonwealth History* 34, no. 3 (2006): 389–406.

[32] Anna Bocking-Welch, *British Civic Society at the End of Empire: Decolonisation, Globalisation and International Responsibility* (Manchester, UK: Manchester University Press, 2018).

[33] Sargent Shriver, "Introduction." In Roy Hoopes, *The Complete Peace Corps Guide* (New York: The Dial Press, 1961), p. 1.

[34] William J. Lederer and Eugene Burdick, *The Ugly American* (New York: W. W. Norton & Company, 1958).

drew renewed attention to America's institutionalized racism. Race was significant. All three programs suggested that the image of primarily white volunteers willing to devote themselves to people of diverse races and cultures would help divert attention from, if not directly counter, domestic racial tensions.[35]

National contexts have framed previous historical analysis of development volunteering. Elizabeth Cobbs Hoffman's 1998 monograph skillfully outlined the early institutional history of the Peace Corps and its role in forging America's triumphal self-image as a liberal, beneficent and advanced nation.[36] Recent scholarship has taken a more critical approach to situate the Peace Corps within a broader focus on poverty in the United States and abroad, and within axes of globalization that helped inform American attitudes to foreign places and people.[37] The history of Australia's Volunteer Graduate Scheme has been sketched as part of a history of its successor organization, Australian Volunteers International, and within the biographies and memoirs of its earliest volunteers.[38] In Britain, VSO has been examined within the broader contexts of British attitudes to decolonization and the rise of youth as a political category.[39]

35 For a discussion of race in the Peace Corps, see Jonathan Zimmerman, "Beyond Double Consciousness: Black Peace Corps Volunteers in Africa, 1961–1971." *The Journal of American History* 82, no. 3 (1995): 999–1028.

36 Elizabeth Cobbs Hoffman, *All You Need Is Love: The Peace Corps and the Spirit of the 1960s* (Cambridge, MA: Harvard University Press, 1998); Elizabeth Cobbs, "Decolonization, the Cold War, and the Foreign Policy of the Peace Corps," *Diplomatic History* 20, no. 1 (1996): 79–105. See also Fritz Fischer, *Making Them Like Us: Peace Corps Volunteers in the 1960s* (Washington, DC: Smithsonian Institution Press, 1998).

37 Alyosha Goldstein, "On the Internal Border: Colonial Difference, the Cold War, and the Locations of 'Underdevelopment'," *Comparative Studies in Society and History* 50, no. 1 (2008): 26–56; Sheyda Jahanbani, "'A Different Kind of People': The Poor at Home and Abroad, 1935–1968" (PhD thesis, Brown University, 2009); Rebecca Schein, "Landscape for a Good Citizen: The Peace Corps and the Cultural Logics of American Cosmopolitanism" (PhD thesis, University of California, Santa Cruz, 2008); David S. Busch, "The Politics of International Volunteerism: The Peace Corps and Volunteers to America in the 1960s," *Diplomatic History* 42, no. 4 (2017): 669–93.

38 Peter Britton, *Working for the World: The Evolution of Australian Volunteers International* (Melbourne: Australian Scholarly Publishing, 2019); Jemma Purdey, *From Vienna to Yogyakarta: The Life of Herb Feith* (Sydney: UNSW Press, 2011); Agnieszka Sobocinska, "A New Kind of Mission: The Volunteer Graduate Scheme and the Cultural History of International Development," *Australian Journal of Politics and History* 61, no. 3 (2016): 369–87.

39 Jordanna Bailkin, *The Afterlife of Empire* (Berkeley, CA: University of California Press, 2012), pp. 55–94; Anna Bocking-Welch, "Youth against Hunger: Service, Activism and the Mobilisation of Young Humanitarians in 1960s Britain," *European Review of History* 23, no. 1–2 (2016): 154–70; Bocking-Welch, *British Civic Society at the End of Empire*; Georgina Brewis, "From Service to Action? Students, Volunteering and Community Action in Mid Twentieth-Century

Rather than a disparate group of national programs, I contend that development volunteering is more fruitfully viewed as a transnational phenomenon that leapt borders.[40] Development volunteering was related not only to national dynamics but also to the Cold War's division of the globe into three distinct worlds; and the division between colonizers and former colonies. In the two decades from 1950, development volunteering programs were launched in Australia, New Zealand, Britain, Canada, the United States, France, Belgium, the Netherlands, Germany, Austria, Norway, Sweden, Denmark, Finland, Israel and Japan, before being taken up by the United Nations in 1971. Volunteers also came from the so-called Second World: in 1964, East Germany launched the *FDJ-Brigaden der Freundschaft* (Friendship Brigade of the Free German Youth). Similar organizations, including Bulgaria's National Committee of Volunteer Brigades and Czechoslovakia's Coordinating Committee for Voluntary Service, soon followed. Taking a step back, and viewing development volunteering as a global phenomenon, allows us to see the size and scale of this movement, and its purchase across the so-called developed world. Volunteers from single programs were often limited by the boundaries of their nation's foreign relations, but, taken as a whole, there were few places that volunteers did not go. Uncovering this broader history situates development volunteering at the heart of international development and humanitarianism during the 1950s and 1960s.

A global framing brings drawbacks as well as benefits. As with all global histories, taking a wide view can preclude careful attention to the granular contexts of individual communities affected by volunteers. Recent accounts of the Peace Corps in specific places, notably Ghana, Ethiopia, the Philippines, Iran and Latin America, have shown the value of research that is deeply embedded in historical, cultural and political contexts.[41] The account of

Britain," *British Journal of Education Studies* 58, no. 4 (2010): 439–49 See also Georgina Brewis, *A Social History of Student Volunteering* (New York: Palgrave Macmillan, 2014), pp. 176–7; Ruth Compton Brouwer, *Canada's Global Villagers: CUSO in Development, 1961–1981* (Vancouver: UBC Press, 2013).

40 Agnieszka Sobocinska, "How to Win Friends and Influence Nations: The International History of Development Volunteering," *Journal of Global History* 12, no. 1 (2017): 49–73.

41 Julius A. Amin, "The Perils of Missionary Diplomacy: The United States Peace Corps in Ghana," *Western Journal of Black Studies* 23, no. 1 (1999): 35–48; Jasamin Rostam-Kolayi, "The New Frontier Meets the White Revolution: The Peace Corps in Iran, 1962–76," *Iranian Studies* 51, no. 4 (2018): 587–612; Christa Wirth, "The Creation of a Postcolonial Subject: The Chicago and Ateneo De Manila Schools and the Peace Corps in the Philippines, 1960–1970," *Journal of the History of the Behavioural Sciences* 54, no. 1 (2018): 5–24; Fernando Purcell, *The Peace Corps in South America: Volunteers and the Global War on Poverty in the 1960s* (London: Palgrave Macmillan, 2019); Beatrice Tychsen Wayne, "Restless Youth: Education, Activism and the Peace Corps in Ethiopia, 1962–1976" (PhD thesis, New York University, 2017).

development volunteering in this book is intended to complement and situate both domestic-focused accounts of national programs and studies of their impacts in particular places. Development volunteering existed on multiple scales; it was a movement that was simultaneously local, national, transnational, international and global.

Bringing in the People

Some three years before Helen Rosenberg arrived in Nigeria, American Elinor Dobbins boarded a Pan Am jet to Manila. The twenty-two-year-old Cornell graduate was headed for Mayabon, a small beach town on the southern island of Negros Oriental, as part of the Peace Corps' first Philippines contingent. In a press interview conducted not long before boarding her flight, Elinor Dobbins opined that the Peace Corps was "wonderful" because it gave her "a chance to be active rather than passive in world affairs and an opportunity to do something for yourself and your country."[42] Dobbins was not alone in her desire to become personally involved in international relations. As Christina Klein and Anna-Bocking Welch have shown with relation to America and Britain, and my previous work has shown in Australia, many otherwise ordinary citizens came to think of themselves as agents in international relations in the post-war period.[43] The existential threats represented by the Cold War and nuclear weapons, and the sense that the world was growing smaller through improved travel technology, supported the belief that "ordinary" people across the Western world had a new role to play in international affairs.

Most histories have depicted international development as a top-down affair – the "Triumph of the Expert" in Joseph Hodge's memorable rendering – but interest and involvement in international development went beyond a narrow technocratic elite.[44] This book argues that development volunteering brought a longer history of public engagement in humanitarianism to bear on international development. By the early 1960s, a convergence of media and popular interest in development volunteering prompted a flood of applications, donations and other tokens of public support. Those who couldn't personally volunteer sent in cash, or wrote songs and poems, or submitted flags and logos, or asked what else they could do to help. The overwhelming popular response points to a rich seam of non-elite engagement in

[42] "Miss Dobbins Goes to the Philippines" in "Press Clippings, 1961," Papers of Elinor Capehart, John F. Kennedy Presidential Library (henceforth JFKL): Returned Peace Corps Volunteers Collection (henceforth RPCV), Box 102.

[43] Christina Klein, *Cold War Orientalism: Asia in the Middlebrow Imagination, 1945–1961* (Berkeley, CA: University of California Press, 2003); Bocking-Welch, *British Civic Society at the End of Empire*; Agnieszka Sobocinska, *Visiting the Neighbours: Australians in Asia* (Sydney: UNSW Press/NewSouth, 2014).

[44] See Hodge, *Triumph of the Expert*.

international development that has largely escaped historical attention. In the late 1950s, one of the earliest Australian volunteers noted, "Perhaps the most hopeful aspect of this recent trend is the fact that it is involving sizable numbers of ordinary citizens in the Western countries," and as a result, "relations with India, Ghana or Indonesia are no longer merely the concern of governments."[45] Uncovering the history of development volunteering thus challenges the top-down technocratic model of development and helps bring "the people" into international history, a field that still largely favors political and cultural elites.[46] It reveals that public involvement was an essential, but largely overlooked, component of international development from the 1950s; not just in a single national context, but across much of the world.

Development volunteering agencies did not just respond to spontaneous eruptions of popular sentiment; they also helped shape popular knowledge. We still know very little about the public's engagement with foreign aid and international development before the 1980s.[47] How did Western publics come to understand global poverty and international development? How did mainstream assumptions about the needs of "underdeveloped" nations arise? And what were the political ramifications of these assumptions? These questions are closely tied to representations, and particularly to the images crafted and broadcast by development volunteering agencies and the mass media. From the late 1950s, development volunteering agencies devoted substantial resources to publicity and media coverage. The Peace Corps was particularly preoccupied with public relations; Chapter 5 of this book reconstructs the vast and elaborate public relations structure that inaugural Director R. Sargent Shriver began to construct even before the agency had been formally established. Content was carried in traditional news formats as well as in mainstream cultural productions such as cartoons, plays, novels and even television sitcoms, which oversimplified international development by rendering it into a narrative of Western goodwill and benevolence. Development volunteering entered popular culture in a way that few other humanitarian or international development initiatives ever would;

[45] Herb Feith, "The Volunteer Graduate Scheme Idea – Could it Work Elsewhere?" *Djembatan*, Vol. 2, no. 4, p. 29.

[46] Richard Ivan Jobs, "Where the Hell Are the People?" *Journal of Social History* 39, no. 2 (2005, Winter): 309–14.

[47] Emerging work in this area includes O'Sullivan, "Humanitarian Encounters"; Anna Bocking-Welch, "Imperial Legacies and Internationalist Discourses: British Involvement in the United Nations Freedom from Hunger Campaign, 1960–70," *Journal of Imperial and Commonwealth History* 40, no. 5 (2012, December): 879–96; Agnieszka Sobocinska, "Popular Causes: The Volunteer Graduate Scheme, the Freedom from Hunger Campaign and Altruistic Internationalism in Australia," *Journal of Australian Studies* 43, no. 4 (2019): 509–24.

tracking what images it portrayed is therefore vital to our understanding of Western public engagement with humanitarianism and international development at mid-century.

This book suggests that development volunteering helped forge a popular humanitarian sensibility across the Western world that laid the groundwork for subsequent developments. Scholars of contemporary foreign aid have pointed to the importance of the "public faces" of development.[48] Development volunteering helped shape popular ideas about humanitarianism, international development and the Global South in particular ways by appealing to certain kinds of "ordinary" citizens. While it is true that volunteers and other supporters came from all walks of life, there was a distinct overrepresentation of white, middle class, educated youth in all three agencies across the time period under examination in this book. Development volunteering gave a broader constituency, including Elinor Dobbins, a chance to be active in world affairs, but they did not operate entirely outside wider structures of inequality in mid-twentieth-century Australia, Britain and America.

Young female volunteers attracted a disproportionate amount of media attention. The media's interest in attractive, young and white volunteers helps explain why a press photographer was there to capture the moment Elinor Dobbins boarded her flight to the Philippines. Moments before boarding, the "girl" volunteers were separated out, arranged on the stairs leading up to the plane, and directed to wave and smile at the Associated Press camera. Much of the media coverage focused on volunteers' appearance and good intentions, without paying much attention to where they went, what they actually did, or how local people responded to their presence. To use historian Mary Louise Pratt's term, the image of attractive volunteers helped narrate a story of "anti-conquest" that camouflaged the spread of Western hegemony.[49] In the 1960s, the good intentions and friendly demeanors of development volunteers could be used to put a positive and well-meaning face on the expansion of Western economic, political and cultural power at the moment of decolonization.

Coverage such as this made development work sexy, helping to pave the way for subsequent cultures of humanitarianism marked by celebrity activism and the glamorization of aid.[50] It also simplified the fraught and contested space of

[48] Matt Smith and Helen Yanacopoulos, "The Public Faces of Development: An Introduction," *Journal of International Development* 16, no. 5 (2004): 657–64.

[49] Mary Louise Pratt, *Imperial Eyes: Travel Writing and Transculturation* (Abingdon: Routledge, 1992).

[50] John Cameron and Anna Haanstra, "Development Made Sexy: How It Happened and What It Means," *Third World Quarterly* 29, no. 8 (2008): 1475–89; Michael K. Goodman and Christine Barnes, "Star/Poverty Space: The Making of the 'Development Celebrity'," *Celebrity Studies* 2, no. 1 (2011): 69–85; April Biccum, "Marketing Development:

development intervention, and directed attention away from the places and people whose apparent needs had motivated development volunteers in the first place. Focusing on volunteers' good intentions rather than outcomes, popular images of development volunteering directed the public's attention away from the voices and demands of the "underdeveloped" themselves, and helped foster public support for a "maximalist" model of development intervention.

The "Maximalist" Model of Development Intervention

The good intentions and good looks of volunteers like Elinor Dobbins and Helen Rosenberg attracted a great deal of attention, but what did volunteers actually do? As the first chapter of this book demonstrates, Australia's Volunteer Graduate Scheme, Britain's VSO and the United States Peace Corps came from different genealogies, but they had essentially the same idea. They would send young volunteers to work across the "underdeveloped" world, at levels of pay below those typically enjoyed by Western expatriates. The Volunteer Graduate Scheme's original idea was to place volunteers as mid-level bureaucrats in the Indonesian public service, an expansive category encompassing teachers, translators, academics, scientists, doctors and librarians. Britain's VSO expanded the terrain by also placing volunteers in community development schemes, in elite private schools and hospitals, and in the colonial bureaucracies of British dependencies. The Peace Corps did all this and more, but the majority of all development volunteers went as teachers, with the greatest number teaching English.

Significantly, the jobs that volunteers performed were only one part of their task. Even before the first development volunteer, Australian Herb Feith, went into the field in 1951, he had begun to think that "the gesture value of such projects," meaning "the motive rather than the immediate practical effect" was "all-important."[51] An early Volunteer Graduate Scheme pamphlet noted that "our most important job in Indonesia, more important even than what we do at work, is just to live normally and naturally in the Indonesian world, and to make friends among Indonesians."[52] More radical volunteers saw this as a way to subvert colonial distinctions based on race; others thought it would help improve their nation's image abroad. But they all agreed that building positive interpersonal relations, and maintaining a good reputation, were even more

Celebrity Politics and the 'New' Development Advocacy," *Third World Quarterly* 32, no. 7 (2011): 1331–46.

51 Herb Feith to Betty Evans, June 20, 1951, National Library of Australia (henceforth NLA): MS 2601, Box 6, Folder 1.

52 "The Scheme for Graduate Employment in Indonesia: An account of the way the scheme works, and a letter from Indonesia to interested volunteers," 1954 edition, National Archives of Australia (henceforth NAA): A1893, 2032/5/4 Part 1.

important than the jobs the Indonesian government had asked them to perform.

The Peace Corps and VSO also thought that a volunteer's real task lay beyond their day jobs. Both organizations articulated a culturalist vision of development, in which "underdevelopment" was caused not just by lack of technical skills, but also by backwardness in personal attitudes. As the London *Times* reported, "the real object is to strike sparks in the minds of the people where the attitude of mind is the real key to the problem of economic and political development."[53] As a result, how well volunteers performed at their jobs was not a primary consideration. Rather, as one British MP reported to the House of Commons, "any good [volunteers] do comes from their own personalities and principles."[54] The Peace Corps also defined volunteers' roles more broadly. Sargent Shriver claimed that "The Peace Corps is more of a cultural, an educational, and social operation than it is an economic one."[55] As one early report noted, "We have the skills, the habits, the attitudes of technology which are the result of living in a technological society," and "they need these."[56] Even though developing nations specifically asked for skilled and specialized personnel, both VSO and the Peace Corps preferred to send generalists. Sargent Shriver's successor as Peace Corps Director, Jack Hood Vaughn, claimed that "the liberal arts graduate with a decent education and lots of ambition" was "the special hero of the Peace Corps."[57] In effect, development volunteering worked on the assumption that young people from "developed" nations were capable of uplifting "underdeveloped" ones simply by their presence, rather than by virtue of their knowledge or skills. Despite its good intentions, development volunteering was an expression of longstanding assumptions about European and North American superiority over "native" populations, which had colonial and racial origins.

Development volunteering therefore articulated a maximalist model of development intervention, by which not only specialist or technical expertise but also social, cultural and psychological models had to be imported from the Global North. The assumptions it supported, of Westerners as enthusiastic go-getters and poorer communities as stagnant and backwards, shifted blame away from structural inequality – from the legacies of colonialism and the

53 "A Year in the Commonwealth for Young Volunteers," *The Times*, December 1, 1959, p. 4.

54 House of Commons Debates, December 12, 1962, Vol. 669, cc423–81.

55 "The Peace Corps: Hearings before the Committee on Foreign Relations, United States Senate, Eighty-Seventh Congress, June 22 and 23, 1961" (Washington, DC: US Government Printing Office, 1961), p. 66.

56 Cited in Samuel P. Hayes, *An International Peace Corps: The Promise and Problems* (Washington DC: Public Affairs Institute, 1961), p. 38.

57 Roy Hoopes, *The Peace Corps Experience* (New York: Clarkson N. Potter Inc., 1968), pp. 3–4.

continued inequity of global trade systems – and placed it on the shoulders of the poor. This logic reinforced colonial-era images of African, Asian and Latin American "backwardness" and justified Western development intervention in a postcolonial period. As one US Senator warned in 1961, the Peace Corps had to balance a desire for international friendship with a responsibility to model a more advanced way of life. "Let's not carry it too far by getting down to their level," he warned, as "there will be little likelihood of their changing their system of government and improving themselves, if we are going to go over there and leave the impression that we are on a par with them and they are on a par with us." Volunteers would have to model American norms to ensure they were not "reducing our people to their level."[58] Development volunteering, often regarded as a pure example of altruism and idealism, carried darker undercurrents, as discourses of development, imperialism and control existed alongside those of youthful idealism and national benevolence.

A diffuse cultural mission also provided welcome cover for development volunteering agencies that were never quite able to prove that their volunteers were having any demonstrable benefit at all. After all, how could one measure whether an individual volunteer had helped instill ambition, a desire for progress or a willingness for service? Even in 1972, after fifteen years in the field, VSO's Executive Committee thought that "it was almost impossible to give any real assessment of the value of the work done," although "it was generally felt that the large quantity of money that had been spent . . . had been well used."[59] The lack of specialized techniques of monitoring and evaluation in the 1960s only contributed to a general sense that the benefits brought by volunteers were impossible to measure, but no less valuable for being so.

Development volunteering agencies were masters in constructive ambiguity. The Volunteer Graduate Scheme, VSO and the Peace Corps each underwent a multiplication of aims, as programs' original intentions were added to and modified by shifting leadership, donor demands and changes in government policy and strategy. This led to some confusion about precisely what volunteers were supposed to do in the Philippines, or Ghana, or Colombia. As a 1961 editorial in the London *Telegraph* asked, "Is voluntary service overseas intended primarily for the benefit of underdeveloped countries or to benefit young volunteers from Britain? Charity, or education, or diplomacy?"[60] The confusion was widespread, both within and beyond development volunteering organizations. But far from being a weakness, this ambiguity expanded the potential bases for support. Some supporters saw development volunteering as a way to

58 Senator Homer E. Capehart, "The Peace Corps: Hearings before the Committee on Foreign Relations, United States Senate, Eighty-Seventh Congress, June 22 and 23, 1961," pp. 87–8.

59 Minutes of the VSO Executive Committee, July 4, 1972, VSO Archive, Box 31.

60 "Charity at Home?" *Sunday Telegraph*, March 12, 1961, p. 14.

end colonialism and colonial attitudes, but others saw it as a means to perpetuate colonial influence, or even expand neocolonial structures. Some supporters regarded development volunteering as a way to eradicate racial prejudice, but others saw a means to display the supremacy of their own nation, race or way of life. Some saw a means towards world peace, others a way of waging Cold War. The ambiguity of development volunteering – its capacity to accommodate multiple views and motivations – contributed to its astounding popularity, at home if not always abroad. As one Columbia University senior commented to the *New York Times*, "The Peace Corps? It's like existentialism. Everybody's for it but nobody quite knows what it means."[61]

On the Ground

Although planned in Washington or London, humanitarianism and international development were enacted by and amongst individuals in Abeokuta, Mayabon and thousands of other villages, towns and cities across half the globe. Building on the contribution of New Diplomatic History, this book seeks to complicate our understanding of international relations by arguing that the embodied, on-the-ground experience of international development is just as significant as organizational or national policy. The later chapters of this book look beyond the government plans, agency rhetoric and media representations that informed the majority of histories of humanitarianism and international development to date. They trace the experience of development volunteering on the ground, as lived by both volunteers and locals, as a step towards unearthing "actually existing development" from the 1950s to the 1970s.

As Anna Lowenhaupt Tsing has noted, universals such as development may be imagined as global, but they "can only be charged and enacted in the sticky materiality of practical encounters."[62] The space between the universal and the particular was replicated in tensions between planning and delivery; between intentions and on-the-ground realities. Acknowledging the embodied nature of the development encounter requires sensitivity, not only to programs' rhetoric but also to policies guiding the quotidian aspects of development volunteering and how they were experienced by individuals on the ground. That means paying attention to the everyday details: what jobs volunteers performed; where they lived and with whom; how much money they had and how they spent it; and how – and with whom – they socialized. Feelings are also significant, both of volunteers and their hosts. Tracing the experiences and

61 "Project gains backing of most undergraduates; women eager," *New York Times*, March 6, 1961, p. 1.

62 Anna Lowenhaupt Tsing, *Friction: An Ethnography of Global Connection* (Princeton, NJ: Princeton University Press, 2005).

emotions of development volunteering helps us begin to understand the affective landscapes of humanitarianism and international development in the 1950s through the 1970s. To really understand the nature of international development, and international relations more broadly, we need to trace its history both from above and below; to trace the government and agency policies that directed volunteers, the experiences that volunteers had on the ground, and how the two impacted and interacted with each other.

Looking at ground level exposes a chronic tension between ideals and reality. We can see something of this tension in Elinor Dobbins' experiences. Work as a middle-school teacher in a Philippines backwater was not exactly the adventure she'd imagined, and despite her best intentions, Dobbins found the work of cross-cultural communication tedious and difficult. Occasional moments of elation were overshadowed by a rising frustration, which she directed at pupils, townsfolk and most often at herself. Like Helen Rosenberg in Nigeria, Elinor Dobbins stuck close to the other Western volunteers in town, who understood her motives and shared her frustrations. They lived together and ate most of their meals at home, prepared by a Filipino housekeeper who also cleaned their large and comfortably appointed house. And like Helen Rosenberg, Dobbins soon began to doubt the value of her posting. "For a few people to speak American English, which is out of place here, the Peace Corps is spending a lot of money," she confided in her diary; moreover, "our influence seems quite limited."[63]

With her faith in the Peace Corps fading, Elinor Dobbins focused her energy on extracurricular activities, albeit not the ones encouraged by Peace Corps headquarters in Washington. Young and admittedly "a little horny," Dobbins negotiated a number of intimate relationships with Filipino men, each of which proved a minefield as her expectations – shaped by American norms of dating and low-key sexual experimentation – repeatedly came into tension with Filipino customs.[64] Other volunteers experienced more direct conflict. Although volunteer agencies' rhetoric emphasized international friendship, in reality volunteers navigated innumerable disputes with host communities. Volunteer teachers in Ghana and Ethiopia, for example, found themselves at the receiving end of countless micro-aggressions, and occasionally overt defiance, from students who regarded their presence as a form of neocolonial domination. Classrooms became virtual battlegrounds as volunteer teachers suffered organized campaigns of misdemeanors designed to undermine their authority, which sometimes extended to physical violence. Volunteers were regularly driven to tears and occasionally to more serious breakdowns; but students regarded their actions as grassroots resistance to Western

[63] Diary entry, December 13, 1961, in Papers of Elinor Capehart, JFKL: RPCV, Box 102.

[64] Elinor Dobbins to Alex Veech, undated 1961, in Papers of Elinor Capehart, JFKL: RPCV, Box 102.

intervention. The tension between the rhetoric of international friendship and the reality of chronic conflict was a challenge for many individual volunteers that was rarely acknowledged at the level of policy.

Looking at the level of experience also underlines the key importance of gender to the development volunteering experience. Development volunteering represented the major avenue for Western women to become involved in international affairs during the 1950s through 1970s, especially in countries practicing systematic sex and gender discrimination for foreign service employment.[65] In terms of numbers alone, women dominated Australia's Volunteer Graduate Scheme, represented almost half of British VSO volunteers, and accounted for roughly one-third of US Peace Corps volunteers throughout this period (although management positions in all three agencies were almost exclusively reserved for men). Molly Geidel has argued that the Peace Corps rewarded certain kinds of performative masculinity and made a fetish of the femininity of women volunteers.[66] We have already seen the significant work performed by media representations of female volunteers. But the personal conduct and intimate relationships of female volunteers were also a particular site of contestation and control. While the image of young women forming close bonds across race and culture was celebrated, in reality female volunteers were subjected to multiple levels of scrutiny. Policing of volunteers' sexual behavior was especially gendered. Elinor Dobbins was lucky that her romantic adventures never came to the attention of the Peace Corps Representative in the Philippines. Other women faced severe consequences for intimate relationships that were deemed a threat to national prestige.

Looking at ground level also helps us to better understand the complex workings of power in development volunteering. Viewed in wide-lens, the humanitarian-development complex can appear totalizing, as a Western-led intervention that took only cursory account of the desires of nations and communities across the Global South. But things can look very different in close-up. Reading the diaries and letters of volunteers like Elinor Dobbins, and accessing sources produced by their interlocutors in receiving nations, it is apparent that North–South interaction played out in complex and sometimes surprising ways. Arriving in a new town or village, volunteers may have benefited from Western geopolitical and cultural power; but at ground level, locals set the terms of engagement. Individual volunteering experiences played

65 Beatrice Loftus McKenzie, "The Problem of Women in the Department: Sex and Gender Discrimination in the 1960s United States Foreign Diplomatic Service," *European Journal of American Studies* 10, no. 1 (2015): 1–21. Australia imposed a marriage bar on female employment in the Commonwealth Public Service, including diplomatic service, through the Public Service Act until 1966.

66 Molly Geidel, *Peace Corps Fantasies: How Development Shaped the Global Sixties* (Minneapolis, MN: University of Minnesota Press, 2015).

out in often unexpected ways, as desire and resistance, and love and hate, intermingled in relationships that were simultaneously personal and political.

Resisting the Humanitarian-Development Complex

Development volunteering found critics across the Global South and, from the late 1960s, in the West as well. Resistance could be articulated at the local level, as when students misbehaved or when residents undermined or sabotaged a volunteer's community development projects. But it was also deeply rooted in political ideologies including anti-colonialism, nationalism, non-alignment and global communism. Resistance to the Volunteer Graduate Scheme, VSO and especially the Peace Corps was expressed by organized opposition movements, in political pamphlets and in mass media across the Third World. From the early 1960s, negative depictions of development volunteering circulated between nations and continents: criticisms of the Peace Corps originating in Nigeria, for example, featured prominently in the Ghanaian popular press, and vice versa, despite chronic tensions between the neighboring nations. They also traveled to other, more distant places: India, Ceylon (Sri Lanka from 1972), Indonesia and beyond. This circulation of knowledge and rumor brought activists from across Asia, Africa and Latin America into conversation. Opposition to development volunteering helped consolidate transnational coalitions opposing Western development intervention. It also unified critics in the West, bringing together a cast of radicalized development experts, activists and returned volunteers who advanced a robust critique of development volunteering, and development intervention more broadly, that cast shade on the beatific image of development volunteering from the late 1960s.

Opposition to development volunteering was not universal by any means. Volunteering agencies were, after all, formally invited by governments struggling to find qualified manpower in the wake of decolonization, and some communities welcomed volunteers with open arms. But opposition to volunteering agencies was significant and consistent. Third World critics argued that volunteers held neocolonial views and ended up doing work that was unnecessary or unwelcome. Anti-volunteer protests regularly erupted on the streets of Third World towns and cities, and by the early 1970s volunteers had been expelled from dozens of nations including Indonesia, Pakistan, Malawi, Guinea, Mauritania, India and Tanzania.

And yet, each year brought tens of thousands more Western volunteers. Noncontinuity was built into the development volunteering model. Individual volunteers served out their one- or two-year terms, then they went home or moved on elsewhere. Bureaucrats and executives in London, Melbourne or Washington could shrug off or even dismiss conflicts incurred at a granular level, simply making a note not to send volunteers to a certain community or school that had proven unreceptive or openly hostile to Western intervention. Individual volunteers often returned with a greater understanding of the nature of development, and of the complex relationship between Global North and Global South, which went beyond the superficialities of media coverage and popular opinion. But there were always fresh, often naïve applicants ready to take their place. After a decade of crisis in the face of sustained opposition, development volunteering restored its legitimacy as an outlet for well-meaning Westerners from the late 1970s. In subsequent decades, hundreds of thousands of Western volunteers traveled to the developing world. Millions more participated in the related, and highly problematic, practice of for-profit volunteer tourism, or voluntourism, which monetized the positive image of development volunteering to become one of the fastest-growing segments of the tourism industry.[67]

Development volunteering never resolved the tensions at its heart: between altruism and neocolonial power; between image and reality; between volunteers and the communities that received them – and, most importantly, between the Global North and the Global South. Nonetheless, it expanded across the globe and across several generations. Perhaps more than anything else, this fact lays bare the power of the humanitarian-development complex: to sustain itself even in the face of internal contradictions and widespread opposition that stretched across the Third World and back.

Scope of This Book

This book traces the origins and early history of Australia's Volunteer Graduate Scheme, Britain's VSO and the United States Peace Corps. It takes up the story in 1950, when the Volunteer Graduate Scheme was established, and closes in the late 1970s, by which time volunteering had become a core component of the international development system and the humanitarian-development complex was firmly established.

While my lens is global, this book is limited to a close study of three programs. I chose to focus on Australia's Volunteer Graduate Scheme because it was the first modern development volunteering endeavor; Britain's VSO because it bridged colonial and postcolonial eras and systems; and the United States Peace Corps because it was by far the largest and most influential of all development volunteering programs. As with all history, choices about what to include are also choices about what to leave out. The many programs that sprang up across Western nations in the years following the launch of the

[67] Stephen Wearing, *Volunteer Tourism: Experiences That Make a Difference* (Wallingford, UK: CABI, 2001); Mary Mostafanezhad, *Volunteer Tourism: Popular Humanitarianism in Neoliberal Times* (Farnham, UK: Ashgate, 2014); Mary Mostafanezhad, "Volunteer Tourism and the Popular Humanitarian Gaze," *Geoforum* 54 (2014): 111–18 .

Peace Corps are not explored in any depth in this book, but their broader existence is an important fact testifying to the global reach of development volunteering. Agencies including Canadian University Service Overseas (CUSO), *Deutscher Entwicklungsdienst* ([West] German Volunteer Service), *Association Française des Volontaires du Progrès* (French Association of Volunteers for Progress) and *Nihon Seinen Kaigai Kyōryokutai* (Japan Overseas Cooperation Volunteers), among many others, played a part in the global story described in this book, but they do not feature in its pages. Neither do the volunteer programs established by Eastern bloc countries. For all their propaganda significance, these programs were relatively small – in 1964 the largest program, the East German *Brigaden der Freundschaft*, was launched with some forty volunteers deployed to Mali and Algeria; even twenty years later there were still only seventeen brigades, comprising some 340 volunteers, in the field.[68] Other Eastern bloc programs were even smaller, and although volunteer programs' significance can't be reduced to their size, the fact remains that their impact was minor compared with that of the Western programs at the core of this book.

From Australia, the development volunteering idea spread through Anglophone networks to New Zealand, then Britain, Canada and the United States. The fact that Anglophone nations were at the forefront of the development volunteering movement is in itself significant. It suggests the importance of colonial and settler colonial legacies, and the ongoing influence of Anglo-American colonial culture – especially the rhetoric of uplift once known as "the White Man's Burden." It points to an ongoing racial and cultural chauvinism that encouraged vast swathes of "ordinary" Britons, Americans and Australians – even untrained students – to assume they had the capacity, and the right, to intervene in distant corners of the world. It also maps on to geopolitical power at mid-century, as the Anglosphere cooperated to facilitate the global reach and influence of political, economic and military policies, especially in Asia and Africa.

Working on the scale of the global demands some abstraction. Global disparity has been known by many names: First World and Third World; "underdeveloped" and "developed" nations; Global North and Global South; the West and the rest. These terms have different shades of meaning, with referents to the Cold War, modernization theory, and the End of History. But they all refer to much the same thing: rich nations and poor nations, correlating roughly with nations that were former or current colonizers (or established as settler colonies) and those that were formerly colonized. In this book I use the term "Western" to collectively refer to Australia, the United Kingdom, Western Europe and the United States; to the political/economic institutions and cultural trends that

68 Woodrow J. Kuhns Jr., "The German Democratic Republic in the Third World" (PhD thesis, University of Pennsylvania, 1985), pp. 140–2.

spanned these nations; and to the geopolitical and cultural power amassed by the capitalist alliance in the Cold War. Even so, I acknowledge that the invocation of a coherent "West" is spurious, and the term can be critiqued both for obscuring historical and cultural specificities and for creating a specter that appears more formidable for its vagueness.[69] Similarly, I use two abstract terms to refer to the nations of Africa, the Middle East, Asia, the Pacific Islands, the Caribbean and Latin America: Third World and Global South. Postcolonial scholars have explored the simultaneously vague and totalizing nature of these problematic terms, and what they semantically obscure and produce.[70] In this book I use the term Third World to refer to decolonizing nations that actively participated in the "Third World project" during the 1950s, 1960s and 1970s; that is, they were involved in anticolonial networks and non-aligned movements that spanned beyond a single nation or continent.[71] I use the term Global South to refer to those areas of the globe plagued by the legacies of colonialism, irrespective of their politics.

I have tried not only to describe the motives and images of development volunteering, but also the experiences. Although I have followed volunteers all over the globe, the majority of my situated analysis refers to Africa and Asia. At several points in this book, I further narrow my focus to two pairs of neighboring but vastly different nations: Indonesia and Malaysia, and Ghana and Nigeria. This reflects the fact that all three development volunteering programs I examine overlapped in Asia and VSO and the Peace Corps were both heavily invested in Africa. At several points, examining these four nations allows me to explore the divergent dynamics of decolonizing nations in the 1960s and 1970s, and to trace varying responses to Western volunteers. The sections of the book that focus on these nations are intended to illustrate, rather than supplant, broader trends. My aim is to produce a narrative with purchase at both the local and global levels, speaking both to individual experiences and to global dynamics.

Retrieving experiences across multiple scales requires a wide range of sources. In addition to the institutional archives of all the development

69 Anne Phillips, "What's Wrong with Essentialism?" *Distinktion: Journal of Social Theory* 11 (2010): 47–60. See also Edward John Powell, "Postcolonial Critical Perspectives on 'the West': Social Hegemony and Political Participation" (PhD thesis, University of Leeds, 2014).

70 Vicky Randall, "Using and Abusing the Concept of the Third World: Geopolitics and the Comparative Political Study of Development and Underdevelopment," *Third World Quarterly* 25, no. 1 (2004): 41–53; Arif Dirlik, "Spectres of the Third World: Global Modernity and the End of the Three Worlds," *Third World Quarterly* 25, no. 1 (2004): 131–48.

71 For similar usage, see Prashad, *The Darker Nations*. See also "Introduction" in Samantha Christiansen and Zachary A. Scarlett, eds., *The Third World in the Global 1960s* (New York: Berghahn Books, 2013); Anuja Bose, "Frantz Fanon and the Politicization of the Third World as a Collective Subject," *Interventions* 21, no. 5 (2019): 671–89.

volunteering organizations examined in this book, state archives and mainstream and specialized press in three languages. I have accessed the personal diaries, letters, scrapbooks and photographs of hundreds of volunteers, which are held in official repositories and in private archives. Some of this material came from unexpected places: an older couple who handed me an aging photograph album while narrating the story of their courtship while volunteers in 1956; the archivist at VSO who dragged out of storage two large boxes of uncatalogued and unsorted microfiche cards, which turned out to hold correspondence with every VSO volunteer in the 1960s. Although I have spoken to many volunteers and some of their interlocutors in host nations, I have chosen to rely mostly on contemporary sources rather than oral histories or memoirs. This is not to diminish the importance of oral sources, but rather to try and access contemporary views and attitudes wherever possible.

A final word on language. Volunteers and their supporters might find the term humanitarian-development complex, with its evocation of the military-industrial complex, a bit harsh. Indeed, it does not seem to do justice to their genuine goodwill or their hard work. Years ago, I was a development volunteer myself – much later than those examined in this book, but in a program directly descended from the Volunteer Graduate Scheme. I like to think that my time was not wasted. But like many other former volunteers, I have to admit that, once we decenter the gaze from our good intentions and instead look to the places we went, listen to the people we worked amongst and examine the effects of our volunteering, the picture becomes much more complicated. After years of thinking about development volunteering, both from direct experience and during research for this book, I have come to agree with the radical priest Ivan Illich, who in 1968 confronted a group of American volunteers with a speech titled "To Hell with Good Intentions."[72] After seventy years of the humanitarian-development complex, we can and should demand more.

Chapter Structure

The ten chapters that follow are divided into three thematic sections. In them, I attempt to access the multiple scales of development volunteering outlined above. I also try to balance the three separate programs that are the subject of this book. Three chapters in this book take an in-depth look at particular themes as they played out in a single program, with the remainder integrating all three programs. The uneven influence of the larger programs is, nonetheless, replicated in these pages, with VSO and the Peace Corps sometimes overshadowing the far smaller Australian Volunteer Graduate Scheme.

[72] Ivan Illich, "To Hell with Good Intentions," www.uvm.edu/~jashman/CDAE195_ESCI375/To%20Hell%20with%20Good%20Intentions.pdf, accessed February 5, 2020.

The book's first Part, "Intentions," traces the motives and rhetoric of development volunteering agencies, supporters and volunteers. Comprising four chapters, it is largely drawn from material in the institutional archives of the Volunteer Graduate Scheme, VSO and the Peace Corps, as well as the national archives of Australia, Britain and the United States. Chapter 1 charts the origins and contradictions of the development volunteering model, while Chapter 2 traces the international networks that facilitated the spread of development volunteering around the globe. Chapter 3 takes an in-depth look at the non-state actors and organizations that supported development volunteering, with a particular focus on religious groups' support for Australia's Volunteer Graduate Scheme, civic and private sector backing for Britain's VSO and public support for the United States Peace Corps. Chapter 4 explores volunteers' multiple and often overlapping motivations. Based on hundreds of application forms submitted by intending volunteers in Australia, this chapter examines how individual sentiments and emotions were translated into politically significant action on the international stage.

Development volunteering made a significant impact on public opinion about international development, humanitarianism and the North–South divide. This is the subject of the book's second Part, "Images," which analyses media and publicity material depicting development volunteering in the 1950s, 1960s and 1970s. Chapter 5 focuses on the wave of publicity and media attention that attended the establishment of the United States Peace Corps. It argues that publicity and mass media overwhelmingly broadcast a beatific image of volunteers that fostered popular approval for Western development interventionism whilst simultaneously limiting the public's understanding of it. Chapter 6 charts the view from the other side by contrasting press reports from two pairs of receiving nations: Indonesia and Malaysia, and Nigeria and Ghana. Using Indonesian, Malaysian and English-language media sources, it reveals far more critical responses that tied individual volunteers to broader systems of power and spread through activist networks across the Third World.

The third and final Part, "Experiences," shifts the gaze to ground level to trace the embodied experiences of individual volunteers. Bringing personal diaries, private correspondence, photographs and scrapbooks into conversation with archival material, this Part acknowledges that international development and humanitarianism were always an embodied experience that brought individuals into close proximity, sometimes with unexpected outcomes. Chapter 7 focuses on the lifestyles cultivated by British VSO volunteers during the 1960s to probe the tensions and inconsistencies between volunteers' good intentions and the reality of life as a Western expatriate in decolonizing nations. Chapter 8 maps out the emotional economy of humanitarianism and development by connecting the intimate with the organizational; the private with the geopolitical. It explores volunteers' intimate and sexual encounters with locals, and traces how, and why, volunteer agencies attempted to regulate sentiment. Chapter 9 draws out the book's key tension, between the Global North and the Global South, by exploring conflict at both an interpersonal and international level. It reads a raft of minor slights, amply documented in official as well as private documents, as incidents of resistance, and tracks organized anti-volunteer campaigns across the Third World as they grew in number and intensity during the 1960s and into the 1970s.

The book's final chapter explores the decade of crisis faced by volunteering agencies from the late 1960s, as returned volunteers and radical critics declared development volunteering akin to neocolonialism and demanded its cessation altogether. It concludes by tracing the surprising resurgence of development volunteering, as it expanded into the UN system and for-profit voluntourism. Far from collapsing under the weight of its contradictions, volunteering proved to be a developmental phoenix, and the humanitarian-development complex – at once a transnational cultural logic and a tangible system of Western development intervention – proved immutable.

PART I

Intentions

1

An Idea for All Seasons

On a muggy morning in June 1951, the first volunteer with Australia's Volunteer Graduate Scheme disembarked in Jakarta, capital of the recently proclaimed Republic of Indonesia. Twenty-one-year-old Herb Feith was the only passenger to come ashore that morning; the others had been scared off by rumors of riots, shootings and the indiscriminate slaughter of Europeans. They had stared incredulously when Feith told them of his intention to take up a volunteer placement in Indonesia's civil service. They told him he was being reckless and overly idealistic; that he wouldn't survive a week, let alone two years, amongst hostile "natives" and their unsanitary habits.[1] Indonesians, too, were often apprehensive. Many came to suspect that Western volunteers had ulterior motives: to make a profit, or try to convert Indonesian Muslims to Christianity. Others simply shook their heads, unable to see the point of it all. Feith soon became accustomed to incredulity and suspicion, as did the volunteers who followed him to Indonesia.

Precisely ten years after Feith's arrival in Jakarta, in June 1961, the first volunteers were selected for the United States Peace Corps. Far from incredulity, the launch of the Peace Corps had met with widespread excitement and approval: the *New York Times* editorialized that it was "a noble enterprise" and "one of the most remarkable projects ever undertaken by any nation."[2] By this time, VSO had operated in Britain since 1958 and development volunteering programs had also been launched in New Zealand and Canada. Over the following decade, tens and then hundreds of thousands of volunteers set off from wealthy nations to work in some seventy countries across the Global South. In 1971, twenty years after Feith first disembarked in Jakarta, development volunteering was fully integrated into the international system with the launch of United Nations Volunteers.

The genealogies and impetus for the establishment of Australia's Volunteer Graduate Scheme, Britain's VSO and the United States Peace Corps differed, but they had essentially the same idea: to send young volunteers to live and

[1] "Herb Feith to 'Everybody'," June 30, 1951, Papers of Herb Feith, NLA MS 9926, Box 1, Folder 1.

[2] "The 'Peace Corps' starts," *New York Times*, March 2, 1961, p. 26.

work in the "underdeveloped" nations then emerging from colonial rule, at something approximating local standards of living. It was thought that this would have multiple benefits: building the manpower capacity of newly independent nations; expanding a volunteer's understanding of global issues; fostering a new spirit of international and interracial friendship; and cementing the reputation of sending nations as good global citizens. These benefits were assumed rather than proven; attempts to measure volunteers' effectiveness, or their actual impacts on the ground, were rarely attempted during the 1950s and 1960s. Neither were receiving communities' views canvassed before volunteers were dispatched. Western ideals lay at the core of development volunteering and questions about volunteers' impacts or their relationship to unequal systems of global power were routinely elided by agencies unable, or unwilling, to see beyond their good intentions.

Development volunteering programs were flexible with their stated aims – sometimes strikingly so – if it meant gaining support, and funding, from key stakeholders. But multiple and overlapping aims bred confusion and contradiction. Operational decisions needed to be made about where to send volunteers and what kind of applicants were most suitable. Should volunteers be selected based on their technical skills and experience, on their ability to make friends or on their capacity to project a positive image abroad? These key decisions depended on broader questions. Were development volunteering programs intended to provide skilled labor to developing nations or were the benefits to accrue to volunteers themselves? Were volunteers aiming to contribute to world peace or were they intended to project a positive national image? Having too many good intentions made it difficult, if not impossible, to achieve any one goal fully, but development volunteering agencies proved unable to resolve these questions. Over the course of the 1950s and 1960s, the Volunteer Graduate Scheme, VSO and the Peace Corps were beset by internal debates that complicated policymaking and bred confusion, and sometimes disillusionment, among volunteers. But the ambiguity could also be constructive, attracting financial and moral support from across the fabric of Western society. Focusing on volunteers' intentions, rather than their actions or impacts on the ground, development volunteering agencies built popular and elite support for broad-ranging but ill-defined development intervention across the Global South: the humanitarian-development complex.

"Natural and Friendly Relations": Australia's Volunteer Graduate Scheme

Herb Feith's arrival in Jakarta was an important moment in the history of development volunteering, but the story began a year earlier, on board a different ship. In August 1950, two Melbourne University students boarded a steamer bound for an International Student Service conference in Bombay. On board, John Bayly and Adam Hunt got talking to Indonesia's delegate to the conference, Abu Bakar Lubis. Somewhere along the way, conversation turned to whether young Australians might fill some of the skilled positions vacated by departing Dutch bureaucrats and so contribute to Indonesia's postcolonial development. Returning to Melbourne, Bayly and Hunt related their conversation to fellow student Herb Feith, then completing an Honors year under prominent political scientist William Macmahon Ball. Feith was an Austrian Jewish refugee with a deep-seated belief that ordinary citizens had a moral responsibility to become involved in the creation of a better world. He got in touch with Molly Bondan, an Australian anti-colonial activist now working for the Indonesian Ministry of Information in Jakarta.[3] Bondan encouraged Feith to come to Jakarta and arranged a job for him at the Ministry of Information. She was waiting for him as he disembarked on that muggy June morning and she introduced Feith to influential people within the vast bureaucracy working to achieve Sukarno's vision of an independent Indonesia.

The Volunteer Graduate Scheme is remarkable for its early establishment. Although it had roots in the colonial period, the postwar system of international development was only in its infancy in the early 1950s. The preamble to the United Nations had undertaken to "employ international machinery for the promotion of economic and social advancement of all peoples" in 1945.[4] United States President Harry Truman had announced the Point Four program, to make "the benefits of our scientific advances and industrial processes available for the improvement and growth of underdeveloped areas," in January 1949.[5] In 1950, the leaders of Commonwealth nations unveiled the Colombo Plan for technical assistance to Asia.[6] That same year, the United Nations initiated its Technical Assistance Administration (UNTAA).[7] But the network of interlocking national and multilateral development agencies that characterized the international development system was still years off. The Volunteer Graduate Scheme was among the earliest programs, either official or nongovernmental, to begin operating in the field of international development.

[3] Joan Hardjono and Charles Warner, eds., *In Love with a Nation: Molly Bondan and Indonesia* (Picton, NSW: Charles Warner, 1995).

[4] United Nations, Preamble to the UN Charter, signed June 26, 1945, www.un.org/en/sections/un-charter/preamble/index.html, accessed April 1, 2020.

[5] For a discussion of Point Four see Ekbladh, *The Great American Mission*, pp. 77–113.

[6] Daniel Oakman, *Facing Asia: A History of the Colombo Plan* (Canberra: Pandanus Books, 2004).

[7] David Webster, "Development Advisors in a Time of Cold War and Decolonization: The United Nations Technical Assistance Administration, 1950–1959," *Journal of Global History*, no. 6 (2011): 249–72.

The Volunteer Graduate Scheme is also notable for arising from a direct request from an Indonesian source, rather than from Western ideas. The shipboard conversation that sparked the Volunteer Graduate Scheme may have been fleeting but it was significant both to the program (which regularly referred to this conversation in publicity material) and more broadly. Lubis' request for volunteers linked the Volunteer Graduate Scheme to a history of Third World developmentalist thought with origins in anti-colonial struggles of the nineteenth century.[8] Early volunteers were careful to articulate their program's aims in ways that would be acceptable to Indonesians. They studiously avoided paternalistic or patronising language and were careful to avoid embarrassing Indonesia by suggesting it needed Western development assistance or, worse, charity. The Indonesian request for Australian volunteers was evanescent, arising from a casual shipboard conversation rather than a considered proposal based on acknowledged need. But even this was substantially more than many other development volunteering programs, which were propelled exclusively by Western intentions and assumptions about developing countries' needs.

Herb Feith thrived in the optimistic atmosphere pervading the early years of Indonesia's independence. He threw himself into his work, charmed his superiors and began to make friends. He managed to secure jobs for two more volunteers, bacteriologist Gwenda Rodda and radio engineer Ollie McMichael, who arrived in 1952. Back in Melbourne, almost a hundred more students declared that they, too, were ready to follow in his footsteps. The next step was to formalize this outburst of enthusiasm. Herb Feith's close friend (and future wife) Betty Evans was a consummate organizer. Barely in her twenties, she had already served on the committees of multiple student and religious groups. In cooperation with Feith in Jakarta, Evans formed an Executive Committee, decided on the name Volunteer Graduate Scheme and began to lobby influential Australians for support.[9] The Executive Committee set the terms of service: volunteers would work for one- or two-year terms with a branch of the Indonesian civil service. The Executive Committee also determined that volunteers should adopt a middle-class Indonesian lifestyle, with enough money for food, housing and entertainment but not for the lavish life preferred by most expatriates. To this end, they decided that volunteers would

[8] Pankaj Mishra, *From the Ruins of Empire: The Revolt against the West and the Remaking of Asia* (London: Allen Lane, 2012); See also Herbert Feith and Lance Castles, eds., *Indonesian Political Thinking, 1945–1965* (Ithaca, NY: Cornell University Press, 1970).

[9] The program underwent a number of name changes during the 1950s. Although most commonly referred to as the Volunteer Graduate Scheme, other names included Volunteer Employment Scheme, Volunteer Graduates Abroad and Pegawai (the Indonesian word for employee, torturously rendered into the acronym Plan for the Employment of Graduates from Australia to Work as Indonesians). For the sake of clarity, I refer to the Volunteer Graduate Scheme throughout this book.

be remunerated according to the official Indonesian salary scale for public servants. Most volunteers served in specialized, technical roles: as scientists, doctors, university lecturers or English teachers. Their high level of education placed them on the upper rungs of Indonesia's official salary scale, but volunteers in large cities like Jakarta found they had to offer private English lessons to make ends meet, especially as Indonesia's economy suffered runaway inflation from the late 1950s. In essence, this standard of living formed the core of the Volunteer Graduate Scheme mission. As one early pamphlet read, "There's a plan working in Indonesia now for this new kind of European in Asia – the European who lives as a brother and not as a boss . . . but are they 'slumming'? Far from it. They are living in middle-class Indonesian hostels and homes . . . seeing Asian life from the level of the Asian."[10]

Almost immediately, the Executive Committee began to pursue government funds. In December 1950, they approached the Australian Department of External Affairs seeking support for "a comparatively large-scale scheme to employ Australian University men and women for one or two years in Indonesia."[11] Minister for External Affairs Percy Spender rapidly dismissed their request. At this time, Spender was preparing to launch the Colombo Plan, a major government-level development program linking several nations across the British Commonwealth. Rather than well-meaning amateurs, Spender saw a need for technical experts who could enact sweeping changes in developing nations, for which they would "be offered generous terms and conditions of employment." The Department of External Affairs did not see a role for volunteers in development and Spender suggested that university students interested in assisting postcolonial nations would be better off finishing their degrees, getting some work experience and, in due course, registering as Colombo Plan experts.[12] Spender's decision was confirmed by his successor Richard Casey, who received a further petition from the Volunteer Graduate Scheme soon after taking office in May 1951. While claiming to "commend the spirit of the Committee of the students . . . and agree wholeheartedly with the objectives they have in mind," the Minister again refused financial support.[13] Noting that Indonesia was not a party to the Colombo Plan, he suggested UNTAA as the proper vehicle through which Australian contributions should be directed, confirming the view that well-paid experts, rather than well-meaning amateurs, were needed for the international development cause.

Over the course of the following year, the Executive Committee shifted their rhetoric to better appeal to the Department of External Affairs. Recognizing

[10] "Note on 'PEGAWAI' Plan for the Employment of Graduates from Australia to work as Indonesians," NLA: MS 2601, Box 13, Folder 126.
[11] John Bayly to A. S. Watt, December 14, 1950, NLA: MS 2601, Box 2, Folder 9.
[12] W. T. Doig to John Bayly, December 29, 1950, NLA: MS 2601, Box 2, Folder 9.
[13] R. G. Casey to W. S. Kent-Hughes, August 31, 1951, NLA: MS 2601, Box 2, Folder 9.

that they wouldn't convince Casey of the development value of non-experts, they began to define the Volunteer Graduate Scheme in a different way. When the Volunteer Graduate Scheme reapproached the Department of External Affairs for a third time in 1952, their stated goal was now "to establish goodwill and understanding between our two countries" by sending personnel to "assist in the technical and social reconstruction of Indonesia, and at the same time live with and get to know Indonesians." The fact that volunteers would receive Indonesian rates of pay became a key point, as "equality of remuneration seems to facilitate the forming of friendships on the job" and would improve Australia's image in Asia. The Volunteer Graduate Scheme noted that "certainly if an Australian technician or graduate works among his Indonesian fellow-employees on the same salary scale as themselves, they have greater respect for him, and regard him as a real colleague rather than a higher-paid outsider."[14]

The reframing of the Volunteer Graduate Scheme from a technical employment scheme to a form of people-to-people diplomacy was rapid and extensive. This framing was particularly appealing in the context of mounting criticism of the White Australia Policy. Australia's restrictive immigration laws, passed in 1901, were explicitly formulated to keep Asian migrants out. But racial discrimination was coming into disfavor by the 1950s and newly independent Asian nations were particularly critical. Travel writers warned Australians heading to the region "to get ready to be quizzed on the White Australia Policy."[15] Criticism of the White Australia Policy was joined by increasing concern about the treatment of Australia's Indigenous population; again, some of the loudest critiques came from Asian interlocutors.[16] Diplomats and a growing number of concerned citizens found themselves in a bind. The White Australia Policy enjoyed overwhelming support back home, but it threatened Australia's reputation abroad.[17] The Volunteer Graduate Scheme's performance of racial equality, and of Australian goodwill, appeared an ideal solution. It promised to project a positive image of Australians as brimming with goodwill and devoid of racial prejudice, while pointedly drawing attention away from the domestic situation, in which strict immigration restrictions and Indigenous inequality continued apace. This framing proved attractive to the Australian government. Reversing its earlier decisions, from 1952 the Department of External Affairs paid for volunteers' (first class) travel to Indonesia, provided grants to cover a range of personal costs and paid a resettlement allowance upon their return. Presenting the Volunteer Graduate

[14] Don Anderson to A. Watt, August 2, 1952, NLA: MS 2601, Box 2, Folder 9.

[15] Frank Clune, *Song of India* (Bombay: Thacker & Co. Ltd, 1947), p. 234.

[16] Walker, "General Cariappa Encounters 'White Australia'."

[17] David Walker, *Stranded Nation*. See also David Walker, *Anxious Nation: Australia and the Rise of Asia, 1850–1939* (St. Lucia, Queensland: University of Queensland Press, 1999).

Scheme as a contribution to Asian engagement rendered it attractive to the Australian government. But it was a major deviation from its foundational aim of ameliorating Indonesia's post-colonial skills shortage.

At the same time, the Volunteer Graduate Scheme sought ongoing financial support from the Indonesian government. It used a different strategy to convince Jakarta, using the language favored by Indonesia's political class to argue that volunteers contributed to the nation's postcolonial development. This appealed to the Indonesian government, which also agreed to fund Volunteer Graduate Scheme volunteers in 1952. As Indonesian Ambassador to Australia Dr. R. H. Tirtawinata noted several years later, "every aspect of our life needs the stimulus of knowledge, of what the Americans call 'know how'. This is what you are giving us and what we most urgently need."[18] This support was not only gratifying, but essential to the Volunteer Graduate Scheme's financial survival as volunteers' salaries were to be paid by the Indonesian government.

The Volunteer Graduate Scheme presented aspiring volunteers with a different picture altogether. Rather than the work itself, or the projection of a positive national image, they stressed that the most important task for Australian volunteers was "identification and concrete manifestation of color equality views."[19] In an open letter addressed to potential applicants, the Volunteer Graduate Scheme argued that "our most important job in Indonesia, more important even than what we do at work, is just to live normally and naturally in the Indonesian world, and to make friends among Indonesians, showing Indonesians that there are whites who don't stand on superiority ideas, and making whites ashamed of the privileges they continue to enjoy." Volunteers did not have to make an extraordinary contribution to Indonesia's development:

> You are useful, we think, just by fixing your own bike or washing the dishes, by talking to a *betjak* [cycle-rickshaw] driver or giving up a seat in a bus. You are helping to give Indonesians an idea of whites as ordinary humans, helping them overcome the inferiority feelings and disdain for manual work so successfully fostered by centuries of feudalism and of colonialism.[20]

Rather than claiming the benefits of volunteering for the national image, the Volunteer Graduate Scheme presented their actions as an intervention in the racial order bequeathed by colonialism, aiming for a decolonization of mind to

[18] Speech delivered by Dr. R. H. Tirtawinata to the Volunteer Graduate Scheme Conference, Melbourne University, August 23, 1956, NLA: MS 2601, Box 2, Folder 21.

[19] Herb Feith to Betty Evans, June 20, 1951, NLA: MS 2601, Box 6.

[20] "The Scheme for Graduate Employment in Indonesia: An account of the way the scheme works, and a letter from Indonesia to interested volunteers," 1954 edition, NAA: A1893, 2032/5/4 Part 1.

Figure 1.1 Information pamphlet for the Volunteer Graduate Scheme, 1957. Image courtesy of Australian Volunteers International.

run alongside political decolonization (Figure 1.1). An early pamphlet written by Feith, Rodda and McMichael in Jakarta noted that:

> What they do in their actual work is important ... But more important perhaps is the fact that these young people assert by the way they live, that

> racial equality is real. By having natural and friendly relations with Indonesians on a basis of mutual respect, they help to do away with the colonial legacy of mistrust and misunderstanding, which to so large an extent continues to affect relations between coloured people and whites.[21]

In emphasizing the potential for racial equality, the Volunteer Graduate Scheme addressed a growing constituency of progressive youth who wished to overturn the legacies of racism and colonialism.

From the 1950s, many Australians came to regard international development as an important weapon in global efforts to keep Indonesia from turning to Communism.[22] Yet, the Global Cold War played a surprisingly minor role in the Volunteer Graduate Scheme's rhetoric. Ollie McMichael was unusual in framing his contribution through the lens of the Cold War, writing in a personal letter that "there is still terrible poverty ... and if the people lose hope they'll turn to the Communists – like China."[23] He was the exception that proves the rule: the voluminous archives of the Volunteer Graduate Scheme, and even Australian government records, make little reference to the Cold War context for development volunteering. Even in 1962, with the Cold War heating up across Southeast Asia, the Volunteer Graduate Scheme held that its aim was to subvert *colonial* divisions, so that "by sharing in manual labour, washing dishes, splashing down muddy kampong tracks and so on, one is protesting against the perpetuation of hierarchies fostered by feudalism and colonialism."[24]

The Volunteer Graduate Scheme therefore began with three distinct, albeit overlapping, objectives, which they emphasized at different times to different audiences. To the Indonesian government, the Volunteer Graduate Scheme claimed to be a technical assistance program that would help ameliorate the manpower shortage hampering the nation's postcolonial development, at a lower cost than the Colombo Plan or UNTAA. To the Australian government, the Volunteer Graduate Scheme presented itself as a goodwill program that would help make friends for Australia and provide a useful counterpoint to the White

[21] Ibid.

[22] Daniel Oakman, "The Seed of Freedom: Regional Security and the Colombo Plan," *Australian Journal of Politics and History* 46, no. 1 (2000): 67–85; Daniel Oakman, *Facing Asia*, pp. 73–125; Bradley R. Simpson, *Economists with Guns: Authoritarian Development and US-Indonesian Relations, 1960–1968* (Stanford, CA: Stanford University Press, 2008); Odd Arne Westad, *The Global Cold War: Third World Interventions and the Making of Our Times* (Cambridge: Cambridge University Press, 2007).

[23] Ollie McMichael, July 9, 1952, cited in Betty Feith, "Putting in a Stitch or Two: An Episode in Education for International Understanding – the Volunteer Graduate Scheme in Indonesia, 1950–63" (M. Ed. Thesis, Monash University, 1984).

[24] Volunteer Graduate Scheme, *Living and Working in Indonesia* (Melbourne: Volunteer Graduate Association for Indonesia, 1962), p. 6. "Kampong" is the Indonesian word for village.

Australia Policy. To intending volunteers, and amongst themselves, the Volunteer Graduate Scheme emphasized their desire to build international friendship and surmount racial divides, as a step towards true decolonization and world peace.

The Volunteer Graduate Scheme succeeded in appealing to all three distinct audiences. By the mid-1950s, the Australian Department of External Affairs had nothing but praise for the program; as one official wrote, "in our view the scheme tapped a useful source of energetic talent from which we profited at a cheap rate."[25] Recognizing the positive national image portrayed by eager young volunteers, the Australian government soon co-opted volunteers into its nascent public diplomacy program.[26] Influential journalist Peter Russo lavished praise on the Volunteer Graduate Scheme: "if there is any better way than that of 'showing the flag' in Asia, any surer way of dispelling Asia's lingering distrust of colonial taints," he wrote, "I have not heard it." In uncertain times, Russo thought volunteers were "our leading insurance salesmen in Asia."[27]

The Volunteer Graduate Scheme also won approval at the highest levels in Indonesia. During a second volunteer assignment, Herb Feith worked as a Presidential translator and speechwriter during the 1955 Afro-Asian Conference in Bandung. Sukarno later personally conveyed his best wishes for the continued success of the Volunteer Graduate Scheme and invited newly arrived volunteers to his palace.[28] Assessing the scheme in 1956, the Indonesian Ambassador to Australia declared that "nothing which has been done to help my country in the eleven years since we gained our independence, has so appealed to the hearts and minds of my countrymen as the graduate employment scheme."[29] Many employers were also pleased. Kurnianingrat Ali Sastoamijoyo managed several volunteers while deputy head of the English Language Inspectorate. In 1959, she wrote of her "deep appreciation for the Volunteer Graduate Scheme," especially in contrast with other foreign aid programs, as "it is often forgotten that we certainly cannot have fought for our independence to be dictated to again in building up the country, no matter how well meant this dictatorship may be."[30]

25 Patrick Shaw to L. J. Arnott, March 15, 1955, NAA: A1893, 2032/5/4 Part 1.

26 Agnieszka Sobocinska, "Hearts of Darkness, Hearts of Gold," in *Australia's Asia: From Yellow Peril to Asian Century*, edited by David Walker and Agnieszka Sobocinska, pp. 173–97 (Crawley, Western Australia: UWA Press, 2012). See also David Lowe, "Canberra's Colombo Plan: Public Images of Australia's Relations with Post-Colonial South and Southeast Asia in the 1950s," *South Asia* 25, no. 2 (2010): 183–204.

27 Peter Russo, "The students don't need advice," *The Argus* (Melbourne), January 12, 1956, p. 2.

28 "Lemonade with the President," *Djembatan*, Vol. 1, no. 1, July 1957, p. 2.

29 Speech delivered by Dr. R. H. Tirtawinata to the Volunteer Graduate Scheme Conference, Melbourne University, August 23, 1956, NLA: MS 2601, Box 2, Folder 21.

30 Jo Kurnianingrat, "An Indonesian opinion on the V.G.S.," *Djembatan*, Vol. 2, no. 4, September 1959, p. 15.

Convincing coworkers and other non-elite Indonesians of their genuine and disinterested desire for Indonesia's development was more difficult. Chapter 9 of this book examines the tension and ambivalence that attended volunteers' day-to-day interaction with Indonesians. "Experience in Indonesia indicates how difficult it is initially for our volunteers to establish a relationship of identification with the local people," noted one internal report in 1958. "Also, because this type of Scheme has no precedent in the experience of Asian peoples, we are aware of how readily Indonesians have sought to explain it in terms of motives other than the real ones of the volunteers."[31] Personal letters betrayed disillusionment and distress as volunteers faced the unrelenting suspicion of coworkers and neighbors. Much of this tension was related to the Volunteer Graduate Scheme's multiple aims, which bred confusion and ambiguity. Were volunteers supposed to put most effort into their jobs in order to help Indonesia's development, or was it more important to build relationships with locals and to act as a bridge between Australia and Indonesia; "European" and "native"; white and brown? In its broadest terms, was development volunteering supposed to help "them" or "us?"

The core question of objectives was never resolved, but the Volunteer Graduate Scheme's small size and enthusiasm carried it through the 1950s. The following decade proved more difficult as bilateral relations deteriorated. Although Australia had initially supported Indonesia's independence, the relationship grew tense after the conservative Menzies government threw its support behind the Dutch claim for West New Guinea.[32] Public approval of Indonesia in Australia, and vice versa, plummeted.[33] Attitudes to the Volunteer Graduate Scheme further soured amidst accelerating political and economic crises in Indonesia. Rapid increases in the cost of living and severe inflation exacerbated xenophobia and bolstered calls for autarky.[34] Foreigners came under increased scrutiny. The trickle of volunteers to Indonesia slowed and the Volunteer Graduate Scheme turned its attention to expansion beyond Indonesia, as explored in the following chapter. With Indonesia undergoing vast internal upheaval, the Volunteer Graduate Scheme was gradually folded into larger successor programs, the Overseas Service Bureau and Australian

[31] Jim Webb, "Extension of Volunteer Graduate Scheme, 1958," NLA: MS 2601, Box 3, Folder 32.

[32] Hiroyuki Umetsu, "Australia's Response to the West New Guinea Dispute, 1952–53," *Journal of Pacific History* 39, no. 1 (2004): 59–77; Hiroyuki Umetsu, "Australia's Action Towards Accepting Indonesian Control of Netherlands New Guinea," *Journal of Pacific History* 41, no. 1 (2006): 31–47; Stuart Doran, "Toeing the Line: Australia's Abandonment of 'Traditional' West New Guinea Policy," *Journal of Pacific History* 36, no. 1 (2001): 5–18.

[33] Agnieszka Sobocinska, "Measuring or Creating Attitudes? Seventy Years of Australian Public Opinion Polling About Indonesia," *Asian Studies Review* 41, no. 2 (2017): 371–88.

[34] Feith and Castles, *Indonesian Political Thinking, 1945–1965.*

Volunteers Abroad, from the mid-1960s.[35] The last Australian volunteer serving under the Volunteer Graduate Scheme, Harold Crouch, departed Jakarta in December 1969.

"Adventure in Discovery": Britain's VSO

In 1957, Ailsa Zainu'ddin, a Volunteer Graduate Scheme veteran who now edited the organization's magazine, *Djembatan*, received a letter from the Director of Education in the British colony of Sarawak (later part of Malaysia). He congratulated Zainu'ddin on the Volunteer Graduate Scheme and advised that his brother, Alec Dickson, was "anxious to develop something of the kind in the United Kingdom, for voluntary overseas service by young people."[36] The following year Alec Dickson, a former colonial functionary who had moved into the emerging field of international development, launched Voluntary Service Overseas, commonly known as VSO. Dickson's wife, Mora, wrote of the 1957 visit to Sarawak as a turning point in his conception of VSO. The trip "acted as a catalyst," Mora Dickson wrote, as "from that moment Alec Dickson saw a real possibility of putting some of his ideals into practice and began to work towards that end."[37] In a recent retelling of VSO's origins, historian Jordanna Bailkin thought this was because "Alec and Mora were deeply impressed by the integration of young people in Sarawak into the communal life" and "through VSO they would seek to replicate that experience for young Britons."[38] Their coming awareness of Australia's Volunteer Graduate Scheme was likely a more direct source of inspiration. In a 1973 survey, based on interviews and direct correspondence, author Robert Morris located VSO's origins in Dickson's having "been strongly impressed by the work he had seen being done by these young Australian volunteers," after which he "worked steadily through the summer of 1958 to put flesh to these thoughts."[39] The 1957 correspondence involving Dickson, his brother and Ailsa Zainu'ddin is further evidence that Dickson was keenly interested in the Volunteer Graduate Scheme. Not normally known for his prescience, Prince Philip (later VSO's Patron) was surprisingly close to the mark: "I remember thinking at the time that like all really good ideas it was so essentially simple. So obvious and so simple in fact that I couldn't help wondering why on earth no-one had thought about it before."[40]

35 Britton, *Working for the World*, pp. 23–8.
36 A. H. Borthwick to Ailsa Zainu'ddin, December 18, 1957, NLA: MS 2601, Box 2.
37 Mora Dickson, ed. *A Chance to Serve* (London: Dennis Dobson, 1976), p. 83.
38 Bailkin, *The Afterlife of Empire*, p. 69.
39 Robert C. Morris, *Overseas Volunteer Programs: Their Evolution and the Role of Governments in Their Support* (Lanham, MD: Lexington Books, 1973), pp. 43–4.
40 Foreword by Prince Philip, Michael Adams, *Voluntary Service Overseas: The Story of the First Ten Years* (London: Faber and Faber, 1968), p. 7.

Popular interest in VSO followed the publication of a letter in London's *Sunday Times* in March 1958. The letter, signed by the Bishop of Portsmouth but cowritten with Dickson, proposed development volunteering as a way for young Britons to fill in the "gap year" that many school-leavers spent waiting for a place at university as the tertiary education system struggled to meet post-war demand. Juvenile delinquency and "Angry Young Men" had aroused a good deal of anxiety in 1950s Britain. Voluntary Service Overseas promised a way for young people to channel their energies into meaningful activities, just as National Service was phased out. They would also derive personal benefit from the experience: as Conservative Party MP Sir John Maitland enthused, VSO was "of great value to those taking part in it. They leave this country as boys and girls, and come back as men and women."[41] For this reason, VSO was initially aimed at eighteen-year-olds fresh out of school, whose characters were thought to be not yet fully formed and who would therefore derive the most benefit. A 1959 report in the *Times* described it as "a situation that would enable bright young people to do a good job of work and at the same time satisfy their spirit of adventure."[42]

Voluntary Service Overseas proposed one-year terms for volunteers, most of whom were employed as teachers, civil servants or in community development in current or former British territories in Africa, Asia, the Caribbean and the Middle East. Where the Australian program ensured that volunteer salaries were identical to those of local counterparts, VSO failed to establish a clear policy, leaving host institutions to set rates of remuneration until the mid-1960s. As Chapter 7 of this book explores in more detail, VSO stipends at this time were often determined by expatriates accustomed to colonial standards of living. Voluntary Service Overseas liked to portray an ascetic image, claiming that volunteers lived rugged lives amongst "backwards" people. In reality, however, many volunteers ended up living in considerable comfort. Where VSO's rhetoric emphasized the spirit of sacrifice, in practice it ensured that volunteers were not financially disadvantaged by the decision to volunteer abroad.

Like the Volunteer Graduate Scheme, VSO's aims multiplied as the organization sought support from different sources. Initially, Dickson approached the Minister for Education, David Eccles, to request funds for what he called "adventure scholarships" on the basis that VSO was an educational program benefiting British students. Eccles was not convinced and repeatedly refused Dickson's proposals, having "reached the conclusion that it provides primarily for service, and not for education."[43] Dickson presented VSO in a rather

[41] House of Commons Debates, December 12, 1962, Vol. 669, cc423–81.

[42] "A Year in the Commonwealth for Young Volunteers," *The Times*, December 1, 1959, p. 4.

[43] David Eccles to Lord Perth, September 1, 1960, The National Archives at Kew (henceforth TNA): CO 859/1445.

different way to the Colonial Office, emphasizing the benefits to Britain's reputation and to the development of decolonizing territories, rather than to British youth. This approach found its mark. From 1958, VSO received regular and increasing grants from the Colonial Office under its Colonial Development and Welfare scheme, and from the Commonwealth Relations Office. Responsibility for VSO shifted to the Department of Technical Cooperation in 1961.

The government's enthusiasm for VSO was folded into a broader belief that development assistance offered a way for Britain's imperial legacy to be a productive possibility, rather than a liability.[44] Launched in 1958, VSO emerged at a time when many Britons still wanted to believe in their nation's greatness. Rather than guilt, many wanted to be proud of their imperial achievements and responsibility for former and current dependencies.[45] Voluntary Service Overseas proposed one way in which Britons could carry out this responsibility and retain the best of the colonial spirit, while avoiding charges of imperialism. Honorary Treasurer of VSO Sir George Schuster felt "most strongly that there is no need to be depressed about our nation," as "we are still a great nation whose example can mean something to the world." He supported VSO because it would not only "arouse a spirit of adventure in our young people" but also "maintain this country's prestige and influence in the world."[46] This belief was widely shared. Conservative MP Gilbert Longden thought that "Our countrymen have been doing this work for generations – although such success as they have had has been denigrated by our enemies and purblind friends as 'colonialism'." He continued, "To hundreds of millions of our fellow creatures we have brought peace, justice, and greater prosperity than they would have known without us," but now the time had come "to fulfil our long-declared purpose and give them sovereign independence." In a changing world, "Voluntary Service Overseas provides one way in which we can give that help."[47] Evoking a positive reading of Britain's colonial past was not the prerogative of Conservatives alone. Labour MP (and future Secretary of State for Commonwealth Affairs) George Thomson noted that "We are a great nation, with a great imperial past. The real challenge which faces us is that of transforming this imperial past into new methods of

[44] See Bocking-Welch, "Imperial Legacies and Internationalist Discourses," p. 20.

[45] Stuart Ward, ed. *British Culture and the End of Empire* (Manchester, UK: Manchester University Press, 2001); Paul Gilroy, *After Empire: Melancholia or Convivial Culture* (Abingdon: Routledge, 2004); Bocking-Welch, *British Civic Society at the End of Empire*; Bocking-Welch, "The British Public in a Shrinking World: Civic Engagement with the Declining Empire, 1960–1970" (PhD Thesis, University of York, 2012).

[46] George Shuster to Dennis Vosper, September 30, 1962, TNA: OD 10/4.

[47] Gilbert Longden, "Draft letter to Chairmen of District Councils in Hertfordshire South West Constituency," May 1961, TNA: CO 859/1446.

exercising our sense of responsibility for people overseas." To answer this challenge, Thomson thought, "There are no better causes than VSO."[48]

Voluntary Service Overseas articulated a maximalist vision of development, by which British youth were useful not because they had technical skills but simply because they had the mindset and habits instilled by life in a "developed" society. In Dickson's view, international development was not just about economic levers and the push to take-off, as "In essence the problems are, in fact, not so much of a technical nature, as of an attitude of mind."[49] He believed that VSO's contribution would be psychological and sentimental, arguing that "the manner in which assistance is given, and still more received, may be more important than the actual amount involved."[50] Dickson's view found some support in Whitehall. The Commonwealth Relations Office noted in June 1961 that, "In so far as the psychological effect on Africans … VSO might be a more effective form of 'technical assistance' than forms of technical assistance which fitted more precisely into a narrow definition of this."[51] The Department of Technical Cooperation was focused on development goals and its officers disagreed, dismissing Dickson's sentimental views as "a new sort of romantic evangelism."[52] Despite internal disputes regarding VSO's effectiveness, the Department's financial support for VSO increased substantially in the mid-1960s.

Like the Volunteer Graduate Scheme, VSO advanced the additional claim that it would improve Britain's reputation in decolonizing nations. A 1960 pamphlet claimed that, in one Caribbean territory, volunteers "have done more than anything else to create a pro-English feeling in the two districts where they are stationed," concluding that "Our two boys have been worth more than any Information Service." In West Africa, it was claimed, "Their warm and friendly sympathy with the people … has made all the difference in the world and added greatly to the strength of Anglo-African friendship here."[53] When Queen Elizabeth II hosted returning volunteers for tea in 1961, her briefing papers emphasized the extent to which they had been accepted by communities undergoing decolonization. David Brown, recently returned from Sarawak, was presented as having "spent sixteen months teaching at a Mission School in a very difficult area, in which few other white people seemed to be able to stay long." A Northern Rhodesia volunteer, Michael Radford, had been "one of the very few able to move freely in the African community without causing any resentment."[54]

[48] House of Commons Debates, December 12, 1962, Vol. 669, cc423–81.
[49] Dickson, *A Chance to Serve*, p. 70.
[50] Cited in ibid., pp. 83–5.
[51] Note to file, "Voluntary Service Overseas," June 1961, TNA: DO 163/22.
[52] Mr. Terrell to Mr. Smith, January 21, 1960, TNA: OD 10/3.
[53] Pamphlet, "Voluntary Service Overseas," current May 1960, TNA: CO 859/1445.
[54] Notes ahead of VSO reception at Buckingham Palace on Monday September 25, 1961, TNA: OD 10/3.

The VSO Council noted that the Queen "had been clearly impressed by the volunteers" in this capacity; Prince Philip became VSO's official patron the following month.[55]

As in Australia, official support was at least partly motivated by VSO's perceived capacity to mitigate the reputational damage caused by contentious, and increasingly violent, debates about race and citizenship at home. The 1950s saw fierce contests about race in Britain, as rates of Commonwealth immigration rose and as far-right groups such as the White Defence League and Oswald Mosley's Union Movement responded with racist rhetoric and violence.[56] It is striking that the first VSO volunteers departed just weeks after the Notting Hill race riots. The sustained focus on British volunteers' perceived absence of racial prejudice, and their ability to move freely among African, Asian and Caribbean communities, must be read in this context. But VSO spoke to a desire to paper over domestic tensions and counteract their effects on Britain's reputation rather than to confront them directly. Dickson's next project, Community Service Volunteers, attempted to replicate the VSO experience at home by sending volunteers to depressed areas of London and Birmingham. Although it received some government support, levels of enthusiasm and financial support paled in comparison with VSO. The British Government backed VSO precisely because it was outwards facing, directing attention onto the problems of the Global South rather than those at home (Figure 1.2).

Like its Australian predecessor, then, VSO had multiple aims: to provide technical assistance to developing nations, to overcome the "moral crisis" thought to be facing youth in postwar Britain and to raise British prestige in a decolonizing world. In operation, these multiple aims caused considerable tension. The issue was directly addressed at the first meeting of the VSO Council in March 1961. Lord Shackleton, a Labour Party politician and member of Council, inquired "whether it was wise to emphasise – in the first paragraph of VSO's articles – the educational benefit to volunteers: surely it should be the service that they undertook that should be stressed."[57] The same month, a letter in the *Observer* argued that "volunteers should have something to give underdeveloped countries beyond goodwill and enthusiasm . . . apprentice masons, carpenters and mechanics as well as recently qualified teachers and nurses, are often more useful than clever boys and girls who have just left school and are waiting to go up to the university."[58] The tension was

55 Minutes of VSO Council meetings, September 25, 1961 and October 23, 1961, VSO Archive, Box 31.

56 Bailkin, *The Afterlife of Empire*, esp. pp. 23–54; Marcus Collins, "Pride and Prejudice: West Indian Men in Mid-Twentieth-Century Britain," *Journal of British Studies* 40 (2001): 391–418 .

57 Minutes of first (informal) meeting of the members of the proposed Council of Voluntary Service Overseas, held at the Royal Commonwealth Society, March 28, 1961, TNA: CO 859/1446.

58 Letters to the Editor, *Observer*, Weekend Review, March 12, 1961.

Figure 1.2 VSO volunteer leading a scouting pack in Somaliland, *c.*1960. Image courtesy of VSO.

crystallized in a fifteen-year struggle between those who thought that teenage school-leavers made the best VSOs and those who preferred trained university graduates. Dickson held firm to the belief that enthusiastic and well-meaning teenagers could have more impact on African and Asian mindsets than technical experts. The VSO Council, dominated by an aging colonial old guard, tended to agree. But this view held little sway with VSO's major funder, the Department for Technical Cooperation (later part of the Ministry for Overseas Development), which was committed to technocratic development and demanded VSO be limited to university graduates with the knowledge and skills needed by developing nations.

Alec Dickson's views carried progressively less weight in the organization he had created. His querulous personality and combative relations with key government ministers came to be seen as a liability and, in 1962, VSO's Executive Committee toppled Dickson and appointed a new Director. But the debate continued. Later that year, the Minister for Technical Cooperation cut all funding from the school-leaver program and insisted that government funds be used only to support the graduate volunteer cohort. Voluntary Service Overseas' Honorary Treasurer Sir George Schuster was incensed. He agreed that development was important, but argued that the benefit to British youth was "equally or even more important."[59] In a meeting with the Minister for Technical Cooperation, Schuster was so vehement on this point that bureaucrats later quipped he'd "showed another of his cloven hooves."[60] No amount of passion was able to change the Minister's mind, however, and VSO was forced to administer two parallel schemes: a "cadet" VSO program for school-leavers funded by donations and a larger graduate VSO program underwritten by government.

Although the central tension remained unresolved, VSO underwent a gradual but emphatic shift over the course of the 1960s. By the time he evaluated the program in 1968, author Michael Adams was confident that "the primary and immediate purpose must be to provide some of the skills which are so urgently needed in the under-privileged half of the world."[61] This shift reflected government policy. Investment in development aid became an important plank in Britain's strategy to redefine its global role following decolonization. The rapid expansion of the British NGO sector from the 1960s to the 1980s was generously funded and often coordinated by government agencies largely because of this imperative.[62] Funding for VSO came increasingly from government sources, which grew to cover 75 percent of VSO's costs – some £650,000 – by 1965.[63] Development volunteering attracted far more government support than other development NGOs such as Oxfam or the British Freedom from Hunger Campaign, which received a combined total of £100,000 in 1965.[64] The level of government involvement forced VSO to align with the government's focus on development goals, even as a reduced "cadet" scheme, funded from other sources, carried on Dickson's sentimental vision for a further decade.

"Standard Oil Moving In on the Quakers": The United States Peace Corps

The establishment of the United States Peace Corps in March 1961 represented a step change for development volunteering. The Peace Corps was larger, more

59 George Schuster to Dennis Vosper, October 5, 1962, TNA: OD 10/4.

60 Service overseas by graduate volunteers, note of an ad hoc meeting on finance on December 10, 1962, written December 12, 1962, TNA: OD 10/4.

61 Adams, *Voluntary Service Overseas: The Story of the First Ten Years*, p. 16.

62 Ministry of Overseas Development (UK), *Overseas Development: The Work of the New Ministry* (London: Her Majesty's Stationery Office, 1965). See also Gerold Krozewski, "Global Britain and the Post-Colonial World: The British Approach to Aid Policies at the 1964 Juncture," *Contemporary British History* 29, no. 2 (2015): 222–40; Hilton, "Charity and the End of Empire," pp. 502–3.

63 Adams, *Voluntary Service Overseas: The Story of the First Ten Years*, p. 16.

64 Peter Williams and Adrian Moyes, *Not by Governments Alone: The Role of British Non-Governmental Organisations in the Development Decade* (London: Overseas Development Institute, 1964), p. 37.

professional and more prominent than anyone thought a volunteer-sending organization could be. Unlike the Volunteer Graduate Scheme and VSO, which were nominally non-government organizations, the Peace Corps was a government program from the start. Its importance was reflected in the speed with which it was launched: less than four months after the Peace Corps was established by Executive Order and placed under the directorship of John F. Kennedy's brother-in-law R. Sargent Shriver, the first group of volunteers departed for postings in Ghana, quickly followed by deployments to Colombia, Tanganyika and the Philippines. Within five years, the program had over 10,000 volunteers on the ground in dozens of nations in Latin America, Africa and Asia.[65]

The Australian Volunteer Graduate Scheme and British VSO directly influenced the United States Peace Corps. From the mid-1950s, members of the Volunteer Graduate Scheme had begun to lobby American counterparts in student and Christian organizations to pilot an American scheme based on their experiences. In 1956, Hans Schmitt, an American working at the University of Indonesia and an acquaintance of Herb Feith, wrote to the US National Council of Churches proposing a scheme to bring 200 American volunteers to Indonesia each year. He thought this was "an extraordinary opportunity," which could have "far-reaching effects both in this country and in the States."[66] He also brought in an element of national competition, urging Americans that "we're not even pioneering this enterprise; the Australians have done that before us, and I would be a mortified American Christian if we couldn't match them."[67] Herb Feith then undertook a direct lobbying campaign after arriving in the United States to pursue doctoral studies at Cornell in 1957. As he wrote, "I've now decided . . . to take the bull by the horns" by "stimulating such interest in the right quarters."[68] Feith travelled to Washington, DC, and New York City to meet with representatives from World University Service, the Student Christian Movement, the US National Student Association, the American Council for Voluntary Agencies for Foreign Service and the Foundation for Youth and Student Affairs. He also sent dozens of letters to organizations around the country. In one letter to the American Committee on Africa, to take just one example, he encouraged "American-African parallels to the Australian-Indonesian Volunteer Graduate Scheme."[69] In mid-1960, he was put in touch with Congressman Henry S. Reuss, who had recently begun to work towards "some sort of 'Point Four Youth Corps'," and who was later involved in

[65] *Peace Corps, 5th Annual Report to Congress* (Washington, DC: Peace Corps, 1966), p. 6.

[66] Hans Schmitt to Rev. Newton Thurber, November 27, 1956, NLA: MS 2601, Box 6.

[67] Hans Schmitt to Rev. Newton Thurber, January 27, 1957, NLA: MS 2601, Box 6.

[68] Herb Feith to Jim and Merele Webb, February 8, 1959, NLA: MS 2601, Box 7, Folder 67.

[69] Herb Feith to American Committee on Africa, April 23, 1959, cited in Feith, "Putting in a Stitch or Two," p. 27.

the formation of the Peace Corps.[70] The VSO model was also influential. Alec Dickson advised all three of the research teams that President Kennedy tasked with planning a US Peace Corps in early 1961. Several of Dickson's recommendations were eventually built into the Peace Corps model, leading his wife to later make the overblown claim that he had been "acknowledged by Americans to be the 'father of the Peace Corps idea'."[71]

As an executive agency with substantial resources, the Peace Corps differed in key ways from its Australian and British predecessors. Its founding budget of $40 million in fiscal year 1961 eclipsed VSO's budget of £60,000 and was in a different category altogether to the Volunteer Graduate Scheme's modest £5,000 annual operating costs.[72] Yet, like both its predecessors, the Peace Corps accrued multiple aims that complicated its purpose and operations. And again, the Peace Corps' aims were based on Western intentions and assumptions, rather than direct or sustained engagement with communities and stakeholders in the Global South. In late 1960, Kennedy engaged modernization theorist Max Millikan to advise him in the creation of the Peace Corps. Millikan counseled that the only "appropriate rationale" for an American volunteer program was to help fill "serious shortages of educated and trained people" in underdeveloped countries.[73] In his inaugural address, Kennedy confirmed Millikan's priorities: "to those people in the huts and villages of half the globe, struggling to break the bonds of mass misery, we pledge our best efforts to help them help themselves," not because it was politically expedient, but "because it is right."[74] But Millikan had also foreseen additional benefits. Cooperation between Americans and foreigners would lead to "a better understanding by the peoples of the underdeveloped countries of American institutions and of the purposes, values and motivations of Americans." A further benefit was that "a program of this kind can play an important part in building over time a growing reservoir of American citizens with an intimate knowledge and understanding of conditions in other parts of the world," which would be useful "as the world becomes increasingly interdependent."[75] Although not all

70 Herb Feith to "Jim Webb, Don Anderson and Gang," May 1, 1960, NLA: MS 2601, Box 7, Folder 73.

71 Dickson, *A Chance to Serve*, unpaginated frontispiece.

72 Budget figures from *Peace Corps, 1st Annual Peace Corps Report* (Washington, DC: Peace Corps, 1962), p. 64; "Voluntary Service Overseas: Actual Income and Expenditure 1961/62," TNA: OD 10/4; Herb Feith to Ken Thomas, February 6, 1954, NLA: MS 2601, Box 2, Folder 13.

73 Max Millikan, "Proposal on International Youth Service, 30 December 1960," JFKL: MMPP-001-004.

74 John F. Kennedy, Inaugural Address, January 20, 1961, www.jfklibrary.org/Research/Research-Aids/Ready-Reference/JFKL-Quotations/Inaugural-Address.aspx, accessed October 21, 2016.

75 Millikan, "Proposal on International Youth Service."

of Millikan's recommendations were adopted, his report directly inspired the Peace Corps' official aims, which were threefold: "to help the people of these countries meet their needs for trained manpower; to help promote a better understanding of the American people on the part of peoples served; and to promote a better understanding of other peoples on the part of the American people." But where Millikan had thought cross-cultural understanding was a beneficial side effect of the main game of technical assistance, the Peace Corps' three aims were given equal status; if anything, the ideal of mutual understanding was accentuated by comprising two of the three official aims.

These aims came into tension when they were translated into policies, especially those regarding the recruitment and selection of volunteers. In keeping with Millikan's recommendation that volunteers be "selected with a view to their being capable of effectively filling locally felt needs for trained manpower," the Peace Corps initially sought university graduates with the technical skills needed in developing nations.[76] However, in a reversal of the British trajectory, the Peace Corps soon came to prize amateurism over technical expertise. By the mid-1960s, the archetypal Peace Corps volunteer was a recent graduate of the liberal arts, a twenty-something "BA generalist" rather than a skilled technician (although some Peace Corps volunteers were older and more experienced). In a 1968 account, author Roy Hoopes recounted that "In the early days of the Peace Corps it was thought that 'Shriver's ambassadors' would be skilled technicians or people with two or three years' experience in an activity which would be of use in the developing nations. But it quickly became apparent that experienced technicians would not be available in large enough quantities to satisfy the demand." Instead, the Peace Corps was deluged with liberal arts graduates, so it "trained them in a skill and a language, and turned them loose in the great big, awesome developing world." According to Shriver's successor as Peace Corps Director, Jack Vaughn, this had "remarkable results": "We are discovering . . . that the special hero of the Peace Corps is the Forgotten Man of the '60s: the generalist – the liberal arts graduate with a decent education and lots of ambition." By 1968, assessments of the Peace Corps echoed Alec Dickson's language of a decade before: "the highest skill for the Peace Corps volunteer usually is his attitude."[77]

In selecting generalists, the Peace Corps shifted the emphasis away from technical assistance towards a broader cultural mission. Much like VSO, the Peace Corps helped redefine poverty not as an economic issue but as a problem of "backward" habits of mind.[78] Increasingly, the Peace Corps articulated the assumption that Americans should guide those from the developing world, not

[76] Ibid.

[77] Hoopes, *The Peace Corps Experience*, pp. 3–4.

[78] See Jahanbani, "'A Different Kind of People': The Poor at Home and Abroad, 1935–1968," p. 21.

Figure 1.3 Peace Corps volunteer and nurse Elizabeth Halkola visits a "kampong" or village, Tambunan, Malaysia, 1960s. Paul Conklin/Getty Images.

because they had any expertise but simply because "We have the skills, the habits, the attitudes of technology which are the result of living in a technological society. They need these."[79] (Figure 1.3.)

The maximalist model of development was made explicit in policy decisions pertaining to volunteers' jobs. The Peace Corps set a standard two-year term for volunteers and deployed the vast majority as school teachers or in community development. The concept of community development, still in its infancy in the 1960s, was translated in its broadest terms: volunteers were encouraged to rely on their own initiative to devise projects to advance the local community. This allowed volunteers a great deal of discretion, in adherence to the principle that people from "advanced" cultures could improve local communities simply by modeling modern techniques of organization and strategic cooperation.[80] The Peace Corps' cultural mission collapsed the distinction between public diplomacy and development. Kennedy thought that "the influence of the Peace Corps will go far beyond the day-to-day activities of the volunteers if they can impress people with their 'commitment to freedom' and to 'the advancement of the interests of people everywhere'."[81] In essence,

79 Hayes, *An International Peace Corps: The Promise and Problems*, p. 38.

80 Immerwahr, *Thinking Small.*

81 "First 80 Members Hear President on Aim of Peace Corps," *Washington Post*, August 29, 1961.

spreading a positive image of the United States would inspire people in "underdeveloped" countries to seek capitalism and democracy, and so constituted development in and of itself. As Sargent Shriver announced to a group of volunteers heading to Ethiopia in 1962, "You are revolutionary agents," as "you are agents of social change. You will have a big effect by just being yourselves."[82]

Although it was not mentioned in the Peace Corps' official aims, the Cold War was also crucial to its formation. The Cold War was far more prominent in the Peace Corps than in the British or Australian programs. The first speech in which Kennedy heralded the Peace Corps, delivered in November 1960 while still a Presidential candidate, presented it as a counter to the USSR's foreign aid program. As the United States sat on its hands, "teachers, doctors, technicians and experts desperately needed in a dozen fields by underdeveloped nations are pouring forth from Moscow to advance the cause of world communism." With the Peace Corps, Kennedy argued, "I am convinced that our young men and women . . . are fully capable of overcoming the efforts of Mr. Khrushchev's missionaries."[83] The Cold War objective of capturing hearts and minds across Africa, Asia and Latin America was folded into the Peace Corps' mission.[84]

For the propaganda benefits to flow to the United States, the Peace Corps had to claim development volunteering as something that was distinctly American – even though it was modeled on Australian and British schemes.[85] Kennedy and Shriver claimed the idealism and apparent selflessness of development volunteers as uniquely American characteristics and this message was amplified by contemporary media reports, as examined in Chapter 5 of this book. Intellectual elites followed in lock step. Famed anthropologist Margaret Mead claimed the Peace Corps was "extraordinarily American in its strengths and in its weaknesses."[86] In a book titled *The Peace Corps and American National Character*, Lawrence Fuchs claimed that "the Peace Corps taught me more about American values and character and American government and politics than I had learned in ten years of teaching American Civilization and Politics at Harvard and Brandeis universities."[87]

82 "Shriver says that World Integration is Main Goal," *Washington Post*, July 11, 1962.

83 "Excerpts from Kennedy's speech urging US 'Peace Corps'," *New York Times*, November 3, 1960, p. 32.

84 Westad, *The Global Cold War*; David C. Engerman, "The Romance of Economic Development and New Histories of the Cold War," *Diplomatic History* 28, no. 1 (2004): 23–54; Engerman, *The Price of Aid*.

85 Sobocinska, "How to Win Friends and Influence Nations."

86 Margaret Mead, Foreword to Robert B. Textor, ed. *Cultural Frontiers of the Peace Corps* (Cambridge, MA: MIT Press, 1966), p. vii.

87 Lawrence H. Fuchs, *Those Peculiar Americans: The Peace Corps and American National Character* (New York: Meredith Press, 1967), p. 4.

Ignoring overseas antecedents, Fuchs claimed that the Peace Corps "was born out of America's historic sense of mission to protect liberty at home and spread it abroad."[88] He was not alone. References to overseas forerunners were obscured, and the originality of the Peace Corps routinely stressed, in Peace Corps publicity material and media reports. The 1961 *Complete Peace Corps Guide*, to give one further example, claimed it as "a new and inspiring approach to international relations."[89]

Projecting a positive national image played well to a domestic audience. The early 1960s engendered widespread soul-searching amidst rising critiques of American mass culture. As Shriver put it, there was a "widespread belief that many Americans have gone soft" and the concomitant doubt "whether America is qualified to lead the free world."[90] The bestselling 1958 novel *The Ugly American* had drawn a harsh portrait of Americans working in developing nations.[91] The Peace Corps was presented as a corrective: as Shriver went on, "the exciting thing about the Peace Corps is that we are finding the Americans who have the faith and the conviction."[92]

In addition, the Peace Corps was regarded as a salve to charges of American neocolonialism. During the 1950s and 1960s, European complaints about America's cultural hegemony were joined by increasingly vocal Third World critiques of its political and military incursions.[93] As the *New York Times* reported in early 1961, "native peoples in many areas have the idea that America is the inheritor of the colonial tradition, that Americans like to keep on a plane of superiority far from them."[94] Shriver responded by claiming that "the Peace Corps is concrete proof that Americans stand ready and eager to work and live on equal terms with peoples of all races, creeds and cultures."[95] The image of egalitarian volunteers thrilled academics and experts as well as tens of thousands of young people across the United States. Renowned sociologist David Riesman maintained that "these mostly young and well-educated Americans come with a certain humility and not with the cultural arrogance and superciliousness of many previous generations of conquerors, traders, missionaries and diplomats."[96] He thought that "the egalitarianism of the

[88] Ibid., p. 11.

[89] Roy Hoopes, *The Complete Peace Corps Guide* (New York: The Dial Press, 1961), p. vii.

[90] Sargent Shriver, "Introduction" to Hoopes, *The Complete Peace Corps Guide*, p. 1.

[91] Lederer and Burdick, *The Ugly American*.

[92] Shriver, "Introduction" to Hoopes, *The Complete Peace Corps Guide*, p. 1.

[93] Prashad, The Darker Nations. See also Emily S. Rosenberg, *Spreading the American Dream: American Economic and Cultural Expansion, 1890–1945* (New York: Hill and Wang, 1982).

[94] Gertrude Samuels, "A Force of Youth as a Force of Peace," *New York Times*, February 5, 1961.

[95] Sargent Shriver, "Introduction" to Glenn D. Kittler, *The Peace Corps* (New York: Paperback Library, 1963), p. 5.

[96] Foreword to Fuchs, *Those Peculiar Americans*, p. xii.

volunteers is perhaps the most revolutionary, if impalpable, value that they bring."[97] As the later chapters of this book demonstrate, the truth was far more complicated than such rhetoric suggests; entangled within the Peace Corps' declarations of egalitarianism were threads of Western cultural chauvinism.

The Peace Corps also promised to counter international condemnation of domestic race issues.[98] Like the Volunteer Graduate Scheme and VSO, the Peace Corps arose amid domestic foment around questions of race and citizenship. The Civil Rights movement had been underway for decades, but the rise of direct action strategies from the mid-1950s imbued it with a new force that also drew international attention to America's institutionalized racism. This was of particular concern in the context of the Cold War.[99] It is notable that some of the most enthusiastic press coverage of the Peace Corps, explored in more detail in Chapter 5 of this book, took place simultaneously with the Freedom Rides, which focused domestic and global attention on the inequity of Jim Crow America. The Peace Corps' stated mission – to live with and among people of different nationalities and races – appeared as an answer to charges of racism levelled at the United States.

Although it was rarely made explicit, a final aim lay in extending commercial opportunities for American business and exporting the capitalist model to new areas. Speaking before an audience of businessmen at the Commonwealth Club of California in October 1963, Sargent Shriver claimed the Peace Corps was "an example of free enterprise at work," that "exemplifies and even generates private enterprise." Not only was the Peace Corps premised on individual volunteers' initiative, but more to the point, volunteers helped organize local people into corporations and cooperatives so that they could compete in larger markets. He gave examples of volunteers who had helped standardize local produce and marketed it for export, redirected local labor to increase production, or established savings and loan associations and credit unions. Peace Corps volunteers were exporting the logic of capitalism: as Shriver continued, "we often find that they have become the Wright Brothers or Edisons or Fords of the world in which they are living."[100]

Even more than the Volunteer Graduate Scheme and VSO, then, the Peace Corps manifested a multiplication of aims. The *Washington Post* captured this fact in a report claiming the Peace Corps variously represented a way "to serve the United States ... to alleviate suffering ... to aid mankind ... to sell democracy ... to fight communism ... to help solve world problems ... to

97 Ibid., p. xiv.

98 Cobbs Hoffman, *All You Need Is Love*, p. 27.

99 Mary L. Dudziak, "*Brown* as a Cold War Case," *Journal of American History* 91, no. 1 (2004, June): 32–42.

100 Speech by R. Sargent Shriver to The Commonwealth Club of California, October 11, 1963, NLA: MS 9347, Box 2, Folder 6.

trade cultures . . . to practice diplomacy on the level of the people."[101] Again, this multiplication of aims caused tensions and practical difficulties, especially in selection of volunteers. The basic question was: should volunteers be selected because they had the technical skills required by developing nations, or because they would spread a positive image of America? Shriver settled on charm over expertise in the early 1960s and elected to send BA generalists over technical specialists. But this policy was widely criticized by receiving nations, who questioned the benefits of English teaching or community development projects and requested volunteers with specific technical skills. In 1969, incoming Director of the Peace Corps Joe Blatchford introduced a "New Directions" platform. Rather than liberal arts majors, the Peace Corps now sought to attract "Irrigation specialists, automotive mechanics, and electricians . . . architects, economists and city planners."[102] Relevant experts proved far more difficult to recruit, however, and this policy was again rolled back in the 1970s.

Such problems notwithstanding, the multiplication of aims was, overall, a strength that allowed the Peace Corps to capture support across the American political spectrum. Although the Peace Corps was generally received with great enthusiasm, it also met some powerful opponents. Republican Congressman H. R. Gross of Iowa famously derided it as a "haven for draft dodgers," a view backed by then-Vice President Richard Nixon.[103] Congresswoman Frances Bolton, a Republican from Ohio and member of the House Foreign Affairs Committee, thought the Peace Corps was "a terrifying thing" that had the potential to "wreck the whole world."[104] The Peace Corps' multiple aims provided Shriver with the flexibility he needed to win over critics. In the weeks before the Peace Corps' first budget appropriation was due to go to Capitol Hill in August 1961, Shriver hosted special breakfasts for Senators and members of Congress. To some, Shriver emphasized the benefits accruing to developing nations, others were sold on the benefits to American youth, while others still were won over by the program's promise as a weapon in the Cold War. The almost gymnastic flexibility of the Peace Corps meant that it had something for everyone: both Congress and the Senate overwhelmingly voted in favor of the Peace Corps.[105] Ongoing support saw the Peace Corps' appropriation soar to $114 million by 1966.[106]

[101] Julius Duscha, "Fate of Peace Corps Hangs on its Vanguard," *Washington Post*, August 27, 1961.

[102] Peace Corps, *Tenth Annual Report* (Washington, DC: Peace Corps, 1971), p. 6.

[103] "Peace Corps Assailed as Draft Dodge," *Washington Post*, March 11, 1961.

[104] Marie Smith, "Peace Corps Disturbs her Peace of Mind," *Washington Post*, March 9, 1961.

[105] Jerry Kluttz, "Peace Corps Weathers Hill Barrage with Few Feelings Hurt at Hearing," *Washington Post*, August 5, 1961.

[106] *Peace Corps, 5th Annual Report to Congress*, p. 69.

As Chapter 3 of this book reveals, the strategic flexibility of the Peace Corps allowed it to capture supporters from across civil society too. In a report to Kennedy in 1961, Samuel Hayes stated that

> Some saw the Peace Corps as mainly an agency to help the nations of Africa, Asia and Latin America step up the pace of their economic and social development. Others saw in it a means of helping to train the youth of the United States and of other countries for responsible citizenship; or of building increased mutual understanding among peoples of different nations; or of helping the United States with some of its own problems of education and social welfare; or of training a pool of young people for later international careers.[107]

Whichever worthwhile goal an individual believed in, the Peace Corps was the answer. As Maurice L. Albertson noted, "the Peace Corps means many things to many people," but far from a weakness, "one of the great strengths of the Peace Corps lies in the multiplicity of purposes it can serve."[108] The Peace Corps had turned constructive ambiguity into an art form but, notably, its imagined interlocutors were nearly always Western. Support for the Peace Corps in the Global South was assumed rather than actively forged. Although the Peace Corps sought formal invitations from national leaders and set out to charm some elites, little effort was made to ascertain what kinds of assistance volunteer-receiving communities actually wanted and how this might vary in strikingly different contexts across half the globe. The Peace Corps was devised in Washington as a response to American motivations. Communities and stakeholders across the Global South had little input into its formation, rationale or operations.

Conclusion

In the two decades from 1950, development volunteering grew from the bright idea of a handful of Australian students to a global phenomenon. Australia's Volunteer Graduate Scheme, Britain's VSO and the United States Peace Corps had different genealogies, forms of organization and spoke to different national contexts. But all three adopted the same basic model of development volunteering, by which mostly young volunteers left home to work abroad on long-term postings at rates of pay below those typically enjoyed by expatriates. All three programs enjoyed the critical support of their national governments from an early stage and all three held multiple aims that created a fundamental and ongoing tension between the desire to help others, to help themselves and

107 Hayes, *An International Peace Corps: The Promise and Problems.*

108 Maurice L. Albertson, Andrew E. Rice and Pauline E. Birky, *New Frontiers for American Youth: Perspective on the Peace Corps* (Washington, DC: Public Affairs Press, 1961), p. 14.

to improve the national image at a time of domestic and international crises regarding race, decolonization and the Cold War.

Development volunteering proved to be remarkably flexible as it moved from grassroots idea to global movement. As one Peace Corps report noted, development volunteering was "An Idea for All Seasons."[109] Australia was a settler colony and a middle-power, Britain was a waning Empire and the United States was a superpower at the peak of its hegemony, but all found the development volunteering concept appealing. Development volunteering attracted different constituencies for different reasons: some valued the promised contribution to development, others thought it would benefit their youth and others still hoped to improve their nation's image, or build international understanding, or stimulate trade. The multiplication of aims complicated the day-to-day operation of the three programs, but it functioned strategically to elicit support from across the political spectrum and secure funding from the Australian, British and United States governments. Development volunteering agencies assumed that their good intentions would be just as appealing to nations and communities in the Global South. As this book's later chapters show, the reality was far more complicated. But receiving communities' ambivalent responses to volunteers rarely figured in decisions made in Melbourne, London or Washington. Throughout the 1950s and 1960s, development agencies were resolutely focused on Western intentions and neglected to either measure actual impacts on the ground or seek out viewpoints from recipient communities across varying political, cultural and economic contexts in the Global South.

Although development volunteering was widely praised as a way to improve international relations, the Volunteer Graduate Scheme, VSO and the Peace Corps articulated a hierarchical vision of international society in which the "developed" world had much to teach the "developing" world. The cultural mission of development volunteering was explicit in VSO's desire to send teenaged school-leavers in the belief that, in development, character was more important than skills – even as developing nations insisted otherwise. It was also explicit in the Peace Corps' selection of recent BA graduates, who comprised some 85 percent of volunteers in 1966.[110] Development volunteering helped articulate a maximalist vision of development that was not only economic and technical but also cultural and psychological. This maximalist vision proposed that individuals, as well as entire societies, were "underdeveloped" and therefore targets for development projects. It also expanded the scope for Western intervention across the Global South, which is the subject of the following chapter.

[109] Peace Corps, *5th Annual Report to Congress*, p. 4

[110] Peace Corps, *5th Annual Report to Congress*, p. 58.

2

Conquering the Globe

Australia's Volunteer Graduate Scheme, Britain's VSO and the United States Peace Corps were expansionist enterprises. Even when they were not sure of their own objectives, let alone effectiveness, each program was determined to expand across the globe. They sought to expand in two ways: by placing volunteers in more developing nations and by influencing other developed nations to establish programs in their image. It is surprising just how quickly the Volunteer Graduate Scheme, VSO and the Peace Corps began to explore, and then pursue, the goal of extending their spread and influence; indeed, each of these programs set down this path *before they had a single volunteer on the ground.* Initially, it took a good deal of effort to convince people of volunteers' value. Even the Peace Corps did not have an easy time of it: entire wings of the agency were tasked with persuading developing nations to accept American volunteers and convincing other developed nations (and the United Nations) to start their own development volunteering programs.

Rather than an inexorable moral force, development volunteering spread because individuals and groups wanted to conquer the globe and they had worked hard towards achieving that goal. By the mid-1960s, their success was not in any doubt. By that time, volunteers from nations across the Global North could be found in every corner of the Global South. The humanitarian-development complex was in train.

"Pioneers": Australia's Volunteer Graduate Scheme

Australia's Volunteer Graduate Scheme was initially imagined as an experiment that was limited in both scope and duration. It had been sparked by an Indonesian request for Australian help to mitigate a skills shortage caused by the rapid departure of Dutch colonial bureaucrats. The Dutch colonial administration had neglected "native" education to such an extent that, at independence, only a small number of Indonesians possessed the necessary skills for modern governance.[1] As a result, as Volunteer Graduate Scheme Honorary

[1] Christiaan Lambert Penders, "Colonial Education Policy and Practice in Indonesia, 1900–1942" (PhD thesis, Australian National University, 1968). See also Suzanne Moon,

Secretary Jim Webb reflected, "We are inclined to think that there is no other country as suited to the experiment as Indonesia."[2] Most volunteers assumed that their tenure in Indonesia would be brief. Australian volunteers would help fill positions until Indonesian replacements could be trained up, a process that would take several years at most. By 1960 some volunteers had begun to think that "the weaning process is now reaching the stage where it should be finished off completely."[3]

It is remarkable, then, just how quickly the Volunteer Graduate Scheme's Executive Committee turned to the question of expansion, and how tenaciously they pursued the goal. Even before Herb Feith disembarked in Indonesia in June 1951 – before anyone could know whether such an experiment would work, let alone provide any benefit – he and fellow Executive Committee members were already planning its extension to other nations. In May 1951, they asked high-ranking Australian diplomat Tom Critchley which other nations might be willing to receive volunteers; Critchley suggested Burma, India and Malaya.[4] Within a month of arriving in Jakarta, and after only one week at work, Herb Feith thought of his experience as "a forerunner of possible other similar ventures in other parts of South-East Asia," ideally in collaboration with UN agencies.[5] Before long, horizons expanded to Burma, India, Pakistan, Ceylon, the Gold Coast (colonial Ghana) and Nigeria.[6] By 1954, the Executive Committee had begun to think globally, claiming "There is no reason why ... countries other than Australia should not consider the whole group of underdeveloped countries as their field." Jim Webb began to carve up the developing world by zone of influence, as "it would obviously be more economical to achieve some rationalisation and for European [organizations] to see the underdeveloped countries of the Middle East and African regions as their more specific field."[7]

Burma would be the first step. Countless hours and substantial sums of money were spent on "pioneering a Graduate Scheme for Burma."[8] Over the course of the 1950s, the Executive Committee of the Volunteer Graduate Scheme pursued every possible avenue to try and establish a volunteer program in Burma. They leveraged student networks to lobby Burmese student

Technology and Ethical Idealism: A History of Development in the Netherlands East Indies (Leiden: CNWS Publications, 2007).

2 Jim Webb to John Thompson, September 28, 1954, NLA: MS 2601, Box 2, Folder 19.

3 Ken V. Bailey, "Comments on the Volunteer Graduate Scheme," February 8, 1960, NLA: MS 2601, Box 12, Folder 117.

4 Tom Critchley to Betty Evans, May 24, 1951, NLA: MS 2601, Box 4, Folder 39.

5 Herb Feith to G. S. McDonald, July 26, 1951, NLA: MS 2601, Box 6, Folder 55.

6 Jim Webb to John Thompson, September 28, 1954, NLA: MS 2601, Box 2, Folder 19.

7 Jim Webb to John Thompson, August 13, 1954, NLA: MS 2601, Box 2, Folder 19.

8 Jim Webb to NUAUS Council, "Scheme for Graduate Employment in Indonesia," February 1955, NLA: MS 2601, Box 1, Folder 2.

leaders who had risen to prominent positions in the nation's postcolonial government.[9] The head of the National Union of Australian University Students, Chev Kidson, visited Burma in 1955, as did his successor in 1957; both made enthusiastic representations on behalf of the Volunteer Graduate Scheme. Contacts forged through the World Student Christian Federation and World Council of Churches were also pursued, leading to meetings with several Burmese Christian leaders. The Volunteer Graduate Scheme made further approaches through multilateral organizations, targeting Australians working for the United Nations in Rangoon, as well as the regional heads of UNICEF. The indefatigable Jim Webb also lobbied Australian diplomats, from the Secretary for External Affairs down to relatively junior bureaucrats. In 1961, the Volunteer Graduate Scheme decided to ramp up efforts, sending a "Field Secretary" on a four-week trip to Burma, Thailand, Malaya and Singapore to drum up interest.[10] To pay for this trip, the Volunteer Graduate Scheme sought contributions from former volunteers and other supporters through a special Development Fund.

Very little eventuated despite the investment of time and money. It soon became apparent that, "although individual Burmese people may show a polite interest in general, a number of key people don't really want a scheme and in fact may be quite suspicious of any approaches made."[11] Burmese interlocutors were wary of volunteers who claimed to be independent but were actually funded by their national government. Returning from Burma in 1955, Kidson reported that he had met "From people at a lower level in Government Departments a stoginess [*sic*] related to national pride which meant in practice considerable suspicion of our motives."[12] A 1958 report cautioned that "Any approach to Burmese about a Volunteer Graduate Scheme must take due account of the fact that it is not initially easy for people in a post-colonial situation to accept the idea that young Australians are really prepared to live and work in their country on the basis of equality." Such responses "have so far not led us to believe that there is any very favourable indication that Australian graduates would be very welcomed in Burma."[13] Even the considerable expense incurred by the 1961 tour came to nothing: the Field Secretary reported Burmese fears that the Volunteer Graduate Scheme "would infringe on Burma's eastern oriented neutralism."[14] Despite years

[9] James Thomas to Jim Webb, December 20, 1956 and February 24, 1958, NLA: MS 2601, Box 3, Folder 28.

[10] Jim Webb to Michael Rubbo, November 9, 1961, NLA: MS 2601, Box 10, Folder 103.

[11] Jim Webb to James Thomas, August 16, 1957, NLA: MS 2601, Box 3, Folder 32.

[12] Chev Kidson to Jim Webb, July 29, 1955, NLA: MS 2601, Box 3, Folder 32.

[13] Jim Webb, "Extension of Volunteer Graduate Scheme, [undated] 1958," NLA: MS 2601, Box 3, Folder 32.

[14] Michael Rubbo, "Investigation of the Volunteer Graduate Scheme in Indonesia as a Preparation for Taking up the Position of Field Secretary in Australia this Year," undated, *c.*1962, NLA: MS 2601, Box 10, Folder 103.

of effort, the Volunteer Graduate Scheme never achieved its aim of expanding to Burma, or indeed anywhere beyond Indonesia.

Jim Webb had better luck establishing new volunteer programs, which looked beyond Indonesia from the start. Webb launched the Overseas Service Bureau in 1962; by this time development volunteering had caught on abroad, paving the way for greater success. The Overseas Service Bureau had a broader remit from the start: its first Bulletin advertised volunteer positions and paid jobs in the Pacific, Southeast Asia and Africa. Webb then went on to play a key role in the formation of Australian Volunteers Abroad (AVA), the immediate successor organization to the Volunteer Graduate Scheme. With Webb as Director, the first group of AVA volunteers departed in 1964 to Papua New Guinea, the Solomon Islands, Tanganyika and Nigeria. By 1966 they were posted to ten countries across Asia, Africa and the Pacific Islands.

The Volunteer Graduate Scheme also had more success spreading the volunteering model to other Western nations. From early 1951, again before fielding their first volunteer, the Volunteer Graduate Scheme initiated contact with the New Zealand University Students' Association and the New Zealand Student Christian Movement, suggesting that they establish a volunteer program of their own. The correspondence continued and, in 1955, Jim Webb found himself sharing a flight from Indonesia with New Zealand's Minister for External Affairs and the Department's Secretary. By the time the plane touched down, Webb had convinced the Secretary, who became "very keen" about a potential volunteer scheme.[15] Within months, the New Zealand Volunteer Graduate Scheme was formally established, funded by the New Zealand government but with strong ties to its Australian counterpart.

In 1954, young Canadian Lewis Perinbam heard of the Australian scheme through the World University Service and decided to set up a similar program. Perinbam visited Indonesia in 1955 to see the scheme in action and build the necessary contacts, but soon decided that Ghana would be a more appropriate partner for Canada. Ghana was in the Commonwealth, which he thought would make the scheme an easier sell politically, and it was on the cusp of decolonization. As Perinbam wrote to the Canadian government, "Arising from the Australian experience, it is suggested that a similar program be established with Ghana . . . in whose progress and prosperity Canada is greatly interested."[16] Perinbam's initiative ultimately developed into Canadian University Service Overseas (CUSO), of which Perinbam became founding Executive Director in 1961.[17]

15 Jim Webb to Herb and Betty Feith, May 1, 1955, NLA: MS 2601, Box 1, Folder 57.

16 "Information letter, Canadian Volunteer Graduate Program," Papers of Herb Feith, undated, *c.*1959, NLA: MS 9926, Box 20.

17 For a full account of CUSO, see Ruth Compton Brouwer, *Canada's Global Villagers: CUSO in Development, 1961–86* (Vancouver and Toronto: UBC Press, 2013); Ian Smillie, *The Land of Lost Content: A History of CUSO* (Toronto: Deneau Publishers, 1985).

These early successes should not be taken as evidence that spreading development volunteering beyond Australia was straightforward, or even simple. The Volunteer Graduate Scheme explored every possible avenue for expansion and, while there were some triumphs, hundreds of other contacts proved to be dead ends. In its first decade, Volunteer Graduate Scheme discussed its activities with the World's Student Christian Federation headquartered at Geneva, the World Council of Churches, the North American Office of the World Council of Christian Education and with several branches of the Student Christian Movement in the US, Canada and the UK. Secular student and educational organizations including UNESCO, World University Service in the United States and Canada, and the National Union of Students in the Netherlands also expressed interest in the Australian scheme.[18] Discussions with hundreds of organizations and individuals in nations including the United States proved fruitless throughout the 1950s.

Nonetheless, the idea that the Volunteer Graduate Scheme was a forerunner for a global movement was vigorously pursued. In 1954, Herb Feith reflected that

> More and more we have been thinking of the [volunteering] idea as something with not merely temporary and local significance, and worth pushing as a pattern of one type of relationship between Western and Asian (and perhaps also African) countries ... It seems that we have a responsibility to open up more 'spheres of investment' not only for Australians but for others.[19]

These "spheres of investment" extended both to other developing nations ("the receiving end") and Western countries ("the recruiting end").[20] Feith and other members of the Executive Committee regarded Australians as natural pioneers who could open up new areas for Europeans or Americans. "We are fortunate in this country in having a high degree of social mobility and a strong egalitarian tradition," Webb noted, and "It may be that graduates from some older European nations would find the adjustment process far more difficult." He went on: "This is one reason why we are keen to 'pioneer' Burma as soon as possible – to help open up the field for others."[21] As Herb Feith added, "Imagine a German bloke trying to make his way to Burma or the Gold Coast ... Australians could help open up the field for people of other nationalities. It will be so much easier for us."[22] The desire to expand across the West

[18] "Correspondence with Overseas Contacts, 1953–1959," NLA: MS 2601, Box 2, Folder 19.

[19] Herb Feith to "Djakartans etc.," June 21, 1954, NLA: MS 2601, Box 5, Folder 49.

[20] Herb Feith to Alison Frankel and Ollie McMichael, May 14, 1954, NLA: MS 2601, Box 6, Folder 62.

[21] Jim Webb to John Thompson, September 28, 1954, NLA: MS 2601, Box 2, Folder 19.

[22] Herb Feith to Don Anderson and Jim Webb, August 27, 1954, NLA: MS 2601, Box 5, Folder 48.

was partly due to a genuine belief in the benefits of development volunteering. But there was also an element of national pride and a desire to claim a legacy. References to Feith and the Volunteer Graduate Scheme as "pioneers" occur as early as 1954. By 1959, Herb Feith declared that "None can usurp Australia's position as pioneer in this important scheme and it is natural that she should be jealous of her accomplishments."[23]

Maintaining Britain's Prestige

In an echo of the Australian program, VSO's founders were determined to expand even before the departure of the first group of volunteers in 1958. Mora Dickson, Alec Dickson's wife, recalled that "We saw the departure of the very first volunteers not as a climax but as a first step in something that might grow to proportions which we could not at that moment visualise."[24] Even though he was still unsure of VSO's purpose or contribution, Alec Dickson began to think that "expansion was not merely possible, it was virtually inevitable."[25] Britain's imperial history facilitated Dickson's ambitions. The first contingent of twelve VSO volunteers were posted to Sarawak, a British crown colony until the formation of Malaysia in 1963. In its second year, VSO volunteers worked in four African nations – all British colonies, trust territories or former colonies – as well as Sarawak. The following year, volunteers were posted to eighteen countries and the year after that, 1961, volunteers were placed in twenty-seven countries across Africa, Asia, the Middle East, the Caribbean, the Pacific Islands and the outlying Falkland Islands.[26] Voluntary Service Overseas grew quickly and its sights soon expanded beyond the former British Empire. As the Foreign Office put it in 1960, so far volunteers "have gone exclusively to Commonwealth or Colonial territories. But there is no reason why they should not also be sent to a foreign country if some reputable organisation in that country asks for them."[27] The Department of Technical Cooperation agreed, suggesting that VSO's graduate program should follow "a division as between Independent Commonwealth Countries, Dependent Commonwealth countries and others in the proportion of 48:28:24."[28] In 1962–3, the program nearly doubled to 320 volunteers across 53 countries.[29] The following year,

[23] "The Volunteer Graduate Scheme Idea – Could it Work Elsewhere?," *Djembatan*, Vol. 2, no. 4, 1959, pp. 29–31.

[24] Mora Dickson, *A World Elsewhere: Voluntary Service Overseas* (London: Dennis Dobson, 1964), p. 15.

[25] Adams, *Voluntary Service Overseas: The Story of the First Ten Years*, pp. 64–5.

[26] "Volunteers – 1960–61," VSO Archive, Box 698.

[27] Anthony Haigh to Charles Johnston, June 7, 1960, TNA: CO 859/1445.

[28] Minutes of Lockwood Committee Meeting, September 26, 1962, London School of Economics Women's Library (Henceforth LSE): RVA Records, Box 40.

[29] Report of the VSO Council for year ended March 31, 1963, VSO Archive, Box 31.

VSO sent 502 volunteers to 57 countries, and although the majority went to former British nations, some worked in "foreign" nations including Algeria, Bolivia, Iran and Mali.

After Dickson's departure in early 1962, VSO's expansion was prompted by the British government rather than by the organization itself. Whitehall supported VSO at least in part because of the assumption that it would improve Britain's standing in current and former colonies. The British Council, the government's public diplomacy arm, was tasked with overseeing VSO's activities abroad from 1962 due to the assessment that VSO was "a valuable means of exercising influence" across the decolonizing world.[30] Such views also held in Westminster. The House of Commons debated a proposal to increase government support for VSO in December 1962. The motion passed easily; indeed, many MPs overstepped the brief by insisting that the government encourage VSO to expand its activities faster and further than proposed. As Conservative MP John Maitland argued, "Only by the Government providing organisation and public money on the scale that is required can we get an expansion of this work to the extent that is needed." He thought that "we owe a duty – perhaps more than any other country – to the vast areas of the world which in the past we have guided, governed and, finally, led to independence." Voluntary Service Overseas was, he thought "one of the most worth-while things we do" and "it is certain that a good deal more could be done to extend it." His views were echoed across the aisle. Labour MP Reg Prentice urged that "we must do more in technical assistance and to encourage people to go from the more developed countries to the less developed countries in considerable numbers . . . I hope that there will be a very big expansion of this sort of thing."[31]

Within a decade, VSO had broadened its remit beyond the boundaries of the former British Empire to "the under-privileged half of the world."[32] The boundaries of the "under-privileged half of the world" were rarely defined. In the absence of precision, assumptions about which nations were "developed" or "underdeveloped" were carried over from the colonial period. MP Jo Grimond's contribution to the 1962 Parliamentary debate on VSO is typical in its lack of precision: Grimond argued that "the greatest and most urgent task of the Western world . . . is to provide the skills to assist these people to run their own countries."[33] Grimond's failure to define who "these people" were, where "their own countries" were situated, or indeed which nations constituted "the Western world," was so customary as to avoid comment. Yet, it was laden with colonial-era presumptions about the nature and location of backwardness,

[30] K. R. Crook to D. M. Smith, June 8, 1961, TNA: DO 163/22.
[31] House of Commons Debates, December 12, 1962, Vol. 669, cc423–81.
[32] Adams, *Voluntary Service Overseas: The Story of the First Ten Years*, p. 16.
[33] House of Commons Debates, December 12, 1962, Vol. 669, cc423–81.

now rephrased as underdevelopment. Moreover, his assumption that "developed" nations were also "Western" reflected the twin contexts of decolonization and the Cold War that framed international development during the 1950s and 1960s.[34]

Voluntary Service Overseas' desire to reach as many places as possible was not entirely uncontested. After a glittering military career, VSO Council member General Sir Gerald Templer knew a thing or two about strategy. In 1963, he wrote a stinging memorandum berating VSO for sending volunteers to "foreign" countries. He felt it "absurd" that a volunteer had been sent to Iran, "Where he could not hope to make any impact," and equally "absurd that we should only send 1 school leaver to Hong Kong." Sending volunteers to "countries where British influence has in the past been negligible," he argued, was simply "a waste of money," and by doing so, VSO "spread our small amount of butter too thinly on too many slices of bread." Instead, he demanded that VSO gave "more prominence to the Commonwealth and what was left of the Empire."[35] Yet, Templer's opposition was the exception rather than the rule: far from scaling back, VSO pursued the goal of expansion throughout the 1960s. By the end of the decade, VSO volunteers could be found in numerous "foreign" nations, especially those that had become flashpoints in the Cold War. As VSO Director D. H. Whiting noted in 1963, "While it is not desirable that the motives of volunteers should be consciously political, it is clear that in many instances – Algeria is a case in point – if we fail to respond Moscow or Cairo will be approached."[36] As Templer had noted, this spread came at the expense of effectiveness; often only a single volunteer was posted to a foreign nation. For VSO, the desire to extend the organization's reach triumphed over volunteers' capacity to make a genuine impact in any one nation.

Voluntary Service Overseas also sought to influence other developed nations, particularly in the Commonwealth. Dickson thought it only natural that a British scheme should serve as inspiration for others. A five-year plan tabled in 1960 anticipated a gradual and orderly expansion: twenty-five volunteers recruited annually from Canada from 1962, joined by a further twenty-five from India and Australia the following year, twenty-five from New Zealand and Ceylon from 1964, and twenty-five from South Africa and "other Commonwealth countries" from 1965.[37] Dickson held particular hope for this final step, as "some of our volunteers from this country might succeed

[34] Westad, *The Global Cold War* and David C. Engerman, *The Price of Aid: The Economic Cold War in India* (Cambridge: Harvard University Press, 2018).

[35] "Memorandum on VSO policy touching distribution of volunteers," Minutes of VSO Executive Committee, October 1, 1963, VSO Archive, Box 31.

[36] D. H. Whiting, "Distribution of School Leavers," Minutes of Executive Committee, September 23, 1963, VSO Archive, Box 31.

[37] "Annual Report and Forecast for 1960," TNA: CO 859/1445.

in touching a chord in the hearts and minds of the locally-born young Whites in Kenya and Rhodesia, so that they in turn might also find adventure in undertaking similar kind of work amongst Africans in their own territories."[38] The racial undercurrent to Dickson's thinking – that white citizens of the Commonwealth would become volunteers in order to mentor their dark-skinned compatriots – was unusual only for being expressed so bluntly. Dickson's plans clarified what was usually left unsaid in the expansionary schemes of development volunteering programs of the 1960s. The Executive Committee that took over after Dickson's departure trod with greater caution. They believed that, with expansion, "the question at once arises: Are we to divide the Commonwealth, or perhaps the world, into spheres of influence and arrange that Australian volunteers, for instance, should both monopolise and confine themselves to territories between Singapore and the Central Pacific, while British and other Commonwealth volunteers cater for the other countries?" The idea was logical, but aroused a great deal of opposition, with the fear that Britain's influence in Southeast Asia and the Pacific would be supplanted by Australia's.[39] In the end these questions proved moot; VSO's attempts at Commonwealth expansion were rebuffed, with every interlocutor expressing a "wish to be independent of us."[40] Rather than coordinating a Commonwealth-wide program, VSO had to make do with British volunteers alone.

Far from assuming global leadership of development volunteering, VSO came to feel increasingly embattled as the launch of the United States Peace Corps threatened to eclipse its activities. Dickson observed the Peace Corps with considerable disquiet. As Mora Dickson related, the Peace Corps "alternately depressed and exhilarated him. He saw the fruition of a vision that had once seemed unrealizable, but in a country other than his own."[41] The long-standing transatlantic rivalry between the United States and United Kingdom only sharpened the sense that, with the rise of the Peace Corps, "the opportunity for Britain to lead in this field was gone."[42] Speaking on the issue as the Peace Corps launched in early 1961, Welsh MP Eirene White warned of the "unflattering comparison ... between the vigorous and youthful leadership given on the other side of the Atlantic and the rather effete gamesmanship that we have on this side."[43] The Minister of State for Colonial Affairs, Lord Perth, called for "appropriate publicity to be given to 'Voluntary Service Overseas' as

[38] The Thomas Holland Memorial Lecture by Alec Dickson, February 23, 1960, TNA: CO 859/1445.
[39] E. R. Chadwick, "VSO Regional Organisations," May 1962, TNA: OD 10/4.
[40] Minutes of a Meeting of the Executive Committee of VSO, April 2, 1963, VSO Archive, Box 31.
[41] Dickson, *A Chance to Serve*, p. 109.
[42] Ibid., pp. 105–6.
[43] House of Commons Debates, March 9, 1961, Vol. 636, cc679–82.

being the original concept which either actually inspired President Kennedy's Peace Corps or at any rate resembles it closely." He recognized that "it is not, of course, possible for the UK government as such to take credit for voluntary endeavour," but wanted more people to know about VSO "as part of the projection of Britain."[44] Plans were hatched for a surge in volunteers to "maintain a foothold in territories which would otherwise turn exclusively to America."[45] The *Observer* ran a lengthy article under the headline "Britain has its own 'peace corps': Pioneer of Kennedy's scheme."[46] But it was too late. In the House of Commons, MP Reginald Prentice railed that "this is typical of what happens in so many different fields. A good idea is started in Britain and is copied and developed on a bigger scale in America." He feared that this pointed to a wider ineptitude, as "we often lack the drive and the capacity to carry through our good ideas until they operate on a sufficiently big scale."[47]

Such anxiety reveals the extent to which VSO had become a site for British national pride. The fear that American prestige had supplanted British power in former colonies also shadowed VSO's concern. As Dickson wrote, "What thoughts must possess an Englishman on hearing that Jamaica and North Borneo are now among those supplicating for the services of the Peace Corps?"[48] In private, Dickson was more forthright. In April 1961, Dickson bumped into Minister of State for the Colonies Lord Perth at a luncheon engagement. The chance encounter soon turned into an "attack . . . about how we had sold out to America in regard to graduates to East Africa." Perth recounted that "I was pretty short with him and told him that it really was not possible to keep the whole of educational development of East Africa to ourselves, and indeed that the Americans had filled a very serious gap and we should all be extremely grateful." Dickson failed to see it that way; for him, VSO was a matter of national pride and so "He looked pretty miserable and made no comment on my strong reply to him."[49] Dickson's mood further soured: despite his early enthusiasm for the Peace Corps, by early 1962 he had begun to think that its impact was "anti-British."[50] Only his ousting from VSO avoided further escalation of transatlantic tensions.

As well as the loss of national pride, Dickson's personal legacy was endangered by the rise of the Peace Corps. More than a decade after his departure from VSO, Mora Dickson published a biography of her husband that claimed the development volunteering model as his personal legacy. She declared that

44 O. H. Morris to Mr. Wilshire, March 27, 1961, TNA: CO 859/1445.

45 Viscount Amory to Iain Macleod, April 21, 1961, TNA: DO 163/22.

46 Robert Stephens, "Britain has its own 'peace corps': pioneer of Kennedy's scheme," The *Observer*, March 5, 1961.

47 House of Commons Debates, December 12, 1962, Vol. 669, cc423–81.

48 Alec Dickson, "A great voluntary movement," *The Guardian*, January 29, 1962.

49 Lord Perth to Mr. Rogers, April 24, 1961, TNA: CO 859/1446.

50 C. A. Hankey to P. Rogers, February 2, 1962, TNA: OD 10/4.

"tens of thousands of people who have come face to face with human needs in the Third World . . . owe their experience to one man – Alec Dickson." She went on to state that he was "acknowledged by Americans to be . . . 'both the guru and the doyen' of the volunteer movement."[51] Echoing the language of the Australian Volunteer Graduate Scheme she seized particularly on the word 'pioneer,' writing that "Voluntary Service Overseas was . . . the pioneer of an increasing list of 'export' volunteer organisations."[52] Claiming leadership of development volunteering remained a matter of some importance for VSO even after Dickson's departure. In a book recounting VSO's first decade, author Michael Adams noted that "The volunteer movement is one of the strikingly hopeful phenomena of the postwar world – and it is a movement in which Britain gave the lead." Again, the word "pioneer" featured prominently, with Adams claiming that "Voluntary Service Overseas . . . pioneered this movement."[53]

Dickson's pique notwithstanding, the rise of the Peace Corps was in fact a boon to VSO. The Peace Corps' budget and scope gave rise to substantial political pressure to further increase government funding for VSO. Although VSO always remained nominally independent, it was largely underwritten by the Department of Technical Cooperation, which became "anxious to extend this work and increase the number of overseas volunteers."[54] A 1962 Department of Technical Cooperation White Paper noted that, when it came to development volunteering, "All this work needs to be expanded, intensified and co-ordinated."[55] Government funding rose, in percentage and real terms, over the course of the 1960s; so much so that Treasury lodged multiple objections about VSO's suspected "sumptuous balance."[56] From 1962, VSO's graduate program was placed under the purview of the Lockwood Committee, a government apparatus tasked with steering the British Volunteer Program. The Lockwood Committee also viewed the expansion of British volunteer programs across the developing and developed worlds as a matter of "great urgency."[57]

As a result, VSO expanded further and faster than anticipated. Its first five-year plan, produced in 1960, had projected 450 volunteers in the field by 1965, of whom 350 would come from Britain and 100 from other Commonwealth nations. In reality, 550 volunteers were posted in 1963, all from Britain. That year, VSO revised its 1965 target to 1,100 volunteers, more than double

51 Dickson, *A Chance to Serve*, unpaginated frontispiece.
52 Ibid., p. 19.
53 Adams, *Voluntary Service Overseas: The Story of the First Ten Years*, pp. 13–14.
54 House of Commons Debates, December 12, 1962, Vol. 669, cc423–81.
55 Cited in Williams and Moyes, *Not by Governments Alone*, p. 36.
56 R. L. Baxter to C. N. F. Odgers, September 13, 1962, TNA: OD 10/4.
57 Lockwood Committee Minutes, 1962–1969, Minutes of Meeting June 21, 1962, LSE: RVA Records, Box 40.

the original.[58] From a trickle of volunteers posted to current or former British dependencies, by the mid-1960s VSO had expanded its reach across much of the Global South.

"Practically All Parts of the World"

Like the Volunteer Graduate Scheme and VSO, the Peace Corps was eager to expand across both recipient and donor nations. And again, this expansion was planned before a single volunteer had been deployed. Announcing his Executive Order to establish a Peace Corps on March 1, 1961, John F. Kennedy said, "Let us hope that other nations will mobilize the spirit and energies and skill of their people in some form of Peace Corps – making our own effort only one step in a major international effort to increase the welfare of all men and improve understanding among nations."[59]

The Peace Corps quickly achieved a truly global scope that was in keeping with the United States' power. The same month that the Peace Corps was launched, Sargent Shriver explained that he was exploring possibilities "in practically all parts of the world, South America, Africa, India, Southeast Asia, and the Far East."[60] In keeping with his global vision, Shriver immediately organized his Office of Program Development and Operations into four geographic divisions: Latin America, Far East, Africa and Near East-South Asia, as well as a Division of UN and International Agency Programs. By 1964, just three years after its launch, Peace Corps volunteers had been placed in forty-five countries across Latin America, Africa, Asia and the Middle East. By 1971, volunteers had been placed in seventy different countries.[61] Maps visually expressed the program's growing reach (Figure 2.1). One 1965 map represented the countries hosting Peace Corps volunteers – a vast swathe straddling the equator – by coloring them green.[62] This inverted the color scheme favored by cartographers of the British Empire, but the message was much the same: the sun never set on the Peace Corps.

This expansion was intimately connected both to colonial legacies and the Cold War. Alongside Ghana, the earliest Peace Corps volunteers departed for the Philippines, which was a former US colony, Tanganyika, still a British trust territory in 1961, and Colombia, which had a long history of US domination. The *1st Annual Peace Corps Report* proudly noted that "both the so-called 'neutralist' nations and those more commonly called our 'allies' requested

[58] Lord Amory to Sir Andrew Cohen, June 16, 1964, VSO Archive, Box 31.

[59] Peace Corps, *Peace Corps Fact Book* (Washington, DC: Peace Corps, 1961), p. 28.

[60] United States Senate, Committee on Foreign Relations, *Nomination of Robert Sargent Shriver to be Director of the Peace Corps*, March 21, 1961, p. 3.

[61] Peace Corps, *Tenth Annual Report*, p. 9.

[62] Aaron J. Erickson, ed. *The Peace Corps: A Pictorial History* (New York: Hill and Wang, 1965).

Figure 2.1 Sargent Shriver with map of Africa. Getty Images.

Volunteer programs."[63] The number of volunteers on the ground, however, told a different story. Of the first deployment of 1,051 volunteers in 1961–2, only seventy-seven served in formally nonaligned nations (ones that had sent delegates to the 1961 Conference of Nonaligned Countries in Belgrade).[64] Throughout the 1960s and 1970s, the vast majority were placed in nations with proven allegiances to the Western bloc, with the largest numbers posted to the Philippines, Colombia and Malaya.[65] No volunteers were posted to Eastern bloc nations during this time and the shifting alliances of unaligned nations were reflected in decisions to accept or expel the Peace Corps.

Following an astonishing few years, the Peace Corps' expansion across the Third World slowed in the 1970s. By its tenth anniversary in 1971, the Peace Corps had been expelled from Ceylon twice, as well as from Cyprus, Indonesia,

[63] Peace Corps, *1st Annual Peace Corps Report*, p. 32.

[64] In 1961/62, there were fifty-one volunteers in Ghana and twenty-six in India. A further forty-six volunteers served in Bolivia and forty-three in Brazil, which had sent observers but not delegates to the Belgrade Conference. See ibid., p. 77.

[65] Ibid., p. 76.

Pakistan, Guinea, Gabon, Mauritania, Libya, Tanzania, Somali Republic, Nigeria, Bolivia, Panama and Guyana. More expulsions would come over the following decade, including from major nations such as India, Iran and Ethiopia. In some years during the early 1970s, the Peace Corps suffered negative growth as more countries threw out the Peace Corps than invited them in. This retraction reflected rising opposition to American power as military involvement in Vietnam and US-sponsored coups from Congo to Indonesia sharpened Third World critiques of the United States. It also reflected growing disenchantment with development volunteering, as explored in more detail in this book's final chapters. Nonetheless, the Peace Corps' initial expansion into the Global South was extraordinary. In just a few years, the Peace Corps had grown in a way that the Volunteer Graduate Scheme and VSO could never hope to. Its expansion reflected the extent of American power – political, economic, military and cultural – in the 1960s. As the United States settled into the role of superpower and global hegemon, its influence was both mirrored and extended by the Peace Corps.

Like the Volunteer Graduate Scheme and VSO, the Peace Corps was eager to claim leadership of development volunteering and worked hard to spread its influence among other "developed" nations. It was assisted in this task by the vast wave of publicity that accompanied the Peace Corps' launch, as detailed in Chapter 5 of this book. Within weeks of the Peace Corps' establishment, and following substantial media coverage, Germany, Sweden and Japan began to explore the question of development volunteering. Somewhat ironically, demands for a "local Peace Corps" were also put to governments in nations with preexisting development volunteering programs, including Britain and Australia.[66] Its own debt to the Volunteer Graduate Scheme and VSO forgotten, American reports crowed that "other nations are now emulating the Peace Corps idea."[67] As the sense of ownership grew, the same language of "pioneering" used by Australian and British programs found its way into the Peace Corps. As the 1971 Annual Report claimed, "The Peace Corps idea is spreading around the globe, and America cannot be more proud to have pioneered it."[68] As one internal report had it, "The proposal to internationalize the Peace Corps concept is, in plain English, 'America's baby'."[69]

The Peace Corps devoted substantial resources to promoting the spread of development volunteering. In 1962, the Peace Corps sponsored the Conference on Middle Level Manpower, which, at 160 delegates from forty-

[66] "Letter to the editor: peace army," *The Times*, March 7, 1961; "Australia's version of America's Peace Corps," *Sydney Morning Herald*, March 8, 1962; "Letter to the editor: an Australian 'Peace Corps'," *Sydney Morning Herald*, March 12, 1962.

[67] Pauline Madow, ed. *The Peace Corps*, The Reference Shelf, Vol. 36, No. 2 (New York: The H. W. Wilson Company, 1964), p. 4.

[68] Peace Corps, *Tenth Annual Report*, p. 9.

[69] "The United Nations and the Peace Corps," in JFKL: Papers of Sargent Shriver, Box 36.

three nations and several international organizations, claimed to be "the largest high-level conference, outside the United Nations, ever devoted to any aspect of economic development."[70] It also represented America's best chance for selling the Peace Corps. In Shriver's analysis, "the conference gave an enormous impulse to the world-wide spread of the concept of volunteer service – the Peace Corps idea."[71] At its conclusion, twelve nations declared their intention to launch or expand development volunteering programs, and an International Peace Corps Secretariat was established to stimulate and encourage "an increased flow of volunteer assistance to the developing nations of the world."[72] Later renamed the International Secretariat for Volunteer Service, this agency encouraged new Peace-Corps-style programs until its dissolution in 1976. As the conference came to a close, Shriver predicted that "from the Puerto Rican Conference will flow an ever-swelling torrent of men and women" undertaking voluntary work in the Global South.[73]

Thanks in part to Shriver's evangelizing, development volunteering programs came to be seen as a marker of a nation's status. In 1973 alone, some 23,000 volunteers worked for the government-funded development volunteering programs of twenty-four nations, including most of Western Europe and Israel, Japan, Australia, Canada and New Zealand. Interest in development volunteering had also been aroused in the Eastern bloc, and the first South–South development volunteering program was launched with the Philippines' Operation Brotherhood. By one estimate, at this stage volunteers accounted for nearly a quarter of all technical assistance personnel worldwide.[74]

While national programs represented the most fertile ground for the Peace Corps' expansion, Shriver also began to lobby the United Nations, first to accept Peace Corps volunteers to work on UN projects, and then towards the ultimate goal of a multilateral volunteering scheme bearing the imprimatur of American leadership. An early report on the Peace Corps had found three key reasons to favor a multilateral Peace Corps under the auspices of the United Nations: to strengthen the UN and its specialized agencies; to avoid the danger of the Peace Corps appearing as "intervention" or "a more sophisticated sort of imperialism"; and, third, widening the source of talent and sharing the financial cost.[75] But establishing the global legitimacy and significance of

[70] Francis W. Godwin, Richard N. Goodwin and William F. Haddad, *The Hidden Force: A Report of the International Conference on Middle Level Manpower, San Juan, Puerto Rico, October 10–12, 1962* (New York: Harper & Row, 1963), p. xii.

[71] Ibid., p. xv.

[72] Ibid., p. xv.

[73] Ibid., p. xvi.

[74] Morris, *Overseas Volunteer Programs*, p. 2.

[75] Maurice L. Albertson, Andrew E. Rice and Pauline E. Birky, *New Frontiers for American Youth: Perspective on the Peace Corps* (Washington, DC: Public Affairs Press, 1961), pp. 58–9.

development volunteering, and therefore the Peace Corps, was a further motivation. Immediately upon assuming his role as Director, Shriver began to explore the possibility of linking the Peace Corps with the UN's cultural body, UNESCO, and the United Nations Economic and Social Council (ECOSOC), appointing a Special Assistant for International Organization Affairs to coordinate approaches to various UN bodies. His successors continued to push for a United Nations volunteer agency throughout the 1960s.

Again, steps towards this goal were taken well before a single Peace Corps volunteer had set foot in a foreign nation. On April 25, 1961, US Ambassador to the United Nations Adlai Stevenson sent a memo to Secretary General Dag Hammarskjöld proposing he consider "The use of volunteer workers in the operational programs of the United Nations and related agencies designed to assist in the economic and social development of the less-developed countries."[76] The proposal excited a great deal of debate: as the Chairman of the US Delegation to ECOSOC reported, "this turned out to be the most bitterly fought issue of the session." In an unusual move signaling its perceived importance, the "long and exhaustive" debate was conducted by Heads of Delegation. The Soviet bloc opposed the proposal; according to the US delegation, "this became a matter of prestige and politics" and introduced "an outright blatant political attack with all of the earmarks of the cold war."[77] Rancorous debate delayed the proposal for years. In the end, the United Nations Volunteer Program (UNV) was not launched until 1971, well after the first flush of enthusiasm for the Peace Corps had passed. But it represented the most dramatic ascent of the development volunteering model and a significant marker of its legitimacy.

Although later chapters of this book unearth opponents, the rise of development volunteering was initially greeted with overwhelming enthusiasm, especially in the Global North. Among the more striking aspects of the 1962 Conference on Middle Level Manpower was the certainty with which government representatives spoke of the benefits that development volunteering had already brought, and the vigor with which they declared the need to recruit and deploy more volunteers. The Conference's delegates were unanimously "convinced of the value and urgency of the Peace Corps idea" and agreed that the Peace Corps and other volunteer organizations had "demonstrated beyond doubt" that volunteers "can make an enormous contribution to the need for skilled manpower in economic development while, at the same time, increasing understanding and

[76] "Peace Corps Plan to go before U.N.," *New York Times*, July 9, 1961, p. 53.

[77] "Report of the Chairman of the United States Delegation to the 32nd Session of the UN Economic and Social Council (July 5–August 4, 1961)," JFKL: Papers of Sargent Shriver, Box 36. See also "Peace Corps Plan to go before U.N.," *New York Times*, July 9, 1961, p. 53.

friendship among nations."[78] This certainty came despite an almost complete absence of data regarding the Peace Corps' impacts, as opposed to its intentions. Early enthusiasm was tempered as time passed. However, the initial outburst of excitement for the Peace Corps, premised on good intentions and persisting even in the absence of evidence, helped forge a near-consensus regarding the value of development volunteering and the desirability of Western development intervention in the Global South more broadly.

Conclusion

Despite internal tensions and contradictions, Australia's Volunteer Graduate Scheme, Britain's VSO and the United States Peace Corps all worked hard to spread the development volunteering model around the world. It is striking that each program began to work towards its expansion before even a single volunteer had left home. Although they had no way of knowing whether their volunteers would succeed, the organizing committees of all three agencies held an evangelical zeal about the concept of development volunteering, and worked to ensure its spread across the developing and developed worlds. From a surprisingly early point, the global expansion of development volunteering became an end in itself. Throughout the 1960s, program evaluation was complicated by agencies' ambiguous and multiple aims and the lack of sound methods for monitoring and evaluation. In the absence of other forms of evaluation, the multiplication of volunteers across the globe came to be seen as a marker of success, and programs competed for the claim of having "pioneered" the volunteering phenomenon.

Development volunteering programs in the early 1960s helped arouse widespread enthusiasm regarding the value of Western volunteers. This was an essential first step in the creation of the Humanitarian-Development Complex. The next step was binding this nexus with the support of civic society, the public sector and the public, a process explored in the next chapter.

[78] Godwin, Goodwin and Haddad, *The Hidden Force*, p. xv.

3

Buying into the Humanitarian-Development Complex

Support for development volunteering cut across the social fabric of mid-century Australia, Britain and the United States. This chapter takes an in-depth look at backers below the government level. Seeing beyond the state, it reveals the vast scope of civil society's engagement with international development during the 1950s and 1960s. Support for the Volunteer Graduate Scheme, VSO and the Peace Corps cut across traditional social boundaries. Sponsors came from left and right, young and old; from the stalwarts of established society to progressive reformers. If development volunteering was an idea for all seasons, it was also one that appealed to many audiences.

Different groups supported development volunteering for different reasons. Churches and faith-based groups saw the potential for lay missionary activity, civic groups variously saw a way to maintain Western prestige or promote higher standards of living abroad, private corporations identified an opportunity for new markets and ordinary people found a worthy cause that spoke to rising concerns about global inequality. For the sake of brevity, this chapter cultivates a focus on faith-based support for Australia's Volunteer Graduate Scheme, civic organizations' and private sector backing for Britain's VSO and public enthusiasm for the United States Peace Corps. Based on the institutional archives of all three organizations, and especially their financial records and correspondence files, these case studies are intended to illustrate the range and breadth of support for development volunteering in all three nations, not to limit it. The Volunteer Graduate Scheme, VSO and the Peace Corps each drew support from across these categories, and more. The extraordinary range of support for development volunteering is testament to its conceptual flexibility and strategic ambiguity. Multiple aims spoke to different constituencies; together they ensured support for development volunteering from across Western society.

Support for development volunteering brought state and non-state actors into close alignment regarding the desirability of increased Western intervention in the Global South. Development volunteering brought together the machinery of the government sector, the private sector, organized religion and civil society: a formidable coalition of political, financial and moral power. This helped forge a wide-ranging agreement that "underdeveloped" nations required Western intervention beyond the provision of funds and technical expertise, but extending to broad and ill-defined social, cultural and psychological assistance rendered by volunteers across the Global South. The substantial coalition of support for volunteers was critical to forging the humanitarian-development complex.

Religion and Faith-Based Groups

Humanitarianism and religion have long been intertwined. The relationship between churches, humanitarianism and Empire has provided fertile ground for historians.[1] Recent scholarship has also drawn out connections between religion and decolonization.[2] Established ties between religious groups and humanitarian agencies continued, and new ones were forged, amid decolonization at mid-century. Religion played a particularly significant role in the rise of Australia's Volunteer Graduate Scheme. The strongest ties were with the Student Christian Movement (SCM), a university-based ecumenical movement founded in 1896 with links to the World Student Christian Federation and the World Council of Churches. In the postwar period, the Australian SCM espoused Christian intellectualism that related theology to current political, social and cultural questions. Its brand of progressive Christianity was notable for its early opposition to the White Australia Policy and support for closer ties with Asia.[3] It was also well-funded, fielding a number of full-time staff and offering grants to fledgling movements and organizations that aligned with its beliefs.

The relationship between the Volunteer Graduate Scheme and organized Christianity was so close that, at least in the early years, it can be difficult to pull the two apart. The Volunteer Graduate Scheme arose as an initiative of individuals who were already members of SCM, and the relationship between the two organizations was organic and mutually supportive. The key figures of the Volunteer Graduate Scheme's first decade – founder of the Executive Committee Betty Evans, first volunteer Herb Feith, Honorary Secretary Jim

[1] Hilary M. Carey, *God's Empire: Religion and Colonialism in the British World, c. 1801–1908* (Cambridge: Cambridge University Press, 2011); Tyrrell, *Reforming the World*; Andrew Porter, *Religion Versus Empire? British Protestant Missionaries and Overseas Expansion*, 1700–1914 (Manchester, UK: Manchester University Press, 2004).

[2] Bocking-Welch, "The British Public in a Shrinking World"; Melani McAlister, *The Kingdom of God Has No Borders: A Global History of American Evangelicals* (New York: Oxford University Press, 2018).

[3] Renate Howe, *A Century of Influence: The Australian Student Christian Movement 1896–1996* (Sydney: UNSW Press, 2009); Renate Howe, "The Australian Student Christian Movement and Women's Activism in the Asia-Pacific Region, 1890s–1920s," *Australian Feminist Studies* 16, no. 36 (2001): 311–23; Meredith Lake, "Faith in Crisis: Christian University Students in Peace and War," *Australian Journal of Politics and History* 56, no. 3 (2010): 441–54.

Webb, Chairman Don Anderson and editor of the scheme's magazine Ailsa Zainu'ddin – balanced their positions with involvement in the SCM.[4] One of the first things the newly formed Executive Committee did was contact Secretary General of the Australian SCM, Rev. Frank Engel, for advice and support. Engel eagerly received these overtures. As Don Anderson recalled, Engel saw "the volunteer graduates thing as part of the mission of the Church. He saw the mission of the Church as helping people, and big items on the agenda of course were the developing countries' inequality."[5]

In addition to moral and spiritual support, the Student Christian Movement offered tangible funding to the Volunteer Graduate Scheme. While volunteers' expenses were covered by the Australian and Indonesian governments, the program's administrative costs were paid by the Australian SCM. The Student Christian Movement also offered access to a large and engaged network. Australian SCM conferences and events proved to be key recruiting grounds for volunteers. In 1953, SCM launched "Operation 20+" to secure twenty new volunteers for the Volunteer Graduate Scheme as part of the "overseas missionary work of the Churches."[6] In 1957, Frank Engel reported that "the ASCM has been the principal organization in Australia interested in the development of the scheme."[7] Indeed, until the late 1950s, every single Volunteer Graduate Scheme participant was also a member of the Australian Student Christian Movement.

Although ties were strongest with the SCM, the Volunteer Graduate Scheme was situated within a broader network of progressive Christian organizations. The Australian Council of the World Council of Churches offered their support as early as October 1950, when the Volunteer Graduate Scheme was little more than an idea.[8] After Minister for External Affairs Richard Casey initially refused government support, the Australian Council of Churches wrote to commend the Volunteer Graduate Scheme in "the warmest possible terms."[9] The relationship between the two organizations remained close throughout the decade. In 1959, Volunteer Graduate Scheme Chairman Don Anderson offered a copy of the scheme's magazine, *Djembatan*, to each of the 500 delegates of the Australian Council of Churches conference (at considerable cost), believing that "the contents of the magazine might be useful

[4] Herb Feith was Jewish but became influenced by progressive Methodism during the early 1950s. See Purdey, *From Vienna to Yogyakarta*.

[5] Author's interview with Don Anderson, Canberra, May 2, 2016.

[6] Handwritten notes for AVA Briefing on the Origins of the Overseas Service Bureau, January 18, 1983, Papers of Rev. Frank Engel, NLA: MS 9073, Box 17, Folder 1.

[7] Unaddressed fragment of letter from Frank Engel, January 14, 1957, NLA: MS 2601, Box 1, Folder 3.

[8] Australian Council for World Council of Churches to Betty Evans, October 18, 1950, NLA: MS 2601, Box 1, Folder 8.

[9] Herb Feith to Betty Evans, October 14, 1951, NLA: MS 2601, Box 6.

reference material for your commissions on 'The Evangelical task of the Australian churches in their world setting'."[10]

The core reason for progressive Christian support of the Volunteer Graduate Scheme was a fundamental alignment regarding questions of international fellowship and missionary endeavor. Unlike many of the established churches, groups such as the Australian Student Christian Movement and Australian Council of Churches thought that overt missionary activity should be replaced with nominally secular service that was nonetheless conducted in the spirit of Christ. Opportunities for evangelizing could be followed during the course of such service, however missionary activity was seen as a corollary rather than the motivation for overseas service, which was offered primarily in the spirit of human fellowship. But the missionary potential of the Volunteer Graduate Scheme was not entirely overlooked. In 1953, the heads of all the major Protestant Churches with the exception of the Presbyterian Church penned an open letter drawing "attention to the missionary challenge presented to Australian Christians by the present situation in South-East Asia" and demanding a "spiritual Colombo Plan" to match the secular foreign aid program.[11] Support for the Volunteer Graduate Scheme was folded into this missionary enterprise. The World Council of Churches, an ecumenical fellowship of over one hundred Christian churches, wrote in 1955 to support the scheme, regarding it as "one of the best expressions of a new missionary endeavour" conducted by "non-professional missionaries in areas of younger churches and mission fields."[12]

As an organization, the Volunteer Graduate Scheme retained a secular posture that would make it acceptable to Indonesia's majority Muslim population. Inevitably, however, there were slippages between volunteers' Christian beliefs and their work for the secular Volunteer Graduate Scheme. Gwenda Rodda was the second volunteer ever fielded by the Volunteer Graduate Scheme, arriving in Jakarta in June 1952. During her time in Indonesia, Rodda wrote a treatise on "Pegawais [volunteers] and Christian Witness in Indonesia," discussing how volunteers could proselytize and seek to convert Muslims in the course of their work.[13] She believed that "Christians among 'pegawais' can be used by God to further His purpose in Indonesia." She went on: "This is a missionary situation. Only about 4% of the 77 million Indonesians are Christians," and "There is a great need for more Christian workers." Rodda thought that Christians could "bear witness by their daily work," and "by disregarding the distinctions of rank, being friendly and polite

[10] Don Anderson to Rev. David M. Taylor, October 5, 1959, NLA: MS 2601, Box 1, Folder 6.

[11] "South East Asia's Challenge to Australians," *The Age*, August 29, 1953, p. 2.

[12] Haris-Reudi Weber to Jim Webb, September 2, 1955, NLA: MS 2601, Box 2, Folder 19.

[13] The word *pegawai*, Indonesian for employee, was commonly used to refer to Volunteer Graduate Scheme volunteers in the 1950s.

to both the bosses and the servants." In this, her rhetoric was identical to the stated aims of the Volunteer Graduate Scheme, as discussed in previous chapters. But Rodda also thought that life as a volunteer presented opportunities for direct evangelizing. "Of course, you meet many people at work," she wrote. "Travelling in the same vehicle, working with them, you . . . often get the chance to talk about God." Moreover, "All sorts of people will ask you for English lessons, and you may use these as general discussion groups or perhaps even Bible study groups." Even contacts that began badly could be turned around for the Christian cause. Many Indonesians were suspicious of volunteers' motives, assuming that they had come to Indonesia for financial gain. Rodda saw an opportunity for proselytizing, as "when they do ask seriously why you came, you can talk about your religious motives."[14]

The Volunteer Graduate Scheme negotiated a fine balance between volunteers' personal beliefs and the organization's need to avoid the appearance of missionary activity. As early as October 1951, Herb Feith wrote, "of course we must be careful to see that neither of the governments come to regard the scheme as something specifically Christian or Protestant."[15] This was particularly important in Indonesia, where influential Muslims feared that the Volunteer Graduate Scheme was a cover for missionary activity. On her first day at the Ministry of Information and Culture, newly arrived volunteer Ailsa Thomson (later Ailsa Zainu'ddin) was interrogated by her immediate superior about whether she was "there to proselytize."[16] More formally, Sugarda Purbakawatja, a senior bureaucrat at the Ministry of Education, made a written submission to the Australian Embassy in Jakarta expressing his opposition "to what he seems to regard as the missionary impulse behind the scheme, and the element of patronage which it seems (to him) to embody."[17]

Despite underlying tensions with the Muslim majority, the Volunteer Graduate Scheme courted the support of prominent Indonesian Christians. Jakarta's small but politically influential Christian population formed an important lobby group. Leading Indonesian Christians such as Minister for Health in the Sukiman Cabinet Dr. Joseph Leimena and Dr. Roem at the Ministry for Information guided the Volunteer Graduate Scheme through the convoluted process of gaining government approval. The Volunteer Graduate Scheme also built and maintained close contacts with the Indonesian branch of the Student Christian Movement, the *Gerakan Mahasiswa Kristen Indonesia* (GMKI). A small and chronically underfunded

14 Gwenda Rodda, "Pegawais and Christian Witness in Indonesia," February 1953, NLA: MS 2601, Box 13, Folder 126.

15 Herb Feith to Betty Evans, October 14, 1951, NLA: MS 2601, Box 6, Folder 55.

16 Author's interview with Ailsa Zainu'ddin, Melbourne, May 14, 2015.

17 Memo by W. A. Vawdrey, December 7, 1954, NAA: A1893, 2032/5/4 Part 1. Indonesian Muslims' opposition to the Volunteer Graduate Scheme is further discussed in Chapter 9.

organization seeking to increase the number of Christians in Indonesia, GMKI approved of the Volunteer Graduate Scheme not only because "we see in it a real unselfish sympathy towards our nation," but also because "it makes an impression on our students when they see that Christians are the first ones to serve in this scheme."[18]

The Volunteer Graduate Scheme became increasingly concerned as Islamic political parties gained strength in Indonesia from the mid-1950s. The Executive Committee urgently sought to attract recruits from outside the Student Christian Movement. This desire was particularly strong among volunteers in Indonesia, who wished to be able to truthfully tell interlocutors that the Volunteer Graduate Scheme was not a Christian group. As Keith Lethlean wrote in 1955 from his posting in Subang in majority-Muslim West Java, "We are all aware of the desirability of some non-SCM person/persons going to [Indonesia] … I don't like an all-SCM group any more."[19] The Volunteer Graduate Scheme was ultimately able to recruit a handful of volunteers from outside the Student Christian Movement, but the close relationship with Christian organizations continued.

Although the Australian case stands out, religious organizations also figured in the rise of Britain's VSO and the United States Peace Corps. Voluntary Service Overseas enjoyed the early support of Christian Aid, the humanitarian arm of the ecumenical British Council of Churches, and its Director Janet Lacey. Aside from government, Christian Aid was VSO's most generous financial backer during its first decade. As VSO's Chairman noted in 1963, "without them and without the personal enthusiasm of Miss Janet Lacey, VSO in its early years would never have got off the ground."[20] Christian Aid's support helped maintain the VSO cadet program for teenage school-leavers after the British government indicated it would only support university graduates. In 1962, Christian Aid provided a grant of £5,400 to the cadet program; by 1964–5, Christian Aid supported 118 of the total 370 cadets, at a cost of £47,000.[21] In 1968, VSO's Honorary Treasurer reported that "the major factor in our financial success so far had been the support of Christian Aid."[22] But Christian Aid grants came with strings attached. Funding was tied to "specific volunteers assisting in approved protestant establishments overseas," and Janet Lacey personally oversaw that funding was not directed elsewhere.[23] All volunteers sponsored by Christian Aid worked for projects and institutions

18 Tine Francz cited in Rev. Frank Engel to Jim Webb, April 9, 1954, NLA: MS 2601, Box 1, Folder 5.
19 Keith Lethlean to Jim Webb, March 28, 1955, NLA: MS 2601, Box 1, Folder 2.
20 Minutes of VSO Second Annual General Meeting, November 21, 1963, VSO Archive, Box 31.
21 Ibid.
22 Minutes of VSO Seventh Annual General Meeting, March 20, 1968, VSO Archive, Box 31.
23 Minutes of VSO Fund-Raising Subcommittee, November 14, 1962, VSO Archive, Box 31.

directly administered by religious organizations, reflecting Christian Aid's expressed aim to extend "the biblical understanding of Christ's service to the church and world."[24] A large number of VSO's cadet volunteers therefore worked on projects established by missionaries and approved by local inter-denominational Christian councils.[25]

Although no other religious organization came close to matching Christian Aid's grants, VSO also received funding from the Methodist, Baptist and Episcopal churches, Catholic Communicants Guilds and the Anglican charity Bishop Creighton House.[26] The World Council of Churches was a generous donor, offering £20,000 in 1962.[27] Voluntary Service Overseas also drew moral support from a broader section of Christian society. The entire March 1960 issue of *Christian Comment*, a periodical devoted to issues of lay education and Christian witness, was devoted to VSO. It presented volunteers in a positive light, claiming they acted on "a Christian determination to give themselves unstintingly to the service of their contemporaries in these under-developed parts of the world."[28] Such rhetoric collapsed the distinction between VSO and progressive Christianity, further sustaining faith-based support for development volunteering.

The Peace Corps was also closely involved with religious organizations. Sargent Shriver's earliest plans proposed that up to half of all Peace Corps projects would be administered by religious groups, on the proviso that "it forswears all proselytizing on the project."[29] This proposal was abandoned after widespread opposition from both religious and secular groups.[30] However, faith-based organizations and individuals continued to formally profess support for the Peace Corps. The youth wing of Jewish organization B'nai B'rith pledged its support in early February 1961, calling it "an historic achievement."[31] Support from Christian groups was more common. Charles W. Forman, Professor of Missions at the Yale Divinity School, thought that the Peace Corps provided an opportunity to rejuvenate missionary work. Much like the Volunteer Graduate Scheme's alignment with the "lay missionary" concept, Forman believed that "Christian mission consists not only of the

24 Cited in Bocking-Welch, "The British Public in a Shrinking World," p. 216.

25 Minutes of VSO Second Annual General Meeting, November 21, 1963, VSO Archive, Box 31.

26 "Contributions received from 1st April 1961 to 1st March 1962" and "Deeds of Covenant," Minutes of the Executive Committee, 1961–1974, VSO Archive, Box 31.

27 Department of Technical Cooperation to A. J. Collier, August 21, 1962, TNA: OD 10/4.

28 Hugh Samson, "A Year of Their Lives," *Christian Comment*, no. 17, March 1960, pp. 1–4.

29 John Wicklein, "Peace Corps ties stir Church issue," *New York Times*, June 19, 1961, p. 1.

30 "The Peace Corps: Hearings before the Committee on Foreign Relations, United States Senate, Eighty-Seventh Congress, First Session on S.2000, June 22 and 23, 1961," pp. 19–21. See also "Any Church role in Corps decried," *New York Times*, June 21, 1961; Theodore Meltzer, "Letters to The Times: Religion and the Peace Corps," *New York Times*, June 23, 1961; "Editorial: A Secular Peace Corps," *New York Times*, July 3, 1961.

31 "Youth Unit Backs Kennedy's Plan," *The Washington Post*, February 7, 1961, p. B1.

explicitly Christian activity carried on by the church but also of the implicitly Christian service carried on by others." He argued that "a new breadth is discovered in the Christian mission as much of what is done by the Peace Corps and similar groups is embraced within its realm."[32]

Others thought the Peace Corps brought more direct benefits for religious and faith-based groups. Samuel DeWitt Proctor was a prominent pastor and educationalist who headed up the Peace Corps' African operations in the early 1960s. "No one should be surprised to see the interest the churches have taken in the Peace Corps," he wrote, as "the Peace Corps has opened a new door for religious, government, and business workers abroad."[33] The view that the Peace Corps opened the world for Christian service was most prominently argued by divinity scholar Roger W. Armstrong. Armstrong lamented that "prospects for church missions as we have known them in the past . . . look very dim" in an increasingly secular world. But "the motives and purposes of the Peace Corps do not have to be explicitly Christian in order for the work of the Corps to be part of the Christian mission." Rather, he regarded the Peace Corps as "a partner in and agent of the Christian mission." "Faith also manifests itself through hope," he wrote, and the global outpouring of hope and optimism that met the program's launch was evidence that "Christian contagion" could be spread through the Peace Corps.[34]

Civic Organizations and the Private Sector

Development volunteering also garnered support from a broad range of secular civic groups, as well as the private sector. In Britain, VSO appealed to three distinct types of organizations: conservative civic groups with ties to Empire, humanitarian and international development NGOs and private businesses. The fact that it successfully cultivated the support of all these groups, despite their varying and sometimes conflicting viewpoints, further underscores the ideological flexibility and widespread appeal of development volunteering in the 1960s.

Voluntary Service Overseas was closely bound to established patterns of British associational life. Its strongest ties were to the Royal Commonwealth Society, originally formed in 1868 as the Colonial Society.[35] The Royal Commonwealth Society was intimately connected to Britain's imperial past; Anna Bocking-Welch has argued that "to become a member was to self-identify as a sympathizer with the empire,

32 Charles W. Forman in Roger D. Armstrong, *Peace Corps and Christian Mission* (New York: Friendship Press, 1965), p. 13.

33 Samuel D. Proctor in ibid., pp. 7–10.

34 Ibid., pp. 65, 81–2, 92–3.

35 Ruth Craggs, "Situating the Imperial Archive: The Royal Empire Society Library, 1868–1945," *Journal of Historical Geography* 34, no. 1 (2008): 48–67.

the Commonwealth, or both."[36] Well into the 1960s, membership was largely drawn from participants in the British imperial project, including former administrators, retired officers and businessmen with colonial interests. As a former colonial officer in Ghana and Nigeria who had transferred his colonial experiences into the new field of international development, Alec Dickson was a model member. When Dickson launched VSO, the Royal Commonwealth Society offered its full support. It housed VSO's administrative staff in its offices at peppercorn rent until VSO outgrew the space at the end of 1963. The Royal Commonwealth Society also gave direct financial grants to VSO, hosted lectures and other promotional activities, and encouraged its members to make personal financial donations in support of volunteers.

The bulk of VSO's early leadership team had forged imperial careers and many were also members of the Royal Commonwealth Society. Voluntary Service Overseas appealed to former colonial officers because it offered a way to productively apply colonial experience at a time when decolonization threatened to render it useless.[37] Office bearers in VSO's Council included Viscount (Alan Lennox) Boyd, a Conservative politician and former Secretary of State for Colonies who was also Chairman of the Royal Commonwealth Society in 1961–3. Council members included former colonial Governors of Uganda, Nigeria and the Falklands, as well as numerous colonial administrators below the gubernatorial level. The Honorary Treasurer of VSO, Sir George Schuster, was formerly Economics and Finance Minister in Sudan and India. Lord (Ellis) Robins, an American-born Briton, controlled considerable business interests in Rhodesia and southern Africa. Field-Marshal Sir Gerald Templer (ex-Chief of Imperial General Staff and notable for his role in putting down the Malayan Emergency) and Sir John Hunt (formerly of the Indian Rifles) brought colonial military experience to VSO's Council.

Yet, VSO was also supported by more progressive organizations. The 1950s and 1960s were pivotal decades in British humanitarianism, as imperial regimes of emergency relief and colonial development were supplemented (and increasingly supplanted) by NGOs seeking to contribute to the economic and social development of newly independent nations.[38] Voluntary Service

[36] Bocking-Welch, "The British Public in a Shrinking World," p. 37.

[37] Uma Kothari, "Authority and Expertise: The Professionalisation of International Development and the Ordering of Dissent," *Antipode* 37, no. 3 (2005): 425–46; Hodge, *Triumph of the Expert*, esp. p. 262.

[38] Akira Iriye, *Global Community: The Role of International Organizations in the Making of the Contemporary World* (Berkeley, CA: University of California Press, 2002), esp. pp. 96–125; Matthew Hilton, "International Aid and Development NGOs in Britain and Human Rights since 1945"; Kevin O'Sullivan, "A 'Global Nervous System'"; Andrew Jones, "British Humanitarian NGOs and the Disaster Relief Industry, 1942–1985" (PhD thesis, University of Birmingham, 2014).

Overseas operated within the emerging network of humanitarian and international development NGOs that helped bridge Britain's imperial legacy with a new rhetoric of global cooperation. Alongside Christian Aid, the largest donors to the VSO cadet program in the 1960s were the Oxford Committee for Famine Relief (Oxfam from 1965) and the British branch of the Freedom from Hunger Campaign (FFHC), a global development initiative of the United Nations Food and Agriculture Organization. Although they also drew on colonial expertise, Oxfam and the British FFHC differed from the Royal Commonwealth Society in their appeal to a wider and mostly younger constituency that was less steeped in imperial nostalgia.[39] Oxfam's politics became increasingly progressive during the 1960s. Among other policies, it supported President of Tanzania Julius Nyerere's call for *Ujamaa*, or African socialism, and eventually adopted the language of social justice to call for a global redistribution of wealth.[40] Alongside the old colonial hands in VSO's Council sat Frank Judd, at that time Chairman of the UK National Youth Committee of FFHC. Judd would go on to a political career, including as Labour Minister for Overseas Development, before becoming Director of VSO and then Oxfam in the 1980s, where he became known for his spirited opposition to Thatcherite politics and denunciation of "the world's fat cats."[41] The tension between progressive members of VSO's Council, such as Judd, and the old guard of colonial officials was ongoing. But VSO continued to elicit financial and moral support from both types of organizations, situating it as a meeting point for conservative and progressive Britons interested in foreign aid. As Uma Kothari has noted, "there has not been a unilateral trajectory from a colonial to a development moment but rather an intertwining of these fields wherein heterogeneous and shifting ideologies and practices were imbricated in each other."[42] This heterogeneity is captured in VSO's lengthy and varied list of civil society backers during the 1950s and 1960s.

Voluntary Service Overseas was also striking in eliciting a broad swathe of support from private businesses. Humanitarianism has long been entangled with capitalism.[43] From the late 1950s, VSO actively sought corporate

[39] Bocking-Welch, "Imperial Legacies and Internationalist Discourses"; Matthew Hilton, "Politics Is Ordinary: Non-Governmental Organizations and Political Participation in Contemporary Britain," *Twentieth Century British History* 22, no. 2 (2011): 230–68; Hilton, "Charity and the End of Empire."

[40] Peter Gill, *Drops in the Ocean: The Work of Oxfam, 1960–1970* (London: Macdonald Unit 75, 1970); Hilton et al., *The Politics of Expertise*, pp. 146–8; Kevin O'Sullivan, "The Search for Justice: NGOs in Britain and Ireland and the New International Economic Order, 1968–82," *Humanity* 6, no. 1 (2015): 173–87.

[41] Frank Judd, "Why the world's fat cats must sit up and listen," *The Guardian*, October 4, 1991, p. 27.

[42] Kothari, "Authority and Expertise," p. 433.

[43] Thomas L. Haskell, "Capitalism and the Origins of the Humanitarian Sensibility, Part 1," *American Historical Review* 90, no. 2 (1985): 339–61; Thomas L. Haskell, "Capitalism and

donations to support development volunteering. In so doing, it provided an early opportunity for the private sector to explore international development as a site for corporate investment.[44] In some years during the late 1950s and early 1960s, VSO received nearly as much funding from corporations as from the government, even without counting in-kind support such as discounted airfares and shipping. In the 1961–2 financial year, the total received from corporations was over £15,500, which was more than VSO's direct government grant of £10,000 (the British Council, a non-departmental public body, donated a further £7,500).[45] This proportion shifted as the British government grant increased in subsequent years. But British business interests continued to invest in VSO well into the 1970s.

Private companies supported VSO for a number of reasons. Some saw a direct benefit to their operations. In 1961, Rolls-Royce signed a seven-year covenant funding ten apprentices to volunteer with VSO each year. By 1963–4, some thirty-three companies, including BP, Bakelite, English Electric and the British Aircraft Corporation did likewise, at a cost of approximately £30,000.[46] They did so from the belief that "it would be of long term advantage to the firms in helping [apprentices] to become eventually more useful, capable and adaptable members of the firms in which they work."[47] Direct profits were also a factor. Voluntary Service Overseas suggested that, by encouraging industrialization and introducing locals to British technology, "this type of volunteer could attract purchases by developing countries from the UK."[48] Positive publicity was a further reason for corporate support of VSO. In 1964, new sponsorships announced by General Electric and Acrow Engineering made the front page of the *Daily Mail*, a national tabloid that had also recently signed a covenant to VSO.[49] The *Daily Mail*'s coverage of VSO skewed towards the experiences of industrial apprentices, who made up a small proportion of volunteers. In late December 1963, the *Daily Mail* profiled a Rolls-Royce apprentice who had "spent more than a year with Ethiopian lepers," and had "returned a wiser, more experienced and better person," ready to take up his

the Origins of the Humanitarian Sensibility, Part 2," *American Historical Review* 90, no. 3 (1985): 547–66; John Ashworth, "The Relationship between Capitalism and Humanitarianism," *American Historical Review* 92, no. 4 (1987): 813–28.

44 For links between humanitarianism and capitalism from the late 1960s, see Sasson, "In the Name of Humanity," pp. 18, 83.

45 Minutes of VSO Finance Subcommittee, May 30, 1961, VSO Archive, Box 31.

46 "List of industrial firms which have sponsored ex-apprentice volunteers, 1963–1964," and "Report on the work of the cadet division of Voluntary Service Overseas, September 1964," Minutes of the Executive Committee, 1961–1974, VSO Archive, Box 31.

47 R. E. Prentice, House of Commons Debates, December 12, 1962, Vol. 669, cc423–81.

48 Minutes of VSO Executive Committee, July 6, 1971, VSO Archive, Box 31.

49 Geoffrey Parkhouse, "Two big firms help the overseas volunteers," *Daily Mail*, June 29, 1964, p. 1.

position as a rocket engineer.[50] Some reports doubled as advertising. When glass manufacturers Pilkington Brothers sponsored three apprentices to volunteer with VSO in 1964, the *Daily Mail* reported that its owner, Mr. Robert Pilkington, was also "on the threshold of an adventure," having just formed a new helicopter charter company "which plans to eliminate the delays in town to town travel."[51] The line between charity and advertising could be fine and support for VSO could be seen as an investment aligning a brand or company with VSO's aura of adventure and goodwill.

Donations from companies with imperial legacies were particularly targeted as part of a strategy instituted by VSO's Finance Subcommittee, with Lord Amory (until recently Britain's Chancellor of the Exchequer) in the Chair. Amory was a true believer in VSO's mission to simultaneously improve British youth and the postcolonial world. He was also impeccably connected. With VSO facing a substantial operating deficit in 1961, Amory decided to target private companies "having interests overseas" to make up the shortfall.[52] At a time of accelerating decolonization, Amory recognized that imperial corporations may wish to contribute to – and be seen to be contributing to – the social and economic development of Africa, Asia and the Caribbean. Amory's strategy suggests that, by mid-century, corporations that had turned a profit through the unequal power relations of colonialism had developed a particular interest in humanitarian and development initiatives. And indeed, VSO's early donor lists represent a who's who of colonial enterprise. In the 1961–2 financial year, VSO received substantial donations (between £1,000 and £5,100) from British South Africa Investments, the Anglo-American Corporation of South Africa, De Beers Consolidated Mines and Imperial Chemical Industries. British American Tobacco and the United Africa Company were also major donors.[53] Smaller amounts came from Shell Petroleum, Esso Petroleum, the Rhodesian Selection Trust, the Borneo Company, Imperial Tobacco Company and Dunlop Rubber.[54] During the 1950s and 1960s, many of these imperial firms sought to rehabilitate their image for a postcolonial context. Some executives worried that decolonizing nations would follow precedents in Egypt and Indonesia and nationalize key industries. Others recognized that Empire Capitalism was no longer tenable and that they would need to appeal directly to African and Asian consumers. Supporting the development of independent nations was an astute marketing move that appealed to Third World aspirations. Voluntary Service Overseas

[50] Daily Mail Reporter, "Homecoming!" *Daily Mail*, December 30, 1963, p. 7.

[51] Richard Herd, "Adventure in the big-game country," *Daily Mail*, June 20, 1964, p. 3.

[52] Minutes VSO Finance Subcommittee, May 30, 1961, VSO Archive, Box 31.

[53] "Amounts promised to VSO in 1962," Minutes of the Executive Committee, 1961–1974, VSO Archive, Box 31.

[54] "Contributions received from 1st April 1961 to 1st March 1962" and "Deeds of Covenant," Minutes of the Executive Committee, 1961–1974, VSO Archive, Box 31.

was particularly attractive for being a non-governmental organization and for its association with individual goodwill. Notably, corporate support for development volunteering rarely came with clear instructions about how their donations were to be used, or where. Their support was motivated less by concern for particular communities or nations, but rather by the anticipated benefits brought by association with well-meaning British volunteers.

At the same time that it attracted support from corporations that had profited from Britain's empire, VSO also appealed to some recent Commonwealth migrants, some of whom had emigrated to escape the inequalities perpetuated by Empire Capitalism. After reading a *Daily Mail* report about industrial apprentices serving as VSO volunteers, Indian-born Ezekiel Moses, who had lived in Britain for a decade and now managed a successful travel agency, decided to donate £300 and offered to become "the 'rallying point' for donations from the 300,000 other Indians living in Britain today." Stating that "I want every one of them to help Britain help India," he also suggested that "every other overseas-born community – the Pakistanis, the Italians, the West Africans, the Jamaicans, the Greeks and the Cypriots – do the same."[55] Although Moses' initiative never got off the ground, the idea that VSO deserved the support of recent migrants from across the former Empire (and beyond) is significant in itself. It underscores the breadth of support for VSO, which ranged from the very cream of Britain's elite to recent migrants. Although their motivations varied, these very disparate groups converged in their support for VSO.

Similar patterns emerged in the United States. The Peace Corps was fully funded by the US government so it did not seek out cash donations in the same way as VSO. Rather, civil society organizations flocked to be associated with the Peace Corps. A lengthy list of non-governmental groups made statements of support for the Peace Corps before the Senate Committee on Foreign Relations in June 1961. Statements came from civic organizations including the 4-H Foundation of America and the Women's International League for Peace and Freedom; from humanitarian and development organizations CARE and the African Research Foundation; from the American Council on Education and Colorado State University; and from labor unions AFL-CIO and the National Farmers Union. Religious organizations including the National Lutheran Council, the National Catholic Welfare Conference, the Friends Committee on National Legislation, the American Friends Service Committee, the Brethren Service Commission and the Mennonite Central Committee also made supporting statements.[56] The breadth of civic support for the Peace Corps demonstrated at Senate and Congressional Hearings was

55 "New plan can boost Britain's volunteers," *Daily Mail*, June 19, 1964, p. 7.

56 "Hearings before the Committee on Foreign Relations on the Peace Corps," United States Senate, Eighty-Seventh Congress, June 22 and 23, 1961.

a factor in the ultimate passing of legislation authorizing and underwriting the Peace Corps.[57]

As with VSO, support from American civil society was based on imprecise statements of volunteers' intentions, rather than on their actual performance or impacts. Not a single Peace Corps volunteer had yet been posted when the Senate Hearings took place; the first volunteers would not leave America for another two months. Moreover, the people and places who would benefit from Peace Corps volunteers had not yet been defined: senators vaguely referred to "a Peace Corps to help the people of interested countries and areas in meeting their needs for skilled manpower."[58] But American civic organizations spoke of the Peace Corps with a confidence that belied its vagueness. The Women's International League for Peace and Freedom claimed that "the Peace Corps program will help to build bridges of understanding where diplomacy and impersonal aid have failed."[59] The National Catholic Welfare Conference stated that "The Peace Corps can be an effective means of directly assisting needy people of Asia, Africa, and Latin America, and other areas, to raise their own living conditions above subsistence levels."[60] The AFL-CIO testified that, in addition, "The Peace Corps . . . can express to the peoples of the world some of the finest aspects of our American heritage."[61] Why were they so eager to become involved? The hope of practical cooperation, in keeping with the Peace Corps' short-lived policy of collaboration with existing private agencies such as universities, religious organizations and NGOs, surely played a role.[62] But even more significant was a more diffuse desire to be associated with a program as popular and well-received as the Peace Corps in its early years. Describing their motivations at Senate hearings, a representative of the Quakers pointed to "the interest and enthusiasm which has been generated for this proposal."[63] The Lutherans spoke of "an active interest among the youth groups and the educational institutions of these church bodies in the progress of the Peace Corps program, and their relation to it." The National Catholic Welfare Conference established a Peace Corps Desk and the National Lutheran Council pointed to "a reservoir of genuine good will among church people for the Peace Corps."[64] Like many of their British counterparts,

[57] "Hearings before the Committee on Foreign Affairs on the Peace Corps," House of Representatives, Eighty-Seventh Congress, August 11 and 15, 1961.

[58] J. W. Fulbright cited in "Hearings before the Committee on Foreign Relations on the Peace Corps," United States Senate, Eighty-Seventh Congress, June 22 and 23, 1961, p. 1.

[59] Mrs. D. Homer Crowley cited in ibid., p. 154.

[60] F. Robert Melina cited in ibid., p. 135.

[61] Harry H. Polak cited in ibid., pp. 111–2.

[62] Heike Wieters, "Ever Tried – Ever Failed? The Short Summer of Cooperation between CARE and the Peace Corps," *International Journal* 70, no. 1 (2015): 147–58.

[63] Edward F. Snyder cited in "Hearings before the Committee on Foreign Relations on the Peace Corps," United States Senate, Eighty-Seventh Congress, June 22 and 23, 1961, p. 115.

[64] Dr. Robert E. Van Deusen, National Lutheran Council, ibid., pp. 118–20.

American civic organizations wanted to forge alliances with the Peace Corps out of genuine enthusiasm and the hope that the Peace Corps' positive image and popularity might reflect well on them.

Alignment with the Peace Corps' positive image also motivated the private sector. Alongside civic and service organizations, the Peace Corps was deluged with offers of cooperation from private firms. Chapter 5 of this book outlines the major contributions of public relations and advertising agencies, running to many millions of dollars over the 1960s. Other major donations came from stalwarts of American business including IBM, AT&T and Caterpillar Tractors.[65] Denim manufacturer Levi Strauss and Co. offered every Peace Corps volunteer a gift certificate for two pairs of Levi's jeans; by March 1963, some 1,900 certificates had been redeemed for 3,800 pairs of trousers.[66] This investment reflected the company's desire to align its brand with the rugged glamor of the Peace Corps, a strategy it continued into the 1990s.[67] The public's enthusiasm for the Peace Corps made aligning a brand with development volunteering a canny marketing move. This is evident in a *Washington Post* cartoon of April 1961 (Figure 3.1), which depicted executives scheming to tie their latest novelty product to the Peace Corps and so make it "a bigger thing than hula hoops!"

The Public

Perhaps the most striking aspect of development volunteering was its capacity to draw in ordinary people. Public support was essential to the Volunteer Graduate Scheme, VSO and the Peace Corps. All three organizations depended on members of the public as raw recruits for their volunteering programs. They also courted popular opinion to draw political strength and moral energy.

It is difficult to overstate the popularity of the Peace Corps in the early 1960s. Even before it had been formally launched, a Gallup poll found that 89 percent of Americans had heard of the Peace Corps, with 71 percent in favor.[68] As the reference to hula hoops in the *Washington Post* cartoon above suggests, the Peace Corps achieved the sort of mainstream popularity normally reserved for popular culture fads. The *New York Times* reported that, from its very infancy, Kennedy's "'peace corps' proposal ... more than any other reached directly into the hearts and minds of thousands of young men and women throughout the country."[69] The public's enthusiasm was palpable. President Kennedy received thousands of

[65] Peace Corps, Memorandum for the President, July 24, 1962, JFKL: RG 490, Box 30.
[66] Peace Corps, Memorandum for the President, March 12, 1963, JFKL: RG 490, Box 30.
[67] "The Quiet American," *The Economist*, November 8, 1997, p. 76.
[68] George Gallup, "American 'Peace Corps' proposal wins broad approval from public," *The Washington Post*, February 1, 1961.
[69] Gertrude Samuels, "A Force of Youth as a Force for Peace," *New York Times*, February 5, 1961, p. SM26.

GRIN AND BEAR IT **By Lichty**

"If we could think of some way to tie our product into it, this 'peace corps' idea could be a bigger thing than hula hoops! . . ."

Figure 3.1 George Lichty, "Grin and Bear It," *Washington Post*, April 6, 1961, p. A19. Used with permission.

letters about the Peace Corps, which as his administrative secretary noted, was the issue that "most consistently produces responses through mail."[70] Heaving mailbags were also dragged into the Peace Corps' Washington offices. Within weeks of its establishment, the Peace Corps office was inundated with more than 40,000 letters, with more people applying to work for the agency than for the rest of government put together.[71] These letters, many of which are held at the National Archives in College Park, are indispensable sources in gauging the breadth of public interest in the Peace Corps. In 1961, letters of support came from across America, from men and women, young and old, rich and poor. Fifteen-year-old New Yorker James Pastena wrote in July 1961 to express his support for this "excellent idea," even though he was

[70] Brandon Rottinghaus, "'Dear Mr. President': The Institutionalisation and Politicization of Public Opinion Mail in the White House," *Political Science Quarterly* 121, no. 3 (2006), p. 465.

[71] Cobbs Hoffman, *All You Need Is Love*, p. 41.

still too young to join.[72] On the other end of the age scale, eighty-two-year-old Walter Robb also backed the Peace Corps, seeing "in it many possibilities that [his] generation did not have."[73]

The extent of the public's enthusiasm can be further gauged by the astonishing breadth of creative engagement inspired by the Peace Corps. Otherwise ordinary Americans devoted hours to designing insignia, symbols and badges for the Peace Corps. One of Senator Henry M. Jackson's Washington State constituents redesigned the American flag so that it better reflected the Peace Corps' objectives.[74] Others wrote poems, stories, songs, anthems, jingles and mottoes by which they hoped to educate "ignorant and apathetic Americans" about world affairs and the need for a Peace Corps.[75] Timmie Rogers, an African-American composer from New York, wrote a song called "Peace" to convey the spirit of the President's plea "not what the country can do for you, but what you can do for the country."[76] Harry Wilson, also from New York, composed "Banners of Peace," which he hoped could be made the Peace Corps' official song.[77] Others offered to undertake unofficial diplomacy by teaching their fellow Americans about the Peace Corps or, more broadly, by travelling "under Peace Corps auspices, spreading goodwill."[78] Leon A. Jaris, an administrator in a California hospital, even proposed "a total PEACE OFFENSIVE," by which "idle factories and farming lands could be turned into training centers here for foreign nationals, staffed by our unemployed as teachers," and "mothball [*sic*] fleet ships could be utilized under student crews . . . and prefabricated hospitals could be set up throughout the world."[79] Letters arriving at the Peace Corps' Washington offices each morning brimmed with suggestions that spoke to hours of thought, discussion and planning. These letters demonstrate something of the extent of public enthusiasm for development volunteering.

Some Americans put their money behind their ideals, even though the Peace Corps never sought public donations. Anna Steiger of Long Island forwarded a check for thirty dollars "to aid the Peace Corps movement," adding that only her two small children prevented her from signing up.[80] Seventh graders from Lincoln Junior High School in Ferndale, Michigan, sent $66.46 in the hope that

72 James Pastena to Peace Corps, March 7, 1961, The National Archives at College Park (henceforth NACP): RG 490, Mail Briefs, Box 1.
73 Walter Robb to Mr. Shriver, May 10, 1961, NACP: RG 490, Mail Briefs, Box 1.
74 Henry M. Jackson to Mr. Shriver, September 18, 1961, NACP: RG 490, Mail Briefs, Box 1.
75 Meredith J. Rogers to Mr. Shriver, June 28, 1961, NACP: RG 490, Mail Briefs, Box 1.
76 Timmie Rogers to the President, March 15, 1961, NACP: RG 490, Mail Briefs, Box 1.
77 Harry L. Wilson to Mr. Shriver, March 27, 1962, NACP: RG 490, Mail Briefs, Box 2.
78 George R. Gish to Senator Alexander Wiley, March 28, 1961, NACP: RG 490, Mail Briefs, Box 1.
79 Leon A. Jaris to Mr. Shriver, May 31, 1961, NACP: RG 490, Mail Briefs, Box 1.
80 Anna L. Steiger to Mr. Moyers, August 13, 1962, NACP: RG 490, Mail Briefs, Box 2.

"the Peace Corps will find it helpful."[81] Fourth graders at the New Lincoln School of New York collected 200 books, which they hoped could be distributed by Peace Corps volunteers in Africa; their efforts were surpassed by the students of Brookline High School in Massachusetts, who collected sixty-five boxes of books.[82] On a slightly different note, the Catholic Youth Organization of New York planned to spend the summer of 1961 growing fruit and vegetables that they would then donate to Peace Corps volunteers heading to Tanganyika.[83] Community groups were similarly enthusiastic. The New York State English Council, the American Vegetarian Party and the American Society of Traffic and Transportation were among scores of groups that wrote to offer their support to the Peace Corps in its early years.[84]

The public response represented a rare outpouring of optimism about America's role in the world and about the future. Even though standards of living were rising and a certain kind of performative cheerfulness dominated advertising and popular culture, domestic and international politics were rarely sites for collective expressions of optimism in the United States.[85] Rather, the Cold War, the threat of nuclear annihilation and the instability entrained by decolonization led many Americans to view international affairs with considerable anxiety during the 1960s.[86] Internal divides, particularly between generations and between races, also tarnished the nation's optimism. The public outpouring of support for the Peace Corps' role in global affairs was all the more significant for being unusual. Of all the manifestations of support for the Peace Corps, Kennedy claimed that "most heartening of all" was the "enthusiastic response by student groups, professional organizations and private citizens everywhere – a convincing demonstration that we have in this country an immense reservoir of dedicated men and women willing to devote their energies and time and toil to the cause of world peace and human progress."[87] As the

[81] Mary Jo Denja to Mr. Shriver, June 3, 1963, NACP: RG 490, Mail Briefs, Box 2.

[82] Group D, Fourth Grade, The New Lincoln School, to Mr. Shriver, April 18, 1963; H. Alan Theran to Mr. Shriver, December 18, 1962, both in NACP: RG 490, Mail Briefs, Box 2.

[83] Rev. Phillip J. Murphy to Mr. Shriver, June 26, 1961, NACP: RG 490, Mail Briefs, Box 1.

[84] Hans Gottschalk to Mr. Shriver, September 14, 1961; Symon Gould to Mr. Shriver, March 27, 1961; A. P. Heiner to Mr. Shriver, May 18, 1961, all in NACP: RG 490, Mail Briefs, Box 1.

[85] Christina Kotchemidova, "'From Good Cheer to Drive-by Smiling': A Social History of Cheerfulness," *Journal of Social History* 39, no. 1 (2005): 5–37. See also Alan J. Levine, *After Sputnik: America, the World, and Cold War Conflicts* (New York: Routledge, 2018).

[86] Levine, *After Sputnik: America, the World, and Cold War Conflicts*. See also Barak Kushner, "Treacherous Allies: The Cold War in East Asia and American Postwar Anxiety," *Journal of Contemporary History* 45, no. 4 (2010): 812–43; Kyle A. Cuordileone, "'Politics in an Age of Anxiety': Cold War Political Culture and the Crisis in American Masculinity, 1949–1960," *The Journal of American History* 87, no. 2 (2000): 515–45.

[87] "President's Message to Congress on the Peace Corps," *New York Times*, March 2, 1961, p. 13.

New York Times editorialized, "Nobody's heart leaps at the thought of intercontinental missiles or of heroic efforts to save our own cities by destroying other peoples [*sic*] cities. The international crisis might come to this. But that isn't what we want." Instead, "What we want in our hearts is goodness and mercy, brotherhood and peace. And it is this yearning that a . . . Peace Corps might help us to satisfy."[88] The nature and reach of publicity and media coverage of the Peace Corps, as investigated in Chapter 5 of this book, was also directly related to the public's outpouring of support.

Of course, not every American approved of the Peace Corps. Charles Pemberton's letter to the *New York Times*, penned six days after Kennedy's inauguration, captured the frustration felt by opponents: "From some of the letters I've read in the newspapers about this fine plan for sending dedicated American young people into the underdeveloped countries, I feel like saying, from a full heart, 'Lord, save it from its friends'."[89] African Americans were far less enthusiastic about the Peace Corps than their white compatriots. Although the Peace Corps declined to collect data about the race of volunteers, historian Jonathan Zimmerman identified only 200-odd Black volunteers and administrators working for the agency in its first decade.[90] Race was not the only factor. Conservative-leaning white Americans protested that the Peace Corps was a waste of money that would be better spent on domestic problems or on building the nation's military capacities. Ted Tsiokas of Illinois was "anti-Peace Corps" because he felt it was "a waste of the taxpayers' money" and two of Senator Ralph Yarborough's Texas constituents sent irate letters "asking why missile engineers are being sent to Africa to build roads when we need so much to close the missile gap."[91] At the extreme end, Mrs. Edward J. Harris of Washington, DC, warned that the "Peace Corps will further the destruction of our great Republic."[92] Letters such as these serve as reminders that some Americans remained staunchly opposed to their nation's assumption of a global role. However, they were vastly outnumbered by expressions of support. Tens of thousands of letters delivered to the Peace Corps offices in the 1960s expressed the overwhelming enthusiasm with which Americans embraced development volunteering.

Public support for the Peace Corps flourished despite widespread confusion about its aims and rationale, or even basic knowledge of what volunteers would do or where they would go. Was its purpose, as Elliot Forbes of the Harvard Glee Club wrote, "to promote world peace"?[93] Or was it another weapon in

88 "Editorial: The Moral Equivalent," *New York Times*, March 5, 1961, p. E10.

89 "Letters to Editor: Charles Pemberton," *New York Times*, January 30, 1961, p. 22.

90 Zimmerman, "Beyond Double Consciousness."

91 Ted Tsiokas to Mr. Shriver, September 1, 1961 and Ralph Yarborough to Mr. Shriver, July 11, 1961, both in NACP: RG 490, Mail Briefs, Box 1.

92 Mrs. Edward J. Harris to Mr. Shriver, March 12, 1961, NACP: RG 490, Mail Briefs, Box 1.

93 Elliot Forbes to Mr. Shriver, February 25, 1961, NACP: RG 490, Mail Briefs, Box 1.

America's Cold War armory? Many Americans thought that the Peace Corps' main purpose was psychological warfare. New Yorker Blair Rogers wrote to say that he thought the "Youth Corps" was "one of the most encouraging developments to people who, like himself, have returned from the Soviet Union with an increasing worry about the need for an ideological fervor in our own people."[94] A New Jersey constituent suggested that "a further step to the Peace Corps" would be a specialist "group of young Americans skilled in debating to act as America's 'intellectual commandoes'."[95] Yet, others thought that the purpose of the Peace Corps was purely humanitarian and protested any suggestion of realpolitik. Pat Montague of Seattle felt "that the Peace Corps should not get tangled in foreign policy and politics." Pointing to the situation in Peru, where a military junta had overthrown the recently elected government, Montague argued that "if the purpose of the Peace Corps is to be humanitarian it should be allowed to go to Peru despite diplomatic relations" as he did "not see why the needs of the people should be denied because the government in power is not to our liking."[96] Yet, a lack of understanding did not detract from the public's enthusiasm. On the contrary, the ambiguity allowed a broad span of American society to see something they liked in the Peace Corps. Progressives supported the Peace Corps' humanitarian motives and contribution to newly decolonized nations; conservatives were attracted by a program that promised to counter Soviet appeal in the Third World and broadcast American power. The popular appeal of the Peace Corps crossed many divides within American society.

Conclusion

Support for the Volunteer Graduate Scheme, VSO and the Peace Corps came from religious and civic organizations, private companies and a broad swathe of the public. Supporters came from the left and the right; from young and old; they were conservatives and progressives; capitalists and workers. In general, these groups had little in common. And yet they were uniform in their support for development volunteering and the maximalist vision of development intervention it entailed. The broad range of support illustrates the flexibility of development volunteering: like beauty, its appeal lay in the eye of the beholder. Opponents did of course exist, but they were strikingly rare and isolated in Australia, Britain and America alike. Until the late 1960s, development volunteering drew the enthusiastic support of ordinary people from

[94] Blair O. Rogers to Mr. Shriver, March 10, 1961, NACP: RG 490, Mail Briefs, Box 1.
[95] Congresswoman Florence P. Dwyer to Mr. Shriver, March 22, 1962, NACP: RG 490, Mail Briefs, Box 2.
[96] Senator Warren G. Magnuson to Mr. Shriver, August 6, 1962, NACP: RG 490, Mail Briefs, Box 2.

across the fabric of Western society – even if many of them did not know what volunteers actually did or where they did it.

The unusually broad base of material and moral support cultivated by development volunteering represented a significant step in forging a political and moral consensus in support of Western humanitarian and development intervention in the Third World. The mixed economy of development volunteering helped bind the humanitarian-development complex by placing individuals, civic organizations and churches into cooperation with private corporations and the government. In 1965, the *Daily Mail*, a British tabloid newspaper and public limited company, sponsored two school-leavers to volunteer with VSO. Eighteen-year-old Veronica Whitty would work in a home for destitute children in Madras run by the Indian civic organization Guild of Service. Seventeen-year-old Richard Cook was to be placed with a Colombo Plan medical team in Laos. The *Daily Mail* article that announced their selection was relatively short, but it revealed an extraordinary nexus of state and non-state power, by which members of the public worked in concert with national governments, multilateral agencies, religious organizations, secular NGOs and the private sector across several nations.

Notably, the vast outpouring of support was for the idea and not the practice of development volunteering. The good intentions of development volunteering agencies, and of volunteers themselves, were prized – but little attention was devoted to what volunteers actually did during overseas postings, what their impacts were or how recipient communities regarded them. Critical questions about how volunteers would render assistance, and towards what end, were rarely asked by the long lists of supporters and donors amassed by the Volunteer Graduate Scheme, VSO and Peace Corps. The benefits of development volunteering were assumed to be self-evident but, as later chapters of this book reveal, there was often a vast gulf between assumptions and on-the-ground experience. Few supporters troubled themselves to uncover this gulf; for most, good intentions were enough.

4

Sentimental Radicals and Adventurers

Development volunteering demanded ordinary people leave the comforts of home to spend one, two or more years in previously unfamiliar reaches of the Global South. Why did tens of thousands of Australians, Britons and Americans respond to this call and why were they so enthusiastic about it? At the heart of this question lies a broader problem: how and why did private individuals seek to become involved in international political action? To closely engage with the motivations of volunteers, this chapter is based primarily on a cache of application questionnaires and correspondence from intending candidates for the Volunteer Graduate Scheme. Scattered across 112 boxes in the National Library of Australia, this collection includes virtually every application the scheme received from its establishment in 1950 to its final disbanding in 1969. The total number of applications is relatively small – in the hundreds rather than the tens of thousands received by the Peace Corps – but because of this, questionnaires were descriptive and provided space for volunteers to ruminate about their motivations, often at length. The much larger pool of applicants for VSO and the Peace Corps demanded a more systematic process for application and selection; prospective Peace Corps volunteers took standardized tests based largely on multiple choice questionnaires. While this was efficient, it necessarily removed most of the nuance behind an applicant's motivations to make it legible to a computer.

Although it draws largely on Australian sources, this chapter addresses all three programs, using contemporary sources about volunteers' motivations for VSO and the Peace Corps, particularly psychiatric reports and aggregate studies, to supplement the primary cache of evidence relating to the Australian program. It reconstructs volunteers' multiple and often overlapping motivations and reveals that, in the 1950s and 1960s, international affairs were not limited to elite actors, nor to rational calculations of interest and strategy. Rather, ordinary citizens across the Western world came to feel personally involved in international relations and their engagement was emotional as well as rational.

Historians and political scientists have taken an affective turn over the past decade.[1] Research into emotions, and their relationship to political decisions,

[1] Sara Ahmed, *The Cultural Politics of Emotion* (Edinburgh: Edinburgh University Press, 2004); Lila Abu-Lughod and Catherine A. Lutz, "Introduction: Emotion, Discourse, and

has flourished.[2] Whereas the history of humanitarianism has long recognized the significance of affect in evoking concern for distant others, historians of international development have mostly focused on state-based interventions and economic models that are assumed to be free of emotion. This approach has dominated histories of postwar Western intervention in the Global South. Yet, the history of development volunteering cannot be told without looking at affect. This chapter reveals that many individuals became part of politically significant global movements precisely because the emotional pull was strong enough to overcome the anticipated material and emotional hardships of volunteering in a distant nation. Many aspiring volunteers demonstrated a heady affective cocktail of concern and optimism. This affective register was distinctive and set development volunteering apart from other forms of humanitarianism, in which empathy is typically expressed in a mood of despair.[3] Individually, these feelings were intense enough to drive otherwise ordinary citizens to seek involvement in international affairs. Collectively, they formed the moral justification for the humanitarian-development complex.

This shared emotional experience was culturally specific to the Global North. Optimism arose from the sense that intervening in others' lives and societies was unquestionably the right thing to do, if it brought them closer to development. This depended on Western logics of improvement and was a legacy of colonialism's will to rule. This is at least part of the reason why volunteering grew so quickly in the North–South configuration, but was an abject failure for South–North volunteering and was slow to take off in South–South contexts.[4]

Goodwill was not the whole story. Many volunteers' good intentions were encouraged and enabled by the rapid expansion of travel and tourism. Vast swathes of new territory were brought into the tourist industry during the 1950s and 1960s, including many nations undergoing decolonization in Asia, Africa and the Caribbean.[5] Development volunteering represented a rare way for young people to access travel and adventure without spending their own

the Politics of Everyday Life," in Lila Abu-Lughod and Catherine A. Lutz, eds., *Language and the Politics of Emotion* (Cambridge: Cambridge University Press, 1990), pp. 1–23; Ruth Leys, "The Turn to Affect: A Critique," *Critical Inquiry* 37, no. 3 (2011): 434–72.

2 Janice Bially Mattern, "On Being Convinced: An Emotional Epistemology of International Relations," *International Theory* 6, no. 3 (2014): 589–94; Emma Hutchison and Roland Bleicker, "Theorizing Emotions in World Politics," *International Theory* 6, no. 3 (2014): 491–514.

3 Susan Sontag, *Regarding the Pain of Others* (London: Penguin, 2004); Lilie Chouliaraki, *The Spectatorship of Suffering* (London: SAGE, 2006). See also Ariella Azoulay, *The Civil Contract of Photography* (New York: Zone Books, 2008).

4 Busch, "The Politics of International Volunteerism"; Matt Baillie Smith, Nina Laurie and Mark Griffiths, "South–South Volunteering and Development," *The Geographical Journal* 184, no. 2 (2017): 158–68.

5 Agnieszka Sobocinska, "Following the 'Hippie Sahibs': Colonial Cultures of Travel and the Hippie Trail," *Journal of Colonialism and Colonial History* 15, no. 2 (2014).

money. As this chapter shows, development volunteering was reliant both on Westerners' good intentions and the burgeoning tourism industry. The intersection of Western structures of feeling with accelerating globalization and the extension of transnational capitalism saw development volunteering rendered into a social norm, even a rite of passage, in subsequent decades.

Sentimental Radicalism

As we have seen, the global roots of development volunteering can be traced to a small number of Australian students who set about addressing the problem of Indonesia's postcolonial skills shortage from 1950. The first volunteer, Herb Feith, was a political science graduate who went on to a glittering academic career. Feith thought a great deal about the relationship between individuals and political systems. He held sentiment and political activism in equal regard and believed the two had to be mutually sustaining: during his first year in Jakarta, he defined his political philosophy as "sentimental radicalism."[6] Feith drew on his personal experience as a refugee from Nazi-occupied Austria, as well as inspiration from Christian theologian Friedrich Bonhoeffer and progressive Methodism. In Indonesia, his sentimental radicalism was sharpened through friendship with Molly Bondan, an Australian who had become an anticolonial activist during World War Two, and by the emotionally charged political climate of Indonesia's first post-Independence decade.[7] Feith thrived in this climate, in which emotion and politics were mutually sustaining, and spoke approvingly of the "sense of unity and purpose and enthusiasm which characterised the period of revolution."[8]

Although Herb Feith was uniquely capable of expressing his political philosophy, other volunteers were similarly emotionally engaged. The emotional draw was so strong that several early volunteers spoke of development volunteering as a "calling," drawing on language typically used by organized Christianity. This emotional template had to be accepted by larger groups if development volunteering was to thrive. In the long term, this did happen. But in its earliest years, Australia's Volunteer Graduate Scheme struggled to attract applicants. At times, the Executive Committee reported that "we are depressingly short of applicants," particularly outside their home city of Melbourne.[9] By 1958, the Volunteer Graduate Scheme had inspired the formation of Britain's VSO; but attracting students in Australia's regions was proving more difficult. That year, the Tasmanian Volunteer Graduate Scheme

6 Herb Feith to Macmahon Ball, December 10, 1952, NLA: MS 2601, Box 4, Folder 43. See also Purdey, *From Vienna to Yogyakarta*.

7 Hardjono and Warner, *In Love with a Nation*.

8 Herb Feith to Noel Wathen, September 24, 1953, NLA: MS 2601, Box 1, Folder 5.

9 Ivan Wilson to Don Anderson, December 3, 1959, NLA: MS 2601, Box 2, Folder 11.

representative reported that "there has been very little enthusiasm on the subject."[10] At the University of Tasmania he wrote, "Student apathy [regarding] international affairs seems to be worse here than anywhere."[11]

This slow start points to the novelty of development volunteering and also to the perceived disincentives of volunteering in a distant country. Most obvious, perhaps, were the anticipated financial sacrifices. Chapter 7 of this book reveals that most volunteers enjoyed a relatively comfortable lifestyle; but many assumed they would have been financially better off staying at home. At a time of low unemployment across Australia, Britain and the United States, most young people were assured of steady jobs. Potential applicants feared that volunteering would delay or otherwise harm their career prospects and financial wellbeing. Many worried about falling behind relative to colleagues who had remained at home, worked their way up the career ladder and saved money towards a home.

In addition to financial disadvantages, volunteers had to make social sacrifices by leaving family, friends and romantic partners behind. The anticipation of loneliness was bad enough, but many applicants were particularly wary of deferring marriage. The possibility of "missing out" on the marriage market felt more real in the 1950s and 1960s than it does today, reflecting that period's unusually high rate of marriage and early age at marriage.[12] The pressure to find a spouse was felt particularly by young women, many of whom expected to retreat from paid work to focus on the unpaid labor of running a home and raising a family. Choosing the right mate was a significant financial as well as emotional investment. Some young women felt that one or two years out of the marriage market could materially hurt their prospects; even some of those who did end up volunteering felt anxious about whether any eligible men would be left by the time they returned home.[13] This remained true well into the 1960s. One 1965 study exploring the barriers to applying for the United States Peace Corps found the two most significant issues preventing application were "desire to pursue career" and "desire to get married."[14]

These attitudes and the slow start of numbers demonstrate just how novel and confronting the development volunteering concept was. The Volunteer Graduate Scheme committee believed that a willingness to sustain personal

[10] Christina O'Farrell to Jim Webb, April 9, 1958, NLA: MS 2601, Box 2, Folder 14.

[11] Ian Newman to Jim Webb, August 20, 1958, NLA: MS 2601, Box 11, Folder 110.

[12] Willard L. Rodgers and Arland Thornton, "Changing Patterns of First Marriage in the United States," *Demography* 22, no. 2 (1985): 265–79; Betsey Stevenson and Justin Wolfers, "Marriage and Divorce: Changes and Their Driving Forces," *Journal of Economic Perspectives* 21, no. 2 (2007), p. 31.

[13] Diary, Papers of Elinor Capehart, JFKL: RPCV, Box 102.

[14] "The Peace Corps and the College Senior," New York: Young and Rubicam, 1965, cited in Charles C. Jones, "The Peace Corps: An Analysis of the Development, Problems, Preliminary Evaluation, and Future" (PhD thesis, West Virginia University, 1967), p. 86.

sacrifice for a greater good was rare among Australian youth and so "do not consider that a huge flow of volunteers will ever come forward. Instead, schemes like these, if true to the conceptions we regard as central, can never attract more than a tiny percentage of students or graduates, the tiny percentage of 'cranks', albeit the practical ones!"[15] And yet, numbers did grow, and not only in Australia. Britain's VSO never struggled for applicants; as Mora Dickson recounted in a biography of her husband, "Alec Dickson did not doubt that the young people would be forthcoming."[16] In 1958, Alec Dickson personally invited twelve individuals to volunteer with VSO. The following year sixty were recruited and by 1963 502 volunteers were selected from more than 1,500 applicants; the numbers climbed steadily before plateauing at some 1,500 volunteers, drawn from an applicant pool of around 4,500, from 1966.[17] Voluntary Service Overseas sent its 10,000th volunteer in 1971.[18] The multitude of applicants for the Peace Corps is legendary. In March 1961, just as the Peace Corps was launched, the *New York Times* interviewed students from universities across the United States. They found a majority were enthusiastic about the idea, with women as eager to join as men.[19] In all, 11,269 applicants fronted for placement examinations during the first year.[20] In the 1965 recruiting year, this had risen to 42,639 applications.[21] By the end of the decade, more than 300,000 Americans had applied for a term with the Peace Corps.

It is important to emphasize that not all those who applied were selected. Development volunteering was a negotiation between applicants' motivations and the program's priorities. Every prospective volunteer was carefully screened and if their attitudes did not match those of the selection committee, those of their national government and sometimes those of the receiving government, their applications were denied. The Volunteer Graduate Scheme estimated that one volunteer was sent for every twenty applications; VSO estimated that roughly one in three applicants were successful; for the Peace Corps the number was more like one in four.[22] Viewpoints expressed in

15 Jim Webb to John Thompson, September 28, 1954, NLA: MS 2601, Box 2, Folder 19.

16 Dickson, *A Chance to Serve*, p. 91.

17 Dick Bird, *Never the Same Again: A History of VSO* (Cambridge: Lutterworth Press, 1998), p. 201.

18 Minutes of VSO Executive Committee Meeting, October 5, 1971, VSO Records, Box 31.

19 "Project Gains Backing of most Undergraduates; Women Eager," *New York Times*, March 6, 1961, p. 1.

20 Peace Corps, *1st Annual Peace Corps Report*, p. 10.

21 George Nash and Patricia Nash, "From which Colleges come the Peace Corps volunteers?" Columbia University Bureau of Applied Social Research, JFKL: RG 490, Series 1, Box 2.

22 The Australian estimate comes from "Scheme for Graduate Employment in Indonesia," Report to Council of National Union of Australian University Students, February 1955, NLA: MS 2601, Box 1, Folder 2. The British estimate is from "Minutes of Second Annual

application questionnaires and correspondence, therefore, capture a broader range of views than those of volunteers who were ultimately accepted into the Volunteer Graduate Scheme, but this breadth allows us to probe at the reasons why otherwise ordinary young people decided to take the extraordinary step of signing up to volunteer in a distant nation from the early 1950s.

Altruistic Internationalism

A large number of applicants to the Volunteer Graduate Scheme expressed a form of sentimental internationalism, articulated as a desire to build personal ties across national boundaries. Sentimental aspirations for friendship across the barriers of geography, nation and culture had previously found expression in student exchange schemes and other forms of cross-cultural interaction across Europe, North America and Australasia.[23] By the 1950s, growing numbers of Americans became committed to winning over Asian hearts and minds in the context of the global Cold War.[24] In Britain, decolonization brought out a similar desire to forge links with citizens emerging from British rule.[25] In Australia, the need to build contacts with Australia's Asian "neighbors" also became commonplace.[26] The Volunteer Graduate Scheme's Honorary Secretary Jim Webb quipped that "Friendship with Asia … is a fashionable theme now in Australian university circles," and it was a theme that the Volunteer Graduate Scheme tapped into.[27]

A sentimental desire for cross-cultural friendship was exceedingly common in applications to the Volunteer Graduate Scheme. Harold Whitfield, soon to complete a Master of Science degree and applying to lecture at Gadjah Mada University in Yogyakarta in 1953, explained that "I believe that this scheme …

General Meeting of VSO, 21 November 1963" and "Report of Council, Year Ended 21 March 1964," VSO Archive, Box 31. The Peace Corps figure is from Nash and Nash, "From which Colleges come the Peace Corps volunteers?" p. 1 and Peace Corps, *5th Annual Report to Congress*, p. 18.

23 Tamson Pietsch, "Many Rhodes: Travelling Scholarships and Imperial Citizenship in the British Academic World, 1880–1940," *History of Education* 40, no. 6 (2011): 723–39; Sam Lebovic, "From War Junk to Educational Exchange: The World War II Origins of the Fulbright Program and the Foundations of American Cultural Globalism, 1945–1950," *Diplomatic History* 37, no. 2 (2013): 280–312; Alice Garner and Diane Kirkby, *Academic Ambassadors, Pacific Allies: Australia, America and the Fulbright Program* (Manchester, UK: Manchester University Press, 2019).

24 Klein, *Cold War Orientalism.*

25 Anna Bocking-Welch, *British Civic Society at the End of Empire.*

26 David Walker and Agnieszka Sobocinska, eds., *Australia's Asia: From Yellow Peril to Asian Century* (Crawley, Western Australia: UWA Press, 2012), pp. 1–23; Sobocinska, "Hearts of Darkness, Hearts of Gold".

27 Jim Webb, "Why not work in Indonesia?" undated, *c.*1954–8, NLA: MS 2601, Box 13, Folder 133.

will foster mutual understanding between the people of our countries."[28] Lois Griffiths, who applied for a posting as an English teacher in 1954, wrote that "nothing could be of greater value than cooperation and understanding between Australia and neighbouring countries."[29] David Marchesi applied stating a "general will to promote international understanding at an inter-personal level."[30] Perhaps John O'Grady, applying to work as a pharmacist, put it most directly in his application, describing a wish "to meet and talk with as many Indonesians as possible" because "I like Asians, and wish to spend some time working with and getting to know these our nearest neighbours."[31]

Christina Klein has shown that, in the 1950s, "Middlebrow intellectuals often presented the Cold War as something that ordinary Americans could take part in, a set of activities in which they could invest their emotional and intellectual energy."[32] This was partly premised on the view that "ordinary" people could become political agents if they banded together; that collective influence, expressed through public opinion, could impact domestic and international policy. Volunteer applicants went a step further, indicating a belief that they could have a direct impact on international affairs, not just as a collective "public" but as individuals. An optimistic faith in the power of the individual was expressed in numerous applications. Judith Gregory, twenty-one years old and applying in 1955 to work as a pharmacist, aspired to "make a personal contribution towards better international relations."[33] Thomas Riddell believed that by working as a teacher he "would also be influencing political developments."[34] Twenty-one-year-old Glenda Baker felt "a responsibility ... to do my best to promote understanding and better relations between the people of SE Asia, esp. Indonesia, and Australia, in fact between all countries."[35] As Ken Thomas noted in his 1955 application, "by working and living with Indonesia, learning [the] language and becoming as much a part of Indonesia as possible I may be doing my share in promoting international understanding."[36]

[28] Harold Whitfield to the Government of Indonesia, August 1953, NLA: MS 2601, Box 3, Folder 26.

[29] Lois Griffiths to Committee for Graduate Employment, NUAUS, July 23, 1954, NLA: MS 2601, Box 1, Folder 5.

[30] Application questionnaire - David Terence Marchesi, December 10, 1961, NLA: MS 2601, Box 1, Folder 8.

[31] Application questionnaire - John O'Grady, September 21, 1955, NLA: MS 2601, Box 4, Folder 38.

[32] Klein, *Cold War Orientalism*, p. 7.

[33] Application questionnaire - Judith Anne Gregory, August 29, 1955, NLA: MS 2601, Box 1, Folder 8.

[34] Application questionnaire - Thomas Frederick Riddell, December 24, 1955, NLA: MS 2601, Box 1, Folder 2.

[35] Application questionnaire - Glenda Baker, August 19, 1962, NLA: MS 2601, Box 9, Folder 93.

[36] Ken Thomas to the Government of Indonesia, undated 1954, NLA: MS 2601, Box 2, Folder 13.

Some applicants expressed a more specialized form of altruistic internationalism, in which the desire to forge international connections met a wish to help others. As Graham Edmiston wrote in 1953, "We in Australia are extremely well off, whereas in Indonesia many things are still lacking. I have a mind to contribute something towards the betterment of Indonesia, through my own work and by giving freely of my time and knowledge."[37] Medical graduate Agnes Warren applied in 1956 because "I feel there is a job I can do – mentally & spiritually as well as physical – to help this young nation."[38] Brian Phillips applied in 1960 because "Here is also the chance to help in a small way a young country which is not as well off materially as our own."[39] The language of altruism – of "helping," "contributing" or "improving" – reveals genuine goodwill towards Indonesians and the Indonesian nation. The history of humanitarianism has been premised on the mass mobilization of empathy and compassion.[40] Typically, public empathy has been evoked in an atmosphere of despair, caused by vivid, and often shocking, representations of the pain and suffering of distant others.[41] Development volunteering was unusual in combining empathy with optimism. As we have seen, this optimism was private, in the sense that it reflected a belief that an individual could positively affect international relations. But it was also structural, related to the mutually affirming ideologies of decolonization and development. Independence movements across Asia and Africa were marked by a striking optimism that freedom from colonial rule would bring both social justice and economic growth. This feeling was further encouraged by the optimism surrounding international development and modernization theory. As David Engerman notes, both North and South were caught up in the "romance of development."[42] Economic development theorists, and the multilateral and national agencies seeking to guide decolonizing nations towards economic development, were optimistic about their prospects – perhaps unduly so, considering the vast shortages of capital and expertise, as well as the extraction basis of their economies, which were a legacy of colonialism.

Where many applicants wrote of a general desire to "help," a smaller number expressed their altruistic impulses in the technical language of international development. Harold Whitfield wrote that "From the books and magazines I have read and from contacts I have had with Indonesian students in Australia I have become aware of the reconstruction and industrial

37 Graham Edmiston to Dr. Oetoyo, July 22, 1953, NLA: MS 2601, Box 3, Folder 26.

38 Application questionnaire – Agnes Grace Warren, October 8, 1956, NLA: MS 2601, Box 1, Folder 8.

39 Application questionnaire – Brian Douglas Phillips, undated 1960, NLA: MS 2601, Box 3, Folder 26.

40 Barnett, *Empire of Humanity*; Tyrrell, *Reforming the World*.

41 Sontag, *Regarding the Pain of Others*; Chouliaraki, *The Spectatorship of Suffering*.

42 Engerman, "The Romance of Economic Development," p. 29.

development taking place in Indonesia and other Asian nations," and he felt he could contribute.[43] Lois Griffiths noted that "I have long followed with interest the achievements of the Indonesian people in developing their country ... I feel that I could make no better use of the professional knowledge which I have than in such a country."[44] Vern Bailey stated that "I believe that technically qualified people can contribute significantly to Indonesia's national development and to the building of firmer friendship between Australia and Indonesia."[45] Perhaps the most conceptually sophisticated application came from twenty-six-year-old Hugh Francis Owen, who applied in 1959 to work in a teaching or economics advisory capacity. He listed a number of reasons for applying, the first being "Because I understand that a trained person can help Indonesia in its economic 'take off'."[46] Coming a year before Walt Rostow's *The Stages of Economic Growth* popularized the concept of economic "take-off," this reflected a cutting-edge understanding of contemporary development economics that underpinned a personal desire to contribute to Indonesia's growth.

Although few expressed it in such sophisticated language, the combination of internationalism, altruism and faith in economic development was common to many volunteer applications. Alison Williams, who applied to work as a biochemist in 1955, stated her reasons as "1) to help in a situation where trained, and experienced graduates are needed. 2) to live with, and make friendships among the Indonesian people, and to gain an understanding of our nearest Asian neighbour."[47] Architect Reginald Smart described himself as "Essentially an idealist," with a desire to use his skills "to make the lives of people richer in many ways." Like many others, Smart's altruistic desire was grounded in internationalism: "I believe that all men are brothers, and are one." Smart went on, writing that

> For too long, Australia has been considered, and has considered herself, a 'Western' nation. I believe, however, that the destiny of all Pacific countries is closely linked and that Australia should work for and with her neighbours. Hence, I should like to do all that I can to promote better understanding between our countries and to help discharge Australia's undoubted responsibilities towards her Asian neighbours.[48]

43 Harold Whitfield to the Government of Indonesia, August 1953, NLA: MS 2601, Box 3, Folder 26.

44 Lois Griffiths application letter, August 1, 1954, NLA: MS 2601, Box 3, Folder 26.

45 K. Vern Bailey application letter, September 16, 1954, NLA: MS 2601, Box 3, Folder 26.

46 Application questionnaire – Hugh Francis Owen, undated 1959, NLA: MS 2601, Box 3, Folder 26.

47 Application questionnaire – Alison Jessie Edith Williams, undated 1955, NLA: MS 2601, Box 2, Folder 15.

48 Reginald K. Smart to Government of Indonesia, October 22, 1952, NLA: MS 2601, Box 4, Folder 40.

As Glenda Sluga reminds us, internationalism in the mid-twentieth century coexisted with nationalism.[49] This was true for many hopefuls applying to the Volunteer Graduate Scheme. As well as speaking to a desire for international cooperation, applicants routinely expressed a wish to bolster Australia's national interest. Australia's history of institutional racism became a major point of tension in the context of Asian decolonization.[50] Some Australians came to think that building personal friendships with Asians would demonstrate their nation's lack of racism and so improve bilateral relations. This logic collapsed the distinction between interpersonal and international relations. Janice McPhee's October 1955 application listed a desire to befriend Indonesians in order to "help in bettering Australian relations with our Asian neighbours."[51] Keith Lethlean, working as a doctor in Indonesia from 1955, regarded the Volunteer Graduate Scheme as "a scheme which increases the friendship between Indonesia and Australia as it makes its contribution to the former's national development."[52] Thomas Errey wrote that "I conceive myself to be both a proud and patriotic Australian and still appreciative of the remarkable traditions, present qualities and potential renewed greatness of the Indonesian people & therefore a suitable person to promote goodwill between the two peoples."[53]

Although such statements were common in Volunteer Graduate Scheme applications, they were exceptional in the broader context of 1950s Australia. Only a minority of Australians opposed the strict immigration restrictions of the White Australia Policy; much of the population still looked north with trepidation.[54] National media emphasized Indonesia's instability and growing tensions over West New Guinea led to increasingly alarmist reporting over the course of the 1950s.[55] Volunteer applicants were unusual in expressing a desire for closer personal and national relations with Indonesia and in believing that

49 Glenda Sluga, *Internationalism in the Age of Nationalism* (Philadelphia, PA: University of Pennsylvania Press, 2013).

50 Walker, *Stranded Nation*.

51 Application questionnaire – Janice Mary McPhee, October 22, 1955, NLA: MS 2601, Box 1, Folder 5.

52 A. Keith Lethlean to Government of Indonesia, September 30, 1954, NLA: MS 2601, Box 3, Folder 26.

53 Application questionnaire – Thomas George Errey, December 4, 1955, NLA: MS 2601, Box 6, Folder 62.

54 Gwenda Tavan, *The Long, Slow Death of White Australia* (Melbourne: Scribe Publications, 2005).

55 Prue Torney-Parlicki, *Somewhere in Asia: War, Journalism and Australia's Neighbours, 1941–75* (Sydney: University of New South Wales Press, 2000); Ross Tapsell, *By-Lines, Balibo, Bali Bombings: Australian Journalists in Indonesia* (Melbourne: Australian Scholarly Publishing, 2014). See also Simon Philpott, "Fear of the Dark: Indonesia and the Australian National Imagination," *Australian Journal of International Affairs* 55, no. 3 (2001): 371–88.

this would benefit the Australian nation. Significantly, they did so years before the government, or indeed a majority of the population, articulated similar views.

Many applicants also expressed anticolonial attitudes. Thelma Ashton wrote that "My interest in Indonesia was originally stimulated by the Revolution of Independence of the Indonesian people, and I wished to lend what assistance I could to further the security and independence of Indonesia."[56] When Thomas Errey wrote to apply in late 1955, he referred to Australian unionists' support for Indonesian independence, which resulted in an extensive "Black Ban" on Dutch shipping during the 1940s.[57] Stating that "my sympathies at the time being wholly engaged on behalf of the Indonesian aspirations for the Republic," Errey now considered the Volunteer Graduate Scheme as a natural next step. As he wrote, "Believe me that I have been from its beginning a fervent supporter of the young Indonesian republic (courting much unpopularity at certain times and in certain places by maintaining it)."[58] Partly, such statements were penned in recognition that the Indonesian Government (which had the right of veto over applications) was fiercely anticolonial in the 1950s. But it was also genuine and spontaneous, rooted in a desire to build international friendships that were simultaneously personal and political.

Altruism, internationalism, nationalism and anticolonialism often coexisted without any apparent tension in volunteer applications. In 1956, Hugh Reeves wrote that "my training should make me useful in a country needing trained people more than most, I am anxious to show that Australians have no racial prejudices and will treat Indonesia as a sovereign nation and I should like to do a little to improve understanding between Australia and Indonesia." He also wrote of a desire for "partly repaying the debt which I think the people of the West owe to those of the East."[59] In addition to supporting Indonesia's economic take-off, Hugh Owen listed a second reason for volunteering: "I believe that Australia's self-interest and that of the West & the world at large, lies in helping i) to raise the standard of living in underdeveloped countries and ii) to prove that the period of colonialism is really passing, if not past."[60] As well as reflecting the multiple aims of development volunteering, the overlapping motivations of applicants spoke to the complex political landscape of the 1950s and 1960s.

[56] Thelma Ashton to the Government of Indonesia, May 23, 1954, NLA: MS 2601, Box 3, Folder 26.

[57] See Rupert Lockwood, *Black Armada: Australia and the Struggle for Indonesian Independence, 1942–49* (Sydney: Hale & Iremonger, 1982).

[58] T. G. Errey to Jim Webb, November 15, 1955, NLA: MS 2601, Box 2, Folder 14.

[59] Application questionnaire – Hugh Reeves, March 19, 1956, NLA: MS 2601, Box 10, Folder 104.

[60] Application questionnaire – Hugh Francis Owen, undated 1959, NLA: MS 2601, Box 3, Folder 26.

Religion

A significant proportion of Volunteer Graduate Scheme applicants cited religious beliefs among their motivations. The previous chapter explored the close ties between development volunteering and organized religion in Australia. A small number of applicants viewed a volunteer posting as a straightforward opportunity for missionary endeavor. But, for most, the issue was more complicated. Progressive Christianity had undergone significant changes in the early decades of the twentieth century and, by the postwar period, the liberal Christianity of organizations such as the Australian Student Christian Movement (SCM) extended to supporting international development projects, and not just because they offered a missionary opportunity.[61] When it came to the "underdeveloped" nations, the views of the SCM mirrored the secular altruistic internationalism described above, except for the fact that international brotherhood and aid were regarded as steps towards "the ultimate realization of a social order consistent with Christianity."[62]

Previous chapters detailed the considerable overlap between the Volunteer Graduate Scheme and the Student Christian Movement in the 1950s. The first significant influx of applications for the Volunteer Graduate Scheme came after its Chairman Don Anderson presented at the 1951 SCM National Conference. In the following weeks, some 100 delegates submitted preliminary expressions of interest; among them were several individuals who went on to volunteer posts, including Gwenda Rodda, Ollie McMichael and Ian Doig.[63] Subsequent SCM conferences elicited further lists of "interesteds."[64] The SCM also led direct recruitment campaigns for the Volunteer Graduate Scheme, including "Operation 20+" that aimed to send twenty volunteers to Indonesia by 1955 and was coordinated by the General Secretary of the Australian SCM, Rev. Frank Engel. Numerous SCM-aligned applicants declared a special desire to work in Christian institutions (even though Indonesia was overwhelmingly Muslim); even Betty Evans, one of the scheme's founders, submitted a specific request to work in a Christian school ahead of her posting in 1954.[65]

It is perhaps unsurprising, then, to find religious motivations intertwined with secular beliefs in applications to the Volunteer Graduate Scheme. Many applicants referred to strong Christian beliefs and expressed a desire to work in Indonesia "in the name of Jesus Christ" or "in some capacity of service for

[61] Howe, *A Century of Influence*; Lake, "Faith in Crisis."

[62] Joan Mansfield cited in Lake, "Faith in Crisis," p. 444.

[63] "ASCM Volunteers for Graduate Employment in Indonesia, Jan '52," NLA: MS 2601, Box 1, Folder 5.

[64] "Interesteds, 1954 SCM Conference," NLA: MS 2601, Box 6, Folder 62.

[65] Herb Feith to Gwenda Rodda and Alison Frankel, March 16, 1954, NLA: MS 2601, Box 6, Folder 62.

Christ's sake."[66] John Francis applied because "I have been 'called' to do Medical Missionary service overseas" and "have decided, after much prayer and deliberation, to offer my services to the Indonesian government to do work there."[67] Some were unsure of anything apart from their Christian calling: as Eleanor Johnson wrote in 1954, "I have been thinking rather seriously of answering a call which I have had to go to Indonesia in the service of Christ, and am a little worried, as I know nothing whatsoever about the conditions there, or those under which I would be working. I do not even know in what capacity I could go."[68] In his applicant questionnaire, twenty-three-year-old mechanical engineer Adrian Muller noted his motivation simply as "Matthew 28: 19–20," the biblical passage known as the Great Commission: "Therefore go and make disciples of all nations, baptizing them in the name of the Father and of the Son and of the Holy Spirit, and teaching them to obey everything I have commanded you."[69]

The Volunteer Graduate Scheme's Executive Committee was not kindly disposed towards those claiming a missionary "calling." As Jim Webb wrote to the World Student Christian Federation in Geneva, "One difficulty has been in dealing with applications from militant 'missionary' types who distinguish sharply between their profession and their vocation as evangelists, rather than seeing their professional work in terms of Christian vocation."[70] Ronald Johnson applied in 1954, declaring that his motives were "closely wrapped up with his Christian faith." This declaration provoked extended discussion by the Executive Committee, who were determined to make a distinction between those who wanted to go primarily as missionaries and those whose altruistic internationalism was underpinned by religious sentiments. This was relatively straightforward in Johnson's case: he flatly declared a "considerable dislike of the idea of saying that his motives were 'humanitarian' when in fact they were Christian." Assessing his application, Herb Feith noted that "Ron's attitudes towards the scheme and Indonesia are definitely considerably different from those of the rest of us. He would not I think be interested in finding out about Indonesia generally, except inasmuch as this seemed to have a direct bearing on his missionary possibilities." Summing up, Feith declared that "All things considered I do not think that Ron should go . . . he'd be unpopular and a bit of a drag on the scheme."[71] Honorary Secretary Jim Webb elaborated that "the danger is that a Christian who conceives his missionary vocation in very

[66] Application questionnaire – John Graham Francis, August 18, 1954, NLA: MS 2601, Box 1, Folder 5; Fay Bannister to Jim Webb, March 8, 1959, NLA: MS 2601, Box 1, Folder 4.

[67] John Francis to Jim Webb, July 28, 1954, NLA: MS 2601, Box 2, Folder 13.

[68] Eleanor Johnson to Jim Webb, August 26, 1954, NLA: MS 2601, Box 2, Folder 13.

[69] Application questionnaire – Adrian Gordon Muller, undated 1958, NLA: MS 2601, Box 2, Folder 12.

[70] Jim Webb to Philippe Maury, August 14, 1954, NLA: MS 2601, Box 2, Folder 19.

[71] "Confidential memorandum on Ronald Johnson," April 27, 1954, NLA: MS 2601, Box 5, Folder 47.

narrow terms – 'spreading the Gospel' verbally and with supreme confidence in his own superiority as knowing The Whole Truth – may be a real menace in any society, particularly Indonesia."[72] Johnson's application did not advance to the next stage.

Yet, the Volunteer Graduate Scheme never disapproved of Christian motivations – far from it – but rather filtered out applicants who betrayed a conservative missionary theology of conversion rather than a desire for "service in Christ." The distinction could be very fine. B. J. Richards was training for the Church of Christ Ministry when he inquired about a volunteer posting, declaring he was "interested in further information concerning Christian Missionary activity amongst those who have never had the opportunity to learn of Christ."[73] Far from rejecting his application, Herb Feith personally replied, noting that, although the Volunteer Graduate Scheme could not support proselytizing, "Almost certainly if you decided to go to a Christian hospital in Indonesia as a pharmacist your theological training would not be wasted . . . you'd perhaps be able to do all sorts of work in the Church community, particularly among young people."[74] Similarly, Sydneysider Peter Shedding wrote in 1959 that "I have felt for some time that God would have me carry out my employ as a Chemical Engineer in the South East Asian area where we could have the opportunity to tell others about the Lord Jesus Christ and to aid them in physical and material ways."[75] Volunteer Graduate Scheme Chairman Don Anderson quickly replied, providing encouragement, further information and suggesting Shedding contact the local volunteer representative to take his application to the next stage.[76]

Although these specific applicants came from Australia, many candidates for the British and American development volunteering agencies also held religious beliefs or even missionary motivations. The previous chapter outlined numerous ties between VSO, the Peace Corps and religious or faith-based groups. In a preface to a 1965 book titled *Peace Corps and Christian Mission*, Former Associate Director of the Peace Corps Samuel D. Proctor wrote that "This new image of the American abroad must not be regarded as something in conflict with the work of foreign missions, but rather as a very worthwhile extension of it." The book described the numerous ways in which volunteer service could be used to further missionary goals. In Africa, some volunteers "are teaching catechism or church school classes, acting as lay readers, playing the organ or piano for services, teaching the Bible in their homes and even preaching."[77] Britain's VSO also had close links with the

[72] Jim Webb to Michael Schneider, July 29, 1955, NLA: MS 2601, Box 3, Folder 23.
[73] B. J. Richards to Miss Evans, November 5, 1953, NLA: MS 2601, Box 2, Folder 15.
[74] Herb Feith to B. J. Richards, November 18, 1953, NLA: MS 2601, Box 2, Folder 15.
[75] Peter Shedding to Jim Webb, October 19, 1959, NLA: MS 2601, Box 3, Folder 26.
[76] Don Anderson to Peter Shedding, October 29, 1959, NLA: MS 2601, Box 3, Folder 26.
[77] Armstrong, *Peace Corps and Christian Mission*, pp. 9, 30.

Church of England and Christian Aid, who funded large numbers of cadet volunteers placed in missions and other religious institutions. Early volunteers included people like Martin Garner, who worked in Sarawak and India before returning to Britain to be ordained into the Church of England. As Anna Bocking-Welch notes, "Garner's time abroad was informed by a Christian ideology of duty and service … For him, the Gospel told the original VSO story: Jesus volunteered to leave the safety of home for those in need and there was 'no greater thrill than following Jesus'."[78] In the United States and Britain, as in Australia, spiritual and secular motivations for development volunteering were intertwined in complex and deeply personal ways.

Invitation to Adventure

Idealistic and spiritual reasons were often joined by more down-to-earth motivations. The opportunity to gain professional and educational experience routinely accompanied applicants' statements of altruistic internationalism or religious beliefs. Agnes Warren applied to the Volunteer Graduate Scheme in 1956 because "I feel there is a job I can do … to help this young nation to take its place in the world – while furthering my own medical experience, under new conditions."[79] Colin Jones applied in 1957 giving two reasons: "1. To help Christian Church in Indonesia" and "2. Architectural Experience."[80] A number of applicants regarded volunteering in Indonesia as an ideal way to gather data towards academic dissertations. The Volunteer Graduate Scheme's first volunteer, Herb Feith, balanced his duties at the Ministry of Information with research towards a graduate thesis in political science. Among his reasons for signing up, Neale Hunter listed a desire "To learn the Indonesian (+ possibly Javanese) language, customs, religious character" and "To possibly amass the material for an MA Thesis on some aspects of Indonesian linguistics."[81] Antoinette Barrett applied in 1960 because she was "studying for an MA in Indonesian Studies in the field of Javanese and Indian inscriptions," and was "desirous of attaining a better knowledge of Bahasa Indonesia + Javanese if possible."[82]

Applicants who couldn't draw direct career benefits often listed a desire to gain more personal experience. Twenty-year-old Colin Black applied because

78 Bocking-Welch, "The British Public in a Shrinking World," pp. 253–4.

79 Application questionnaire – Agnes Grace Warren, October 8, 1956, NLA: MS 2601, Box 1, Folder 8.

80 Application questionnaire – Colin Arthur Herbert Jones, January 15, 1957, NLA: MS 2601, Box 1, Folder 8.

81 Application questionnaire – Neale James Hunter, November 4, 1956, NLA: MS 2601, Box 1, Folder 8.

82 Application questionnaire – Antoinette Mahree Barrett, undated 1960, NLA: MS 2601, Box 2, Folder 12.

"The scheme offers me an opportunity to gain a 1st hand knowledge of an important area of which I now know nothing. In addition the idea of working in another language is one that particularly interests me."[83] Scot Chaston similarly noted that "I would consider it to be an invaluable part of my education to work in Indonesia for a few years."[84] Ken Tucker submitted a list of motivations:

> 1) Because I have a great interest in people; 2) Because I think that it would be advantageous to me in widening my education and outlook, and also increase my interest and knowledge of world events. 3) To do my share of strengthening Asian-Australian relationships and understanding. 4) To gain experience of both an industrial nature and of how other people live. 5) Perhaps a trivial reason, but I feel that I would very much like to go.[85]

It is notable that, apart from "strengthening Asian-Australian relationships and understanding," the rest were personal benefits.

Many applicants also yearned for travel and adventure. The Volunteer Graduate Scheme's Executive Committee disapproved of such motivations, derisively noting "We have to distinguish carefully between people who are really interested in Indonesia and adventurers or joy riders who desire to go to Indonesia for travel and pleasure or to gain something for themselves."[86] Like many contemporaries, they spurned tourists as frivolous and self-serving, even if tourists themselves often declared internationalist motivations behind their journeys.[87] And yet, even the Executive Committee couldn't deny the lure of exoticism and adventure. In 1953, suspicion about the "real motives" of a pair of applicants led to a spirited debate about the relationship between volunteering and tourism. One concerned member wrote to Honorary Secretary Jim Webb to protest that "One can't deny that there is a certain amount of adventure involved – it can't be avoided." Moreover, "adventure of the right sort perhaps is applicable – and then again one does not expect to be worked to death, there is something of the holiday present" for even the most idealistic and zealous volunteer.[88] This tension was never resolved. Although the

83 Application questionnaire – Colin Murray Black, May 6, 1956, NLA: MS 2601, Box 4, Folder 38.

84 Application questionnaire – Scot Henry Herbert Chaston, undated 1959, NLA: MS 2601, Box 2, Folder 12.

85 Application questionnaire – Kenneth John Tucker, May 6, 1956, NLA: MS 2601, Box 1, Folder 5.

86 Jim Webb to John Thompson, August 13, 1954, NLA: MS 2601, Box 2, Folder 19.

87 Agnieszka Sobocinska, "Visiting the Neighbours: The Political Meanings of Australian Travel to Cold War Asia," *Australian Historical Studies* 44, no. 3 (2013): 382–404; Jenifer Van Vleck, *Empire of the Air: Aviation and the American Ascendancy* (Cambridge, MA: Harvard University Press, 2013).

88 Keith Buckley to Jim Webb, November 9, 1953, NLA: MS 2601, Box 2, Folder 13.

Executive Committee protested any suggestion that volunteers were holiday-makers, articles in the Volunteer Graduate Scheme magazine *Djembatan* mirrored travel writing, if not tourism promotion, with titles like "Holiday in Tapanuli," "A Trip to Java and Bali" and "Impressions of Bali."[89] Descriptions of Bali, Indonesia's famed holiday island that had just risen to fresh prominence as the mythical Bali Hai in the Rodgers and Hammerstein musical *South Pacific*, were a frequent feature and directly echoed tourism promotion literature: volunteer doctor Ray Mylius' piece ended with, "Let me recommend to you a holiday in Bali."[90] Moreover, it is notable that the authorized "history of the V.G.S," published in a UNESCO-funded special issue of *Djembatan* in 1959, was titled "Invitation to Adventure."[91]

A desire for travel and adventure was expressed in numerous Volunteer Graduate Scheme applicant questionnaires. In 1953, Ian Spalding wrote to inquire about volunteering, explaining that "My thoughts have occasionally drifted to the possibility of wandering off to the East for a while to see what life is like there."[92] Michael Bradley, applying to work as a teacher in 1956, stated "I want a chance of seeing the country & people of Indonesia at first hand."[93] Jillian Vial applied in 1960 because, among other reasons, "I want to travel and experience life, conditions and customs of Asia."[94] Although the desire for travel and adventure is often conflated with youth, older applicants were not immune. Substantially older than most applicants at fifty-six, H. Robinson simply noted "Why I am making this application: I like the colour and life in Asian countries."[95] Many applicants mentioned a desire to see the world near the end of a long list of more "worthy" or serious reasons. We can assume that other applicants felt a desire for adventure but preferred not to mention it in their applications, perhaps aware of the Volunteer Graduate Scheme's policy of filtering out "adventurers" or afraid of being regarded as frivolous. But, as Herb Feith admitted, even for the most committed volunteer "idealism would not be their only motive for coming here. Others would be the desire to go abroad and the desire to get experience."[96]

89 Hugh Reeves, "Holiday in Tapanuli," *Djembatan*, Vol. 1, no. 2, November 1957, pp. 2–4; Mrs. Reeves, "A Trip to Java and Bali," *Djembatan*, Vol. 2, no. 2, December 1958, pp. 12–13; Ray Mylius, "Impressions of Bali," *Djembatan*, Vol. 2, no. 1, September 1958, pp. 12–14.

90 Ray Mylius, "Impressions of Bali," *Djembatan*, Vol. 2, no. 1, September 1958, p. 14.

91 "Invitation to Adventure: A History of the V.G.S.," *Djembatan*, Vol. 2, no. 4, September 1959, pp. 5–6.

92 Ian Spalding to Betty Evans, October 1, 1953, NLA: MS 2601, Box 2, Folder 15.

93 Application questionnaire – Michael Charles Bradley, undated 1956, NLA: MS 2601, Box 2, Folder 13.

94 Application questionnaire – Jillian Claire Vial, undated 1960, NLA: MS 2601, Box 3, Folder 26.

95 H. Robinson to Herb Feith, October 2, 1956, NLA: MS 2601, Box 1, Folder 8.

96 Herb Feith to Dr. Darmasetiawan, November 16, 1951, NLA: MS 2601, Box 6, Folder 55.

The tourism industry both encouraged and enabled volunteers' wanderlust. Historians of travel have pointed to the 1950s and 1960s as key decades in the rise of mass tourism. Travel technology devised for warfare in World War Two was turned to commercial uses following the war's end, and a global explosion in the number of air and sea routes, travel agents, hotels, currency exchange centers and other tourist infrastructure coalesced into a new tourist industry. Globally, the number of people taking an overseas trip grew from 25 million in 1950 to 166 million in 1970.[97] The rising prominence of tourism stoked a growing desire for travel experiences: travel writing regularly topped best-seller lists across the West, the number of publications devoted to travel and adventure surged and tourist advertising became a feature of mainstream magazines and press.

This was true in Australia as in other parts of the world. Australians had long been enthusiastic travelers.[98] The period following World War Two saw such a surge of international travel that Australia suffered negative migration in the immediate postwar years despite refugee and migrant arrivals.[99] The number of Australians taking an overseas trip nearly tripled every five years between 1960 and 1975.[100] Although Australian travelers had historically looked to Britain and Europe, a growing number chose to travel to Asia. Since at least the mid-nineteenth century, many Australians had regarded Asia as a place of overwhelming misery and pestilence, from which they attempted to insulate themselves with stringent immigration restriction legislation.[101] From the 1950s, however, tourist imagery began to portray places like Singapore, Malaysia and Japan as exotic and desirable destinations. Although Indonesia was often regarded with trepidation, from the 1950s Australian tourism to Bali began to escalate.[102] Intending volunteers were slightly ahead of the curve, but their desire for travel and adventure in Asia fell into broader patterns of postwar tourism consumption in the Western world.

Development volunteering was therefore closely related to the rise of the tourist gaze and the new identities and mindsets enabled by the tourism

[97] United Nations World Tourism Organization, *Yearbook of Tourism Statistics* (1988).

[98] Agnieszka Sobocinska and Richard White, "Travel and Connections." *In The Cambridge History of Australia, Volume 2: The Commonwealth of Australia*, edited by Alison Bashford and Stuart Macintyre, pp. 472–93 (Melbourne: Cambridge University Press, 2013).

[99] Commonwealth of Australia, *Official Year Book of the Commonwealth of Australia*, No. 37(1946–7), p. 1293.

[100] Australian Bureau of Statistics, *Year Book Australia* (1977–8), p. 702.

[101] Greg Watters, "Contaminated by China" in Walker and Sobocinska, *Australia's Asia*, pp. 27–49.

[102] Adrian Vickers, *Bali: A Paradise Created* (Ringwood, Victoria: Penguin Books, 1989), pp. 187–192. See also Sobocinska, *Visiting the Neighbours: Australians in Asia*, pp. 169–188.

industry.[103] Travel and tourism often evoked images of luxury hotels and first-class service; but the tourist industry also glamorized the idea of "roughing it" in order to capture a broader range of consumers. The 1950s saw several well-publicized and generously sponsored "expeditions" to distant, exotic locales in the developing world, which rendered physical hardship and colonial-style adventure desirable for the mass market.[104] Budget travel to destinations in North Africa, the Middle East, South Asia and Southeast Asia became popular at roughly the same time as development volunteering took off; by the mid–late 1960s, the "overland route" or "hippie trail" attracted hundreds of thousands of (mostly young) Western travelers every year.[105] The two phenomena were connected: as long-time VSO employee Dick Bird recounted, "when the Beatles discovered India in the 1960s, so did application forms to VSO."[106]

The desire for independence represented a further motivation for some applicants, particularly young women. Parental and societal expectations that young women would marry and settle into family life could be stifling for those with an adventurous streak. Although growing numbers of women did access leisure travel during this period, many parents put up emotional, financial or even physical barriers to a daughter's departure. The organized nature of development volunteering programs, and the lofty rhetoric that underpinned them, could render a volunteering placement an easier sell than other forms of travel. Young women hinted at these reasons in applications and in personal letters to the Volunteer Graduate Scheme's Executive Committee. To take just one example, Thelma Ashton's parents initially opposed her application to become a Librarian with the Volunteer Graduate Scheme in 1954.[107] But they relented after assurances that the scheme was supported by the Australian government and that previous women volunteers had felt safe in Jakarta. Ashton was free to see the world.

Across Place and Time

The core motivations cited by Australian applicants were mirrored, with some regional variations, by British applicants to VSO and American applicants to

103 John Urry, *The Tourist Gaze*, 2nd ed. (London: SAGE Publications, 2002); Dean MacCannell, *The Tourist: A New Theory of the Leisure Class* (London: Macmillan, 1976).

104 Ruth Craggs, "'The Long and Dusty Road': Comex Travel Cultures and Commonwealth Citizenship on the Asian Highway," *Cultural Geographies* 18, no. 3 (2011): 363–83; Agnieszka Sobocinska, "The Expedition's Afterlives: Echoes of Empire in Travel to Asia." In *Expedition into Empire: Exploratory Journeys and the Making of the Modern World*, edited by Martin Thomas, pp. 214–32 (Abingdon: Routledge, 2015).

105 See Sobocinska, "Following the 'Hippie Sahibs'."

106 Bird, *Never the Same Again*, p. 62.

107 Thelma Ashton to Herb and Betty Feith, April 23, 1954, NLA: MS 2601, Box 5, Folder 47.

the Peace Corps. In a report synthesizing thousands of application forms for the Peace Corps in 1962, Suzanne N. Gordon and Nancy K. Sizer found that "what most of them want to do is to 'help people' … To them, serving as a volunteer is a way to work for peace, serve the United States, help to improve international relations, or participate in the progress of developing nations." They also noted that "More than half of the applicants mention potential advantages to themselves – experience, knowledge, a chance to develop as individuals and to further their careers or vocations," but that "The advantage mentioned most often, however, is the opportunity the Peace Corps provides for learning about other cultures … and becoming familiar with different customs, philosophies and ways of life."[108] Although systematic research was never conducted, VSO volunteers were also thought to bear similar motivations. In 1963, the Lockwood Committee, tasked by the British government to oversee overseas volunteering programs including VSO, reported that "there was no single motive underlying overseas service by volunteers," but "A basic factor was the undoubted need in developing countries for the temporary assistance of trained young men and women." Moreover, "It was considered that there was a strong element of mutual advantage in this service. Whilst fulfilling a need overseas it was providing a positive opportunity to the volunteers concerned."[109] The rising reputation of VSO brought further benefits to individual volunteers. In 1967, the London *Telegraph* advised ambitious teenagers that "To line yourself up for a seat in Parliament, today's swingingest qualifications are a working-class father, a grammar school education, an Oxbridge degree and a pair of hands horny from VSO work."[110]

Perhaps more significant than differences between programs was change over time, particularly in the context of broader cultural and political changes in the late 1960s and 1970s. The fervor surrounding the early years of the Peace Corps marked a high point of enthusiasm for development volunteering. During the late 1960s and into the 1970s, youth across North America, Europe and Australia began to lose faith in Western intervention in the Third World, a phenomenon examined in this book's final chapter. As Alec Dickson noted, "When I founded VSO the angry generation had not yet emerged: that was a period of awakening, when one could appeal more easily to an unsophisticated idealism." By the late 1960s young people seemed to think differently; Dickson believed that they had not only become more assertive, but had also lost hope in ideals.[111]

108 Suzanne N. Gordon and Nancy K. Sizer, *Why People Join the Peace Corps* (Washington, DC: Institute for International Services, 1963).

109 "Service Overseas by Volunteers – Weekend Conference at Farnham Castle, 22–24 February 1963," Lockwood Committee Minutes, 1962–1969, LSE: RVA Records, Box 40.

110 Violet Johnstone, "Young Topics," *The Telegraph*, January 21, 1967, p. 11.

111 Dickson, *A Chance to Serve*, p. 130.

Although applicant numbers did fall, the individuals applying for volunteer postings in the 1970s professed motivations broadly similar to those of their predecessors. Applicants still nurtured an idealistic desire to help those worse off than themselves and many also betrayed a desire for travel and adventure. A VSO Executive Committee meeting in 1974 reported that the primary motivations for applicants were "practical altruism" and the "aim to respond to a need," although one selector noted she was "glad to see that many candidates were not afraid of admitting that they wished to see the world."[112] The similarity to discussions of ten and even twenty years before, despite vast shifts in global politics and youth culture, is striking. It suggests significant continuities in volunteers' motivations over time, which helped sustain the humanitarian-development complex beyond the first flush of enthusiasm.

Conclusion

From the early 1950s, young people across the West began to express a desire to become personally involved in international affairs. Application forms submitted by intending volunteers articulated a desire to build personal friendships across boundaries of nation, culture and race. Applicants also expressed a desire to help distant others and bring about development and modernization. This altruistic internationalism was felt as much as thought; Herb Feith's term "sentimental radicalism" captured both its affective and political elements. As with humanitarian concern, the major emotion of development volunteering was empathy but, unusually, it was expressed in a mood of optimism. Applicants conveyed an optimistic belief that they could contribute to better international relations, or even to world peace. They were also optimistic about the potential of international development to improve millions of people's lives. This emotional palette was appealing and encouraged hundreds of thousands of Australians, Britons and Americans to apply for volunteer postings in distant corners of the Global South.

No matter how deeply felt, altruistic internationalism was only one of a number of mutually sustaining motivations. Applicants often listed their aspiration to help in the same breath as expressing a desire for travel and adventure. From the 1950s, the global tourist industry began to portray distant corners of the Global South as ripe for Western adventure. In volunteering, young people saw an opportunity for travel that, for most, was otherwise unattainable. Development volunteering was, in this sense, enabled by the spread of the tourism industry, by globalization and the export of Western capitalism across the globe. The allure of development volunteering – of helping disadvantaged people and strengthening international ties while also

[112] Minutes of VSO Executive Committee meeting, January 7, 1974, VSO Archive, Box 31.

enjoying a once-in-a-lifetime adventure – was so strong that it continued despite rising critiques in the late 1960s and 1970s. While returned volunteers debated whether development volunteering should be curtailed or even banned, new cadres of idealistic and mostly young people sought out VSO and the Peace Corps with the same core motivations: to help others, to spread international goodwill and to seek adventure.

Emotions were a glue that cemented the humanitarian-development complex. Individually, the empathy and optimism of development volunteering drove many otherwise ordinary citizens to seek a volunteer placement in spite of potential personal and financial deterrents. Collectively, these emotions represented a moral justification for the humanitarian-development complex. It is notable that few applicants ever wondered about whether their intervention would be welcomed by recipient communities. Like the civic organizations and private companies explored in the previous chapter, many volunteers exhibited an immense optimism about development volunteering as a cause. This optimism sent them to distant countries armed with little more than determination and the deep-seated belief they could help save the world. Volunteers' motivations were almost always a projection of their own desires and rarely engaged with the stated demands of people and governments in the Global South. Good intentions were enough to justify Western intervention in distant nations.

PART II

Images

5

The Publicity Machine

In March 1961, a young Clint Eastwood wrote to President Kennedy to offer his services for the United States Peace Corps. Eastwood's star was on the rise; the CBS series *Rawhide*, which brought him to fame, was already one of the highest-rating television programs in America. Eastwood did not know much about the Peace Corps, but he knew he wanted to be involved, so he offered to create "a volunteer entertainment group to supplement the work of the Peace Corps."[1] Eastwood's letter provoked some discussion but he was ultimately turned down. Even in its infancy, the Peace Corps exuded a strong appeal, drawing in celebrities and suburbanites alike. Countless hours and millions of dollars were spent further publicizing and advertising the Peace Corps over coming years, bringing development volunteering, and international development more broadly, to wider prominence than ever before. In 1965, sociologists gave its appeal a name that reflected both the Peace Corps' glamor and the fact that, like Eastwood, many people remained unsure about what it actually did or what its impacts were: the "Peace Corps mystique."[2]

This chapter focuses on the wave of publicity and media attention that attended the establishment of the Peace Corps and its reception in the Global North. Australian and British volunteer programs attracted some media coverage from the early 1950s, but their efforts were eclipsed by the public relations campaigns of the Peace Corps. Involving corporate advertising and public relations agencies as well as in-house specialists, the Peace Corps was a publicity machine that reached mass audiences in the United States and around the world.

This publicity was important for several reasons. First, the vast swathe of civic and public support for development volunteering, outlined in previous chapters, was closely connected to its high profile. So too were the rising numbers of applicants. In 1965, over forty thousand Americans applied to become Peace Corps volunteers.[3] As we saw in the previous chapter, applicants brought multiple and often overlapping motivations; however, it is difficult to

[1] Eric Fleming and Clint Eastwood to The President, March 29, 1961, NACP: RG 490, Incoming Mail Briefs 1961–1963, Box 1.

[2] Textor, *Cultural Frontiers of the Peace Corps*, p. 3.

[3] George Nash and Patricia Nash, "From which Colleges come the Peace Corps volunteers?" Columbia University Bureau of Applied Social Research, JFKL: RG 490, Series 1, Box 2.

imagine a similar surge of enthusiasm without the widespread publicity the Peace Corps attracted in its early years. Publicity was significant for a further reason. By reaching a broad and receptive audience, the images broadcast by and about the Peace Corps helped shape popular and elite opinion, not just about development volunteering but also more broadly about the Global South and the nature and necessity of international development. Public support was an essential ingredient binding the humanitarian-development complex; tracking the images that influenced many people's assessment of international development and mapping out public responses to them is therefore essential to our understanding of this phenomenon.

The Peace Corps provided a space for ordinary citizens to think about global poverty and international development; for many, it provided an impetus to think about these issues for the first time. Based on a close reading, this chapter posits that Peace Corps publicity was as significant in its occlusions as its inclusions – that what was left out of the frame was just as important as the image itself. The Peace Corps focused on volunteers and their intentions, while cultivating a strategic vagueness about what they actually did, the places they did it and what impact they had. This helped forge public opinion that was distinctly unbalanced and served to build popular support for the humanitarian-development complex.

Madison Avenue to Malawi

The Peace Corps actively sought publicity from the moment of its creation. Both John F. Kennedy and first Peace Corps Director R. Sargent Shriver were masters of publicity.[4] Even before the Peace Corps was formally constituted, Shriver had engaged public relations experts to sketch the basic outline of a vast publicity strategy.[5] The Peace Corps soon boasted a full-time Associate Director of Public Affairs; within a couple of years, the Public Affairs section had grown to accommodate separate departments for Public Information, Communications and Radio and Television. Shriver also forged close relationships with corporate public relations and advertising agencies. The United States government had begun to use corporate advertising agencies during World War Two and this became increasingly common as propaganda activities were centralized during the Cold War.[6] Shriver brought the talent and

[4] Joseph B. Berry, *John F. Kennedy and the Media: The First Television President* (Lanham, MD: University Press of America, 1987); Aniko Bodroghozy, "The Media." In *A Companion to John F. Kennedy*, edited by Marc J. Selverstone (Chichester: Wiley Blackwell).

[5] Bill Moyers to Sargent Shriver, February 27, 1961, NACP: RG 490, Incoming Mail Briefs 1961–1963, Box 3.

[6] Rosenberg, *Spreading the American Dream*; Laura A. Belmonte, *Selling the American Way: U.S. Propaganda and the Cold War* (Philadelphia, PA: University of Pennsylvania Press, 2008).

glamor of both Hollywood and Madison Avenue to bear on the Peace Corps' image. He looked for people with Hollywood connections to add glamor to his agency and poached well-connected creatives to act as in-house publicists. Terry Turner, the Peace Corps' Director of Radio and Television in the mid-1960s, described his trajectory as "From Madison Avenue to Malawi."[7] In addition to in-house staff, Shriver engaged external consultants including J. Walter Thomson and the National Advertising Council contributed by appointing corporate agencies such as Young & Rubicam to work for the Peace Corps as part of their public service contribution. By the mid-1960s, the Peace Corps had the second largest public service campaign in the United States, trailing only the Traffic Safety campaign with an estimated annual dollar value of $25 million in 1966.[8]

Peace Corps advertisements were carried in hundreds of national, regional and college publications and across the nation's airwaves. The Peace Corps was also eager to capitalize on the growing influence of television. Terry Turner thought that "television is the primary medium of communication in the modern world," and so "we should be able to use the tools of television to relay our story."[9] In 1965, almost two billion impressions of Peace Corps television advertisements were broadcast into American homes.[10] Shriver maintained a punishing schedule of appearances on television news and current affairs shows, at a time when such appearances were unusual for the head of a government agency (Figure 5.1). Shriver's energy, telegenic appearance and personal charm helped extend the Peace Corps' appeal. Peace Corps Washington also encouraged and supported program-length documentaries, the first of which, *Peace Corps in Tanganyika*, began production immediately after the Peace Corps' launch and aired on NBC in late 1961. Screened on national television and replayed at numerous university campuses and high schools, filmed documentaries were regarded as an important recruitment tool.[11] Many of these programs were syndicated and broadcast in other English-speaking countries, extending the Peace Corps' reach across the world. *Peace Corps in Tanganyika*, for example, was broadcast on free-to-air television in Sydney, Australia, within weeks of its US premiere.[12]

[7] Terry Turner to Martha Crane, September 28, 1966, NACP: RG 490, Radio and Television Files, Box 1.

[8] Advertising Campaign, April 14, 1966, NACP: RG 490, Radio and Television Files, Box 4. Note that this figure does not include the value of donated agency time.

[9] "Film Unit," September 21, 1965, NACP: RG 490, Radio and Television Files, Box 8.

[10] "Advertising Campaign," April 14, 1966, NARA: RG 490, Radio and Television Files, Box 4.

[11] Modern Talking Picture Service, *What do audiences say about your film? The Peace Corps in Tanganyika*, NACP: RG 490, Radio and Television Files, Box 5.

[12] "Guide to TV Programs on all Channels," *Sydney Morning Herald*, February 12, 1962, p. 12.

Figure 5.1 Sargent Shriver (on the right) interviewed on KTBC-TV, *c*.1962. NARA: RG 490, Radio and Television Files, Box 5.

The Beautiful Americans

The expansive reach of the Peace Corps publicity machine imbued it with the power to shape public opinion. Historians and scholars of development studies have shown that the "public faces" of international development shape the popular and political contexts in which foreign aid policy and programs are devised.[13] What images did the Peace Corps broadcast and what messages did these images convey? Throughout the 1960s, Peace Corps publicity was tightly focused – some might say fixated – on volunteers. It focused on who they were rather than what they did and specifically highlighted their good looks, good intentions and optimistic mindsets. This was unusual in the broader context of media coverage of international development, which was sporadic and tended to focus on large-scale problems and projects rather than individual actors below the elite level. It was also unusual in the history of humanitarian publicity.

[13] Smith and Yanacopoulos, "The Public Faces of Development: An Introduction," p. 663; Cameron and Haanstra, "Development Made Sexy: How It Happened and What It Means"; Lisa Rideout, "Representations of the 'Third World' in NGO Advertising: Practicalities, Colonial Discourse and Western Understandings of Development," *Journal of African Media Studies* 3, no. 1 (2011): 25–41.

Humanitarian imagery has historically focused on pain and suffering in order to awaken empathy and build a disposition to engage with and care for distant Others.[14] Yet, distant suffering was rarely depicted in Peace Corps publicity; in fact, very little attention was devoted to recipient communities at all. Instead, Peace Corps publicity relentlessly reproduced the image of American volunteers who were simultaneously altruistic and glamorous; who set out to do good and looked good in the process.

In print, on radio and on TV, publicity emphasized volunteers' good intentions, whilst omitting details about the work they would do or why it was needed. One of the earliest official Peace Corps publications, the *Peace Corps Fact Book*, began with the question, "Why a Peace Corps?" As an answer, the *Fact Book* simply stated that "the Peace Corps idea ... has demonstrated a strong appeal to the idealism and altruism of Americans."[15] Neither in this instance nor in the vast majority of publicity did the Peace Corps explain the need for American intervention abroad, or indeed clarify what Peace Corps volunteers would be doing. Volunteers were shown to be well-intentioned and ready for hard work and that was justification enough.

This reductive focus was the product of official policy. The nature and intention of publicity material generated a great deal of discussion at Peace Corps headquarters in Washington. Early on, the Public Affairs section decided that publicity material was to be directed at young Americans and that it was to make them feel empowered, to "say that in the Peace Corps you will be heard and that you will have an opportunity to put your ideas to practical use."[16] This resulted in publicity in which American intentions were repeated and amplified, and other viewpoints muted. A radio advertisement produced in early 1962, by Chicago-based advertising agency Doherty, Clifford, Steers & Shenfield, ran:

> Probably no public activity has ever captured the imagination and interest of the country – and the world – as quickly, as has the Peace Corps. Many see it as a way in which America can help in the world-wide fight for freedom among new and rising nations – and it is. Many see it as a way to serve humanity in the battle against poverty, ignorance and hunger – and it is that, too. Still others feel about the work of the Peace Corps as their

[14] Sontag, *Regarding the Pain of Others*; Chouliaraki, *The Spectatorship of Suffering*; Christina Twomey, "Framing Atrocity: Photography and Humanitarianism," *History of Photography* 36, no. 2 (2012): 255–64. See also Michael Lawrence and Rachel Tavernor, eds., *Global Humanitarianism and Media Culture* (Manchester, UK: Manchester University Press, 2019) and Johannes Paulman, ed., *Humanitarianism & Media: 1900 to the Present* (New York: Berghahn Books,2019); Kevin Rozario, "'Delicious Horrors' Mass Culture: The Red Cross, and the Appeal of Modern American Humanitarianism," *American Quarterly* 55, no. 3 (2003): 417–55.

[15] Peace Corps, *Peace Corps Fact Book*, p. 3.

[16] "Peace Corps Copy Policy," NACP: RG 490, Radio and Television Files, Box 4.

> ancestors felt about the opening of our own West – and it is true that many of the same traditional American characteristics are needed for Peace Corps work as were needed then. Today, Peace Corps volunteers are working, teaching, helping people in Africa, Asia and South America – and requests are pouring in for more.[17]

In this radio spot, American motivations were explored at length and from multiple angles. So much attention was devoted to intentions that little time remained for volunteers' actions and their reception, and no time at all for their impacts. Indeed, what volunteers *did*, rather than what they *intended*, was simplified to "working, teaching, helping," with the suggestion that this was beneficial because "requests are pouring in for more." This was a one-minute radio spot; others in the same series were shorter at 30 seconds, 20 seconds and 10 seconds, and they only heightened the same pattern, emphasizing abstract intentions to the exclusion of on-the-ground realities.

The same focus on volunteers' motivations was also common in articles, books and pamphlets written about, but not commissioned by, the Peace Corps. The line between publicity and reportage was frequently blurred. Dozens of Peace Corps staff collaborated with journalist Roy Hoopes to produce the 1961 *Complete Peace Corps Guide*. In tone and content, Hoopes' work was virtually indistinguishable from official publicity and the line was further muddied by an introduction penned by Shriver. Like official Peace Corps publicity, Hoopes located the purpose of the Peace Corps in its ideals rather than its effects. "Whether or not we . . . have a significant impact on the economic lot of the countries where they will serve does not make any difference," he wrote. "The point is that thousands of young Americans are willing to help and are willing to make sacrifices to do so; the principal purpose of the Peace Corps is to provide the organization through which this desire can be channeled."[18] The focus and tone devised by the Peace Corps' in-house publicity team also influenced mainstream media. Thousands of articles, editorials and profiles followed the pattern set by the Peace Corps in focusing on well-meaning, optimistic volunteers. Even *Vogue* magazine enthused that the Peace Corps volunteer was "a cool, heroic figure in a non-heroic age."[19] As the first Peace Corps *Annual Report* noted, "press comment on the Peace Corps has been generally favorable" and at times it was "overwhelmingly so."[20]

Foregrounding American motivations was politically important for the Peace Corps. It served to bolster political support and helped draw together a broad coalition of civil society backers. More broadly, it also served to

[17] "General one-minute radio spot #3," Doherty, Clifford, Steers & Shenfield, Inc., February 1962, NACP: RG 490, Radio and Television Files, Box 1.
[18] Hoopes, *The Complete Peace Corps Guide*, p. 50.
[19] "Vogue's Eye View of a Loving Sign," *Vogue*, February 1, 1963, p. 91.
[20] Peace Corps, *1st Annual Peace Corps Report*, p. 58.

counter rising critiques of American culture. Hollywood producer Michael Abbott thought the Peace Corps was "without doubt, the most potent public relations tool ever devised," as "for those parts of the world inflamed with anti-Americanism, America's Peace Corps will be the salve and the counter-irritant to the infectious spread of the 'ugly American'." This was a riposte to Lederer and Burdick's influential 1958 novel *The Ugly American*, in which American haughtiness and indolence was contrasted with Soviet aid experts who won villagers over to the Communist cause by sheer hard work.[21] Although the term "Ugly American" was used ironically by Lederer and Burdick, by the early 1960s it had coalesced into a derisive image of Americans held by cultural elites at home and abroad. Abbott thought that the Peace Corps was America's answer. Far from ugly Americans, the Peace Corps would be "beautiful Americans ... bringing hope and trust and self-esteem."[22]

Peace Corps publicity focused on volunteers' beauty in a literal sense too. Unlike many international issues, the Peace Corps was a visual phenomenon. Articles and books on the Peace Corps were liberally illustrated and introduced a certain rugged glamor to the previously technocratic field of international development. Photographs depicted volunteers at training, work and leisure. The centerpiece of a 1963 Paperback Library volume titled *The Peace Corps*, intended for mass distribution at a low cost, was a sixty-four-page collection of photographs contributed by the Peace Corps.[23] The vast majority of images depicted young, attractive and energetic volunteers. A large number depicted volunteers performing back-bends and rappeling during pre-departure training at a facility in Puerto Rico. Whilst the photographs were clearly staged, few were posed. Partly, this was designed to appeal to potential volunteers, many of whom were attracted to the Peace Corps precisely because of its promise of travel and adventure. However, the parade of youthful, attractive young bodies also underscored the notion that America's best and brightest were eager to devote themselves to international development.

The mainstream press took its mark from Peace Corps publicity. Many reports were illustrated with photographs taken at the Puerto Rico training camp. One 1962 article in *The Atlantic Monthly*, illustrated with photographs of a young, blonde female volunteer rappeling during training, claimed that "volunteers must be sturdy, have the skills of pioneers and a proud team spirit."[24] The relationship between rappeling and a volunteer posting in a Filipino school (to take one of the most common positions in the early years) was always problematic and, internally, Program Directors worried that

21 Lederer and Burdick, *The Ugly American*.
22 Michael Abbott, "The Peace Corps," NACP: RG 490, Radio and Television Files, Box 4.
23 Kittler, *The Peace Corps*.
24 Hilda Cole Espy, "What you should know about the Peace Corps," *Atlantic Monthly*, August 1962, NACP: RG 490, Public Relations Publications, Box 2.

"the jungle camp experience tends to produce in the trainee an inappropriate sense of confidence . . . verging on arrogance, [which] is exactly the opposite of the humility which ... should be the hallmark of the good PCV."[25] Nonetheless, this training formed a core element in the public imaging of the Peace Corps, reproduced in numerous articles. The image of fit, attractive, young volunteers, ready to take on the world, was endlessly reproduced.

The media's preference for glamorous volunteers is apparent in the substantial media attention that accrued to selected individuals. Janet Hanneman was a twenty-five-year-old nurse from Kansas when she volunteered for the Peace Corps in 1962. She was one of more than four thousand volunteers sent overseas that year, but her media profile was entirely disproportionate to those numbers. Tall and striking, and with more than a passing resemblance to Jackie Kennedy, she caught the eye of photographers even before departure. The *New York Post* ran a photograph of her rappeling at the Puerto Rico training camp in March 1962. The official Peace Corps newsletter ran a different photo of Janet rappeling taken at the same time. These images were also part of a photo-essay in the 1963 Paperback Library edition on the Peace Corps. Unusually, the interest in Hanneman continued after training, when she began her placement in Pakistan. An official Peace Corps photographer followed Hanneman over several days and took roll after roll of photographs (Figure 5.2). The images were arresting. Hanneman's appropriation of Pakistani clothing and jewelry were emphasized and every photograph depicted Hanneman as composed and stylish, even in the midst of disorder. That year, her photographs appeared over six pages in the *Second Official Peace Corps Report*. She was profiled in multiple illustrated *New York Times* articles, some of which were forwarded to President Kennedy, and in the *Kansas City Times*.[26] A different set of photographs illustrated an article in the *American Journal of Nursing*. Hanneman's time in the Peace Corps was the subject of a multi-page photo-essay in the *Rotarian*, which opened by introducing her as "Pretty Janet Hanneman, of the Peace Corps." On her return, *Life* magazine profiled Hanneman in a liberally illustrated report on the so-called "re-entry crisis" faced by Peace Corps volunteers returning to the United States.[27]

By foregrounding attractive volunteers like Janet Hanneman, the Peace Corps brought a new kind of glamor to international development. The Peace Corps' publicity and media coverage glamorized American altruism and transposed this glamor to international development contexts. Publicity

[25] cited in Textor, *Cultural Frontiers of the Peace Corps*, p. 23.

[26] "Peace Corps Nurse on Rounds of Pakistani Hospital," *New York Times*, "Weekly Report to the President, Dec. 1963," JFKL: RG 490, Box 30. See also Thomas F. Brady, "Peace Corpsmen Crack the Bengali Barrier," *New York Times*, September 29, 1963, p. 29.

[27] Kenneth J. Coffey, "Nurses and the Peace Corps", *American Journal of Nursing*, 62, no. 7 (1962), pp. 50–2; Janet Hanneman "PCV in Pakistan", *The Rotarian*, June 1964, pp. 12–15; Richard B. Stolley, "The Re-Entry Crisis", *Life*, March 19, 1965, pp. 98–110.

Figure 5.2 Peace Corps volunteer and nurse Janet Hanneman stands with patients at the Government Mental Hospital, Lahore, Pakistan, 1963. Paul Conklin/Getty Images.

and reportage were particularly focused on good-looking women.[28] In 1968, seven years after collaborating with the Peace Corps on the *Complete Peace Corps Guide*, Roy Hoopes returned to the subject with a pictorial collection, *The Peace Corps Experience*. Part of the collection was devoted to a photo-essay titled "Pretty Girls: The Peace Corps has its share." Running over four pages, this depicted ten female volunteers teaching classes in Africa, Asia and the Middle East. The text accompanying the photographs claimed that "Everybody remembers falling in love with the pretty young teacher at one time or another in their school days, and the boys who have Peace Corps teachers will no doubt face the same hazards."[29]

Why were attractive women so prominent in publicity and media coverage? On the one hand, such coverage reflected the fact that over one-third of Peace Corps volunteers were female. Yet, this coverage was not merely a reflection of reality: after all, most volunteers did not look like Janet Hanneman and their experiences proved of little interest to the media. Instead, depictions of attractive volunteers, with whom the locals "no doubt" fell in love, were strategically deployed to suggest that development intervention was not only benevolent but also eagerly desired. To borrow

[28] For a further discussion of depictions of women in the Peace Corps see Geidel, *Peace Corps Fantasies*, pp. 79–94.

[29] Hoopes, *The Peace Corps Experience*, pp. 113–7.

Mary Louise Pratt's term, the Peace Corps narrated a story of anti-conquest that camouflaged the spread of US hegemony and the maintenance of global economic inequality.[30] By the early 1960s, the Cold War extended across the globe as the USA and USSR battled for influence in the Third World.[31] These battles were both military (with US Army involvement in Vietnam escalating) and strategic. The establishment of the Peace Corps was intimately related to US economic, military and cultural power; more broadly, it was also related to the maintenance of an unequal global economic system that benefited the Global North. The 1960s saw the rise of dependency theory and concomitant calls for a restructure of global economic and financial systems to overcome the distorting legacies of colonialism. Third World independence movements advanced some of these economic concepts into the political field, proposing colonial reparations and schemes for global economic redistribution that climaxed with the New International Economic Order (NIEO).[32] The Peace Corps did not support redistribution. Instead, as we have seen, it presented development as a matter of adopting American mindsets and it suggested this was achievable at the level of individuals and not systems. Peace Corps volunteers embodied the maintenance and extension of an unequal system of power. Portraying this power as an attractive proposition – as a pretty young woman with whom locals instantly fell in love – papered over the hard edges of global inequality and narrated a story in which US power and Northern hegemony was not only benign but vehemently desired. Attractive Peace Corps volunteers put an appealing face on the spread of American power and on development politics in general (Figure 5.3).

The Great Humanitarians

Peace Corps publicity also helped blur the boundaries between humanitarianism and international development, effectively depoliticizing Western intervention in the Global South in the overlapping contexts of decolonization and the Cold War. By the 1960s the division between humanitarian projects run by non-governmental organizations and charities (putatively motivated by altruism) and international development projects overseen by government agencies (motivated by political interests) had begun to blur.[33] Publicity material and media further muddied this division by portraying Peace Corps volunteers, who were deployed expressly for the purpose of economic and community development, as humanitarians who had made significant personal sacrifices in order to help others. In 1963, *Time* magazine ran a cover story that claimed

30 Pratt, *Imperial Eyes*, pp. 38–84.

31 Westad, *The Global Cold War*.

32 Prashad, The Darker Nations; Vijay Prashad, *The Poorer Nations: A Possible History of the Global South* (London: Verso, 2014).

33 Barnett, *Empire of Humanity*.

Figure 5.3 Cover of *Peace Corps Facts* pamphlet issued by the Peace Corps, May 1, 1964.

the Peace Corps as "a US Ideal Abroad." The article acknowledged the image of the Peace Corps as Beautiful Americans and began by noting that "from the front porches of the US, the view of the Peace Corps is beautiful." However, *Time* wrote, "as so often happens, the image is glossier than the reality." Across several pages, the article depicted volunteers who had "been racked by illness and bedded down in squalor," who "wrestled with tongue-twisting languages [and] gagged on incredible foods containing everything from cat meat to sheep intestines to fish heads," and who "cursed the mistakes of their superiors and muttered in fury at the ignorance and inertia of the natives they are trying to help."[34] Fetishizing the difficulties of Peace Corps life, the *Time* article countered fears that young Americans would be unable to cope with the reality of

[34] "The Peace Corps: Almost as Good as its Intentions," *Time*, July 5, 1963, pp. 18–22.

life in the Global South. It also emphasized the notion that volunteers were willing to make substantial personal sacrifices in order to help others.

By portraying development volunteering as a sacrifice, *Time* aligned Peace Corps volunteers to the popular image of humanitarianism rather than international development. This was an important distinction. As a state agency, the Peace Corps was directly involved in the international development paradigm. As we have seen, it was linked to geopolitics and profoundly implicated both in the Cold War and in the spread of Northern economic hegemony.[35] Humanitarianism, on the other hand, was popularly thought to be removed from politics. Publicity that presented volunteers as humanitarians therefore served to depoliticize the Peace Corps, decoupling it from political and economic power and symbolically realigning it with altruistic intentions. On the ground, Peace Corps volunteers were routinely identified with US state power rather than with compassionate and apolitical humanitarianism. As this book's later chapters show, organized opposition movements against the Peace Corps arose across the Third World during the 1960s. But Western publicity and media representations elided the complex reality in which the Peace Corps operated by focusing on the volunteers' ideals, and their willingness to endure rough conditions, without reflecting the heavily politicized contexts in which they operated.

Time took it for granted that attractive Americans who willingly gagged on foreign foods would be well received by host communities. As with official publicity, *Time* measured the Peace Corps' success by volunteers' good intentions rather than by what they actually achieved. Indeed, it decreed the Peace Corps a stunning triumph as, "in scores of small ways, through their own zeal and ingenuity, the Peace Corpsmen have made a disproportionate number of friends for the US." Because of this, *Time* dubbed the Peace Corps "probably the greatest single success the Kennedy Administration has produced."[36]

Far from informing the public, the narrow focus cultivated by Peace Corps official publicity, and retained by independent media coverage, essentially limited the public's understanding of development volunteering and of international development more broadly. The Peace Corps strategy of focusing on volunteers' good intentions, its partiality for glamor and physical beauty and the media's habit of likening volunteers to humanitarians resulted in a close up on volunteers that was so tight as to exclude any broader context. Why volunteers were needed, what work they did, how they were received and whether they were making any palpable difference to local communities were important questions, but they were not pursued with anywhere near the degree of interest as volunteers' backgrounds, motivations and living conditions. Undoubtedly, this simplified rendition of a politically, economically and

[35] Engerman, *The Price of Aid*; Latham, *The Right Kind of Revolution*.
[36] "The Peace Corps: Almost as Good as its Intentions," *Time*, July 5, 1963, pp. 18–22.

culturally complex activity brought in a wider audience and cultivated broad swathes of public support and enthusiasm at a politically critical time. However, the tight focus on volunteers effectively stymied the potential for informed discussion of the necessity and ethics of development interventions, thwarted debate about its impacts and excluded voices from the Global South altogether.

Peace Corps executives recognized that its publicity material, and the media coverage that followed its lead, failed to inform audiences about the program's aims, methods or effects. Starting with *Peace Corps in Tanganyika*, audience responses to Peace Corps documentaries were routinely measured, often by multiple publicity and market research firms. Sargent Shriver also requested personal feedback from friends and acquaintances across the country, revealing a deep and abiding interest in public reception. Respondents regularly pointed to the lack of concrete information beyond volunteers' motivations and identified it as a real problem that impeded their understanding of the Peace Corps. A Kansas focus group reported that *Peace Corps in Tanganyika* was "a good show," but it needed "greater emphasis on the NEED for the Peace Corps" and more scenes of "the Peace Corps in actual operation," that is, working with Tanganyikans rather than just talking about their motivations.[37] In effect, audiences were critiquing the decision to focus on volunteers' intentions rather than their actions. This feedback was echoed in personal letters. Late in 1961, Shriver's former colleague on the Kennedy campaign, William C. Battle, urged him to change tack, as "I think that the sight of trainees swinging on ropes and climbing mountains has by now pretty well lost its appeal." He advised that "most people are interested in the ultimate results of the work of the Peace Corps" and requested more information about what volunteers did, how they were received and their impacts on local communities.[38] Shriver forwarded several letters, including Battle's, to Peace Corps Deputy Director Bill Moyers, but they had little impact. The Peace Corps' publicity policy remained unchanged and shots of rope-swinging were endlessly repeated in documentaries and other forms of publicity throughout the 1960s.

As well as failing to inform audiences, the Peace Corps mystique had concrete impacts on volunteers. Returned volunteers complained that "the gap between what they felt they ought to achieve and what they were actually achieving was so great as to produce, in many cases, considerable anxiety and guilt."[39] As Shriver noted, "the most unsettling challenge the volunteer faces is his publicity."[40] That being said, many volunteers were eager coproducers of the Peace Corps mystique – so much so that internal documents referred to some as "publicity

[37] Joyce C. Hall to Sargent Shriver, January 2, 1962, JFKL: Papers of Sargent Shriver, Box 12. Emphasis in original.

[38] William C. Battle to Sargent Shriver, December 18, 1961, JFKL: Papers of Sargent Shriver, Box 12.

[39] Cited in Textor, *Cultural Frontiers of the Peace Corps*, p. 52.

[40] "The Peace Corps: Almost as Good as its Intentions," *Time*, July 5, 1963, pp. 18–22.

hounds."[41] In 1962, NBC planned a Christmas special featuring ten Peace Corps volunteers. Executives held some initial concern that volunteers might "think they are being exploited for publicity purposes."[42] They need not have worried: within a month, eager volunteers had sent in tape recordings from El Salvador, the Philippines, Tunisia, Bolivia, Sierra Leone, Thailand and Ethiopia.[43] Many volunteers went further by generating their own publicity, most commonly by writing articles and dispatches for hometown newspapers. Countless articles penned by individual volunteers demonstrate considerable enthusiasm for the Peace Corps' public profile and a desire to align themselves with the Peace Corps mystique.

The image of the Beautiful American endured, perpetuating the narrative of anticonquest even in the context of rising opposition to America's overseas interventions in the late 1960s and beyond. The return of volunteer Barkley Moore, who had worked in Iran for five years from 1966, provided the space for coverage so positive it verged on hagiography. The *National Observer* profiled Moore in a 1971 article titled "The Beautiful American." With a particular focus on his motivations and personal qualities, the article depicted Moore in superhuman terms: he was "able to move people to accomplish what they said was impossible." Unsurprisingly, the *National Observer*'s assessment hinged on Moore's personal characteristics and capacity to inspire: one former supervisor was quoted as saying, "He's the only person I've ever met ... who makes you want to say, 'I'll follow you anywhere'."[44] This assessment was by a fellow American; Iranian views were not canvassed. This article was written at a high point of anti-Peace Corps sentiment, as described in this book's final chapters, and at a time when proponents of a New International Economic Order were extending the critique of Western hegemony to include the international development system. The one-sided nature of the *National Observer*'s coverage, even in this broader context, speaks to the dominance and tenacity of the Peace Corps mystique.

Those Countries

The Peace Corps' fixation on attractive volunteers meant that relatively little attention was devoted to exploring the other side of the equation – that is, the people and places receiving Western volunteers. When Kennedy first announced the Peace Corps in late 1960, he merely noted that volunteers would serve "abroad." This imprecision was preserved in the Peace Corps

41 Kellogg Smith to Pat Kennedy, November 20, 1962, NACP: RG 490, Radio and Television Files, Box 1.

42 Ibid.

43 Norman Shavin to Doug Kiker, December 26, 1962, NACP: RG 490, Radio and Television Files, Box 1.

44 J. Hampton, "The Beautiful American," *The National Observer*, February 1, 1971.

Act, passed by Congress in September 1961, which failed to define the Peace Corps' area of service, referring to it only as "these countries."[45] The ambiguity of terms such as "these countries" was in keeping with the development discourse of the 1960s, which subsumed economic and regional specificities to a binary between "developed" and "underdeveloped" nations.[46] But it went further, creating an essential ambiguity about which nations required Western development intervention. Removing specific context allowed the media to run with crude assumptions. Many reports assumed that volunteers would live in mud huts far from civilization. A common trope removed them even further. In an article for *Atlantic Monthly*, Hilda Cole Espy thought that the distance between America and "underdeveloped" countries was so great that it could only be expressed in temporal, rather than geographical, terms. She depicted the Peace Corps volunteers as having gone "backwards in time," where they grappled with "the realities of life in primitive places."[47] This depiction of underdeveloped nations as "backwards in time" was echoed in numerous reports. The *Complete Peace Corps Guide* from 1961 claimed that the Peace Corps served in parts of the world where "history has not happened."[48] The Paperback Library edition of *The Peace Corps* wrote of volunteers serving in places where "time seemed to have stopped."[49]

Often, the Global South was portrayed as a tabula rasa upon which the Peace Corps could inscribe its achievements. In 1962, the *New Yorker* interviewed Harris Wofford, Special Representative for the Peace Corps in Africa. In an article titled "Pioneers," Wofford claimed that "the greatest future for the Peace Corps is in Africa," because "It's so wide open. And limited only by our imagination. It's an empty continent." He went on: "You get a feeling that must be like what the people who first saw America felt . . . They're starting out with a clean slate."[50] Such statements were far removed from reality. Rather than pioneers starting with a clean slate, Peace Corps volunteers were placed in established communities with rich histories. The largest number of volunteers worked as teachers, usually delivering existing curricula in conventional schools. Many volunteers were based in cities and enjoyed at least some modern comforts. Yet, neither the publicity nor media acknowledged this fact, instead preferring to portray volunteers as "pioneers" in the ambiguous category of "those countries."

[45] Peace Corps, *1st Annual Peace Corps Report*, pp. 4–5.
[46] Rist, *The History of Development*, pp. 75–6.
[47] Hilda Cole Espy, "What you should know about the Peace Corps," *Atlantic Monthly*, August 1962.
[48] Hoopes, *The Complete Peace Corps Guide*, p. 49.
[49] Kittler, *The Peace Corps*, p. 11.
[50] Lillian Ross, "Pioneers," *The New Yorker*, June 23, 1962, reproduced in Pauline Madow, ed., *The Peace Corps*, New York: The H. W. Wilson Company, 1964, pp. 81–5.

Although this chapter has focused on the publicity surrounding the Peace Corps, many of the same tropes were common to British coverage of VSO. In its first year, VSO sent volunteers to dependencies and former colonies in Africa and Asia, and within a decade VSO had broadened its remit to "the under-privileged half of the world."[51] The boundaries of the "under-privileged half of the world" were rarely defined and ambiguous reporting and crude assumptions flourished in news coverage. The London *Times* reported that "Boy Volunteers" worked "among backward peoples" in "backward communities in the under-developed territories of the Commonwealth."[52] The more progressive *Guardian* also depicted VSO in ambiguous terms, as sending volunteers to the "outback" or, even more broadly, "overseas."[53] The tabloid *Daily Mail* similarly wrote of VSOs working "in the mountains, in the bush, in shanty towns"; most commonly, articles simply stated they worked "overseas" or "abroad."[54] In the absence of precision, assumptions were carried over from the colonial period. Sites hosting VSOs were assumed to be places of misery: "the land of the lost" or of "the sick and the starving."[55] The media commonly reiterated colonial truisms and language: one *Sunday Telegraph* report even wrote of VSO "getting ready to invade Africa."[56] The failure to define where "backward communities" were situated was so customary as to avoid comment. Yet, it was laden with colonial-era presumptions about the nature and location of backwardness, now rephrased as underdevelopment. It was also laden with assumptions about the necessity for Western intervention across vast swathes of the globe.

Volunteers in Popular Culture

The Peace Corps mystique was so powerful that it entered into popular culture. Researcher Molly Geidel has calculated that the Peace Corps featured in at least fourteen novels and two plays during the 1960s.[57] Just as significant was its

51 Adams, *Voluntary Service Overseas: The Story of the First Ten Years*, p. 16.

52 "Boy Volunteers Return Home: Year Spent Among Backward Peoples," *The Times*, September 29, 1959.

53 "Young volunteers back from the outback," *The Guardian*, September 29, 1960, p. 2; "Adventure Overseas," *The Guardian*, October 23, 1968, p. 7.

54 Peter Lewis, "In the mountains, in the bush, in shanty town . . . I meet six boys and a girl who are proving themselves the hard way," *Daily Mail*, October 29, 1963, p. 8; "Two big firms help the overseas volunteers," *Daily Mail*, June 29, 1964, p. 1; "Wanted: 1600 youngsters to help overseas," *Daily Mail*, May 27, 1965; "How the young ones can help abroad," *Daily Mail*, December 10, 1964; "Young volunteers will stay abroad longer," *Daily Mail*, August 9, 1966.

55 "Young Britons helping the sick and the starving," *Daily Mail*, August 16, 1966, p. 4; Nicholas Lloyd, "A year alone in the land of the lost," *Daily Mail*, August 23, 1966, p. 4.

56 "Sunday morning with Mandrake: Getting ready to invade Africa," *The Sunday Telegraph*, August 15, 1971, p. 5.

57 Geidel, *Peace Corps Fantasies*, p. 83.

presence on television, which emerged as the dominant media format in the 1960s.[58] As Shriver declared, "I am 1000 per cent in favor of television broadcasting."[59] Shriver was eager to capitalize on the publicity potential of television and TV executives were attracted by the promise of a broad audience. It seemed a natural match. The Westinghouse Broadcasting Company (WBC), which owned a number of television stations across the United States, was the first to offer its services. Ten days after the Peace Corps launched in March 1961, WBC presented President Kennedy with a Peace Corps-based television concept that would blur the lines between fact and fiction and bridge popular entertainment, private profit, domestic politics and international relations. The Westinghouse Broadcasting Company predicted that such television programming could have a broad impact, including helping to "strike a new force for American prestige in the international field."[60]

Throughout 1962–3, the Peace Corps' Radio and Television Division contemplated commissioning a semi-fictional TV serial to serve as a flagship for Peace Corps publicity. Several production companies competed for the rights to this program; *Variety* reported that "everybody wants to get into the act." Hollywood producer Danny Mann drew together support from Universal-Revue and NBC and recruited Kaiser Aluminum as a potential sponsor. *Variety* speculated that Mann had also hired famed writers including James Mitchener, Carl Sandburg and Archibald MacLeish, briefing them that "the language ... should be deep feeling."[61] Although Mann regarded this as a "coup for Hollywood," he also considered a semi-fictional TV program about the Peace Corps to be the "best way to channel our American way of life to the world."[62] Mann's treatment built on the premise that "Peace Corps is people" and proposed to focus on the human drama of cross-cultural encounter rather than on the detail of the work done. "The way in which a Peace Corps volunteer, for example, may help another human being to irrigate a rice field is interesting," Mann's pitch went, "but not nearly as arresting as a revelation of the emotional conflicts that arise between the two." That conflict would not only be dramatic, but also didactic: "The resolution of those conflicts will reveal to our audience the capacities of human beings

58 J. Fred MacDonald, *One Nation under Television: The Rise and Decline of Network TV* (New York: Pantheon Books, 1990); Lynn Spigel, *Welcome to the Dreamhouse: Popular Media and Postwar Suburbs* (Durham, NC: Duke University Press, 2001).

59 Sargent Shriver to George A. Heinemann, February 7, 1962, NACP: Radio and Television Files, Box 1.

60 WBC to President Kennedy, March 10, 1961, NACP: RG 490, Radio and Television Files, Box 1.

61 Army Archerd, "Just for Variety," *Variety*, October 26, 1962.

62 Army Archerd, "Just for Variety," *Variety*, October 15, 1962.

to live and learn and share a common experience that brings together men's minds as well as there [*sic*] heart."[63]

Mann's proposal aroused a great deal of debate at Peace Corps headquarters in Washington. The Radio and Television Division thought highly of the pitch, at one point noting that the proposed format "would be perfect."[64] However, the proposal to blur politics and entertainment provoked difficult questions. Should the Peace Corps lend its official endorsement to a fictionalized drama? Should it demand script approval? Doug Kiker and Norman Shavin from the Radio and Television Division recommended caution. The Peace Corps should "endorse nothing officially," they argued, for the simple reason that "the show might, despite all our efforts, be a dog."[65] Peace Corps Deputy Director Bill Moyers disagreed. "Any weekly TV show that carries the name 'Peace Corps' or deals with the Peace Corps will in the public's mind have Peace Corps approval, whether a trailer credit is carried on each episode or not," he wrote. "That being true, we will be responsible, in the public's mind, for the proper projections of the Peace Corps." Moyers recommended the Peace Corps demand strict controls, including script approval rights, for any program dealing with relevant subject matter.[66] In the end, the debate didn't amount to much. Mann's sample script did not measure up to expectations; Kiker assessed it as "a lot of crap . . . full of big words and fuzzy ideas."[67] The project was quietly dropped.

While plans for a flagship TV serial never eventuated, the Peace Corps featured in numerous variety shows, serials and sitcoms throughout the 1960s. The popular *Gertrude Berg Show* ran an episode with a Peace Corps plotline in 1962. *The Patty Duke Show* aired the episode "Patty and the Peace Corps" to a nationwide ABC audience on November 11, 1964. Unlike Mann's proposal, the Peace Corps had no power of veto over these productions; indeed, it is possible that Peace Corps Washington was unaware of these programs before they were aired. Yet, even in the absence of oversight, depictions did not stray far from the official script. In *The Patty Duke Show* episode, Patty – a loveable teenager who was always getting into scrapes – secretly signed up to the Peace Corps. Patty's success in being chosen for the program was portrayed as a great honor; in the episode, she was interviewed for the local

63 Daniel Mann and Ray Wagner to John Horton, Peace Corps, October 27, 1962, NACP: RG 490, Radio and Television Files, Box 1.

64 Doug Kiker to Sargent Shriver, October 22, 1962, NACP: RG 490, Radio and Television Files, Box 1.

65 Doug Kiker to Sargent Shriver, October 26, 1962, NACP: RG 490, Radio and Television Files, Box 1.

66 Bill Moyers to Sargent Shriver, October 26, 1962, NACP: RG 490, Radio and Television Files, Box 1.

67 Doug Kiker to Sargent Shriver, undated: "Saturday night," NACP: RG 490, Radio and Television Files, Box 1.

newspaper and even her teenage nemesis, Sue Ellen, thought Patty's assignment was "the most exciting thing I've ever heard of!" As in the official publicity, the show's focus was on volunteers' motivations rather than the effects of their work on the ground. Explaining why she signed up, Patty dreamily likened Peace Corps volunteers to "the great humanitarians. Albert Schweitzer, Clara Barton, Betsy Ross." And as in official publicity, the location, nature and effects of the Peace Corps' work were glossed over, and the role of the Peace Corps oversimplified, for a popular audience. Explaining what an unqualified teenager, still in high school, could offer the developing world, Patty replied that "a little skill can go a long way in those countries." She continued, "I'm teaching English but that's just the beginning. Once I get there I'm going to spread around some good old American know-how."[68]

When it came to receiving nations, *The Patty Duke Show* rehashed stereotypes that bordered on caricature. Patty assumed that the Peace Corps would send her to Africa, which the sitcom portrayed as "a primeval paradise . . . Man pitted against raw nature." References to Africa as the "dark continent" were recurrent and Patty explained that "I want to light a candle in the darkness." In preparation for her posting, Patty decorated her suburban bedroom with masks and shields, learned to drum the message "take me to your leader" and practiced a "tribal" dance by throwing a spear at a dartboard. Patty also attempted to prepare "native" foods, as "we have to live like the natives . . . share the same kind of living accommodation, eat the native food." Patty claimed that "in certain parts of Africa grasshoppers are a rare delicacy" and so she set out to capture one – before finding that she could not bring herself to kill an insect. She then went on to make grass soup from the cuttings of her lawn, which unsurprisingly proved to be no more palatable than the grasshopper.

Although it was produced without agency approval, "Patty and the Peace Corps" adhered to the pattern set by the Radio and Television Division of the Peace Corps and the mainstream press. *The Patty Duke Show* portrayed the Peace Corps in a positive light by specifically focusing on volunteers' good intentions, rather than on their actions and impacts. In positioning Peace Corps volunteers amongst the "great humanitarians," it represented international development as an act of altruism. It also justified its interventionist logic as "a little skill can go a long way in those countries" and America possessed a great deal of "know how." *The Patty Duke Show* further elided discussion of what the Peace Corps would actually do or where it would go. Its continent-level representation of Africa as a stereotypical place of darkness and "natives" elided the complex political situation in decolonizing nations of the 1960s. It also shut off the possibility of African agency. Mirroring Peace

[68] Sidney Sheldon, "The Patty Duke Show: Patty and the Peace Corps – typescript," New York Public Library, Performing Arts Research Collection, CTR 366E.

Corps publicity and media reports, and further simplifying their themes to reach a primetime audience, popular culture representations of the Peace Corps encouraged audiences to approve of the Peace Corps, while limiting their understanding of it.

Public Responses

So far, this chapter has traced publicity, media and popular culture portrayals of development volunteering. But how did the public receive and understand those images? Gauging audience responses is notoriously difficult, but the tens of thousands of letters that arrived at the White House and the Peace Corps' Washington offices offer some insights into the diffusion of official publicity and portrayals in popular culture. They also allow a rare glimpse into public opinion about the Peace Corps, and about international development more broadly, during the early 1960s. It is impossible to pinpoint the exact extent to which Peace Corps publicity and popular culture portrayals shaped the views held by correspondents. Yet, letters certainly reveal an audience attuned to Peace Corps publicity. Elwyn Owen, a Minister at the Congregational Church of Lima, Ohio, hosted a screening of *Peace Corps in Tanganyika* in November 1962. He was certain that "the young people who saw the picture will be 'witnesses' for the effectiveness of the Peace Corps and that they will speak a good word for it wherever they are."[69] This was confirmed by other correspondents. Among them was President of the University of Notre Dame, Theodore Hesburg, who wrote to tell Sargent Shriver that the Peace Corps was getting "lots of press coverage, radio and TV time" and that, on campus, "everybody is talking about it."[70] A number of correspondents engaged directly with Peace Corps publicity, confirming its personal impact as well as extensive reach. On the whole, their letters suggest a receptive audience for publicity material. However, some thought that the involvement of corporate advertising and popular entertainment degraded the Peace Corps. In early March 1961, John Kirby from Georgia sent a telegram to inquire if it was necessary "that the PC be corrupted" by appearing on the panel game show *What's My Line*. A small number of astute correspondents also reflected on the bias they perceived in Peace Corps publicity. Katherine Stone Philipp of New York telephoned Sargent Shriver after watching a television program about the Peace Corps in early December 1961. Shriver's secretary took notes, making this otherwise ephemeral interchange with a member of the public accessible. In Stone Philipp's view, the Peace Corps mystique was unhelpful:

[69] Rev. Elwyn Owen to Robert Ruben, November 5, 1962, NACP: RG 490, Radio and Television Files, Box 4.

[70] Theodore Hesburg to Sargent Shriver, March 20, 1961, NACP: RG 490, Incoming Mail Briefs, Box 1.

there was "Too much emphasis in the TV program on what a rather patronizing and not too popular Uncle Sam could show the rest of the world." In particular, she was critical of the fact that the locals who were hosting Peace Corps volunteers "seemed not to have a chance to say a word" in the TV program. In her view, Americans "could make more friends" if they approached the world in a spirit of mutual exchange, rather than creating a fetish object of the Beautiful American.[71]

Correspondence that did not directly refer to publicity material or media coverage nonetheless echoed its language and imagery and mirrored its ambiguities. Perhaps unsurprisingly, considering the imprecision of publicity and recruitment material, many Americans were confused about the countries where Peace Corps volunteers would serve. While some letters used the technical language of "developed" and "underdeveloped" nations that was current at the time, others used vernacular terms such as the "poor" or "have not" nations. Some correspondents freely admitted their confusion. Texan Ray Greene, for example, wrote specifically to request "information from the Peace Corps on underdeveloped nations."[72] Others made telling assumptions about where Peace Corps volunteers would go. New Yorker A. W. Dawson thought that the Peace Corps sent youngsters to "the wilds of Africa" and other places "without the convenience of modern civilization."[73] However, many letters revealed a widespread confusion about the precise location of "those countries." Californian John F. Spence wrote to seek a Peace Corps placement in Japan.[74] Others hoped to be sent to Germany, Hungary or Israel. In late 1961, two of Congressman William Cramer's Florida constituents separately wrote to express their desire to work with the Peace Corps in the United Kingdom.[75] These letters, amongst many more, confirm a generally low level of knowledge about the nature and location of development volunteering. They also point to common blind spots and assumptions about international development, which reflected the elisions and ambiguities of the Peace Corps' rhetoric and publicity material.

Many correspondents expressed support for Western development intervention despite the confusion. Previous chapters of this book explored the

[71] Katherine Stone Philipp to Mr. Shriver (telephone), December 12, 1961, NACP: RG 490, Incoming Mail Briefs, Box 1.

[72] Lindley Beckworth to Peace Corps, received March 15, 1961, NACP: RG 490, Incoming Mail Briefs, Box 1.

[73] Senator Kenneth B. Keating to Mr. Shriver, March 21, 1962, NACP: RG 490, Incoming Mail Briefs, Box 2.

[74] Senator Thomas Kuchel to Peace Corps, March 13, 1961, NACP: RG 490, Incoming Mail Briefs, Box 1.

[75] Senator Karl E. Mundt to Mr. Shriver, April 21, 1961 (re: Europe); James H. Robinson to Mr. Shriver (re: Germany), June 12, 1961; Senator Warren Magnuson to Peace Corps, March 15, 1961 (re: Hungary); William C. Cramer to Peace Corps, November 14, 1961 (re: Britain), all in NACP: RG 490, Incoming Mail Briefs, Box 1.

outpouring of public support that accompanied the launch of the Peace Corps, arguing that ambiguity about the program's goals only bolstered its popularity. Publicity and media coverage regarding volunteer-receiving nations were similarly vague, often bundling dozens of nations together as "those countries," and this vagueness was also productive. Presenting vast swathes of the globe as a tabula rasa encouraged Americans to project their own visions of global development onto the Peace Corps and built public support for Western development intervention across the Global South.

Global Reach

The content, style and tone of Peace Corps publicity reached far beyond the United States. In an increasingly interconnected global media landscape, American stories about the Peace Corps were syndicated across the English-language press and beyond. The syndicated nature of these articles meant that audiences had direct access to American points of view and were provided with American justifications for the Peace Corps. Even reports that were not directly syndicated often reproduced the style and tone of American publicity, pointing to the effectiveness of the American mass media as an agent of soft power and extending the influence of the humanitarian-development complex across the Global North.[76]

The American publicity model directly impacted upon and influenced other development volunteering programs. The Australian Volunteer Graduate Scheme had maintained a complicated attitude towards publicity throughout the 1950s. On the one hand, the Executive Committee recognized that publicity was necessary for recruitment. They also sensed that "As part of the nation's small corporate conscience we need publicity because publicity makes public opinion."[77] On the other hand, they worried that too much publicity might embarrass Indonesians by exposing their relative poverty and need for foreign assistance. As Herb Feith wrote in 1961, "the scheme has to some extent consciously shunned publicity . . . lest Indonesians come to regard it as 'another Western effort that we're supposed to be grateful for'."[78] This ambivalence had produced a half-hearted approach to publicity; only a trickle of articles in university magazines and metropolitan newspapers in Australia and Indonesia profiled the Volunteer Graduate Scheme in the decade from its establishment in 1951.

[76] See Sönke Kunkel, *Empire of Pictures: Global Media and the 1960s Remaking of American Foreign Policy* (New York: Berghahn Books, 2016); Jason C. Parker, *Hearts, Minds, Voices: US Cold War Public Diplomacy and the Formation of the Third World* (New York: Oxford University Press, 2016).

[77] Stewart Lipscomb to Jim Webb, November 15, 1962, NLA: MS 2601, Box 8, Folder 82.

[78] "Work and Identification in Indonesia," Herb Feith, *In Unity*, December 1961.

Publicity efforts were redoubled after the launch of the Peace Corps. The excitement attending the launch of the American agency led to calls for an "Australian Peace Corps" from as early as March 1961.[79] Such demands revealed a broad lack of recognition of the Volunteer Graduate Scheme's achievements and the Executive Committee worried that it would be overlooked if the government launched a new flagship volunteering scheme. In response, the Volunteer Graduate Scheme stepped up its publicity campaign, using the moment to position themselves as the "Australian Version of America's Peace Corps."[80] The major outcome was a book-length account, *Indonesia Face to Face*, published in 1964. Like contemporary accounts of the Peace Corps, *Indonesia Face to Face* focused on individual volunteers' intentions rather than the broader political context of development. The Volunteer Graduate Scheme funded a significant portion of author Ivan Southall's research trip to Indonesia and facilitated access to past and present volunteers. But many volunteers objected to the final outcome, which they felt was too American in its aggrandizement of the scheme and too sentimental in its focus on individuals' good intentions and personal relationships. Volunteer George Hicks thought *Indonesia Face to Face* gushed "banal trivialities in a style that would be an insult to the intelligence of 'True Romance' readers." He also thought that focusing on volunteers was in poor taste because it relegated Indonesia into "a backdrop in which the volunteers are soon to parade larger than life."[81] Criticism was most intense from volunteers on the ground at the time of the book's publication, who worried that American-style publicity could backfire by turning Indonesian opinion against them. As Mary Johnston wrote from Solo in Java, "I enjoyed reading it," but "I feel kind of embarrassed about it. Now that I've finished it I've put it away as I wouldn't like to lend it to friends."[82] Three more volunteers wrote from Jakarta to "express our disapproval of any book written about the scheme," arguing that "It seems hardly necessary to elaborate on our desire to work quietly and unobtrusively away from the glare of publicity, especially personal publicity."[83] These volunteers' concerns reveal that they felt insecure in Indonesia and hint at the ongoing tensions volunteers experienced on the ground. As the following chapters examine in more detail, many Indonesians became critical of the

[79] Letters to Editor: M. J. Holmes, "Aid for Indians," *Sydney Morning Herald*, March 8, 1961, p. 2; "Announcement of Joint Policy," *Sydney Morning Herald*, August 14, 1961, p. 5; "Overseas Workers Wanted," *Canberra Times*, April 6, 1964, p. 4.

[80] "Australian Version of America's Peace Corps," *Sydney Morning Herald*, March 8, 1962, p. 2. This was done in cooperation with the Volunteer Graduate Scheme's partner organization, the Overseas Service Bureau.

[81] George Hicks to Jim Webb, November 1, 1964, NLA: MS 2601, Box 7, Folder 75.

[82] Mary Johnston to Jim Webb, November 6, 1964, NLA: MS 2601, Box 7, Folder 77.

[83] George Hicks, John James and Bernard Lionnet to Jim Webb, July 27, 1964, NLA: MS 2601, Box 4, Folder 36.

Peace Corps in the early 1960s. In this context, publicity that drew attention to Western development intervention was seen as a liability rather than a strength.

In Australia, *Indonesia Face to Face* achieved respectable sales and positive reviews. Far from embarrassment, some young people were inspired by its depiction of Australian volunteers in Indonesia. As one intending volunteer wrote, "It is hardly necessary to comment on the great value of this text . . . It is the best briefing that I could have received!"[84] But the experiment was never repeated. Although initial inspiration for the Peace Corps had come from Australia and Britain to the United States, the tide of influence turned irreversibly in the wake of the Peace Corps' superior publicity. Throughout the 1960s and beyond, Australian volunteer programs were routinely referred to as "Our Peace Corps." From this time on, American publicity helped shape Australian ideas about development volunteering and the development sector more broadly.[85]

Conclusion

Rather than public information, the Peace Corps' publicity machine, finely tuned to the glamor of Hollywood and Madison Avenue, set about promoting the "Peace Corps mystique." From its launch in early 1961, the Peace Corps drew upon a small army of publicists, advertisers and public relation experts. Together, they curated an image that emphasized the good intentions of American volunteers, portraying Peace Corps volunteers as embodiments of the Beautiful American – both literally and figuratively. For the most part, mass media and popular culture representations closely followed the pattern set by Peace Corps policy. At times, independent reportage was indistinguishable from public relations and popular culture depictions only distilled and accentuated the official message. The *National Observer* was an independent publication, yet its depiction of Iran volunteer Barkley Moore as a "Beautiful American" outstripped official publicity in its one-sided zeal. *The Patty Duke Show* may have been light entertainment, but its depiction of the Peace Corps effectively refined the official message and broadcast it to a prime-time audience. The Peace Corps publicity machine was wildly successful. Throughout the 1960s and beyond, the Peace Corps became shorthand for a certain type of virtuous and idealistic American; even in the 1987 film *Dirty Dancing* the idealistic Baby was set to join the Peace Corps before she met Johnny.

84 Russell Edmunds to Jim Webb, November 11, 1964, NLA: MS 2601, Box 9, Folder 94.

85 See, for example, "Our Peace Corps sends more volunteers abroad," *Sydney Morning Herald*, November 12, 1964, p. 2; "Orange Teacher in 'Peace Corps'," *Sydney Morning Herald*, December 28, 1964, p. 8.

By focusing so closely on volunteers' good looks and good intentions, Peace Corps publicity and media effectively obscured the broader contexts of international development. Far from informing the public, the tight focus of Peace Corps publicity consigned volunteers' actions, impacts and receptions outside the frame. Broader contexts, including structural causes of global poverty and systemic inequalities, were effectively excluded from public and elite discussion. This systematic occlusion was politically significant. Deconstructing the monolith of public opinion, this chapter argues that popular views about the Peace Corps and international development were built on scraps of information and a generally positive sentiment. Across the United States and beyond, citizens enthused that the Peace Corps was an unequivocal force for good, but many remained uncertain about what the program did, where it did it or what impact it had. The vagueness of the Peace Corps' publicity and media coverage, which focused on volunteers' motivations rather than their actions and on individual good intentions rather than the structural changes required to mitigate global poverty, effectively built enthusiasm and support for the interventionist logic of international development, while simultaneously limiting the public's understanding of it.

Imaging the Peace Corps in this way had further ramifications. Bringing glamor to humanitarianism and with a particular focus on young, attractive women, the Peace Corps popularized an anticonquest narrative that put an attractive face on Western power. Reaching a broad audience, privileging American viewpoints and eliding competing visions and critical appraisals, Peace Corps publicity helped normalize and glamorize the logic of intervention embedded in the global system of international development. The absence of local voices speaking for themselves left little room for contradiction. Yet, as the following chapter shows, many nations regarded volunteers in entirely different ways and media reportage across many Third World nations was ambivalent, if not explicitly critical, of Western volunteers.

6

The View from the Other Side

The previous chapter tracked the overwhelmingly enthusiastic coverage enjoyed by development volunteers in the mass media of the Global North. But how were volunteers and their organizations regarded in recipient nations? This chapter charts the view from the other side by analyzing press reports from two pairs of volunteer-receiving nations: Indonesia and Malaysia, and Ghana and Nigeria, from the early 1950s until the mid-1960s. Both pairs of countries were geographical neighbors who underwent divergent political, economic and social trajectories during decolonization. Yet, there were marked similarities in media reports about development volunteering. In contrast to the mainstream media of the Global North, the press of many receiving nations was not in thrall to young volunteers. Rather, Western development intervention was often assessed through the critical lens of anti-colonialism. Where volunteers' good intentions had drawn enthusiastic praise at home, people in countries with recent colonial histories were just as likely to regard Western volunteers with caution, if not outright suspicion. By the early 1960s, development volunteering was also stitched into the politics of the Cold War. Perceptions of Western volunteers were tied to attitudes to the Capitalist bloc and to the United States as a rising hegemon. As a result, where Western media doted on volunteers as embodiments of their nation's ideals, newspapers in the Global South were just as likely to ask critical questions. Unlike much of the Western media, these questions spoke to a recognition that development was rooted in ideology and that good intentions did not always lead to good outcomes.

The four nations examined in this chapter underwent divergent trajectories in the 1950s and 1960s. Indonesia declared independence from the Dutch in 1945 and experimented with constitutional democracy and "Guided Democracy" under Sukarno, before a 1965 coup installed Suharto's New Order regime. Malaysia's path to independence from Britain was less confrontational than Indonesia's, with a working relationship with the former colonizer even after independence in 1957.[1] Ghana declared independence from Britain the

[1] This chapter uses the term "Malaysia" for the sake of continuity. Malaysia was formed in 1963 when the Crown Colony of North Borneo, the Crown Colony of Sarawak and Singapore merged with Malaya. Singapore left Malaysia in 1965.

same year, but unlike Malaysia's Tunku Abdul Rahman, President Kwame Nkrumah pursued a radical path to decolonization, characterized by socialism, modernity and pan-Africanism, before his ousting in 1966. Meanwhile, Nigeria's declaration of independence from Britain in 1960 began a long struggle to forge unity amidst a large and diverse population, which devolved into civil war by the end of the decade.

In all four nations, the 1950s and 1960s were periods of intense debate about the meaning and nature of decolonization, national identity and the future of relations between postcolonial states and former colonial powers. Attitudes to Western volunteers were tied to these broader debates. In 1952, Indonesia's Vice-President Mohammad Hatta warned his nation to "be cautious and selective in the face of foreign cultures," and to "take the core of foreign culture and throw away the peel."[2] Determining what was core and what was peel was the subject of intense debate not only in Indonesia but across the decolonizing world. A desire for economic development and modernization was attended by pervasive anxieties about Western cultural influence that was most often expressed in opposition to American films, music and clothing. Development volunteering articulated a maximalist vision of development: volunteers were to impart not only specialist or technical expertise, but also social, cultural and psychological models. Local reception of Western volunteers was therefore closely related to broader debates about Western cultural influence, as well as questions of geopolitics and development.

The press played an important role in mediating these debates. As literacy rates grew, national presses helped construct the imagined communities of postcolonial nationhood.[3] Sukarno and Nkrumah styled their nations as beacons of postcolonial independence and sections of the press in Indonesia and Ghana took on an educative role designed to school populations in postcolonial citizenship.[4] In both nations, government and party-aligned newspapers were stridently anticolonial and regarded Western involvement in their nations with suspicion. The press in Nigeria and Malaysia was less directly regulated by government, but here, too, the nature and extent of foreign intervention was contested. In both nations, the 1960s were marked by intense debates about how to leverage cultural, economic

[2] Mohammad Hatta, "Take the Core of Foreign Culture and Throw Away the Peel (1952)," in Feith and Castles, *Indonesian Political Thinking, 1945–1965*, p. 290.

[3] Benedict Anderson, *Imagined Communities: Reflections on the Origin and Spread of Nationalism* (London: Verso, 1991); Derek R. Peterson, Emma Hunter and Stephanie Newell, eds., *African Print Cultures: Newspapers and Their Publics in the Twentieth Century* (Ann Arbor, MI: University of Michigan Press, 2016).

[4] Andrew Goenawan, "The Indonesian Press, Indonesian Journalism and Guided Democracy." In *The Indonesian Press: Its Past, Its People, Its Problems*, edited by Paul Tickell (Melbourne: Monash University Annual Indonesian Lecture Series, 1987); Jeffrey S. Ahlman, *Living with Nkrumahism: Nation, State and Pan-Africanism in Ghana* (Athens, OH: Ohio University Press, 2017); See also Frank Barton, *The Press of Africa: Persecution and Perseverance* (New York: Africana Publishing Company, 1979).

and political advantage from former colonial powers and rising hegemons without falling into new patterns of dependency and domination. Different viewpoints found expression in newspapers intended for different audiences: in Nigeria, separate newspapers served different ethnic and linguistic groups within the Western, Northern and Eastern regions; in Malaysia, newspapers in English, Malay, Chinese and Tamil addressed different ethnic constituencies living alongside each other. Media responses to development volunteers were folded into these broader contests that went to the heart of postcolonial nationhood.

Historical accounts of development volunteering have largely overlooked receiving nations' media responses. Focusing on program and volunteer intentions rather than their receptions, historians of Australia's Volunteer Graduate Scheme and Britain's VSO have not closely examined Global South press responses.[5] Elizabeth Cobbs Hoffman, whose 1998 book remains the authoritative account of the Peace Corps, noted that "in Ghana, the press harped on American neo-colonialism," but, she continued, "it is equally true that the government and people of Ghana chose the volunteers" as part of a campaign to diminish "tribal rivalries." Cobbs depicted a scenario in which Peace Corps volunteers were eagerly desired and went on to claim that much of Ghana's development success was "due in important part to the convergence of the free world and African goals that brought Kwame Nkrumah together with the Peace Corps."[6] This chapter uncovers a far more ambivalent response. Far from agreeing that progress lay in "convergence" with the "free world," the arrival of the Peace Corps (and other foreign volunteers) was hotly contested. Although the governments of Ghana, Nigeria, Indonesia and Malaysia issued formal invitations to development volunteers, this did not mean volunteers were desired by the broader community: even the ruling political parties sometimes disagreed with leaders' requests for volunteers.

This chapter seeks to decenter Western accounts of development volunteering and take account of the view from the other side. It is based on close examination of the major English-language newspapers from all four countries, as well as the Indonesian and Malay vernacular press (subsequent chapters explore how volunteers were received by host communities themselves). Tracing press depictions of development volunteering in the Global South, it uncovers a greater resistance to development volunteering than has previously been recognized and reveals that the humanitarian-development complex was contested from the very beginning.

First Reports

The media profile of the first development volunteering program, Australia's Volunteer Graduate Scheme, was limited. As we have seen, the Scheme's

[5] See Britton, *Working for the World*; Bailkin, *The Afterlife of Empire*; Bocking-Welch, *British Civic Society at the End of Empire*.

[6] Cobbs Hoffman, *All You Need Is Love*, pp. 149–151.

Executive Committee was concerned that excessive coverage might offend Indonesian sensibilities by broadcasting the nation's need for foreign assistance. They approached publicity in Indonesia with sensitivity and emphasized aspects of their scheme that they knew would appeal to Indonesian audiences. As a result, the Volunteer Graduate Scheme was depicted in only a handful of articles in Indonesia during the 1950s. Significantly, many of these presented Australian volunteers in Indonesia in a positive light.

Indonesian language media articles put special emphasis on the fact that Australian volunteers received the same wages as their Indonesian counterparts, in accordance with the official salary scale for public servants (*Peraturan Gaji Pegawai Negeri Republik Indonesia 1948*, or PGP). This was unusual enough to be headline news in both mainstream and left-wing newspapers. A February 1955 headline in *Harian Umum*, a mainstream daily published in Yogyakarta, emphasized that Australian graduates were willing to be paid according to the PGP.[7] The headline for a January 1956 article in *Pedoman Minggu*, the Jakarta newspaper of the Indonesian Socialist Party, also foregrounded this fact.[8] The article noted that "Foreign workers, especially those arriving from outside Indonesia, usually live luxurious lives in this country. Those who send them, both governments and private companies, must be prepared to pay high wages ... many times above the PGP." But, the article continued, "there are also several foreign workers in this country who do not enjoy luxuries, who are in the same boat as domestic employees. It is somewhat surprising that they want to live on the PGP, especially as they are white people accustomed to a higher standard of living."[9] The Volunteer Graduate Scheme considered their willingness to live on PGP salaries as a centerpiece of their program. This was also a major point of interest for Indonesians: as *Harian Umum* noted, "What really attracts attention ... is their willingness to work in Indonesia ... and be paid according to the PGP 1948. Specifically, they are willing to receive the same pay as Indonesian workers of a similar education."[10]

The Indonesian language press also emphasized Indonesian agency in the origins of the Volunteer Graduate Scheme. As noted in Chapter 1, the initial idea had sparked from a shipboard conversation between Australian and Indonesian delegates to an international student conference in 1950. Although this encounter was fleeting and Indonesians were never substantially involved in the planning or coordination of the Volunteer Graduate Scheme, it played a significant role in the Indonesian media's retelling of its history.

[7] "Sardjana Australia Sanggup Dibajar menurut P.G.P.," *Harian Umum*, February 2, 1955, NLA: MS 2601, Box 14. All translations from Indonesian are mine.

[8] Amir Daud, "Pemuda2 Australia memberikan tenaganja di Indonesia: Mereka hidup setjara PGP," *Pedoman Minggu*, January 15, 1956, NLA: MS 2601, Box 14.

[9] Ibid.

[10] "Sardjana Australia Sanggup Dibajar menurut P.G.P.," *Harian Umum*, February 2, 1955, NLA: MS 2601, Box 14.

Pedoman Minggu placed the initiative firmly in Indonesian hands, claiming that Abu Bakar Lubis had encouraged the Australian delegates to participate in the development of Indonesia, to which they passively responded, "We are ready."[11] A January 1955 report in the Muslim Masyumi Party's organ, *Abadi*, also traced the Volunteer Graduate Scheme's origins to this Indonesian request and a June 1956 report in *Merdeka*, a pro-Sukarno paper owned by the Jakarta media magnate B. M. Diah, emphasized that "The proposal was first put forward by an Indonesian delegate."[12]

The emphasis on Indonesian agency and Australians' practical demonstration of wage equality engendered largely positive coverage of the program's diplomatic intentions. Noting that one of the Volunteer Graduate Scheme's aims was "to destroy unnecessary obstacles between East and West," *Pedoman Minggu* noted that "If we remember that the Australian government bought the 'White Australia Policy', then it is really encouraging that these Australian students have a more advanced way of thinking." The report noted that the potential "to bring sympathy and good relations between Indonesia and Australia in the future actually lies more with them [than the government], because they know and associate more with the people; a kind of association that Australian diplomats don't have here."[13] *Merdeka* noted that the Volunteer Graduate Scheme "will only make a small contribution to Indonesian development, but it can be of greater value in bringing the young people of the two countries closer together, and give Australians some understanding of Indonesia's ideals and difficulties, and about the hopes and worries of its people." Moreover, it continued, "here is shown in a small way that Australia and Asia can join hands to overcome the barriers of tradition, color and culture."[14]

The positive tone of Indonesian press coverage was encouraged by the Volunteer Graduate Scheme's sensitivity to Indonesian attitudes. Herb Feith, the program's first volunteer, returned to Jakarta after marrying Betty Evans in 1954. He worked at the Ministry of Information, served as an official speechwriter to Sukarno during the 1955 Afro-Asian Conference at Bandung and later wrote a magisterial account of Indonesian politics.[15] Feith was closely

[11] Amir Daud, "Pemuda2 Australia memberikan tenaganja di Indonesia: Mereka hidup setjara PGP," *Pedoman Minggu*, January 15, 1956, NLA: MS 2601, Box 14.

[12] "Pemuda2 Australia ikut membangun Indonesia," *Abadi*, January 14, 1955 and "Presiden Soekarno dihormati kaum intelek dan disembah oleh massa: Seorang Australia tentang Indonesia," *Merdeka*, *c.*June 17, 1956, NLA: MS 2601, Box 14.

[13] Amir Daud, "Pemuda2 Australia memberikan tenaganja di Indonesia: Mereka hidup setjara PGP," *Pedoman Minggu*, January 15, 1956, NLA: MS 2601, Box 14.

[14] "Presiden Soekarno dihormati kaum intelek dan disembah oleh massa: Seorang Australia tentang Indonesia," *Merdeka*, *c.*June 17, 1956, in NLA: MS 2601, Box 14.

[15] Herbert Feith, *The Decline of Constitutional Democracy in Indonesia* (Ithaca, NY: Cornell University Press, 1962).

attuned to Indonesian attitudes: even in the afterglow of the Bandung conference, Herb Feith warned that "the more extreme nationalism becomes and the more difficult it is for foreigners to work here, the more important will be the contribution of the scheme as showing that 'there are also good foreigners'."[16] Ailsa Zainu'ddin, formerly a tutor in history at Melbourne University and recently married to an Indonesian diplomat, was also an influential member of the Volunteer Graduate Scheme Executive Committee. Like the Feiths, Zainu'ddin was well-versed on Indonesian political and social attitudes and approached contacts with Indonesian media with an unusual degree of subtlety.

The positive tone of Indonesian reports was also the product of Indonesia's political climate in the mid-1950s, which was uniquely receptive to international cooperation in the period between the Bandung Conference and the anti-foreigner campaigns that followed a CIA-backed uprising in Sumatra in 1958. This brief flowering of internationalist sentiment opened the door to newspaper stories about well-meaning foreigners whose spirit of international cooperation belied the tense diplomatic climate between their countries.

The Peace Corps Moves In

The situated knowledge of the Volunteer Graduate Scheme was difficult to replicate in larger programs extending beyond single nations. The Peace Corps followed a very different publicity strategy. As the previous chapter showed, the agency constructed a vast publicity machine extending across a wide range of media, which was tightly focused on Western perspectives. The Peace Corps paid far less attention to the newspapers of receiving nations; the push for the "hearts and minds" of people in developing nations did not extend to engaging with their press.[17]

In the United States, sustained press interest in the Peace Corps began immediately after President Kennedy's inaugural speech in January 1961. But in many receiving nations media attention came much later, typically after an announcement that Peace Corps volunteers would be arriving in their region. This suggests that decolonizing nations were less interested in the Peace Corps as an expression of American ideals than as a tangible scheme with the potential to make a direct impact on their nation. The earliest sustained coverage came in the wake of Sargent Shriver's first world tour in April–May 1961, during which he visited Ghana, Nigeria, India, Pakistan, Burma, Malaya, Thailand and the Philippines in an attempt to elicit interest

[16] Herb Feith to Don Anderson and Jim Webb, October 21, 1955, NLA: MS 2601, Box 4, Folder 34.

[17] For an analysis on American soft power in developing nations, see Kunkel, *Empire of Pictures*, esp. pp. 80–103, and Parker, *Hearts, Minds, Voices*, pp. 116–39.

and requests for volunteers. After that, a further bump in publicity typically followed the announcement that an agreement to receive Peace Corps volunteers had been signed, then another after volunteers arrived in country.

Ghana was the first place Shriver touched down and his arrival provoked a minor crisis in the ruling Convention People's Party (CPP) after the *Ghanaian Times*, a CPP newspaper, condemned the Peace Corps. "Few organizations could have been presented to the world in more grandiose terms," the *Ghanaian Times* reported, but in fact the Peace Corps was "an agency of neo-colonialism."[18] The report was in keeping with the tenets of Nkrumahism: anticolonialism, modernism and African self-sufficiency.[19] However, Nkrumah looked favorably on the Peace Corps; in this instance, the need for trained teachers in Ghana's burgeoning education system outweighed anti-Western rhetoric.[20] The *Ghanaian Times* was chastened and Nkrumah went out of his way to grant Shriver a warm welcome. Rather than an embarrassing aberration, the *Ghanaian Times*' initial response underscores the extent to which acceptance of the Peace Corps went against established Nkrumahist principles. Nkrumah's invitation to the Peace Corps aligned more closely with opposition party policy, as expressed in its organ, the *Ashanti Pioneer*.[21] Writing of the Peace Corps, *Ashanti Pioneer* columnist Kwame Kesse-Adu wrote that "it is difficult to accept the verdict that it is guilty of one of the 'isms', even before it has had a chance to get started. We are told its aims are peaceful. At least elementary prudence makes it an obligation, on the lovers of peace, not to cry wolf! wolf! when after all, it may actually be a harmless dove of peace."[22]

Contrasting reports about the Peace Corps were folded into widespread and substantive political, ideological and philosophical debates taking place in Ghana. The CPP and *Ghanaian Times* held that all Ghanaians should be ideologically supportive of independence and so they should be prepared to pay for it: independence, they claimed, came at the price of eternal vigilance and financial sacrifice. The *Ashanti Pioneer*, on the other hand, thought that foreign nations should be made to shoulder the responsibility of Ghana's development: it regarded foreign aid more positively, even if it resulted in binding cooperation with the Western bloc. The *Ashanti Pioneer* ran a headline announcing that "We hail the Peace Corps pact," which was "unexpected but Godsent," and represented aid "without strings . . . and there is no reason to entertain doubts and suspicion."[23] The *Ashanti*

18 *Ghanaian Times*, April 25, 1961.
19 See Ahlman, *Living with Nkrumahism*.
20 Cobbs Hoffman, *All You Need Is Love*, p. 155.
21 See Jean Marie Allman, *The Quills of the Porcupine: Asante Nationalism in an Emergent Ghana* (Madison, WI: University of Wisconsin Press, 1993).
22 Kwame Kesse-Adu, "Accra Diary: The American Peace Corps," *Ashanti Pioneer*, May 3, 1961, p. 2.
23 J. S. Kwabena Kumi, "We hail the Peace Corps Pact," *Ashanti Pioneer*, July 26, 1961, p. 4.

Pioneer's praise for the Peace Corps was also tied to opposition to a new raft of government tariffs, which aimed at revenue-raising by placing taxes on consumer commodities and introducing compulsory savings, and which in effect sought to involve a larger part of Ghana's population in financing the country's development program.[24] The contest over the Peace Corps was, therefore, folded into broader debates about who should fund Ghana's modernization.

Nkrumah's decision to invite the Peace Corps to Ghana limited the media's capacity for direct criticism, especially after the August 1961 passage of legislation making it an offense to insult President Nkrumah in print or speech, punishable by up to three years' imprisonment. The arrival of the Peace Corps the same month met with a muted media response. The largest-circulation newspaper in Ghana, the *Daily Graphic*, did not report on the Peace Corps' arrival, nor indeed on its first two years in Ghana. The *Ghanaian Times* ran short snippets reporting the bare facts of the volunteers' arrival. Even the *Ashanti Pioneer* was relatively circumspect, marking the Peace Corps' arrival with a single article.[25] But a shadow debate took place in ongoing critiques of foreign expatriates in post-colonial Ghana. In August 1961, just days before the first contingent of Peace Corps was due to arrive, the *Ghanaian Times* ran an editorial demanding "Stop these experts." It declared that "Ghana has arrived at a stage in her development when it must pause, look left and right, and find out if all the British expatriates and other foreigners parading in the country as experts are really experts." Claiming that many were in reality "greenhorns," the *Ghanaian Times* called for the nation "to be rid of the humbuggery of these fake experts."[26] Even the pro-Western *Ashanti Pioneer* condemned some of the "experts from abroad" who failed to make a genuine contribution to Ghana and called on the government "to see whether something cannot be done about the present policy of allowing our Ghanaian experts to go abroad, whilst we at home go abroad looking for expatriate experts and teachers."[27] Although the Peace Corps was never referred to by name, the debate about "greenhorn" Western expatriates in Ghana was obliquely tied to the arrival of the first Peace Corps contingent.

Nkrumah's acceptance of Peace Corps volunteers imposed a de-facto ban on negative reporting of the program in Ghana. In this context, opposition to Western volunteers in Ghana was rarely made overt in the media (although, as Chapter 9 of this book reveals, it was more common at grassroots level). Alongside the shadow debate regarding the desirability of Western "experts,"

[24] Norman Mosher, "Taxes and Forced Savings in Ghana," *West Africa Report* 6, no. 9 (1961, October), p. 8.

[25] "Peace Corps volunteers arrive in Ghana," *Ashanti Pioneer*, September 2, 1961, pp. 3–4.

[26] "Editorial: Stop These Experts," *Ghanaian Times*, August 12, 1961, p. 2. See also E. F. Aspro, "Readers write ... Check these foreigners," *Ghanaian Times*, March 27, 1962, p. 2.

[27] "Editorial: The Contrast of Experts," *Ashanti Pioneer*, September 29, 1961, p. 2.

broader ambivalence regarding development volunteers in postcolonial Africa was expressed in Ghanaian reports of Peace Corps activities in neighboring Nigeria. These reports took on additional significance following the Postcard Incident, which took place just days after the Peace Corps arrived in Nigeria and six weeks after they had landed in Ghana.

The Postcard Incident

On October 13, 1961, Margery Michelmore, a Peace Corps volunteer recently arrived in Nigeria, dropped a postcard addressed to an American friend on her way to the post office in the Southwestern town of Ibadan. The postcard was discovered by a group of Ibadan university students, who took exception to Michelmore's descriptions of "the squalor and absolutely primitive living conditions" in Nigeria, where "everyone except us lives in the street, cooks in the street, sells in the street and even goes to the bathroom in the street." The following day, the Students' Union staged a protest rally demanding the expulsion of all Peace Corps volunteers, whom they denounced as "agents of imperialism," and beseeching fellow Nigerians to boycott interaction with Peace Corps volunteers. Dapo Falase, President of the Students' Union, dubbed the Peace Corps "an international group of intelligent international secret service spies" and branded the United States as "one of the greatest enemies of Africa."[28]

Outrage quickly spread beyond Ibadan. The Western Region's ruling Action Group party condemned the Peace Corps as "international spies" and "imperialist lions who had invaded our country in the sheep's skins of all forms of peace missions." The Eastern Region's NCNC party demanded an apology from the US Ambassador.[29] Ten days after the incident, the Nigerian Prime Minister, Abubakar Tafawa Balewa, joined the chorus of condemnation, while simultaneously calling for restraint. Michelmore must be "unequivocally condemned" he said, but "not all people are alike and the remark of an individual like the girl could not be taken as representing a whole nation."[30] At a UNESCO conference later the same month, Nigeria's foreign minister, Jaja Wachuku, concluded that America's reputation had been "slightly tarnished" by the incident, which had confirmed suspicions that the United States was gripped by "a general feeling of superiority over the non-White world."[31]

[28] "UCI row: Peace Corps girl says – I quit," *Daily Express*, October 16, 1961, p. 1.

[29] "AG, NCNC on Peace Corps girl," *Daily Express*, October 20, 1961, p. 5. The NCNC (National Council of Nigeria and the Cameroons) was the dominant party in Nigeria's Eastern region at the time.

[30] "PM blames Peace Corps girl," *Daily Express*, October 21, 1961, p. 1.

[31] "US no longer symbol of liberty," *Daily Express*, October 25, 1961, p. 2.

The postcard incident was front page news in Nigeria's major daily and weekly papers, with coverage and debate continuing for weeks. The broad circulation *Sunday Express* and *Sunday Post* both published the postcard in its entirety, along with the home addresses of both Michelmore and the friend for whom the postcard had been intended.[32] The *Sunday Post* published a front-page report punctuated with exclamation points: "Sour! Bitter! These ugly words describe the mood and the temper of students at the University College, Ibadan."[33] In Enugu, the Eastern Region's *Nigerian Outlook* called for "an immediate re-examination of the Kennedy Peace Corps mission in Nigeria."[34] As Professor of Agricultural Economics at the University of Ibadan (and regular columnist for the *Sunday Express*) H. A. Oluwasanmi noted, "wherever two or more Nigerians met last week – at work or in the playing fields, at home or in school – Miss Michelmore's postcard was the topic of heated debate."[35]

Much of the discussion related to the true purpose of the Peace Corps and opened up a space for discussion of the benefits and pitfalls of development aid more generally.[36] The Ghanaian press had already suggested the Peace Corps was a wolf in disguise; now similar analogies became commonplace. The Northern People's Congress Party's *Daily Mail* wrote that "We want friends but not wolves in sheep's clothing as President Kennedy's spies."[37] The Lagos *Daily Express*, aligned with the Action Group, was puzzled by the Peace Corps, claiming that it was unprecedented to have a situation where "the mighty and affluent . . . pay court to the low-downs of the earth." The students at Ibadan, it noted, had "decoded it to read: Beware of the Trojan horse!" but a contrasting "official signal flashes out to reassure the world: Not so, not so, only a band of good Samaritans abroad."[38] The Trojan Horse image was also picked up by H. A. Oluwasanmi, who wrote that, "I am usually tough-minded and septical [*sic*] about Greeks carrying gifts." But, he continued, "I can see no evidence that the Peace corpsmen are spies," but rather "are here in response to our invitation and out of a burning and genuine desire to be of help to us."[39]

Oluwasanmi's piece notwithstanding, the Michelmore incident opened an avenue for broader criticism of American volunteers, and the United States

32 "A Girl's private letter stirs UCI," *Sunday Express*, October 15, 1961, p. 16.

33 "UCI Students Are Angry: Mass Rally Today," *Sunday Post*, October 15, 1961, p. 1.

34 "Margery's Postcard," *Sunday Post*, October 22, 1961, p. 2.

35 H. A. Oluwasanmi, "Peace Corps Guys Aren't Spies," *Sunday Express*, October 22, 1961, p. 7.

36 See Larry Grubbs, "Bringing 'the Gospel of Modernization' to Nigeria: American Nation Builders and Development Planning in the 1960s," *Peace and Change* 31, no. 3 (2006, July): 279–308; *Secular Missionaries: Americans and African Development in the 1960s* (Amherst, MA: University of Massachusetts Press, 2009).

37 Cited in "Margery's Postcard," *Sunday Post*, October 22, 1961, p. 2.

38 "Opinion: Envoys," *Daily Express*, October 17, 1961, p. 4.

39 H. A. Oluwasanmi, "Peace Corps Guys Aren't Spies," *Sunday Express*, October 22, 1961, p. 7.

more generally, in Nigeria's vibrant and relatively unregulated press. A university gossip column snidely offered "a piece of advice for those of the American group still left . . . those not-quite-up-not-quite-down semi-trousers you wear are very unbecoming. Also the worn-out and dirty tennis shoes. Those at least could have been left back home in God's Own Country."[40] Even Oluwasanmi took the opportunity to denounce the "racial arrogance" of Americans after Sargent Shriver dismissed Nigerian opponents as Communist stooges. "We cannot pick a flower without some white father in official Washington telling us that it is a red rose fertilized by Communist manure," he complained, moreover "We cannot urge our people to beg less and build their society upon their own strengths and upon virtue without some wiseacre preaching to us that this is the Communist way of doing things." Frustration with the American tendency to reduce Nigerian postcolonial sentiments to Cold War frames evoked strong opposition: as Oluwasanmi noted, "The implication is clear. It is the same ancient libel in a new garb. The African is a child. He cannot think, cannot act and cannot make the 'right' choices by himself without the directing hands of the Kremlin or Washington."[41]

Margery Michelmore apologised for her postcard and was quickly withdrawn from Nigeria. The *Daily Express* thought that this put an end to the matter and urged readers to build "a calm atmosphere and time for the other young members of the Peace Corps to give a good account of themselves."[42] But its readers were less sanguine. Letters to the editor were unremittingly negative, condemning Michelmore's "anti-black feeling" as being common to "white bigots" who refused to see the positive signs of Nigeria's progress and congratulating the students of University College Ibadan "for their vigilance." One reader called for Michelmore to be "caned for her practical insult on Nigerians." Others thought that suspicion and censure should not be limited to Michelmore but rather extended to all Peace Corps volunteers, as "Heaven knows what the others must have written in sealed letters."[43]

The Michelmore incident played into tensions between Nigeria and the United States and between decolonizing African nations and the West more broadly. It was the latest in a string of incidents to inflame Nigerian resentment against Western racism and condescension in the postcolonial period. Most pressing was the institutional racism experienced by Nigerians living in the United Kingdom and racial slights to senior diplomats in the United States. Just days before Michelmore had dropped her postcard, the Lagos *Daily*

40 Abi Craig, "By the Way! One for the Yanks!" *Sunday Express*, October 22, 1961, p. 4.

41 H. A. Oluwasanmi, "Peace Corps Guys Aren't Spies," *Sunday Express*, October 22, 1961, p. 7.

42 "Opinion: Time to forget," *Daily Express*, October 20, 1961, p. 4.

43 Oamen Diagi, "Dear Sir," *Daily Express*, October 20, 1961, p. 4.

Express had published an editorial warning that "if the West led by the United States of America and Great Britain loses Africa to the East" it would be because of "the race problem" and continuing slights to the "human dignity" of Africans.[44] The postcard incident aggravated already existing grievances. As the *Daily Express* editorialized in its wake, it was the "smugness and mediocrity" of Americans that caused greatest offense and, "from the hoity-toity way things are now going," the Peace Corps was "hoist with her own petard already."[45] More than a month after the postcard incident, a columnist concluded that "Someone ought to tell the Americans that though we can use their help, we are not in desperate need of it."[46]

The postcard incident encapsulated Nigerian frustration with Western attitudes to Africa. Nigerian students, politicians and the media took exception to Michelmore's depiction of Nigeria as "absolutely primitive": Ibadan students were angry that she neglected to mention the university's modernist campus or the educated and thoroughly modern Nigerians she had met. But Michelmore's depiction was entirely consistent with contemporary Western representations of Nigeria, Africa and the "underdeveloped" world. As the previous chapter demonstrated, Western press reports of development volunteering portrayed a distorted image of Global South backwardness. Just three days before Michelmore dropped her fateful postcard, a headline in the London *Times* claimed that "Peace Corps Trains for Primitive Life."[47] Similar media representations would follow. Rather than an isolated incident, the Michelmore affair drew upon the discursive gulf between Global North and Global South. It also highlighted the role of development volunteering as a lightning rod for ongoing, and broader, North–South tensions.

Reports of the postcard incident circulated to other parts of Africa and the Global South. Michelmore's postcard was widely reported in neighboring Ghana. Significantly, reports were overwhelmingly sympathetic to the Nigerian point of view, despite chronic tensions between the two nations that, in 1961, occasionally flared into threats of military conflict. A *Ghanaian Times* headline ran "Peace Corps woman member insults Nigeria" and, in a specially italicized section, it reported that in Nigeria, "the students condemned the Peace Corps programme which 'in fact is a neo-colonialist move directed against the legitimate aspirations of Africans for peace, progress and complete eradication of vestiges of imperialism and colonialism'."[48] In the week following the incident, even the pro-Western *Ashanti Pioneer* ran stories

44 "Opinion: The West and Skin," *Daily Express*, October 7, 1961, p. 4.

45 "Opinion: American Champions," *Daily Express*, October 14, 1961, p. 4.

46 Soba Oyawoye, "The Michelmore Affair: Why Can't Yanks See Anything Wrong?" *Daily Express*, November 12, 1961, p. 4.

47 "Peace Corps Trains for Primitive Life," *The Times*, October 10, 1961, p. 10.

48 "Peace Corps Woman Member Insults Nigeria: We're Living in Primitive State, She Writes," *The Ghanaian Times*, October 17, 1961, p. 3.

directly quoting Nigerian, but not American, viewpoints. Separate articles reported that the Nigerian Union of Britain and Ireland expressed "shock at this hideous distortion of conditions";[49] that Prime Minister Balewa thought that "It is bad of anybody to come and abuse us here in Nigeria";[50] and that the Foreign Minister had declared the United States' reputation tarnished by the incident.[51]

Reporting on negative receptions of volunteers in Nigeria allowed Ghanaian newspapers to critique the Peace Corps without overtly undermining Nkrumah's continued support for the program. In the wake of the postcard incident, the *Ghanaian Times* ran regular articles about volunteers behaving badly in Nigeria. In March 1962, it reported that the *West African Pilot* had declared the Peace Corps "an auxiliary branch of the U.S. secret service" and hinted that "there are some 'not very good' reports about the peace corps members in Ghana" as well.[52] In May 1962, a further report noted that Nigerian students had demanded an investigation into the Peace Corps, as they "would not tolerate the transformation of the University of Nigeria into an American administrative and academic colony."[53] The following month, the *Ghanaian Times* reported that the Peace Corps had also roused suspicion in Tanganyika, with Parliamentarian John Mwakangale arguing that "These people are not here for peace, they're here for trouble" and warning that "if they don't behave, one day they will find themselves in the Indian Ocean."[54]

The postcard incident was one of the earliest instances in which a serving Peace Corps volunteer attracted substantial media attention. Heavily reported in Nigeria, it also drew the attention of other nations that had already signed up to receive development volunteers and those debating whether to extend an invitation to the Peace Corps or VSO. Reports spread far beyond Africa. Over the following years, references to Margery Michelmore's postcard were common whenever opposition to development volunteering was articulated across the developing world.

A Wolf in Sheep's Clothing

Indonesia had welcomed Australian volunteers from 1951, but the climate for development volunteering in Indonesia rapidly deteriorated. Indonesian attitudes to the West soured during the West New Guinea dispute in the 1950s,

[49] "Global Glimpses: London," *Ashanti Pioneer*, October 19, 1961, p. 3.
[50] "Nigerian Fed. Premier Condemns," *Ashanti Pioneer*, October 23, 1961, p. 1.
[51] "US 'Slightly Tarnished' – Wachuku," *Ashanti Pioneer*, October 25, 1961, p. 3.
[52] "Peace Corps Is Branch of U.S. Secret Service – says Nigerian daily," *Ghanaian Times*, March 28, 1962, p. 3.
[53] "Probe Activities of Peace Corps, Nigerian Students Appeal," *Ghanaian Times*, May 25, 1962, p. 4.
[54] "Peace Corps Accused of Subversion," *Ghanaian Times*, June 14, 1962, p. 8.

further declined following the exposure of CIA backing for anti-Sukarno rebels in 1958 and hit a nadir during *konfrontasi* with Malaysia from 1963. Debates about the desirability of Western political and cultural influence became increasingly tense. The communist newspaper *Harian Rakjat*, which enjoyed a mass readership at a time when the Indonesian Communist Party (*Partai Komunis Indonesia*, PKI) was the second largest in the world, consistently opposed Western influence, arguing that "The Indonesian people do not wish to be free from Dutch colonialism and then receive neo-colonialism."[55]

Sargent Shriver arrived in Indonesia in September 1962 hoping to convince Sukarno to accept Peace Corps volunteers as teachers, technical experts and doctors. Over the course of several days and in six cities, he met dozens of officials and bureaucrats and attended numerous banquets. Many of these meetings went well: Foreign Minister Subandrio told Shriver that, although the US had "no chance to compete with the Russians in the field of aid," the "person-to-person friendly approach of the Peace Corps, leaving aside all political considerations, is a means of counteracting the appeal of Communism to the Indonesian common people."[56] As a US Embassy official explained, "That is the justification for the Peace Corps in Indonesia which can get more mileage for less money in a desperate and vital contest."[57] Although Sukarno had stopped short of making a formal request, Shriver departed Jakarta confident that volunteers would follow within a matter of months.

Shriver's visit attracted the attention of Indonesia's media at a time of relative freedom of the press.[58] Reports appeared in newspapers across the political spectrum, with the majority of articles studiously non-committal as reporters awaited Sukarno's decision.[59] But the communist *Harian Rakjat* came out in opposition to the Peace Corps, warning that "based on experience in many countries including Ghana, Nigeria, and others, the Peace Corps is a tool of neocolonialism" with which it would be "impossible to work for peace."[60] Over the following months, *Harian Rakjat* ran an intense anti-Peace

[55] *Harian Rakyat*, September 28, 1961, p. 3.

[56] J. W. Henderson to Sargent Shriver, September 5, 1962, JFKL: Papers of Sargent Shriver, Box 28.

[57] Ibid.

[58] Although government oversight of Indonesian newspapers continued during the period 1960–4, this period was less restrictive than immediately following the imposition of Martial Law in 1957 and the massive media crackdown that followed the 1965 coup. See David T. Hill, "Press Challenges, Government Responses: Two Campaigns in 'Indonesia Raya'." In *The Indonesian Press: Its Past, Its People, Its Problems*, edited by Paul Tickell (Melbourne: Monash University Indonesian Lecture Series, 1987).

[59] See, for example, *Berita Indonesia*, September 5, 1962, cited in US Embassy, Jakarta, "Djakarta Press Summary, 1961–1965," NLA MP 377; "S. Shriver Received by Roeslan Abdoelgani," *Duta Masyarakat*, September 8, 1962; "American Peace Corps Would Operate in Indonesia?" *Warta Berita*, September 8, 1962.

[60] "Pemuda Rakjat: Tolak 'Korps Perdamaian'," *Harian Rakjat*, September 12, 1962, p. 1.

Corps campaign that extended to dozens of articles and editorials. It pointed to African responses to volunteers as evidence that the Peace Corps was a front for American subversion. It also conjured the Michelmore postcard scandal, which it represented as "an insult to colored people."[61] In one of three negative articles in its September 10, 1962 issue, *Harian Rakjat* claimed that the entire Peace Corps was composed of people like "the racist Margery," who look on the people of developing nations as "second class humans."[62] One report directly cited the *Ghanaian Times*, arguing that "the American Peace Corps is an instrument of neo-colonialism, an instrument to destroy the new developing countries and put them under the domination of American imperialism."[63]

Harian Rakjat depicted the Peace Corps as a CIA and SEATO front organization seeking to engage in "espionage activities for the imperialists."[64] It claimed that Peace Corps volunteers were actually military troops in disguise, citing rumors that a Peace Corps agronomist in South Vietnam had "suddenly changed into an army officer of the United States troops" and claiming that this revealed "the real image of the Peace Corps."[65] In the days following Shriver's visit, *Harian Rakjat* claimed that US Secretary of State Dean Rusk had admitted that, for the project of American hegemony, "the presence of American teachers, doctors and engineers in the agreed territories is not less important than the presence of American troops."[66] It reported that Secretary General of SEATO Pote Sarasin had declared his organization was "engaged in [the] non-military field" and had hinted that this engagement took place through the Peace Corps.[67] Finally, it reported that Shriver himself had admitted that the Peace Corps was in fact a US Army sleeper unit that could easily revert into a "War Corps" and that the Peace Corps was infiltrated by active US troops in readiness of this event.[68] As such, *Harian Rakjat* concluded, "The American Peace Corps is nothing other than an instrument of neo-colonialism disguised as a peace promoting organization."[69]

61 "Pengakuan Sargent Shriver: 'Korps Perdamaian' gampang dirubah menjadi 'Korps Perang'," *Harian Rakjat*, October 17, 1962.

62 "Korps Perdamaian," *Harian Rakjat*, September 10, 1962, p. 11.

63 "Pengakuan Sargent Shriver: 'Korps Perdamaian' gampang dirubah menjadi 'Korps Perang'," *Harian Rakjat*, October 17, 1962.

64 "Forbid the Peace Corps to operate in Indonesia," *Harian Rakjat*, September 27, 1962, cited in Djakarta Press Summary 1961–5, NLA MP 377.

65 "The real image of the American Peace Corps: A Peace Corps agronomist turns out to be an officer," *Harian Rakyat*, October 18, 1962.

66 "'Korps Perdamaian' dan SEATO," *Harian Rakjat*, September 10, 1962, p. 1.

67 "Peace Corps dan SEATO," *Harian Rakjat*, September 12, 1962.

68 "Pengakuan Sargent Shriver: 'Korps Perdamaian' gampang dirubah menjadi 'Korps Perang'," *Harian Rakjat*, October 17, 1962.

69 "Oppose the American Peace Corps – E. Java Peace Movement," *Harian Rakjat*, September 28, 1962, cited in Djakarta Press Summary, 1961–5, NLA MP 377.

In representing the Peace Corps as a cover for imperialism, *Harian Rakjat* echoed the vocabulary and analogies of earlier critics in Ghana and Nigeria. "Whatever name you give to your anti-communist effort, our people clearly recognize the face of United States imperialism," ran one article in September 1962, just as "even when a crow bathes in roses, its feathers still remain black."[70] The following month, it reported that American attempts to enter on the premise of peace were "like a lion making the sound of a bird."[71] This was also the premise of a *Harian Rakjat* cartoon depicting the Peace Corps as a dove covering the military apparatus of SEATO, accompanied by a caption declaring that "A wolf is always a wolf" (Figure 6.1).

In the final months of 1962, the newspaper ran dozens of articles – sometimes several a day – reporting on organizations, trade unions and youth groups opposed to the arrival of American volunteers. African experiences with the Peace Corps featured prominently in *Harian Rakjat*'s reports. It claimed that "many experiences in countries such as Ghana and Nigeria have shown that the American Peace Corps is subversive and insulting to the people of those countries."[72] In September 1962, the newspaper reported that the communist youth organization Pemuda Rakjat had declared that "based on past experience in many countries like Ghana and Nigeria, the Peace Corps are a tool for neo-colonialism."[73] A further report declared that "the American Peace Corps had been active in creating disturbances in Africa during the last few years" and that "protests were raised and demonstrations were staged against the Peace Corps in many African countries because the activities and the organization itself was proved to be subversive."[74] Reports urged Sukarno to oppose the Peace Corps because it represented "a form of neocolonialism which has already met resistance from the peoples of Africa."[75]

In addition to African experiences, *Harian Rakjat* drew links with reports from other parts of Asia. In December 1962, after two months of intense opposition, it noted that the "American Peace Corps was only a disguise for American subversive activities and warlike adventures which would sow the seed of discord among the Indonesian people, similar to what happened in South Korea, South Vietnam, and in other Asian countries."[76] It cited Indian

70 "Apa itu 'Korps Perdamaian'?" *Harian Rakjat*, September 10, 1962, p. 1.

71 "Pengakuan Sargent Shriver: 'Korps Perdamaian' gampang dirubah menjadi 'Korps Perang'," *Harian Rakjat*, October 17, 1962.

72 "SBIM Surabaya: Tolak 'Korps Perdamaian' AS" and "PP SBLG tolak 'Korps Perdamaian'," *Harian Rakjat*, October 12, 1962.

73 "Pemuda Rakjat: Tolak 'Korps Perdamaian'," *Harian Rakjat*, September 12, 1962, p. 1.

74 "Oppose Peace Corps' interference in Indonesia," *Harian Rakjat*, September 15, 1962, cited in Djakarta Press Summary, 1961–5, NLA MP 377.

75 "Tolak 'Korps Perdamaian'," *Harian Rakjat*, September 21, 1962.

76 *Harian Rakyat*, December 18 [1962], cited in Djakarta Press Summary, 1961–5, NLA MP 377.

Figure 6.1 "Srigala tetap Srigala [A wolf is always a wolf]," *Harian Rakjat*, September 19, 1962. [*Korps Perdamaian Amerika Serikat* = United States Peace Corps.]

experiences, noting that the *Delhi Times* had reported that "sweet talks on the philanthropic and humanitarian mission of the American Peace Corps were nothing else but a big deceit from the beginning until the end."[77] It also noted that Ceylonese students had declared the Peace Corps to be "Kennedy's Spy Corps," claiming that volunteers "were chosen and specially trained as political agents, tasked with forming an imperialist fifth column . . . and undermining our independence, slandering our neutral and free politics, and finally

[77] "Espionage Lurked Behind Sargent Shriver's Sweet Talks," *Harian Rakjat*, October 10, 1962, cited in US Embassy, Jakarta, Djakarta Press Summary, 1961–5, NLA MP 377.

Figure 6.2 "Colonialism departs through the door; neocolonialism enters through the window," *Harian Rakjat*, September 21, 1962.

dragging us into SEATO."[78] The article appeared alongside a cartoon depicting neocolonialism as a masked bandit sneaking in to burgle Indonesia even as formal colonialism ended (Figure 6.2).

Although the most vociferous coverage appeared in the communist press, the official government news agency, *Antara*, also carried reports criticizing the Peace Corps. It reported that the left-leaning Murba Party had released a statement opposing the Peace Corps because, "as reported by the foreign press, instead of performing peaceful works members of the Peace Corps were engaged in hostile activities in the countries where they were assigned." The report continued, "They have brought into these countries 'cold war', got themselves involved in subversive activities, increased racism and many more unjustified actions which finally forced the countries concerned to oppose the Corps' operation."[79] *Antara* also reported that the Indonesian Student Association (*Concentrasi Gerakan Mahasiswa Indonesia*) had written a letter to President Sukarno and Foreign Minister Subandrio opposing the Peace Corps, noting that "the main reason of its rejection was that the American Peace Corps had been proved to have operated as an instrument of American imperialism in the implementation of the American foreign policy" and concluding that "the Corps was indeed another means of the imperialist to penetrate into the new developing countries."[80]

78 "'Korps Perdamaian', korps mata²," *Harian Rakjat*, September 21, 1962.

79 "Murba Party Statement on the American Peace Corps," *Antara News Service*, September 25, 1962.

80 "CGMI Student Association Opposes the American Peace Corps," *Antara News Service*, October 7, 1962.

Media interest grew as Indonesia's Minister of Higher Education, Thoyib Hadiwidjaja, announced that 100 Peace Corps volunteers would arrive to work as lecturers in the nation's universities in May 1963. Opposition activists redoubled their efforts. In April 1963, *Harian Rakjat* published a lengthy article by Ruddy Mangala, leader of the Indonesian Students' Association, which situated the Peace Corps at the heart of US strategy for world domination. Mangala claimed that, after military failures in South Vietnam and Cuba, America was pursuing a "new strategy" and masking "neo-colonialist infiltration under the guise of 'economic assistance', the Alliance for Mutual Progress, Peace Corps and all sorts of other things that sound sweet and sympathetic." But the peoples of Nigeria, Kenya and Somalia, among others, had seen through the deceit and exposed the "racism, neo-colonialism and anti-Communism" that lay at the heart of the Peace Corps.[81] A *Harian Rakjat* editorial further pointed to anti-Peace Corps demonstrations in the Indonesian towns of Bandung, Semarang and Padang as evidence of widespread popular opposition to the Peace Corps.[82]

Indonesia's left-wing and communist press was not state sponsored in the same way as the *Ghanaian Times*. However, the parties and political alliances that underpinned it were not without influence. Reports pressing for the removal of Peace Corps volunteers were phrased in Sukarno's own language; the incompatibility of volunteers with Indonesia's anticolonial nationalism was overtly tied to Sukarno's key policies of Nasakom (nationalism, religion, communism) and Manipol (a portmanteau term denoting support for Indonesia's constitution, Indonesian socialism, guided democracy, guided economy and Indonesian identity). Opposition was also tied to Sukarno's previous decisions to ban American organizations including the Asia Foundation and Rotary Clubs.[83] Facing sustained domestic opposition, Sukarno decided to walk back his invitation to the Peace Corps. The initial request for 100 volunteers was reduced to just seventeen, who would no longer be placed in universities but rather would work as athletics coaches. Moreover, Sukarno tasked volunteers with training Indonesian athletes for the upcoming GANEFO (Games of the New Emerging Forces), a deeply politicized sporting contest staged in opposition to what Sukarno called "the Old Established Forces" led by the United States.[84] The modified invitation was, in essence, a slight to the United States. Sukarno refused to accept any more Peace Corps

81 Ruddy Mangala, "Peace Corps harus dilawan karena masalah prinsip," *Harian Rakjat*, April 20, 1963.

82 "Editorial: Melawan Peace Corps," *Harian Rakjat*, April 26, 1963.

83 "Editorial: Melawan Peace Corps," *Harian Rakjat*, April 26, 1963.

84 Chris A. Connelly, "The Politics of the Games of the New Emerging Forces (GANEFO)," *The International Journal of the History of Sport* 29, no. 9 (2012): 1311–24; Rusli Lutan and Fan Hong, "The Politicization of Sport: GANEFO – a Case Study," *Sport in Society: Cultures, Commerce, Media, Politics* 8, no. 3 (2005): 425–39.

volunteers after the first seventeen departed in 1965, a decision upheld by Suharto even after the bloody decimation of the nation's Communist Party and left-wing press later the same year. Even though Suharto's regime was far more accepting of American development assistance, the Peace Corps did not return to Indonesia until 2010.[85]

Next Door

Even as Indonesia's left-wing press pursued a vigorous campaign of opposition to the Peace Corps, newspapers in neighboring Malaysia took a more measured approach towards Western volunteers.[86] Many postcolonial nations were enthusiastic about development and modernization and some offset a desire for absolute sovereignty with the need for capital and expertise from industrialized nations. Third World nations balanced development assistance from the Eastern and Western blocs, but other postcolonial states were integrated into a single alliance system. Malaysia was an anticommunist bulwark in Southeast Asia whose leaders resolutely followed a path towards economic development. The First Malayan Five Year Plan, adopted the year before independence, shifted the nation's focus from military to economic goals. It prioritized education, manufacturing and rural development, supported by British, Australian and American expertise and investment. These overarching development goals were broadly retained in subsequent decades, but the withdrawal of British economic and military support East of Suez from 1968 led Malaysia to look towards further American funding.[87]

Malaysia signed up to receive Peace Corps volunteers just days before the postcard incident in Nigeria in October 1961. Critics had already pointed to the potential for the Peace Corps to do "more harm than good": Ungku Aziz, head of the Department of Economics at the University of Malaya, announced on a locally recorded BBC radio program that the Peace Corps could "really cause more trouble than good", primarily because of the "psychological impact on the country they go to."[88] But, on the whole, coverage of the Peace Corps was positive. Although the wide-circulation, English-language daily *Straits Times* reported on the postcard incident, and even published a large

85 For Suharto-era developmentalism, see Simpson, *Economists with Guns*.

86 The period's dynamic political situation meant that some newspapers intended for Malaysian audiences were located in Singapore, either temporarily or as a legacy of the colonial-era Straits Settlements that straddled what became Malaysia and Singapore. The dominant English language newspaper, the *Straits Times*, had bureaus in Singapore, Penang and Kuala Lumpur.

87 Rajah Rasiah, *Foreign Capital and Industrialization in Malaysia* (Basingstoke, UK: Palgrave Macmillan, 1995).

88 "American 'Peace Corps' Can Do More Harm Than Good – Ungku Aziz," *Singapore Free Press*, June 24, 1961, p. 2.

photograph of Margery Michelmore in its pages, it failed to draw a direct link between volunteers in Nigeria and those headed for Malaya. Instead, the bulk of reports were directly syndicated from London newspapers and conveyed Western appraisals of the postcard incident rather than Nigerian responses. In November 1961, for example, a report written by Englishman David Holden represented Michelmore as "the American girl ... who innocently wrote a postcard" and became a victim of "exaggerated" and "youthful militancy" that had no clear political agenda.[89] Unlike reports in Ghana and Indonesia, the misdeeds of volunteers in other nations were not presented as significant to the Peace Corps in Malaysia.

Coverage remained positive as the first Peace Corps group arrived in mid-1962. The *Straits Times* reported that the Peace Corps was a promising experiment in "grassroots diplomacy."[90] Coverage focused on volunteers' good intentions and willingness to learn Malay language and customs; in this it more closely reflected the tone of reports in the United States than those in the Third World.[91] The *Straits Times* asked "what moved them to give up their comfortable city life to travel more than 12,000 miles and work in the jungles and kampongs?"[92]

Rather than mere fawning, however, such coverage was closely linked to Malaysia's demand for skilled expertise. In early 1962, Malaysian bureaucrats were working hard to recruit more foreign experts.[93] The Second Five Year Plan had recently emphasized the need for more middle-level technical workers to progress the nation's development.[94] Media reports made it clear that, while volunteers' skills were desired, their broader "way of life" was not. The *Straits Times* warned the newly arrived volunteers that "the Corps' frankly evangelical name is the first bait to the sceptic," and "it cannot hurt to remind them, without any wish to be churlish, that they are not here to advertise their way of life, which is different from ours, or to offer a lead, which neither Asia nor the rest of the world want, or to exhibit an abstract 'commitment to freedom'; they are here to work, and if they are wise, to learn."[95] Although the Malaysian press eagerly welcomed volunteers in the early 1960s, it

89 David Holden, "The Race for the Leadership of All Africa," *Straits Times*, November 24, 1961, p. 10.

90 "Shriver to look at 'Grassroots Diplomacy' at work in Malaya," *Straits Times*, August 14, 1962, p. 9.

91 See, for example, "P-Corps group go to 'school'," *Straits Times*, January 16, 1961, p. 13; "Three-hour Malay Lessons a Day for the Peace Corps," *Straits Times*, January 29, 1962, p. 5; "U.S. Peace Corps No. 2 arrives and all 31 speak Malay," *Straits Times*, June 2, 1962, p. 24.

92 "IN – Kennedy's Peace Corps: The 26 Volunteers who want to help Malaya – For Free," *Straits Times*, January 13, 1962, p. 9. Note *kampong* is the Malay word for village.

93 "Committee to plan new search for expert staff," *Straits Times*, March 22, 1962, p. 10; "More pay to woo experts from abroad," *Straits Times*, May 13, 1962, p. 7.

94 "Big 'Peace Corps' project for Malaya," *Singapore Free Press*, October 9, 1961, p. 2.

95 "Editorial: Peace Corps," *Straits Times*, January 15, 1961, p. 10.

perceived their contribution through a minimalist conception of development that differed from the Peace Corps' cultural mission.

The media interest extended to British VSO volunteers, who came to be known as the "British Peace Corps," even though articles noted that the organization preceded the American program by several years.[96] Although they attracted less attention, British volunteers generally enjoyed even more favorable coverage than the Peace Corps. The *Malay Mail* in November 1961 reported that VSOs had come "to do their bit for the improvement of Commonwealth relations in Malaya."[97] Profiling two VSOs working in Ipoh on the north-west coast, the *Straits Times* headline asked, "Why can't our children be like these?"[98] The "Woman's World" pages extended the discussion, staging a vox pop with three Malay women to draw out their opinions on whether Malaysia, or Asia more broadly, should launch a Peace Corps program of their own.[99]

It is significant that the most positive coverage appeared in English-language papers at a time when Malay was the primary language of nationalist discourse.[100] Coverage in the vernacular Malay media was more limited. *Berita Harian*, a major Malay-language newspaper, neglected to report the arrival of the first Peace Corps contingent and Margery Michelmore's postcard was not mentioned at all. But interest slowly picked up as subsequent groups arrived from 1962, with the novelty of Western volunteers who were eager to learn the Malay language and eat Malay food a particular point of interest.[101] Such reports served to differentiate Peace Corps volunteers from former colonizers, many of whom had resisted adopting the local language and foods, and from British and Australian military communities then posted in Malaysia who likewise maintained a strict division between Western and "native" language and society until at least the 1970s.[102] The relatively warm media response reflected Malaysia's ongoing political and military ties with Britain, Australia and the United States during the 1960s, and a generally more

96 "British 'Peace Corps' teachers in Perak," *Straits Times*, January 20, 1962, p. 8.

97 "Member of Peace Corps? Not me, says Heather: Voluntary Service Overseas started by UK before US thought of it," *Malay Mail*, November 23, 1961.

98 "Why can't our children be like these?" *Straits Times*, February 18, 1962, p. 3.

99 "Malayan Peace Corps and your children," *Straits Times*, March 18, 1962, p. 14.

100 See Antonio L. Rappa and Lionel Wee, *Language Policy and Modernity in Southeast Asia: Malaysia, the Philippines, Singapore, and Thailand* (New York: Springer, 2006); Azirah Hashim, "Not Plain Sailing: Malaysia's Language Choice in Policy and Education," *AILA Review* 22, no. 1 (2009): 36–51.

101 "31 lagi rombogan derma bakti dari AS tiba," *Berita Harian*, June 2, 1962, p. 1; "Anggota2 Bakti berbahasa Melayu," *Berita Harian*, June 10, 1963, p. 5.

102 Christina Twomey et al. , "Australia's Asian Garrisons: Decolonisation and the Colonial Dynamics of Expatriate Military Communities in Cold War Asia," *Australian Historical Studies* 51, no. 2 (2020): 184–211; Mathew Radcliffe, *Kampong Australia: The RAAF at Butterworth* (Sydney: NewSouth, 2017).

tolerant attitude to Westernization in Malaysia than in some Third World nations.[103]

Yet, even in relatively pro-Western Malaysia, media coverage was sporadic and patchy. This highlights the broader point that development volunteering did not make a major impact on public opinion in the Global South in the same way that it did in the Global North. In early 1961, as major US dailies were running multiple stories about the Peace Corps every day, months could go by without a single mention of the program in Malaysia or in any of the nations that are the subject of this chapter. Other volunteering programs, including Britain's VSO and the Australian Volunteer Graduate Scheme, went unreported for years at a time. Development volunteering programs had assumed that volunteers would arouse intense interest in receiving nations; Sargent Shriver operated on the assumption of "the high visibility of PCVs in a host country."[104] But Western volunteers were typically featured in local media only when they impacted on local concerns or when they did something wrong. In the dynamic political and social contexts of Africa and Asia in the 1950s and 1960s, media attention was often focused on domestic political and economic issues and on substantial shifts in foreign relations, not least amongst them the recurrent confrontations between both Ghana and Nigeria, and Indonesia and Malaysia. Overlaid with the additional global factors of the Cold War, decolonization and development, it is hardly surprising that the press of all four nations rarely commented on the activities of foreign volunteers within their borders or around the world. To a certain extent, this is an obvious point, but too often the assumption is that nations in the Global South were passive recipients of Western – and particularly American – information campaigns.[105] With development volunteering, as with other issues, local perspectives and interests set the media agenda.

Conclusion

The previous chapter revealed that domestic media coverage of the Peace Corps had a sizeable impact on public opinion in the United States. Newspapers in the Global South paid less attention and, when they did, they were usually less flattering to volunteers. Although the earliest coverage of Australian volunteers in Indonesia was positive, by the early 1960s media

[103] Barbara Watson Andaya and Leonard Andaya, *A History of Malaysia* (Honolulu: University of Hawai'i Press, 2001).

[104] "Social Behavior of Volunteers," Peace Corps Training Center, Washington, January 1967. JFKL: RG 490, Box 25.

[105] For a full discussion of US media projection and receptions, see Kunkel, *Empire of Pictures*; Nicholas J. Cull, *The Cold War and the United States Information Agency: American Propaganda and Public Diplomacy, 1945–1989* (Cambridge: Cambridge University Press, 2008).

reports about Western volunteers in Ghana, Nigeria and Indonesia tended towards criticism. Negative stories about development volunteers (and the Peace Corps in particular) were picked up with an undeniable enthusiasm; bad news about the Peace Corps circulated within and between nations across the Global South. Margery Michelmore's dropped postcard became a major international incident largely because of the media attention it received, which continued despite attempts to dampen the flames by governments and ministers. This coverage reveals a significant disconnect between the formal invitations extended to volunteers and public opinion in host nations: it suggests that formal acceptance of Peace Corps volunteers should not be mistaken for enthusiastic reception by local communities.

Suspicion about the true motives and long-term impacts of Western volunteers helped coalesce new networks of Afro-Asian and Third World anticolonial internationalism and strengthen existing ones. Negative reports about the Peace Corps circulated between nations and regions, with similar themes and analogies reappearing in Ghana, Nigeria, Indonesia and beyond. As Chapter 9 of this book explores in more detail, opposition was not limited to the press. From the mid-1960s, anti-volunteer protests erupted in cities across the Global South and volunteers were expelled from key nations including India and Tanzania, among many others. Western observers tended to regard opposition movements as unpredictable, irrational and Communist-inspired, but their origins can be traced to the ambivalent response of Ghanaian, Nigerian and Indonesian media to the arrival of the Peace Corps in the early 1960s. Resistance to Western volunteers was typically articulated at the local level, but it was built upon a concern with anticolonialism, nationalism and nonalignment that was shared across many parts of the Global South – although, as Malaysia's example reminds us, in some places the desire for economic development outweighed demands for freedom from foreign interference.

Even so, there is little evidence that Western development volunteering organizations were paying attention. The United States Information Agency (USIA) compiled a report on Overseas Press Reaction to the Peace Corps in April 1961, only a month after the Peace Corps' launch. The Agency reported that "world press reaction to the Peace Corps" had been "predominantly favorable, except for the Communist press and radio." Negative coverage, it claimed, was based on doubts that young Americans could cope with the hardships of living in "strange lands."[106] The report condensed coverage from across continents, regions and blocs into five short pages, often selecting a single source to depict the attitudes of an entire nation or even continent. More tendentious, however, was the report's timing: after the Peace Corps had

106 United States Information Agency Office of Research and Analysis, "Peace Corps: Overseas press reaction," April 20, 1961, JFKL: Papers of Sargent Shriver, Box 34.

been launched, but before a single receiving nation had been identified. As this chapter has shown, receiving nations' media typically began to pay attention only when it became clear that Peace Corps volunteers would be arriving in their own countries and many of these reports were not at all positive. But, by that time, Peace Corps Washington had stopped paying attention. As the previous chapter showed, the public information section of the Peace Corps was tightly focused on domestic public opinion. This attitude extended to the leadership. Shriver's meticulously organized personal papers include multiple folders of press clippings about the Peace Corps. His collection of articles from the US press was voluminous and extended from early 1961 until his resignation in 1965. The file of overseas press clippings, however, only holds the USIA report of April 1961. This is illustrative of broader patterns. In the main, Peace Corps Washington ignored critical reports circulating in the press of receiving nations; if they couldn't be ignored, as in the case of the postcard incident, they were blamed on Communist subversion or on small pockets of radicalized youth running amok. Shriver and the Peace Corps preferred to not look too closely at the complexities of public opinion in receiving nations, but to regard official invitations from governments as evidence that volunteers were desired and in demand. This situation was mirrored in the London headquarters of VSO, a far smaller outfit with fewer resources to investigate how the mass media in receiving nations responded to British volunteers and also in Australia. The humanitarian-development complex was essentially self-perpetuating and fed off its own publicity rather than considering viewpoints from the Global South, even if, as the following chapters show, things could look very different on the ground.

PART III

Experiences

7

A Little Colony

Twenty-two-year-old Susan Richards, from Kettering in England's east Midlands, applied to VSO in the winter of 1964. Newly qualified as a registered nurse, Richards had read about development volunteering in the *Observer*; it seemed an ideal way to nurture her interest in "the underdeveloped countries" while also working towards a career in international health.[1] Richards arrived in Blantyre, Malawi, on September 6, 1964, two months after the nation declared independence from Britain. The British Council, acting as VSO's "overseas arm," had arranged for Richards to be posted to the government hospital, which was "desperate for nurses." It seemed an ideal arrangement that would promote "goodwill between the people of Britain and the people of Malawi."[2]

Things were rather different on the ground. Instead of nursing African patients in desperate need, Susan Richards was put on a ward for fee-paying European patients, which "even by my standards was overstaffed," with five nurses and five servants for twelve patients. "This really made me see red," she wrote, as "just down the passage there were five wards, each containing approximately 100 [African] patients, with one sister between the five wards." She applied for a transfer, explaining that "I had come out to help the people and the country, and not to nurse some English woman who had decided to have her varicosed veins out in Blantyre," but the British expatriate matron in charge of her ward refused. Things were not much better outside of work. "One of the more disappointing things," she wrote, "is the modern convenient surrounding in which we are placed. I came out imagining that things would be rough and I would have to put up with little money and making the best of it." But instead, "we have a luxurious house and . . . a very good salary, which makes me feel slightly guilty." All in all, Richards felt, the ease and luxury of her VSO year "was a blow to my spirit which was all set for some gastly [*sic*] challenge."[3]

[1] VSO application form, Susan Mary Richards, February 17, 1964, VSO Archive, Microfiche files.

[2] T. S. Tull to B. C. Roberts, June 10, 1970, "VSO Programme in Malawi," TNA: FCO 45/767; Susan Richards to Miss Jones, October 14, 1964, VSO Archive, Microfiche files.

[3] Susan Richards to Miss Jones, October 14, 1964, VSO Archive, Microfiche files.

This chapter is the first of three examining the volunteer experience at ground level. Moving beyond the plans and intentions covered in the book's first Part, and the images and discourses of the second, this third and final Part explores the lived conditions and personal encounters that attended, and indeed defined, development volunteering. Although planned in Western capitals, humanitarianism and international development were executed in countless interactions between groups and individuals in cities, towns and villages across the Global South. Acknowledging this fact requires historians to expand their focus, to pay attention not just to rhetoric and intentions but also to experiences that took place at ground level. For development volunteering that means paying attention to the everyday details: what jobs volunteers performed; where they lived and with whom; how much money they had and how they spent it; and how – and with whom – they socialized.

Tracking what volunteers did on the ground allows us to go beyond the rhetoric of development volunteering organizations. It also allows us to see how individual encounters were shaped by global historical patterns and particularly how volunteers were impacted by already existing expatriate cultures. Scholars have identified a significant overlap in personnel and expertise, and continuities in expatriate spatiality and material culture, between colonialism and postcolonial development in Africa, Asia and Latin America.[4] The social worlds of expatriates at decolonization have attracted less attention. Ann Laura Stoler and others have shown that colonial categories were structured by race and marked by social as much as official boundaries.[5] How did the racially exclusive social circles of colonialism translate into the postcolonial moment? How did volunteers encounter these social circles? And to what extent did volunteer agencies engineer the encounter through decisions about where to place volunteers, amongst which communities and at what standard of living?

To answer these questions, this chapter focuses largely on Britain's VSO in the mid-1960s. It is based on a close examination of records maintained by VSO, the British Council and government departments, as well as volunteers' personal and professional correspondence. Voluntary Service Overseas

[4] Uma Kothari, "Spatial Practices and Imaginaries: Experiences of Colonial Officers and Development Professionals," *Singapore Journal of Tropical Geography* 27 (2006): 235–53; Hodge, *Triumph of the Expert*; Ruth Craggs and Hannah Neate, "Post-Colonial Careering and Urban Policy Mobility: Between Britain and Nigeria, 1945–1990," *Transactions of the Institute of British Geographers* 42, no. 1 (2017): 44–57; Eva-Maria Muschik, "The Art of Chameleon Politics: From Colonial Servant to International Development Expert," *Humanity* 9, no. 2 (2018): 219–44.

[5] Ann Laura Stoler, "Rethinking Colonial Categories: European Communities and the Boundaries of Rule," *Comparative Studies in Society and History* 31, no. 1 (1989, January): 134–61; Ann Laura Stoler, *Carnal Knowledge and Imperial Power: Race and the Intimate in Colonial Rule* (Berkeley, CA: University of California Press, 2002).

required volunteers to write to headquarters at least twice a year, encouraging them to vividly describe their living conditions, work and personal relationships in informal language. Sometime in the late 1970s, all the letters from previous decades were scanned onto microfiche and thrown haphazardly into several large boxes. Uncatalogued and largely forgotten, these letters contain a wealth of granular information about volunteers' conditions and experiences. They reveal that, in the mid-1960s, the lived experience of many volunteers was strikingly different from what they had expected. Although they had departed with good intentions, many volunteers quickly fell in with colonial mores and expatriate norms that effectively distanced them from the local communities they had wanted to help.

Although focused on British volunteers, this chapter speaks to the experience of Western volunteers more broadly. By the mid-1960s, the numbers of Western expatriates in many parts of the Global South had surged. Volunteers from Britain, North America, Australia and Europe worked alongside each other, socialized together and often lived together. There were exceptions, of course, but many volunteers from the US Peace Corps and other Western programs lived in much the same style. Forming tightly-knit communities, Western volunteers effectively bridged the imperial and postcolonial periods across much of the Global South.

The "Old Boy Net"

From its origins in 1958, VSO cultivated an image of young people working hard in remote regions, in basic conditions and at considerable personal sacrifice. As one contemporary report had it, "They lost no time, it was said, in identifying themselves with the people they worked for" and "lived in remote areas where they were the only white people."[6] Despite the popular image of roughing it in primitive conditions, in the mid-1960s the majority of VSO volunteers were posted to established, expatriate-run institutions, many of which had a long colonial history. Well into the 1970s, VSO directed a significant majority of volunteers to British dependencies and former colonies. On the ground, their jobs and lifestyles often provided a point of translation of colonial culture into the postcolonial period.

There are several reasons why VSO sent volunteers to expatriate-run institutions, but administrative convenience was prime among them. During VSO's early years, postings were found through an informal network of colonial bureaucrats colloquially known as the "old boy net."[7] At the center of the old boy net was VSO founder Alec Dickson, who had begun his career in

[6] "Apprenticed to a Nation," undated clipping from *Commonwealth Today*, c.1961, TNA: DO 163/22.

[7] T. J. O'Brien to D. C. Mandeville, November 19, 1960, TNA: DO 163/22.

colonial service before transitioning into international development during the 1950s. Early volunteers were posted to institutions and countries with which Dickson had personal ties: the first contingent went to Sarawak, where Dickson's brother was Director of Education with the British colonial administration. The next groups went to Ghana, Nigeria and the Cameroons, all locations where Dickson had worked during the 1940s and 1950s. The Royal Commonwealth Society facilitated access to former colonial bureaucrats and dignitaries among its members, significantly expanding the old boy net. Postings were also influenced by religious and missionary societies. As we have seen, in the mid-1960s Christian Aid funded almost a third of VSO's cadet program (aimed at recent school-leavers).[8] Cadet volunteers funded by Christian Aid were mostly sent to religious schools and missions that had been established by European missionaries and often continued to be administered by expatriates.

The professionalization of VSO after Dickson's departure in 1962 saw the organization expand beyond the old boy net, but administrative arrangements continued to privilege expatriate-run organizations. The British Council was appointed as VSO's "overseas arm," with responsibility for finding suitable postings, after Dickson's departure. Established to advance English language and culture abroad, the British Council skewed VSO placements towards teaching and particularly the teaching of English in elite schools and colleges. Of the forty-two volunteers posted to India in 1963–4, for example, thirty-seven worked in elite private schools.[9] By the mid-1970s, nearly 70 percent of all VSO volunteers were posted as teachers and almost half of these were English teachers; a significant contribution to the linguistic imperialism of the English language in the postcolonial era.[10]

Finances were a further factor determining why so many VSO volunteers were posted to elite schools and institutions. Although VSO funded volunteers' travel, clothing and some other essentials, volunteers' monthly stipends were paid by the host institution until the late 1960s. Poorer schools, or community-run grassroots organizations, simply couldn't afford volunteers. This was particularly notable in India, where by 1964, VSO worried that "it would

8 Minutes of Second Annual General Meeting of VSO, November 21, 1963, VSO Archive, Box 31.

9 "Voluntary Service Overseas: 1963/64 Volunteers," VSO Archive, Box 698.

10 Of 1,078 volunteers, 673 worked in teaching posts in 1974–5, with 301 working as English language teachers. See "VSO – Educational Recruitment," VSO Archive, Box 699. On linguistic imperialism see Robert Phillipson, *Linguistic Imperialism* (Oxford: Oxford University Press, 1992); Diana Lemberg, "The Universal Language of the Future: Decolonization, Development, and the American Embrace of Global English, 1945–1965," *Modern Intellectual History* 15, no. 2 (2018): 561–92; see also, Ngugi wa Thiong'o, *Decolonising the Mind: The Politics of Language in African Literature* (London: J. Currey, 1986).

appear that demand is levelling off now owing to the inability of educational institutions to meet local volunteer costs."[11] A report from the British Council in Madras stressed "the extreme difficulty experienced by schools and other organisations in this area in raising enough money to pay for the upkeep of volunteers." As the British Council explained, local rates of pay were so low that "what we think of as voluntary aid often appears to the recipient as an expensive commitment – and is sometimes beyond his capacity to pay." Voluntary Service Overseas assessed that schools representing "the most fruitful field for volunteers ... can least afford volunteers and many of them have not asked to have them for reasons of finance."[12] Although particularly acute in India, the situation was replicated across the Global South. Douglas Whiting, VSO's newly installed Director, visited Nigeria and Ghana in 1964. He reported that "We have not perhaps realised in London that the rent of a staff bungalow in Lagos may be £500 p.a.," which was a considerable sum and so, as a result, "Nearly all cadet teachers are working in 'aided' or 'private' Christian schools."[13]

A final factor lay in VSO's preference that volunteers work under expatriate supervisors. Part of this was related to perceptions of volunteers' effectiveness, with the idea that "the best results seem to be obtained when a volunteer is working under the direction of and in close contact with an expert."[14] But it also related to the civilizing mission inherent to development volunteering, as explored in earlier chapters. Following his 1964 visit to Nigeria, Douglas Whiting wrote of an ideal posting he had come across at the Medical School in Lagos, where "The admirable expatriate Matron needs a mature volunteer to act as Junior Warden of the hostel for nurses. The latter are technically well trained, but she needs someone to teach them how to live – to teach English, to supervise general behaviour, to encourage them in games, cultural activities and in home-crafts such as dress-making and cooking."[15] Development volunteering articulated a maximalist vision of development, which was cultural and psychological as well as economic and technical. The notion that volunteers would "teach them how to live" remained current for VSO throughout the 1960s. Despite claims that they would live according to local standards, many volunteers were in fact set up to model a Western way of life.

[11] "VSO – A note on planning for development, 1964," VSO Archive, Box 31.

[12] "Paper on payment of volunteers' costs in India for Executive Committee," January 5, 1965, VSO Archive, Box 31.

[13] "Confidential: Director's Visit to Nigeria and Ghana, October 1964," VSO Archive, Box 31.

[14] "Report on the work of the cadet division of Voluntary Service Overseas," September 1964, VSO Archive, Box 31.

[15] "Confidential: Director's Visit to Nigeria and Ghana, October 1964," VSO Archive, Box 31.

Setting Standards

In its promotional material, VSO emphasized the primitive and challenging conditions endured by volunteers. As we saw in Chapter 5, hardships endured by volunteers were also highlighted by the British and American media. But in reality, VSO was careful to ensure that volunteers did not suffer any privations. During the early years, Alec Dickson left volunteers' "pocket money" to the discretion of the institutions that hosted them. Many organizations considered a basic lifestyle to include expatriate-style housing, food and entertainment. Well-meaning hosts also routinely paid more than agreed. Volunteers employed by the colonial administration in Kenya, for instance, were supposed to receive twenty shillings a week – but in fact routinely received fifty shillings and an additional clothing allowance. As one of the Governors' officials reported, this was "worthwhile as it has given the three of them the feeling that they are able to return hospitality on occasion when it has been given to them" by local expatriates.[16] Some host organizations were even more generous: in 1960, volunteers working in Rhodesia received rent-free accommodation plus a monthly allowance of £35, equivalent to some £2,200 per month in 2020 terms.[17] This was enough to make local politicians "uneasy about the principles of the scheme" as "equal facilities" were not available to local youth.[18]

Although VSO rhetoric claimed that volunteers lived at a similar level as local counterparts, in fact salaries were pegged to those of other expatriates. In 1964, VSO Director George Whiting noted that, in India, "difficulties had arisen already because in some cases our volunteers were being paid more than indigenous workers with equivalent or higher qualifications." But one of his staff, just returned from an inspection tour of India, "felt that it would not be possible for the European, unaccustomed to the climatic conditions or the diet of India, to remain fit and do an adequate job on a comparable salary." Far from addressing the ramifications of volunteers receiving higher salaries than locals, this meeting ended with VSO proposing an even higher subsidy for volunteers.[19] The issue was raised again the following year; this time, Whiting quickly put the matter to rest by insisting "that the 'salary' – i.e. money in lieu of board and lodging – paid to a GVSO was nothing like as much as that paid to an expatriate," and moreover, "Volunteers are encouraged to donate any surplus funds to the project as, for example, books for a library."[20] The VSO

[16] Patrick Denison to Charles Carstairs, August 24, 1960, TNA: CO 859/1445.

[17] Thirty-five pounds in 1960 terms had a relative income value of £2,206 in May 2020: www.measuringworth.com, accessed May 2, 2020. Value is in UK pounds.

[18] Sir Evelyn Hone to Charles Carstairs, October 8, 1960, TNA: CO 859/1445.

[19] Minutes of meeting held September 28, 1964, Returned Volunteer Advisory Committee, VSO Archive, Box 31.

[20] Minutes of meeting held February 1, 1965, Returned Volunteer Advisory Committee, VSO Archive, Box 31.

administration, Executive Committee and Council were overwhelmingly staffed by people with colonial experience, including former colonial bureaucrats; so was the British Council, which was responsible for monitoring volunteers on the ground as VSO's "overseas arm." For many of them, a "local" standard of living was inconceivable; the ideal situation was one in which volunteers received a salary slightly lower than that of other expatriates.

As VSO professionalized during the 1960s, payments made by host institutions were supplemented, and later replaced, by a complex schedule of grants and allowances paid from London. Stipends and other payments trended upwards throughout the decade. Where, in the early 1960s, VSO's rhetoric emphasized the spirit of sacrifice required of a volunteer, by the end of the decade VSO and the British government agreed that "one of the main objects ... is that volunteers should not be out of pocket."[21] This principle was extended to insurance and pensions back in Britain. From the mid-1960s, considerations about remuneration were "guided by the principle that ... a volunteer (as compared with a non-volunteer contemporary) is not worse off, or better off, in respect of ultimate pension rights and general social security entitlements."[22] Volunteers like Susan Richards, who had expected to rough it in primitive conditions, were surprised and often disappointed at the comfortable reality of life as a VSO.

On the Ground

Voluntary Service Overseas policies saw a significant proportion of volunteers posted to teach in elite schools or government agencies, often as part of a large expatriate staff and at relatively high levels of pay. Andrew Richardson signed up for VSO in 1964, at the age of twenty. He was posted to Mayo College in Ajmer in northern India: an exclusive, British-style boarding school founded at the height of the Raj and known colloquially as the "Eton of the East."[23] One of Richardson's tasks was to set up the Duke of Edinburgh Award Scheme; the Duke of Edinburgh personally congratulated Richardson and his students during a royal visit in 1965.[24] In Nigeria, Nigel Turner was posted to the Comprehensive High School at Aiyetoro, a "prestige project" funded by the United States and with a large international staff. "When you enter the compound it is just like entering wealthy English suburbia," Turner wrote, which was "a fantastic contrast with what I have seen so far in Africa." Outside the compound gates were "typical scenes of Africa ... whilst inside are two storey detached houses ... well surfaced roads & street lights."[25]

21 Memo, D. E. Roberts to C. N. F Odgers, July 5, 1967, TNA: OD 8/466.
22 Memo, D. E. Roberts to Mr. Odgers, February 16, 1968, TNA: OD 8/466.
23 "Eton of the East," http://mayocollege.com/Eton.html, accessed July 18, 2019.
24 Andrew Richardson to "John," March 23, 1965, VSO Archive, microfiche files.
25 Nigel Turner to Mrs. Thomas, October 4, 1964, VSO Archive, microfiche files.

In 1964–5, the same year that Andrew Richardson and Nigel Turner were posted, VSOs worked in dozens of elite schools including Trinity College in Ceylon, the Breeks Memorial School in India, Murray College in Pakistan, The Queen's School in Nigeria and Bernard Mizeki College in Rhodesia (which, like Mayo College, was modeled on Eton). Other volunteers worked in Anglican mission schools: nearly all VSOs posted to Papua New Guinea, for example, taught at mission schools and postings to religious organizations were also common in Africa. All these institutions had imperial origins and many employed a large expatriate staff well into the postcolonial period. Although the largest number of VSOs worked as teachers, volunteers doing technical, social or medical work (including Susan Richards in Malawi) could also find themselves working in unexpectedly comfortable conditions. As Nigel Turner concluded, "It is not what I expected . . . this mecca of civilisation."[26]

Many volunteers enjoyed a standard of living considerably higher than that of local populations. Having signed up for the adventure of a lifetime, some volunteers, including Roger Sandifer in Nigeria, were surprised to find that "there is nothing to worry about its just like living at home [*sic*]."[27] Letters from volunteers in 1964–5 overwhelmingly reported unexpected levels of comfort. Susan Rowan, working in the British Overseas Territory of St. Helena in the Caribbean, reported that "Living conditions were very good," and indeed "A great deal better than a volunteer is led to expect."[28] Mary Salton, a teacher in Bougainville, Papua New Guinea, admitted that "It is sometimes hard to believe I am a V.S.O. at all – we live in the lap of luxury."[29] Andrew Rice-Oxley, working at a Quaker school in Beirut, wrote about the "shocking luxury of the place . . . As far as my accommodation goes I cannot boast of a mud-hut," he wrote, and in this, he suspected, "I fall well below the V.S.O standard."[30] Miles Roddis, working at a French-style Lycée in Vientiane, Laos, lived "in a luxurious Embassy bungalow" with "full Embassy privileges" and a living allowance that was "more than adequate, and could be considerably pruned."[31] Evelyn Ross, working at a Methodist Girls' school in West Nigeria, wrote that "I still have not got over my amazement that I should be able to spend a year abroad with all expenses paid."[32] Far from experiencing privations, Ross wrote that "My little flat . . . is far better than anything I'll have at home for years."[33]

[26] Ibid.
[27] Roger Sandifer to VSO, June 9, 1965, VSO Archive, microfiche files.
[28] Final Report, Susan Rowan, 1965, VSO Archive, microfiche files.
[29] Mary Salton to Mr. Isherwood, December 7, 1964, VSO Archive, microfiche files.
[30] Andrew Rice-Oxley to Mr. Haig, November 2, 1964, VSO Archive, microfiche files.
[31] Final Report, Miles Roddis, October 18, 1965, VSO Archive, microfiche files.
[32] Evelyn Ross to Mr. Shaw, August 9, 1965, VSO Archive, microfiche files. Emphasis in original.
[33] Evelyn Ross to Mr. Shaw, March 17, 1965, VSO Archive, microfiche files.

For many volunteers, living comfortably meant hiring domestic servants. Although domestic service had been common in Britain in the pre-war years, by the 1960s it was virtually unknown for all but the wealthiest elite. Most volunteers had never dealt with maids or stewards but, as VSOs, many confronted the "servant question" for the first time. Some volunteers were assigned servants through their employer. This was particularly common for volunteers at elite or mission schools. At Mayo College in India, Andrew Richardson had servants to take care of cleaning, laundry and cooking, with food to order.[34] Mary Salton in Papua New Guinea lived and worked on a Christian mission with "girls waiting on us hand and foot – cooking and serving all our meals and doing all our laundry."[35] But many volunteers working outside of elite, expatriate-run institutions also had servants. In La Paz, Bolivia, John Rosser lived with a wealthy family who maintained a number of servants, a reminder that servants were not only hired by expatriates. Rosser had some difficulty finding the right tone with his servants. Ultimately, he decided it was best to stay out of any difficult conversations as "One thing to be remembered if living with a family is the treatment of servants, they are always very temperamental and should be talked to through the mouth of the people you are staying with."[36] Other volunteers decided to hire domestic servants themselves. At Ifaki in Western Nigeria, Evelyn Ross found that "Life is really very pleasant (apart from History and French) especially as I have ... a houseboy doing all the work."[37] Not far away at Abeokuta, Helen Rosenberg shared a bungalow with a Peace Corps volunteer. Together, they hired an Igbo housekeeper, who was "a very good cook so we live like kings."[38]

The shared servant serves as a reminder that, although the bulk of this chapter focuses on VSO, development volunteers from other programs often enjoyed similar conditions and they too hired servants. In 1966, a report on Peace Corps volunteers' living standards found that "some PCVs live in very comfortable houses, even nicer than their U.S. dwellings." A "large percentage" also "hired local domestic help almost as a matter of course."[39] The Peace Corps contingent arriving in Ethiopia in 1965 were issued $25 per month for "domestic help" as part of their monthly stipend.[40] Sargent Shriver was careful to direct volunteers that "We should always call people by their names abroad, never using such phrases as 'boy' for servant or other

[34] Andrew Richardson to VSO, October 4, 1964, VSO Archive, microfiche files.
[35] Mary Salton to Mr. Isherwood, December 7, 1964, VSO Archive, microfiche files.
[36] Final Report, John Rosser, 1965, VSO Archive, microfiche files.
[37] Evelyn Ross to Mr. Shaw, September 26, 1964, VSO Archive, microfiche files.
[38] Helen Rosenberg to Mr. Haig, September 22, 1964, VSO Archive, microfiche files.
[39] "PCV Housing Allowances and Reimbursement," 1966, JFKL: RG 490, Box 23.
[40] Calculated in Ethiopian dollars. "Section V: Financial Arrangements for PCVs," 1965, JFKL: RG 490, Box 23.

helpers."[41] Yet, the fact that Shriver expected Peace Corps volunteers to hire servants is telling and speaks to the assumption that "Europeans" need not do manual labor in the tropics. This assumption was carried over from colonialism and was one that development volunteering was expressly intended to overcome.[42] Hiring a servant in the midst of decolonization was one vector through which colonial norms were translated into the postcolonial world. That volunteers were part of this process of translation points not only to their high standard of living, which for some volunteers was even higher than at home, but also to ongoing assumptions carried over from the colonial period, as dictated by performances of colonial and racial prestige.[43]

Of course, not every volunteer lived in luxury. School-leaver "cadet" VSOs received lower rates of pay than their graduate counterparts and some found conditions less salubrious. Although instances of true hardship are hard to find, a small number of cadet volunteers wrote to VSO to complain. Diana St John in Nigeria was paid £18 a month and "I know it is an awful thing to say, but I sometimes found it a little hard to live on . . . at times the cost of living seemed more than my salary."[44] For many, the problem did not lie in the standard of living itself, but rather in the comparison between payments made to cadet and graduate VSOs. Philip Taylor, a graduate VSO in Nigeria, lived with a cadet who "is paid less than half as much as myself, and is so much more badly off than the rest of us that I think he finds his position intensely embarrassing." Neither suffered privations, but the gulf in payments appeared unjust in principle and, as a result, "The standard rate VSOs are paid, irrespective of the situations in which they find themselves, is considered here to be both a little foolish and a little cruel."[45] Even so, concerns for cadets' standards of living were rarely borne out. Andrew Richardson, a cadet volunteer at Mayo College in India, was paid 200 Rupees per month, roughly equivalent to £15. He considered this "a good wage for a V.S.O.," as "it should enable one to save a bit for the holidays . . . I should be able to put about £7 per month aside." All in all, he concluded, "I haven't anything to grumble at."[46]

Far from penury, most volunteers, whether graduates or cadets, had enough money left over to pay for lengthy and intrepid holidays, taken during term

41 Director's staff meeting, November 29, 1961, JFKL: RG 490, PC Microfilm, Box 1, 11/1/61–12/23/61. See also Cobbs Hoffman, *All You Need Is Love*, p. 63.

42 Claire Lowrie, *Masters and Servants: Cultures of Empire in the Tropics* (Manchester, UK: Manchester University Press, 2016), p. 1. See also Tim Harper, "The British 'Malayans'." In *Settlers and Expatriates: Britons over the Seas*, edited by Robert Bickers, The Oxford History of the British Empire Companion Series (Oxford: Oxford University Press, 2010), p. 253.

43 See Kothari, "Spatial Practices and Imaginaries," especially p. 246.

44 Final Report, Diana St John, September 13, 1965, VSO Archive, microfiche files.

45 Philip Taylor to Mr. Thomas, September 30, 1963, VSO Archive, microfiche files.

46 Andrew Richardson to VSO, October 4, 1964, VSO Archive, microfiche files.

breaks or at the end of their posting. Voluntary Service Overseas paid particular attention to ensure that volunteers had enough money for leisure travel. As a 1962 newsletter advised, "the main purpose of VSO is to help those who are less fortunate than ourselves ... though where seeing the world can be combined with the job and there are no snags involved we are only too pleased for you to see as much as you can."[47] Voluntary Service Overseas diverted significant and rising resources into travel grants, reflecting the value the organization and volunteers placed on travel and adventure. Until the mid-1960s, volunteers could apply to the British Council for an additional £25 to pay for a holiday, if they were unable to save enough money during their posting. The value of holiday grants rose throughout the 1960s. From 1964, graduate volunteers signing up for two-year terms received a £75 grant to fund a mid-term holiday; from 1966, cadet VSOs who elected to stay for two years also became eligible for a mid-term travel grant, albeit at the reduced rate of £50.[48] Both the Volunteer Graduate Scheme and the Peace Corps also offered additional allowances for holiday travel, which were regularly increased into the 1970s. When combined with generous stipends, travel grants were a further way in which volunteers' lifestyles diverged from those of counterparts in developing nations, for many of whom leisure travel remained out of reach.

The VSO holiday grants funded some impressive journeys. Despite subsidizing the salary of his cadet VSO housemate, Philip Taylor reported that "In terms of money I have been very well off" and with an additional £70 holiday grant "I was able to go on a marvellous trip" across twelve countries in Western Africa. He wrote to VSO to say "Thankyou very much for that – it was a remarkable journey."[49] Tony Thorndike, a teacher in Kano in Northern Nigeria, began his posting with a trip across Niger and into Libya through the Sahara. During his mid-term holidays, he took an eight-week, 5,000-mile journey across Africa, during which he drove a steam train, went skin-diving, shark-fishing and canoeing, not to mention "hunting with bow and poisoned arrows with a pagan tribe." When his VSO term was over, Thorndike decided to give up his seat on a chartered flight and instead come home via Cairo and overland through Europe, all on money he'd saved as a VSO.[50] Some money could even be found for extravagant souvenirs. Jill Roach was a cadet VSO in India, but she had enough for mid-term holidays in Kashmir where, among other things, "I went quite mad and bought a fur jacket, marmot, for £13."[51] John Rogers, also a cadet, travelled through Singapore on his way home from

[47] "To All our Volunteers – News Letter no. 3," February 1962, in TNA: OD 10/4.

[48] Minutes of Executive Committee meeting, November 3, 1964, VSO Archive, Box 31; see also TNA: OD 8/466.

[49] Philip Taylor to Mr. Hollis, April 18, 1965, VSO Archive, microfiche files.

[50] Anthony Thorndike to Mrs. Hooper, June 1, 1965, VSO Archive, microfiche files.

[51] Jill Roach to Mr. Haig, June 29, 1965, VSO Archive, microfiche files.

Malaysia and he "purchased a darned expensive camera there, besides sundry other goods and chattels."[52]

Social Life

Across Asia, Africa and beyond, volunteers arrived in cities and towns that had long hosted an expatriate population, often in established communities with defined social norms and mores. Historians have begun to pay attention to the social and cultural aspects of expatriate life in colonial spaces. As Robert Bickers has shown, expatriate communities had particularities and multifaceted differences, but they could also be regarded as "one world of empire settlement" in which the same people and social mores were encountered and reencountered.[53] Mobility between colonial sites, through imperial careering, sojourning and tourism, helped ensure similarity (though not interchangeability) within empires and, to some extent, between the expatriate cultures of British, French and Dutch colonies.[54] Although there were differences between expatriate society in, for example, India and Egypt, one marked continuity was a strict social divide between "Europeans" and non-white Others, the borders of which were marked by informal, as well as official, forms of inclusion and exclusion. Writing of colonial India, David Washbrook evoked a "hermetically sealed bell-jar" in which "people from the British Isles preferred their own company to that of anybody else and would set up forms of exclusion against the outside world whenever and wherever they could."[55] Peter Mansfield dubbed expatriate culture in colonial Egypt "social apartheid."[56]

By the 1960s, expatriate communities across Africa and Asia appeared destined for demise. But as erstwhile colonists emigrated, their numbers were refreshed by a new cast of postcolonial expatriates including technical advisers, development experts, businessmen, professionals, diplomats – and volunteers. New arrivals were often the beneficiaries of spatial and material cultures forged during empire.[57] The overlap between colonists and

[52] John Rogers to Miss Green, October 12, 1964, VSO Archive, microfiche files.

[53] Robert Bickers, ed., *Settlers and Expatriates: Britons Over the Seas* (Oxford: Oxford University Press, 2010), p. 5.

[54] David Lambert and Alan Lester, eds., *Colonial Lives Across the British Empire: Imperial Careering in the Long Nineteenth Century* (Cambridge: Cambridge University Press, 2006).

[55] David Washbrook, "Avatars of Identity: The British Community in India." In Bickers, *Settlers and Expatriates: Britons over the Seas*, pp. 199, 179.

[56] Peter Mansfield, *The British in Egypt* (New York: Weidenfeld and Nicolson, 1971).

[57] Viviana D'Auria, "More Than Tropical? Modern Housing, Expatriate Practitioners and the Volta River Project in Decolonising Ghana." In *Cultures of Decolonisation: Transnational Productions and Practices, 1945–70*, edited by Ruth Craggs and Claire Wintle, pp. 196–221 (Manchester: Manchester University Press, 2016); Sarah L. Smiley, "Expatriate Everyday Life in Dar Es Salaam, Tanzania: Colonial Origins and

postcolonial expatriates also meant that some norms and behaviors were passed down directly. During the 1960s, expatriate culture was still firmly rooted in colonial patterns even as nations moved towards decolonization. Recent scholarship draws attention to the importance of boundaries – of body, race and gender – for expatriate communities in decolonizing and postcolonial spaces.[58] Although formal colonialism was coming to an end, the informal systems of colonial culture, which powerfully delineated social boundaries based on racial and cultural difference, were translated into a postcolonial context.[59]

Volunteers' letters and diaries reveal the extent to which social life was conducted within enclavic expatriate circles across Africa, Asia and beyond. Returning from a posting in St. Helena, Susan Rowan reported that "People who like parties and colonial-type social life, are adequately catered for."[60] From Malawi, Susan Richards wrote that "The social and high life in Blantyre was terrific."[61] Describing the social life in the famed colonial hill station of Simla in India's north, Jill Roach wrote that "it seemed to me that it would be very easy to forget you were in India after a few months because superficially Simla is like a Western town."[62] The scenario Roach described in Simla in 1965 closely approximated British colonial culture at the hill station, under which social life had been limited to contact with other "Europeans."[63] This was also true beyond former British colonies. Posted to Vientiane in Laos, Miles Roddis found himself "amid a rather incestuous Embassy & Colombo Plan circle."[64] "Most of the Europeans here," he reported to VSO, "seem to live their air-conditioned lives quite obliviously of the Lao. They drink their French wine in French cafes, or order their frozen mutton and Typhoo tea from abroad, while the Americans, with their high-powered, chromium-plated aid scheme, blatantly political in overtones, have their own campus, a village hacked out of the

Contemporary Legacies," *Social & Cultural Geography* 11, no. 4 (2010): 327–42; Anne-Meike Fechter and Katie Walsh, "Examining 'Expatriate' Continuities: Postcolonial Approaches to Mobile Professionals," *Journal of Ethnic and Migration Studies* 36, no. 8 (2010): 1197–210.

58 Anne-Meike Fechter, *Transnational Lives: Expatriates in Indonesia* (Abingdon: Routledge, 2007); Pauline Leonard, *Expatriate Identities in Postcolonial Organizations: Working Whiteness* (Farnham, UK: Ashgate, 2010); Dane Kennedy, *The Magic Mountains: Hill Stations and the British Raj* (Berkeley, CA: University of California Press, 1996).

59 Ruth Craggs and Claire Wintle, eds., *Cultures of Decolonisation: Transnational Productions and Practices, 1945–1970* (Manchester, UK: Manchester University Press, 2016); Kothari, "Spatial Practices and Imaginaries."

60 Final Report, Susan Rowan, 1965, VSO Archive, microfiche files.

61 Susan Richards to Miss Jones, October 14, 1964, VSO Archive, microfiche files.

62 Final Report, Jill Roach, September 27, 1965, VSO Archive, microfiche files.

63 Kennedy, *The Magic Mountains.*

64 Final Report, Miles Roddis, October 18, 1965, VSO Archive, microfiche files.

jungle, 6 [kilometers] out of town."[65] Although he had arrived with good intentions, Roddis found the tight-knit expatriate community impossible to escape.

Racially exclusive expatriate social life took place in larger cities such as Lagos or Vientiane, but also in more isolated locations. Posted to a "bush school" at Ikole, some 200 km from Ibadan in southwestern Nigeria, Diana St John "never imagined that there would be such coming and going between the Europeans."[66] Mary Salton, posted to Buin in Bougainville, on the outer archipelago of Papua New Guinea (an Australian colony until 1975), was about as far from metropolitan life as it was possible to go. But even she experienced a busy expatriate social life, writing of buffet dinners, cocktail parties and balls held for the twenty or so resident "Europeans" and their regular visitors. To social parties Salton typically wore her "best cotton dresses while everyone else had cocktail dresses."[67] The performance of European prestige was expected even at the furthest reaches of Empire.

British volunteers were subjected to the full integrative pressure of expatriate communities. Tony Thorndike spent 1965 in Maru, in a remote part of Northern Nigeria. Far from social isolation, however, the region hosted a tight-knit group of expatriate teachers who tried to reproduce British life in Nigeria. Thorndike thought that Peace Corps volunteers were given some leeway, but VSOs were expected to fall in line with expatriate norms as "I've been told 'they're American and we expect them to do silly things – but you're an Englishman and should act like one'(!)"[68] But other Western volunteers also felt pressured to conform to expatriate standards. Peace Corps volunteer Alex Veech was shocked by the extent of expatriate society in the British colony of Tanganyika upon arriving in 1961. His experience of the Peace Corps was "colored by living in a colonial area where the British have carved for themselves a very sophisticated life. It was a surprise to find the British high life, club, little theater group, dinner parties, and costume New Year's Party in proximity with but still culturally worlds apart from the barefoot, underpaid and sickly African." He felt that "Life was therefore hard for our little group since by Western background we tend towards the British way of comfortable living, but by idealism we feel we should know the African that he may know us." In the end he fell in with expatriate ways, as "the British, standing apart from the African, give us no way of easy contact with the African whose country this is."[69]

65 Miles Roddis to Miss Ball, October 13, 1964, VSO Archive, microfiche files.

66 Diana St John to Miss Harvey, September 18, 1965, VSO Archive, microfiche files.

67 Mary Salton to Mr. Isherwood, October 24, 1964, VSO Archive, microfiche files.

68 Anthony Thorndike to Mrs. Hooper, November 6, 1964, VSO Archive, microfiche files.

69 Alex Veech to E. V. Dobbins, March 11, 1962, Papers of Elinor Capehart, JFKL: RPCV, Box 102.

The pressure to integrate into expatriate society was particularly directed at female volunteers. The following chapter takes a close look at the policing of female volunteers' sexual behavior by volunteer agencies, but this policing took place at the level of expatriate communities too. Arriving in Blantyre, nurse Susan Richards found that "Rumours had got round that there were new single nurses arriving" as "The shortage of girls out here is about 1–10." Richards was overwhelmed with male attention and her expatriate social life became so busy that "really it was most difficult to remember that I was a V.S.O."[70] The rumor mill that notified Blantyre of a volunteer's approach was also a strong socializing mechanism enforcing expatriate mores. In Simla, Jill Roach found navigating her busy social life more fraught than in Britain. In keeping with the expatriate community's sensitivity to questions of British prestige, and their tendency to locate and guard national prestige in the bodies of women and girls, Roach explained that "it is essential to remember that you are not in England and that it is important to uphold some reputation."[71] Although almost thirty years had passed since Independence, much of the colonial culture – including the gulf between "European" and "native," imprinted particularly in social life and policed especially for girls and women – not only remained intact but was in fact perpetuated by the influx of development volunteers. Many volunteers felt pressured to alter their behavior in order to fit in. Carole Revans and Valerie Ratcliffe, graduates in sociology from the London School of Economics and Liverpool University respectively, were sent by VSO to complete a social survey of Fijian living conditions in 1964. But as young, single women, the local expatriate community regarded them simply as "cheap staff to look after European children." As Revans complained, "having come out to do a social survey, contact with 30 riotous planters' offspring was more than we bargained for."[72] Even though they were "the bane of our lives," Revans and Ratcliffe felt powerless in the face of the local expatriate community. The young women acquiesced with the community's gendered social norms and spent significant periods of time caring for the expatriate children, even though this ran counter both to their own inclinations and the knowledge that "their time could perhaps be better spent catering to the needs of the local population."[73]

A small proportion of VSOs did resist falling in with expatriate social circles; others were excluded. Tony Thorndike's arrival in Maru aroused suspicion amongst the local expatriates, who worried that he would undercut their comfortable salaries at the exclusive, Western-style school at which they all taught. As he wrote to VSO, "When I first arrived . . . I was assailed on all sides

70 Susan Richards to Miss Jones, October 14, 1964, VSO Archive, microfiche files.

71 Final Report, Jill Roach, September 27, 1965, VSO Archive, microfiche files.

72 Carole Revans to Mr. Thomas, October 6, 1964, VSO Archive, microfiche files.

73 Final Report, Carole Revans, January 12, 1966, VSO Archive, microfiche files.

by Europeans who could not understand my way of thinking." As a volunteer, rather than a contract worker, "I was treated almost like an outcast & called a 'poor white', 'scrounger' etc. – in other words, persona non-grata." The expatriates also accused him of being "'too sincere' (true quote!) ... [and] spending too much time in the Nigerian establishments ... and not in the European Club."[74] As a result, Thorndike avoided the local "club life which I find unpleasant due partly, of course, to the fact that I'm more-or-less ostracised." Even so, Thorndike's social life was largely conducted with other Europeans; although he avoided the Club, he soon became "pretty friendly with a couple of cotton growers, about four road engineers (mostly Irish with a marvellous sense of humour) and with the local Anglican (CMS) missionary."[75]

Although the largest number of VSOs were sent to expatriate hubs, a proportion were posted far from the major centers of expatriate life. In her "bush" school at Ifaki in Nigeria, Evelyn Ross considered "There is little danger in Ifaki of a volunteer associating with other Europeans to the detriment of her work; there is every opportunity to form friendships with Nigerians." Yet, Ross found the social distance between herself and Nigerians difficult to bridge, writing that "there is a distinct lack of Nigerians who are educated and can understand English well, so that the volunteer is very often lonely."[76] Ruth Searle was posted to a small Anglican Mission in Papua New Guinea, where she was one of only three "Europeans." Like Evelyn Ross in Nigeria, Searle found that "the isolation can be rather wearing. One longs for the sight of a European face after a while."[77] Her sense of isolation was so intense that she measured distance by proximity to other expatriates: "Our nearest European neighbours are six miles away on one side, and eighteen miles on the other."[78] Her loneliness, despite constant contact with Papuans, is telling. Other VSOs actively sought to break out of the expatriate bubble. Mary Schofield, a teacher in Lagos, considered herself "very lucky to have a Nigerian Principal. It means that we meet a lot of Nigerians through her. It would be so easy for one's circle of friends to be all Europeans."[79] Schofield was indeed lucky to have found an entry point into Nigerian social circles. Many volunteers completed their terms with VSO without having made any significant relationships with locals.

As the next two chapters explore in more detail, attempts at friendship and intimate relationships across racial and cultural divides could be fraught. In this vexed scenario and reflecting the norms of the expatriate communities in which they were posted, many VSOs preferred to club together, recreating the grammar schools and scout packs they had left behind in Britain and through

74 Anthony Thorndike to Mrs. Hooper, July 20, 1965, VSO Archive, microfiche files.
75 Anthony Thorndike to Mrs. Hooper, November 6, 1964, VSO Archive, microfiche files.
76 Final Report, Evelyn Ross, 1965, VSO Archive, microfiche files.
77 Ruth Searle to Mr. Haig, December 27, 1964, VSO Archive, microfiche files.
78 Ruth Searle to Mr. Haig, October 10, 1964, VSO Archive, microfiche files.
79 Mary Schofield to Mr. Thomas, October 4, 1963, VSO Archive, microfiche files.

their intimacy avoiding meaningful contact with locals. We can see this at work in a group diary kept in 1964–5 by four young VSO volunteers in Noqub, north of Aden in today's Yemen. Working together building a school for the blind and living in the same house, the four volunteers quickly became close. They ate most meals together and convened weekly formal meetings, complete with agenda, in addition to their constant informal contact. For variety, they held a weekly dinner in "European dress" as well as a "crazy night" in fancy dress. Their intimacy effectively divided them from their local community. Contacts were limited to the "coolies" working for them and did not go beyond the odd invitation to tea or a wedding. Relations were not helped by widespread anticolonial sentiment in the context of the Aden Emergency, the start of which immediately preceded the volunteers' arrival and which almost certainly contributed to the workers' recurrent threats to strike. But neither were they helped by the volunteers' apparent insensitivity to locals' circumstances or feelings (openly eating in front of them during Ramadan, for example, or remaining unmoved by the death of an employee's eighteen-month-old son, one of a pair of twins, opining instead that "it may be a good thing as the other twin should have a better chance to survive"). Perhaps unsurprisingly, the volunteers' initial objective to set up a "Club" facilitating contact between Arabs and VSOs came to nothing. In its absence, nothing approximating a genuine relationship between the four volunteers and locals was ever hinted at in the pages of their diary, much of which reads like a boys' own adventure.[80]

Towards Aidland

By the mid-1960s, some Asian and African nations hosted hundreds or even thousands of volunteers. Their sheer number saw volunteers forge their own variant of expatriate culture, at its peak during holidays when volunteers visited each other but also encompassing their day-to-day lives. In Liberia and Ghana, for instance, Western volunteers accounted for over half of all secondary school teachers.[81] Volunteers also made up some 50 percent of primary school teachers and 30 percent of secondary school teachers in Ethiopia.[82] In such contexts, VSO's Executive Committee perceived "a danger that the volunteer movement would be flooded in developing countries," resulting in "a bad impression of over-supply."[83] For volunteers, however, counterparts from other Western volunteer programs were a major source of

[80] Diary: Roger A. Goodchild, Geoffrey P. Jones, Thomas Mills and David Rendell, Box 31, VSO Archive.

[81] Glyn Roberts, *Volunteers in Africa and Asia: A Field Study* (London: The Stanhope Press, 1965), p. 9.

[82] Glyn Roberts, *Volunteers and Neo-Colonialism*, p. 37.

[83] Minutes from meeting, February 14, 1966, Returned Volunteers' Advisory Committee, VSO Archive, Box 31.

amusement, friendship and even romance. Volunteers frequently shared workplaces, social groups and, sometimes, homes. In Abeokuta in Western Nigeria, VSO Helen Rosenberg shared a flat with Peace Corps volunteer Pat Brown. "Thank heavens for the peace corps," she wrote, as "I'm sure I wouldn't still be here if it wasn't for Pat, she really is a wonderful person to live with."[84] Just down the road, her VSO colleague Philip Taylor lived downstairs from a Peace Corps volunteer and, as a result, "I seem to have met every P.C.V. in Nigeria . . . They are all most kind & friendly."[85] The sheer number of volunteers in Abeokuta presented what Helen Rosenberg called an "Expatriate Dilemma": with three VSOs and "6 or 7" Peace Corps in the region, "We formed a very good group who on the whole didn't mix with the other ex-pats in town."[86]

The exclusive social world of volunteers was in full evidence during holidays. Funded by holiday grants, volunteers set off on expeditions across their regions. Many stayed with other volunteers whenever possible. Helen Rosenberg and Pat Brown went travelling together in late 1964. As Rosenberg reported back to London, "We visited Kaduna, Jos, Zaria, Kano, Minna, Abuja & Keffi and stayed with V.S.O's all the time."[87] Diana St John also travelled around Nigeria with a Peace Corps volunteer; the pair became so close they moved in together after the holiday was over.[88] Rosenberg and St John were presumably among those Nigeria VSOs who celebrated Christmas 1964 with a "large GVSO Christmas party lasting 3–4 days" in Kaduna. One guest reported that "A riotous time followed and everybody had a marvellous time," before the entire group traveled some 380 miles to Ilorin, where two more VSOs hosted a New Year's Eve party, which "was worth going to as well as you can imagine."[89]

Similar rounds of visiting were common in Ghana, India, Malaysia and other nations hosting large contingents of volunteers. Returning through Kaduna several months after the riotous 1964 Christmas party, Tony Thorndike found the hosts "rather fed-up . . . as their house has been indiscriminately used as a hotel/resthouse for VSOs from all over Nigeria and Ghana, the vast majority of whom they have never seen before or heard of even."[90] The Peace Corps found a way to help those "poor Volunteers" whose homes were regularly invaded, establishing some seventy-five hostels across Africa and Asia, including six in Nigeria.[91] Peace Corps hostels were large and

[84] Helen Rosenberg to Mr. Haig, April 20, 1965, VSO Archive, microfiche files.

[85] Philip Taylor to Mr. Thomas, September 30, 1963, VSO Archive, microfiche files.

[86] Helen Rosenberg to Mr. Haig, December 15, 1964, and Final Report, Helen Rosenberg, October 7, 1965, both in VSO Archive, microfiche files.

[87] Helen Rosenberg to Mr. Haig, February 2, 1965, VSO Archive, microfiche files.

[88] Final Report, Diana St John, September 13, 1965, VSO Archive, microfiche files.

[89] Anthony Thorndike to Mrs. Hooper, January 11, 1965, VSO Archive, microfiche files.

[90] Anthony Thorndike to Mrs. Hooper, June 1, 1965, VSO Archive, microfiche files.

[91] Sally Foster, "Case Histories" in "PCV Housing Allowances and Reimbursements," JFKL: RG 490, Box 23.

comfortable – the hostel in Addis Ababa, for example, had thirty beds, including two rooms for married couples, and offered three meals a day in an exclusive dining room.[92] They were also epicenters of volunteer social life, welcoming volunteers from Canada, Britain and other countries as well as Peace Corps volunteers. The hostels proved so popular that volunteers were regularly turned away, leading the Peace Corps to suggest that the burden be shared more equally between the programs.[93] Some members of the VSO Executive Committee wondered whether the Peace Corps' complaint was an opportunity in disguise, as volunteers unable to find a bed in a Peace Corps hostel would be forced to stay in local establishments and thereby get a more "authentic" experience. But VSO's Director George Whiting disagreed; based on his experience, he doubted that volunteers would stay in local hotels or guesthouses. In the Director's view, Peace Corps hostels merely prevented VSOs from "placing a strain on the resources of British Council representatives and their families."[94] Whiting considered the hostels to be a vital resource for VSOs during weekends and holidays and he worked hard to placate American grievances for as long as possible.

The friendships forged between volunteers from different nations represent one kind of internationalism enabled by the rise of development volunteering. But the close networks forged within and between volunteering programs also created a new kind of expatriate community. The social enclavism of volunteer social networks mirrored (and sometimes blurred into) existing expatriate communities. It served to separate volunteers from locals along racial as well as cultural lines, further engraving the divides between "Europeans" and "natives" and between the Global North and Global South. Volunteers' enclavic social life, and attendant infrastructure including hostels, shared accommodation and facilities, also helped consolidate spaces of aid in the Global South, laying the foundations for "Aidlands" by which development practitioners became increasingly physically and culturally separated from the "field" in later decades.[95]

Back to Colonialism?

Some volunteers were perturbed by the relative luxury and social endogamy of their postings. Writing from La Paz, John Rosser betrayed that "I felt sometimes as though my accommodation was too good for a Volunteer."[96] Miles

[92] "Transient Houses" in "PCV Housing Allowances and Reimbursements," JFKL: RG 490, Box 23.

[93] "Report of Director's Visit to Nigeria and Ghana, October 1964," VSO Archive, Box 31.

[94] Minutes of Executive Committee, February 1, 1965, VSO Archive, Box 31.

[95] Lisa Smirl, *Spaces of Aid: How Cars, Compounds and Hotels Shape Humanitarianism* (London: Zed Books, 2015); David Mosse, ed., *Adventures in Aidland: The Anthropology of Professionals in International Development* (New York: Berghahn Books, 2011).

[96] Final Report, John Rosser, 1965, VSO Archive, microfiche files.

Roddis worried that his "'volunteer' status was quickly lost" amidst the luxury of his surroundings in Vientiane. Roddis felt he was "grossly overpaid ... Indeed, it's almost embarrassing to be introduced as a 'volunteer' – and particularly when you meet Lao teachers, of course, earning about 1/8 as much as I do."[97] Mary Schofield, teaching in Lagos, Nigeria, was similarly troubled. "One thing which did annoy me was being called a Volunteer when I was receiving a tax-free salary of £700 a year plus free housing. Most of the 'Volunteers' I met felt the same way about this."[98] Others were more sanguine. Philip Taylor, working in Nigeria, felt that "My living conditions were probably too good for a volunteer, although they may have been about right for a European teacher who wanted to be effective."[99] Ruth Joy, who worked in British Guiana, found her living conditions to be "Of a much higher standard than I had anticipated." When asked whether these conditions "were too good for a volunteer," however, Joy replied that, "I felt that as I was being paid a reasonable salary I might as well live fairly comfortably & it would be hypocritical not to."[100]

The distance between expectations and on-the-ground reality was a particular point of tension. A significant number of volunteers wrote to VSO to convey surprise, and sometimes dismay, at their comfortable postings in elite institutions. Twenty-one-year-old Barry Romeril was posted to the exclusive Sainik School, a military college in Tamil Nadu, India, in 1964–5. Newly graduated from Oxford, Romeril was no stranger to elitism, but even he took exception to his surroundings, complaining that this "is not my idea of what V.S.O should be." Romeril protested that "this is not the place to send VSOs" as "this school can in no sense be called poor" and "there must be higher priorities than this for India."[101] As he explained, "The rich in India often live more comfortably than the rich in advanced western countries due to the abundant supply of poorly paid servants, cooks, bearers etc." He concluded that "VSO should not help to further cushion their comforts by providing cheap English teachers for their sons."[102] Working at Aligarh University in Pakistan, Robin Robbins was similarly surprised at the campus' manicured grounds, well-endowed library and apparently unlimited budget. "The University is well off and spends a lot on equipment and buildings," he wrote, so perhaps VSO should explore "how much better their assistance might be used elsewhere."[103] Nigel Turner also became disillusioned during

97 Miles Roddis to Miss Ball, October 13, 1964, VSO Archive, microfiche files.
98 Mary Schofield to Mr. Thomas, September 8, 1964, VSO Archive, microfiche files.
99 Final Report, Philip Taylor, 1965, VSO Archive, microfiche files.
100 Final Report, Ruth Richardson (nee Joy), November 9, 1965, VSO Archive, microfiche files.
101 Barry Romeril to Mr. Carey, April 29, 1965, VSO Archive, microfiche files.
102 Final Report, Barry D. Romeril, August 16, 1965, VSO Archive, microfiche files.
103 Robin Robbins to Miss Ball, April 6, 1965, VSO Archive, microfiche files.

his "prestige" posting at an American-funded school in Nigeria. A VSO representative reported that "he has had to contend with work and conditions of a very different kind to what he might have expected: the luxury and kudos of a 'prestige' school" and, consequently, "Nigel . . . became slightly cynical under these conditions."[104]

Volunteers working in elite schools were not the only ones to complain. Susan Richards, whose experiences in a Malawi hospital opened this chapter, repeatedly wrote to VSO to express her concern. "On the whole, I have been very disappointed with my work out here," she wrote in October 1964. She felt duped, as "When I was met at the British Council's House by Miss Wessells, the chief of nursing, she said that they were desperate for nurses and just couldn't get enough." The thought that she might be nursing wealthy Europeans had not entered her mind: "I took it for granted that the nurses would be mainly looking after Africans."[105] But when she complained about being put on an overstaffed European ward, Miss Wessells "got most upset and said that the V.S.O documents didn't state which colour I was to nurse with." As Richards wrote, Wessells "completely missed the point and just thought I'd got some anti-white colour bar," and "As she is South African this went down very badly."[106] Volunteers working alongside British contract teachers or nurses, who were paid more for similar work, were also prone to disillusionment. Even those VSO nurses who were put on "over crowded under staffed African wards," Susan Richards wrote, still felt "this would have been splendid if we had not seen plenty of European contract nurses in the same hospital."[107] Andrew Richardson at Mayo College similarly admitted that "I can't help wondering how much use I am here when there are two other chaps doing similar work without any sense of service."[108] As we saw in Chapter 4 of this book, many volunteers had initially been motivated by a sense of goodwill and a sincere desire to help those less fortunate than themselves. Arriving on the ground, many came to think that their goodwill was being wasted and, like Susan Richards, began to feel resentful that they had been "duped" by VSO.

Thinking beyond their own postings, some concluded that VSO as a whole perpetuated, rather than mitigated, global inequality. Near the end of his twelve-month posting, Barry Romeril wrote that "I am of the firm opinion that VSO in India does more to subsidise the rich in India than it does to help the poorer section of the country."[109] He was not alone: this book's final chapter tracks organized opposition groups formed by returned volunteers

[104] D. J. Harvey, "Confidential report on Nigel Turner," December 1, 1965, VSO Archive, microfiche files.

[105] "Report on Nurses in Malawi," October 22, 1964, VSO Archive, microfiche files.

[106] Susan Richards to Miss Jones, October 14, 1964, VSO Archive, microfiche files.

[107] Final Report, Susan Richards, September 27, 1965, VSO Archive, microfiche files.

[108] Andrew Richardson to VSO, November 20, 1964, VSO Archive, microfiche files.

[109] Final Report, Barry Romeril, August 16, 1965, VSO Archive, microfiche files.

in Britain and the United States from the mid-1960s. Following a tour of Southeast Asia in 1966, even VSO Director George Whiting came to think that volunteer numbers should be limited in some cities "because of the dangers of creating a little British colony."[110] Yet, the situation was not systematically addressed; instead, volunteers' colonies grew steadily larger as VSO and the Peace Corps were joined by volunteers from new programs established by other "developed" nations.

Neither was VSO responsive to reports that individual volunteers were living at too high a standard. Susan Richards had come to Malawi expecting a "challenge," but she received an allowance of £640 per annum from the Malawi government, a salary of £36 net per month from her hospital and free accommodation with full board.[111] Voluntary Service Overseas became concerned; volunteers were supposed to pay for their keep out of their annual allowances, so that "If you have not been paying anything and no deductions have been made from your monthly allowance, by this time, strictly speaking, you owe the Malawi Government quite a fortune."[112] Yet, there is no evidence that repayment was either sought or provided: Susan Richards lived it up in Malawi and even saved money towards her return to Britain in 1965.

On the other hand, reports of volunteers living at a standard below that of other expatriates were urgently followed up. In 1964, VSO Director George Whiting personally inquired into conditions at the Anglican Girls' High School at Ughelli in Nigeria after discovering that the original rate paid to VSOs, set at £26 per month by an expatriate headmistress, had been revised down to £20 per month by "the new Nigerian Bishop in Benin or the Indian headmistress." Whiting worried that this rate was "proving insufficient" and that volunteers might suffer some embarrassment as a result.[113] Similarly, VSO repeatedly returned to the vexed issue of payments for teachers in India, believing that "the standard terms of service . . . have a quite different meaning in India from their meaning in Africa" as "The teaching profession occupies a very lowly position in India." In this context, even a volunteer "in a good boarding school" might receive a salary so low that "even allowing for the value of his board and keep he is worse off than we envisage that the volunteers

[110] Minutes from meeting February 14, 1966, Returned Volunteers' Advisory Committee, VSO Archive, Box 31.

[111] In 2019 terms, and converted into British pounds, this amount had a relative income value of £27,080 and was in addition to food, accommodation and VSO's grants and termination payments (in mid-November 1964, Malawi £1,072 had an exchange rate of GBP 539.32): www.measuringworth.com, accessed June 26, 2019.

[112] R. P. K Harrison to Susan Richards, C. Parker and S. Maltby, March 24, 1965, VSO Archive, microfiche files.

[113] "Confidential: Director's Visit to Nigeria and Ghana, October 1964," VSO Archive, Box 31.

should be."[114] Far from pursuing equality of remuneration, VSO kept a close eye on volunteers in India, ensuring that salaries and grants allowed a standard of living well above that of local counterparts.

The Peace Corps was more responsive to reports that volunteers were living lives of undue luxury, especially after Jack Hood Vaughn replaced Sargent Shriver as Director in 1966. Facing a stagnating operating budget, Vaughn began to "tighten the screws on anything that smacks of material comfort or ostentation" in order that "our operation should be as efficient and look as lean as possible."[115] In April 1966 – just weeks after taking up his role – Vaughn decided that the "Peace Corps' overseas hostels are on balance a strong negative factor," for a list of reasons including "expensive, dangerous, wrong image, nuisance, colonial."[116] Far from helping the Peace Corps, Vaughn assessed the hostels as "an apartheid device."[117] Volunteers' living standards also became a matter of open concern. Peace Corps Representatives around the world were instructed to closely look into volunteers' personal finances, to ensure they were not living at too high a standard. Existing policies spelt out that volunteers' stipends "should be checked against prevailing salary levels for counterparts" and that these were "national, not expatriate, counterparts."[118] New policies went further, castigating volunteers who lived in comfortable, expatriate-grade housing on school compounds and asking "how can they be expected to learn anything about these people living and working in a cultural vacuum?"[119]

Vaughn's proposed changes exposed the fundamental tension between volunteers' good intentions and on-the-ground realities. In Nigeria, all six Peace Corps hostels were shut down in mid-1966 and volunteers received notice that their living allowances would shortly be reduced. Volunteers were incensed and wrote "a large number of letters on these subjects, coupled with a series of complaining resolutions and petitions."[120] The issue was extensively debated in the pages of the in-house magazine, *Peace Corps Volunteer*. As one feature article noted, Peace Corps Washington expected Nigeria-bound

[114] Department of Technical Cooperation, "Notes on VSO Projects in India," February 19, 1964, VSO Archive, Box 31.

[115] R. L. Steiner, "Memo to Peace Corps Directors, North Africa, Near East, South Asia Region," October 25, 1966, JFKL: RG 490, Box 23.

[116] Jack Vaughn to Robert Klein, April 22, 1966, JFKL: RG 490, Box 23.

[117] Jack Vaughn cited in "The top issues: hostels, Hondas, 'pay'," *Peace Corps Volunteer*, December 1966, p. 6.

[118] Interim Policy Directive 4.2: Guidance in Determining Subsistence Allowance, September 1, 1961, JFKL: RG 490, Box 23.

[119] "PCV Housing Allowances and Reimbursement," November 1966, JFKL: RG 490, Box 23.

[120] Stuart Awbrey and Pat Brown, "The issues of Nigeria, and beyond," *Peace Corps Volunteer*, December 1966, p. 2.

volunteers to live a simple life amongst Africans, but, in reality, "the Volunteers have been asked to teach in school systems where an estimated 97 per cent of the teachers are expatriates." Moreover, "they are given modern quarters . . . [and] are expected to associate with other teachers (expatriates) and to participate in the activities of the community (at the club)."[121] The Peace Corps' attempt to cut stipends was incompatible with the reality of their postings. One volunteer argued that Vaughn's insistence that volunteers live in primitive conditions was rooted in "overworked and meaningless clichés," whose necessity had "never been adequately explained." As he went on, "the definition of the Volunteer's basic role has too often been shunned and substituted . . . with trappings and incidentals – pictures of the 'mud hut' – which just aren't based on fact with regard to Nigeria."[122] Another reminded Vaughn that the Nigerian government had requested teachers and not community development workers – and so volunteers should live accordingly. By cutting volunteers' stipends and forcing them out of teachers' compounds, "The Peace Corps administration . . . chooses to impose its own conception of what the Volunteers should be doing, rather than accepting the directive of the host government."[123] The resistance was serious enough to induce Vaughn to travel to Nigeria and personally meet with 600 volunteers (from a total of some 700 in the country at the time). Tellingly, the volunteers won: returning to Washington, Vaughn revoked his directive cutting stipends. Volunteers continued to receive high stipends – enough to "cover refrigerators and servants, and savings" – until Nigeria-based volunteers were evacuated amidst the Biafran War in 1967.[124] The "little colonies" established by volunteers in other parts of the Global South endured far longer.

Conclusion

Taking a close look at the lives and lifestyles of volunteers, with a particular focus on VSO volunteers during the mid-1960s, this chapter found that the lived experience of development volunteering diverged from the rhetoric of volunteering agencies and the images perpetuated by Western media. Of course, this chapter can't cover the experiences of every individual volunteer. However, broad patterns are evident and clear. In current dependencies and former colonies, volunteers stepped into roles and lifestyles very recently

[121] Ibid., p. 4.

[122] Robert J. Attaway, "Letter to the Editor: Define the Goals," *Peace Corps Volunteer*, Vol. 5, no. 5. March 1967, p. 22.

[123] Stephen D. Krasner, "A Smug Peace Corps," *Peace Corps Volunteer*, Vol. 5, no. 5. March 1967, pp. 22–3.

[124] Stuart Awbrey and Pat Brown, "The issues of Nigeria, and beyond," *Peace Corps Volunteer*, December 1966, p. 5.

vacated by European colonists; indeed, many were placed within institutions and systems that were little changed from the colonial era. Although volunteers imagined they would live simple lives and had left home genuinely prepared to make sacrifices, the lifestyles they ultimately cultivated were closely aligned with expatriate norms that had been set under colonialism. To their surprise – and occasionally distaste – many volunteers found their standards of living at least as high, and sometimes higher, than back home. Stipends and allowances stretched to comfortable, modern housing and many volunteers employed servants and enjoyed regular holidays. Many volunteers also socialized primarily with other expatriates, including volunteers arriving from across the Global North as development volunteering boomed in popularity during the 1960s. Individual volunteers sought companionship, comfort and entertainment with those who understood them best during a time of personal upheaval; but, in doing so, they collectively created a racially exclusive social world that mirrored colonial norms enforcing distinctions between "European" and "native" through social as well as formal mechanisms.

Looking at ground level, therefore, supports a different interpretation of the impacts and effects of development volunteering than has been advanced to date. Far from being forerunners of postcolonial egalitarianism or representatives of the idealism of the 1960s, development volunteers were early inhabitants of Aidlands in which expatriate aid workers were physically and socially separated from the local communities they sought to help. This separation took place despite volunteers' best intentions and genuine goodwill, and many expressed frustration and blamed VSO for placing them in institutions and locations with a large expatriate population. But the fact remains that most proved unable, or unwilling, to change the situation. This underscores the power of quotidian culture and social norms to modify development plans as they were put into practice. Put simply, the best of intentions were compromised amid the day-to-day strain of life in a foreign environment, especially in the presence of already-existing expatriate populations. Colonial culture did not simply die out with the declaration of political independence across the Global South, but was transmitted into the postcolonial period through a range of complex processes and vectors. Western volunteers were significant among these. In their day-to-day lives, many volunteers bridged the colonial and postcolonial eras. Their experiences point to the difficulty of forging genuine interpersonal relations between volunteers and their host communities, a theme that is continued in the next two chapters.

8

The Intimacy of the Humanitarian-Development Complex

In 1957, Joan Minogue, freshly graduated from a teaching college in regional New South Wales, arrived in Semarang in Central Java. She was there for eighteen months, teaching English under Australia's Volunteer Graduate Scheme. Far from her parents and eager to further the Volunteer Graduate Scheme mission of "identification" with Indonesians, Minogue met and fell in love with Hardjono, a Javanese man living in nearby Bandung. After a slow start complicated by religious differences, declarations were made and the couple decided to marry. Minogue reapplied for another term with the Volunteer Graduate Scheme, which was delighted to have her back, but her application was rejected following a routine security check by the Australian government's Department of External Affairs. Upon application, the Minister, Richard Casey, explained that Minogue was rejected because "you had declared your intention of getting married on your return to Indonesia."[1] For the Australian government, volunteering to help Indonesia's development was one thing, but forging an intimate relationship across boundaries of nation, culture and race was quite another.

Humanitarianism and international development were enacted through countless interactions between individuals. This chapter maps out the emotional economy of development volunteering by connecting the intimate with the organizational; the private with the geopolitical. It looks below the systems level to examine how individuals interacted within the structures of humanitarianism and international development, and to trace the role of affect and intimacy in the humanitarian-development complex. Ann Laura Stoler points to the central role that the regulation of sexual relationships played in the colonial enterprise and the continuing influence of these structures in postcolonial times.[2] This chapter finds a similar scenario in development volunteering agencies during the 1950s and 1960s. These organizations often espoused postcolonial values, but the rhetoric did not always translate on the ground.

[1] Richard Casey to Joan Minogue (copy), August 3, 1959, NLA: MS 2601, Box 10.

[2] Stoler, *Carnal Knowledge and Imperial Power*, esp. pp. 47–78; Ann Laura Stoler, *Duress: Imperial Durabilities in Our Times* (Durham, NC: Duke University Press, 2016), pp. 305–35.

Regular tensions arose between individuals and agencies, and between agencies and governments, as they negotiated the intimate and the global.

The Joan Minogue case was an early example of what became a chronic point of tension for volunteers, agencies and governments: how to define the boundaries of acceptable interpersonal conduct on the ground. It also affords a hint of the kaleidoscopic range of personal and sometimes intimate relationships formed by volunteers abroad and takes them seriously as outcomes of the humanitarian-development complex. Many volunteers lived in relative luxury within the "little colonies" explored in the previous chapter but, even so, encounters with locals did occur in the course of their work or in the broader community. Personal relationships with locals spanned the full human range of emotion from disinterest to wild passion, fond regard to disgust and even hate. A small number of these stories are examined in this chapter, which looks for the seams that stitch the intimate to the systemic as a first step towards mapping the affective landscape of foreign aid during the 1950s and 1960s.

"We Really Mean This Identification Business"

As Chapter 4 of this book demonstrated, volunteers in the 1950s and 1960s were commonly motivated by altruistic internationalism, as well as a desire for travel and adventure. In her application, Minogue had written, "I am most interested in Asian countries, and wish to assist, in as far as I can, in helping these countries."[3] Volunteer agencies and the governments that funded them, however, saw young volunteers in a different light. As we have seen, the Australian, British and US governments each regarded development volunteering as a way to improve their national image in the context of decolonization and the Cold War. Organizations and governments cherished the association between volunteers and the national character. As a result, they became closely concerned with the problem of regulating contacts between volunteers and the communities in which they served. The Volunteer Graduate Scheme, VSO and the Peace Corps all contained a fundamental tension between what volunteers did on the ground and how their actions were variously claimed, utilized, policed or rejected by their sending agency, their government and the media. This brought with it an intrinsic problem: how to inspire the correct emotional response – a blend of sympathy and enthusiastic goodwill – but limit overidentification resulting in romantic love or other forms of "going native."

Joan Minogue's romantic encounter with Hardjono provides an entry point into the complexity and perceived limits of identification and intimacy within the humanitarian-development complex. Minogue's fellow volunteers were hardly surprised when she fell in love with Hardjono. If anything, the

[3] Application questionnaire – Joan Minogue, May 5, 1956, NLA: MS 2601, Box 10.

Volunteer Graduate Scheme actively encouraged volunteers to form affective relationships with Indonesians. In some ways, the Volunteer Graduate Scheme was the most radical of the three volunteer agencies examined in this book. The Scheme aimed for "natural and friendly relations with Indonesians on a basis of mutual respect," which they thought "may help to do away with the colonial legacy of mistrust and misunderstanding, which to so large an extent continues to affect relations between coloured peoples and whites."[4] Early volunteers, who formed the majority of the Executive Committee responsible for setting policy, believed that emotional ties were the strongest signs of identification across boundaries of race and culture. Marriage was entirely consistent with their definition of "natural and friendly relations." The scheme's first volunteer, Herb Feith, wrote in 1957 that intermarriage "has become an important aspect of the scheme – in the eyes of many Indonesians the most convincing proof that we really mean this identification business."[5] By the time Minogue arrived in Java, two volunteers had already married Indonesians. Ailsa Thomson had first met Zainu'ddin, an Indonesian diplomat, in Canberra and had applied to the Volunteer Graduate Scheme in 1954 "with the intention of matrimony."[6] The pair married five months after their arrival in Jakarta. A second volunteer, Thelma Ashton, met Richard Rungkat during her placement as a librarian in Jakarta's Ministry of Education and they married in 1957. Both marriages were happy, seemingly confirming the Volunteer Graduate Scheme's ideological support of affective relationships between Australians and Indonesians. Ailsa Zainu'ddin wrote in the Volunteer Graduate Scheme magazine that "VGS not only entails a risk of becoming involved in inter-racial marriage, but . . . Indeed, it might be said that inter-racial marriage is a logical, although certainly by no means inevitable outcome of the ideals and aims of the Scheme."[7]

Yet, many Australians regarded the matter very differently. As Herb Feith wrote following Thelma Ashton's wedding, "it can't be long before 'Truth' will send a correspondent here to report on 'Colombo Plan Funds for the Breeding of Half-Castes'."[8] Feith's reference to an Australian tabloid publication was tongue in cheek, but it pointed to a broader reality: many Australians defined the boundaries of appropriate affect between Australians and Asians in a very different way. Friendship and brotherly assistance were deserving of support,

4 "The Volunteer Graduate Scheme for Indonesia: An account of the Scheme and a letter from Indonesia to Interested Volunteers," December 1956, NLA: MS 2601, Box 13, Folder 125.

5 Herb Feith to Betty, Mum and Dad and Lotte, July 2, 1957, NLA: MS 2601, Box 4, Folder 35.

6 Author's interview with Ailsa Zainu'ddin, Melbourne, November 5, 2014.

7 Ailsa Zainu'ddin, "The Marriage of True Minds," *Djembatan*, Vol. 3, no. 1, 1959, pp. 13–16.

8 Herb Feith to Betty, Mum and Dad and Lotte, July 2, 1957, NLA: MS 2601, Box 4, Folder 35.

but more intimate relationships were to be discouraged as it was assumed they would cause divided loyalties and threaten racial miscegenation. In the archives we can now see that the decision to refuse Joan Hardjono's reapplication was reached following an intense debate between three sections of the Australian government bureaucracy: the Technical Assistance Branch of the Department of External Affairs, the Southeast Asian Section of the same department and the Australian Embassy in Jakarta. The Technical Assistance Branch saw no obstacle to volunteers marrying Indonesians; if anything, their improved language skills and networks would only increase their capacity to contribute to Indonesia's postcolonial development. The Australian Embassy in Jakarta, however, disagreed. Embassy staff had already expressed distaste at volunteers' attempts at identification with Indonesians. Marriage, for them, was confirmation that volunteers' loyalties were not primarily to Australia. Moreover, there was the White Australia Policy to consider. Back in Canberra, the Southeast Asian Section of the Department of External Affairs agreed. It wrote with concern about "the high proportion of women volunteer graduates who marry Indonesians." It went on: "Mixed marriages always create special problems and . . . I am not sure that we are doing the right thing by idealistic, rather unworldly, young women in officially sponsoring them to go to Indonesia to work under conditions peculiar to the volunteer graduate scheme."[9] The claim that interracial marriage inevitably led to "special problems" reflected broader Australian assumptions of an unbridgeable gulf between races and cultures that flourished under the White Australia Policy.

The gendered assumptions that young women were particularly vulnerable to romantic overtures by the "Other" also harked back to a long history of racism in Australia. David Walker has shown that invasion fiction often depicted women as weak spots by which Asian invaders infiltrated White Australia.[10] In making their decision, the Australian Embassy in Jakarta assumed that "on marriage . . . [Minogue] would be likely to accept the loyalties of her husband and that she is working for Indonesia for quite a different reason than when she was a volunteer graduate."[11] This was despite the fact that the two previous volunteers who had already married Indonesians had not undergone any apparent shift in loyalties; indeed, Ailsa Zainu'ddin and Thelma Rungkat held key administrative posts in the Volunteer Graduate Scheme for several years after their marriage.

Minogue's rejection also signaled a renewal of concern that Australians in Asia maintain a relatively high standard of living that reflected their "prestige"

[9] P. G. F. Henderson to Mr. Quinn, "Memo: Volunteer Graduate Scheme in Indonesia, 5 June 1959," NAA: A1838, 3034/10/20.

[10] David Walker, "Rising Suns," in Walker and Sobocinska, *Australia's Asia*, pp. 73–95; Walker, *Anxious Nation*, pp. 98–112.

[11] P. G. F. Henderson to Mr. Quinn, "Memo: Volunteer Graduate Scheme in Indonesia, 5 June 1959," NAA: A1838, 3034/10/20.

as members of the white race and Western civilization.[12] The Australian Embassy in Jakarta had long disagreed with volunteers' insistence on living at an Indonesian standard. In the debate surrounding Minogue's application it noted that "in Indonesia in particular some white wives of Indonesians have had very difficult times in the past."[13] This echoed a previous Immigration Department decision to refuse departure for a small number of women who had married Indonesians in Australia during the war. The Minister for Immigration, Arthur Calwell, forbade their departure because "life in a native village would be just unthinkable" for Australian women.[14] However, it was only unthinkable for white women: seven "Australian-born coloured" wives of Indonesians, along with their children, were allowed to depart for Java alongside their husbands.[15] Such government decisions marked longer Australian fears regarding the "prestige" of white women, resulting in additional levels of policing deployed in distinctly gendered ways.

The gendered nature of the government's discussion points to continued anxiety about racial miscegenation, which had long been a sensitive issue in Australia. The White Australia Policy was particularly concerned with policing interracial relationships, which were seen as a threat to the prestige and racial fitness of white Australia.[16] In 1952, the Australian Department of Immigration had passed a landmark decision allowing Japanese wives of Australian servicemen to migrate to Australia. This precedent led the Department of Defence to develop a policy of dissuading Australian servicemen serving in the region from marrying Asian women (although many such marriages took place nonetheless).[17] Immigration historian Gwenda Tavan has designated the mid-1950s as a period of "inching towards change."[18] Viewed in this broader context, the Minogue case becomes one of several avenues by which the Australian government attempted to regulate romantic and sexual relationships to maintain the boundaries of White Australia before the race-based immigration policy was finally repealed in 1973.

Yet, Minogue's status as a development volunteer differentiated her from the broader range of immigration cases. Disagreement over the nature of her work in Indonesia and her status relative to other Europeans points to continued ambiguity regarding not only the role of Australians in Asia but also the correct place of development work in international relations. While the

12 Sobocinska, *Visiting the Neighbours: Australians in Asia*, esp. pp. 15–31.

13 P. G. F. Henderson to Mr. Quinn, "Memo: Volunteer Graduate Scheme in Indonesia, 5 June 1959," NAA: A1838, 3034/10/20.

14 A. Calwell to E. J. Ward, April 18, 1947, NAA: A433, 1949/2/4823.

15 "Australian wives of Indonesians," NAA: A433, 1949/2/4823.

16 David Walker, *Anxious Nation*, pp. 181–94.

17 Mathew Radcliffe, "In Defence of White Australia: Discouraging 'Asian Marriage' in Postwar South-East Asia," *Australian Historical Studies* 45, no. 2 (2014): 184–201.

18 Tavan, *The Long, Slow Death of White Australia*, pp. 89–108.

Australian government approved and lauded the Volunteer Graduate Scheme's fraternal and humanitarian sentiments, it deemed romance and a genuine desire to accept aspects of Indonesian life and culture beyond the limit of acceptable engagement. This division was clearly demarcated after a direct appeal to the Minister for External Affairs. Richard Casey personally reviewed and intervened in Joan Minogue's case, pointing to a significant level of interest in the Volunteer Graduate Scheme. As a result of Casey's intervention, Minogue was permitted to return to Indonesia as a member of the Volunteer Graduate Scheme, but only if she promised to remain unmarried for at least a year and to resign upon her marriage. Effectively, Casey reinscribed the place of affect in Australian relations with Asia, limiting it at rhetorical fraternity and censuring genuine intertwining of Australian and Indonesian lives through marriage. This came despite continued protest from volunteers.

When she returned to Indonesia, Minogue faced a choice: to remain a development volunteer, retaining full identification with Australia, or to marry the man she loved. She chose the latter and married Hardjono only a couple of months later. Her marriage was considered an embarrassment by all parties: the Volunteer Graduate Scheme Executive Committee felt that going back on her word to Casey reflected badly on the scheme as a whole; the Australian government felt even more strongly that volunteering posed a threat to naïve young women. As it happened, Joan Hardjono remained in Indonesia for much of her life, working on economic and public policy issues at Universitas Padjadjaran until the 1990s. Her daughter, Ratih Hardjono, became a Presidential secretary to President Abdurrahman Wahid and a journalist at the influential news magazine *Kompas*. She also wrote an influential account of Australian–Indonesian relations.[19]

Volunteers' relations with Indonesians remained an open question into the 1960s. The Australian Embassy in Jakarta continued to rail against individual volunteers who were accused of pursuing relationships with Indonesians rather than Australians or other European expatriates. In late 1961, Pierre Hutton, an Australian Embassy official, summoned Herb Feith to a meeting that quickly became heated. Relaying the meeting to the Volunteer Graduate Scheme's Executive Committee, Feith recounted that "Pierre feels that [volunteers] go out of their way to have nothing to do with the embassy." While they were happy enough to collect their stipends, "they never think it worth their while to talk to the cultural attaches about Indonesian–Australian relations." With an intensity that Feith thought betrayed a surprising depth of emotion, Hutton had demanded, "Is it necessary for people to turn their backs on their own country in order to practice their belief in humanity?" Much like the expatriate

[19] Ratih Hardjono, *White Tribe of Asia: An Indonesian View of Australia* (Melbourne: Hyland House, 1994).

communities explored in the previous chapter, employees of the Australian Embassy in Jakarta lived at a remove from Indonesians. Volunteers were subjected to intense pressure to conform to expatriate mores. Rather than trying to blend into Indonesian society, Hutton demanded, "Why can't the relationship be as with the Peace Corps, whose members are proud to be Americans?" The mention of the Peace Corps, whose first volunteers had entered the field some six months prior (although none would arrive in Indonesia until 1963), pointed to the global context in which the Australian government was now crafting its expectations of volunteers. It also sharpened the belief that Australian volunteers were not performing the task of development volunteering adequately: as Hutton went on, he had become "against the whole scheme in its present form."[20] The Australian government wanted volunteers to be visibly and proudly Australian and they thought that volunteers' desire for close affective relationships with Indonesians compromised their Australianness. Although the Volunteer Graduate Scheme was premised on the notion that volunteers would learn the language, eat the local food and live in a way that mirrored that of Indonesians, Hutton's outburst was a reminder that there were boundaries beyond which a volunteer was considered at threat of "going native" and requiring reprimand. Emotional relationships with Indonesians, which it was feared diluted volunteers' attachment to Australia, lay beyond this boundary.

Springs of Love

The Minogue case had numerous parallels in both the British and American volunteer schemes. As the number of young Westerners serving overseas increased, so did the range and complexity of emotional entanglements. As we have seen, the Volunteer Graduate Scheme was the most progressive of the three volunteer agencies examined in this book. Voluntary Service Overseas and the Peace Corps were never openly supportive of crosscultural romance; unlike the Volunteer Graduate Scheme, they certainly did not regard marriage as a logical or desirable outcome of volunteering. Faced with a striking variety of interpersonal, crosscultural and often interracial relationships, sending agencies and governments attempted to regulate relationships to what they considered appropriate limits and sought ways to police the intimate contacts of volunteers abroad.

Britain's VSO echoed, and even amplified, the Volunteer Graduate Scheme's rhetoric that affect and emotion were a key aspect of development volunteering, but the rhetoric was divorced from realities on the ground. The program's founder, Alec Dickson, believed that foreign aid could only be effective if accompanied by an emotional investment from both donor and recipient. Where the Volunteer Graduate Scheme placed the stress on "identification,"

[20] Herb Feith to Jim Webb, November 16, 1961, NLA: MS 2601, Box 4, Folder 36.

Alec Dickson emphasized love as the emotional register of the VSO experience. Praising one of the earliest VSOs in Sarawak, Alec's wife Mora Dickson wrote that "it was not ultimately his talents or his character or his usefulness to those who asked for him that made the best kind of volunteer, though all these things were important, it was the openness of his heart in loving his fellows and accepting their affection in return." She believed that volunteers' youth was central to their capacity for emotional engagement, as they "were at an age when the springs of love still ran freely outside set channels responding eagerly to the warmth in others and this was their priceless qualification."[21] "Love" in this context meant platonic, brotherly love rather than the romantic variant, a fact considered so obvious that Dickson did not feel the need to define it explicitly. It was also strategically deployed. In the Dicksons' view, British hauteur towards "natives" was a major problem in the context of decolonization. In the future, postcolonial nations would be free to choose their relationships and the Dicksons feared they would cut their ties if Britons continued to act with imperial disdain. The Dicksons recognized that most white Britons felt themselves to be racially and culturally superior and they acknowledged that differences in education and temperament made crosscultural friendship unrealistic. For this reason, they placed their faith in young people: both because they thought that young Britons had not yet imbued the pervasive racism of their society and also because they held that their relative lack of sophistication mirrored that of people in "underdeveloped" nations.

This enhanced potential for "love" was the primary reason why VSO continued to send school-leaver "cadets" throughout the 1960s, even as their lack of skills came under sustained criticism. Chairman of the VSO Council Lord Amory wrote in 1964 that "the young person of 18–19 years is more uninhibited than the person of 21–22 years and, in certain situations, this can be of particular value in the making of friendships."[22] The Dicksons were entirely convinced that VSO was effective on these terms. Alec Dickson decreed VSO a spectacular success even before the first contingent had returned from their year abroad. The Manchester *Guardian* reported in 1959 that Dickson "describes what has been achieved as 'a breakthrough in human relations'."[23] In her study of VSO, Jordanna Bailkin agreed that "the crux of the VSO idea was not technical aid but international friendship," marked by "affective intimacy."[24]

Yet, on the ground, a more complex pattern emerged. As we saw in the previous chapter, volunteers' day-to-day lives were less affected by the

[21] Mora Dickson, *A Season in Sarawak* (London: Dennis Dobson, 1962), p. 192.

[22] "Confidential: Copy of a letter from Lord Amory dated 16th June, 1964 addressed to Sir Andrew Cohen about the future of the Cadet programme," VSO Archive, Box 31.

[23] "Schoolboy Recruits for Central Africa: Improving race relations," *The Guardian*, April 4, 1959, p. 3.

[24] Bailkin, *The Afterlife of Empire*, p. 74.

Dicksons' rhetoric than by the people to whom they were immediately responsible: supervisors in their immediate postings (often part of the colonial "old boy net"), British bureaucrats (locally at High Commissions or Embassies and through the Colonial Office or Commonwealth Relations Office) and the British Council, which took on in-country responsibilities as VSO's "overseas arm" from 1962. Local expatriate communities were also influential. All these groups monitored volunteers and provided advice about local conditions and how to manage them. Some commented or intervened if a volunteer was thought to be rubbing against the boundaries of appropriate conduct; some even reported "delinquent" volunteers to VSO or further up the chain of government. It was these audiences, as much as the Dicksons or VSO headquarters back in London, that really affected volunteers' lifestyles. In this context, "friendship" with locals took on a particular slant. The ideal volunteer was not one who built strong interpersonal relationships based on love, rather it was one who could appear to be an equal while in fact acting as a role model and a leader: someone who "had so identified himself with those around him that they fairly worshipped him."[25] This view took British superiority for granted and was premised on the belief that locals would immediately be charmed by any Briton's performance of equality.

Those volunteers who were suspected of falling outside of this paternalistic model of friendship were censured and sometimes punished. This was particularly true for volunteers who were visibly influenced by contact with locals, even if the influence was relatively trivial. A minor scandal erupted in 1959 when two VSOs in Malaya arrived at a diplomatic function dressed in sarongs: this was interpreted as "going native" and saw the volunteers reprimanded. Alec Dickson recounted the incident in 1960, dismissing it as an indiscretion that was blown out of proportion.[26] However, the fact that it *was* blown out of proportion is important in itself, revealing the distance between London's rhetoric and Kuala Lumpur's norms, by which even a trivial suggestion that volunteers had taken on some "native" ways was perceived as a threat to Britishness. As we have seen, an assumption of cultural superiority over the "backward" peoples of Asia, Africa and Latin America lay at the heart of development volunteering. One early account likened British volunteers in the developing world as akin to "a hothouse plant in a garden overgrown with weeds."[27] "Going native" invoked the possibility of the plant becoming degraded by contact with weeds; it had to be combated.

[25] House of Commons Debates, December 12, 1962, Vol. 669, cc423–81.

[26] "Voluntary Service Overseas: The Thomas Holland Memorial Lecture by Alec Dickson," *Christian Comment*, 17, March 1960, pp. 442–60.

[27] David Wainwright, *The Volunteers: The Story of Overseas Voluntary Service* (London: Macdonald, 1965).

As with the Australian Volunteer Graduate Scheme, the personal conduct of female volunteers was of particular concern to VSO. The behavior of young women was subject to multiple levels of scrutiny to ensure that personal relationships remained within permissible boundaries. Hints of romantic relationships formed between British volunteers and local men regularly surfaced and were inevitably interpreted not as a manifestation of "springs of love," but more critically through the prism of the girl's and Britain's reputation. In November 1961, VSO volunteer Heather Making was depicted as a representative globally minded young Briton in the English-language *Malay Mail.* In a flattering profile, the newspaper reported that she had "arrived in Malaya straight from school . . . to do [her] bit for the improvement of Commonwealth relations."[28] In this instance, Making was given prominence as a figurehead for Britain's desire for better postcolonial relations. Yet, at the same time, the diplomatic channels were full of chatter about her personal conduct. The Malayan High Commission in Kuala Lumpur wrote to the Office of the Deputy High Commissioner in Penang to report that "Miss Making is apparently having an affair with a Sikh whom she met on the boat on the way to Malaya." The High Commission thought that "this is entirely her affair if her relations with the Sikh are conducted outside the college" but "they do cause something of a sensation if they are extended onto the college premises, especially in a college for Malay girls where most of the pupils have been brought up in the traditions of Islam."[29] Making was never consulted about the alleged "affair" nor questioned as to whether she was indeed conducting it on school grounds. Instead, the British representatives in Kuala Lumpur decided that she should be removed from her post and moved to another school (with a British headmaster) at Kuala Kangsar. This removal was ordered despite the fact that colonial officials on the ground in Penang found it "difficult to imagine anything more unlikely than [the] allegations against Miss Making."[30]

As the Making case shows, even potentially baseless rumors about romantic encounters could result in a female volunteer being disciplined or removed from her post. The increased level of scrutiny experienced by young women rendered them more visible; moreover, their behavior was often taken as reflecting on other volunteers, or the entire British nation. As one colonial bureaucrat wrote about Malaya's first VSO contingent in 1961, "Most of the youngsters are doing well but the two girls . . . have caused a certain amount of difficulty," especially as "The more emancipated outlook of young western women has caused a clash with the two Headmistresses." The gossip surrounding these two "girl volunteers" saw the Deputy High Commission in Penang

[28] "Member of Peace Corps? Not me, says Heather. Voluntary Service Overseas started by UK before US thought of it," *The Malay Mail*, November 23, 1961, TNA: DO 163/22.

[29] A. J. Brown to J. R. Williams, November 1961, TNA: DO 163/22.

[30] J. R. Williams to A. J. Brown, December 4, 1961, TNA: DO 163/22.

decree that "the idea of putting VSOs into Malayan schools has not been a success so far."[31]

Voluntary Service Overseas was more direct when it came to romantic relationships that were serious enough to lead to marriage. In 1965, VSO released a rare statement regarding policy on interpersonal relationships within a longer set of practical instructions issued to British Council staff in overseas posts. It suggested that staff should warn volunteers against entering into an engagement during their postings, as "an unwise engagement may lead to repercussions which might affect the volunteer movement in that country."[32] Some volunteers kept their intimate relationships secret for fear of retribution or concealed them until after their return to Britain. Two examples serve to illustrate many more contained within letters in VSO's institutional archives. Ainslie Reeve, who worked for the Melanesian Mission in Bunana, Solomon Islands, forged a romantic relationship with a local man during her posting in 1964–5. The pair planned to marry and he left the Mission (which did not "'approve' of married folk on the staff") in anticipation of the wedding, but by then Reeve's posting was up and she had to return to England. Reeve concealed the relationship from VSO until, still desperate to return to the Solomon Islands three years later, she wrote to ask if there was any way they could send her back. As she explained, "the whole story of connected events is rather complicated . . . suffice it to say that the complication lies in the fact that I'm engaged to be married to a Melanesian." Perhaps unsurprisingly, VSO did not provide any assistance and Reeve wrote a final despondent letter in 1969 informing them that she had received news that her fiancé could not wait any longer and was going to marry a local girl instead.[33] Similarly, Roy Saffhill concealed his relationship with "a Eurasian girl, Bernadette," which had begun while he was a VSO in Singapore, until the couple were already married and living in Cambridge, far from any possible repercussions.[34]

The fact that volunteers concealed their romantic relationships points to some level of self-policing. Yet, volunteers were often less guarded about romances with other "Europeans" and, indeed, VSO rarely intervened in these cases – even when the suitor genuinely did appear inappropriate. Ruth Joy, posted to Georgetown in British Guiana, wrote to advise VSO that she had decided to marry Richardson, a Briton from a Bookers sugar plantation, immediately after he proposed in June 1965. The VSO representatives were surprised at her intention to marry right away, rather than waiting out the remaining month of her posting and marrying back in England. One VSO

[31] Ibid.

[32] Cited in Bird, *Never the Same Again*, p. 90.

[33] Ainslie Reeve to Mr. Carey, January 19, 1969, VSO Archive, microfiche files.

[34] Roy Saffhill to Chris Thomas, October 4, 1966, VSO Archive, microfiche files.

official noted that "it seems strange with only a month or so in it to marry away from home" and suggested "she be asked whether she is not asking her family to sacrifice what would no doubt be a great happiness to them." However, even this delicate suggestion was mooted by another VSO employee, who noted that "Miss Joy's husband to be has probably only recently been divorced – if it is the same man who she was alleged to be friendly with when I was in B. Guiana. This being so I think it might be more prudent to say nothing – particularly as she is now virtually out of our care & will be able to decide her future."[35]

That VSO intervened to curb volunteers' relationships with locals, but not with fellow Britons, shows that it was not romance per se that VSO took issue with, but specifically interracial and crosscultural intimacies. In determining Ruth Joy's relationship a private matter, in which she alone could "decide her future," VSO took a decidedly different approach than with Heather Making, whose alleged romance across national and racial lines was managed from London as an institutional matter. At least part of the reason lay in the potential for "going native." All three development volunteering programs explicitly negotiated this boundary, but the threat of "going native" was particularly powerful in the British context. Although the term did not come into common usage until Kipling's *Kim* was published in 1901, the concept was powerful from as early as the seventeenth century, expressing threats to European imperial power by putting into question the reliability of its own agents.[36] It also expressed fears that contact with the Other might engender a lowering of Western cultural norms or a pollution of the racial stock. This vexed context further compounded volunteers' tendency to turn to other volunteers, or members of the expatriate community, for friendship and romance. The intimacy and closeness of expatriate Europeans could serve to cut off contact between locals and volunteers.

Thus, while the Dicksons wrote of love as the essential ingredient of development volunteering, affective exchanges between British volunteers and the men and women they worked among were often a point of tension. In one of the many speeches and pamphlets Alec Dickson authored about the importance of affect, he made the important qualification that "there must be more not less direct relationship, if not person to person, at least of people to people."[37] This qualification is key, pointing to volunteers as embodiments of rhetorical collegiality and distant sympathy rather than direct and personal affective exchange. The ideal VSO friendship was one of categories not individuals: of white Britons cooperating on friendly terms with nonwhite "natives," rather than the variable and often messy emotional configurations

35 "Ruth Joy – Proposed Marriage," July 7, 1965, VSO Archive, microfiche files.

36 Linda Colley, "Going Native, Telling Tales: Captivity, Collaborations and Empire," *Past & Present*, 168, no. 1 (2000): 170–93.

37 Dickson, *A Chance to Serve*, p. 85.

of interpersonal communication. Some volunteers pursued friendships on these terms. In Papua New Guinea, for example, VSO Ruth Searle wrote that the "friendship of the [Papuan] girls is something I shall miss most of all … we're great friends, not individually, but en masse."[38] This category of friendship was functional, in that it helped boost the reputation of white Britons seemingly eager to do away with colonial-era prejudices, but it left little room for genuine personal relationships based on intimate connection.

Notably, VSO's management of intercultural and interracial intimacy can only be discerned through individual case studies, as revealed in volunteers' letters and diaries, as well as in British bureaucrats' attempts to manage these cases. Voluntary Service Overseas was loath to lay down coherent policy in relation to the personal and intimate relationships formed by its volunteers; the matter was never raised by the Executive Committee or its sub-branches in the course of the 1960s. This suggests that either VSO did not expect intimate contact between volunteers and "natives" to be widespread or commonplace enough to require preagreed principles, or that absolute flexibility was required to allow staff to deal with cases on an ad hoc basis. Significantly, both these scenarios ran counter to VSO's stated aims. In 1963, the Executive Committee restated the importance of the aim "to improve relations and break barriers in a multi-racial world by providing a field in which our young people may make friendships and widen sympathies."[39] However, little interest was ever actually shown in fostering these relationships on the ground. Instead, volunteers' behavior was policed by expatriate communities and bureaucrats working to a different model of intercultural contact. As with so many aspects of development volunteering, VSO was regarded, a priori, as a vehicle for goodwill and friendship. What actually happened on the ground had little bearing on this operational assumption.

Exemplary Conduct

The approach of the United States Peace Corps was very different to that of the Volunteer Graduate Scheme and VSO, reflecting both the increased professionalization and efficiency of its administration and also a greater recognition that young volunteers were likely to establish romantic and sexual relationships over the course of a two-year posting. Peace Corps staff in Washington devoted a great deal of time to devising detailed and prescriptive policy regulating the boundaries of appropriate personal behavior. The agency also posted Peace Corps Representatives – commonly known as Reps – to each host country to closely supervise and manage volunteers' personal conduct.

[38] Ruth Searle to Mr. Haig, June 8, 1965, VSO Archive, microfiche files.

[39] "Memorandum for Executive Committee Meeting to be held on Tuesday 1st October 1963," VSO Archive, Box 31.

The issues of sex, marriage and pregnancy were unusually consuming for the Peace Corps. As one Interim Policy Directive noted in June 1962, "Perhaps no question has been more discussed in the Peace Corps, both formally and informally, than that of an appropriate policy with respect to the marriage of volunteers during overseas service."[40] By the 1960s, sexual expression and some degree of experimentation were accepted parts of American youth culture.[41] In this context, the entire Peace Corps organization recognized that sending young people overseas would inevitably lead to sex and, in some cases, to marriage. However, in the early months and years, many genuinely believed that sex would be kept within the organization. In 1961, Shriver quipped that "Romance Blossoms" in the Peace Corps, with marriages between volunteers so common that "some people are calling us a romance agency." And, he continued, this was no bad thing: "it's probably the safest way you could possibly pick a mate. You can look at a girl and say, 'Here's somebody of good intelligence or she couldn't have passed the test'." He went on: she'd also be "in good physical shape," have passed strenuous psychological and psychiatric testing and even have an FBI clearance. "In normal life," he concluded, "you could not possibly know that much about a girl you were courting."[42] For many volunteers this worked perfectly. Peace Corps weddings were a regular feature of volunteer life. Despite fervent opposition from a small group of policymakers who feared that babies would soften the agency's image, Peace Corps Washington also changed its policy in 1962 to allow volunteers to have children and remain at their posts, as long as both mother and father returned to work soon after having their baby. The Returned Peace Corps Volunteer archive at the JFK Presidential Library holds the records and interviews of hundreds of former volunteers, and a striking number of those recount experiences of courtship with another volunteer followed by marriage, pregnancy and childbirth in the course of their posting.

The Peace Corps was far less enthusiastic about emotional and romantic entanglements between volunteers and "Host Country Nationals." In 1962, after fierce debate, Peace Corps Washington decided not to adopt a flat rule automatically terminating all volunteers who married host country nationals. "But," it warned, "the Peace Corps is aware – and expects each volunteer to be aware – of the very strong possibility that marriage to a non-volunteer may

[40] Interim Policy Directive 3.9, June 19, 1962, JFKL: RG 490, Microfilm NK-14, Roll 2 – Marriage Policy.

[41] Beth Bailey, *From Front Porch to Back Seat: Courtship in Twentieth-Century America* (Baltimore, MD: Johns Hopkins University Press, 1988). See also Beth Bailey, *Sex in the Heartland* (Cambridge, MA: Harvard University Press, 1999); John Modell, *Into One's Own: From Youth to Adulthood in the United States, 1920–1975* (Berkeley, CA: University of California Press, 1989).

[42] "Cupid a Member of Peace Corps," unattributed press clipping, 1961, JFKL: Papers of Sargent Shriver, Box 31.

create so many complications as to make termination of the volunteer's service desirable and necessary."[43] The decision whether to "terminate" a Peace Corps volunteer was left to the discretion of Peace Corps Reps. The path to marriage was not smooth. The policy read that a Rep "must satisfy himself that the volunteer's prospective spouse clearly understands and is fully prepared to act at all times in accordance with the principles of the Peace Corps and the volunteer's responsibilities to the host country and the Peace Corps." Reps were instructed to meet and evaluate a volunteer's prospective spouse and, if they did not personally object to the match, to commission a security screening from the US Embassy, order a comprehensive medical examination and undertake a full evaluation of financial means and family connections. Sometimes, couples had to undergo formal counseling before approval was considered. Financial regulations represented a further hurdle. In essence, a volunteer's spouse could be neither too rich nor too poor, and if they worked then their job had to be approved by the Peace Corps Rep. The Peace Corps forbade the organization supporting nonvolunteers and also forbade financial support from either the volunteer's or the local spouse's family. This meant that volunteers with a local spouse and a child could face real financial hardship trying to survive on a single volunteer's stipend. Finally, the volunteer had to satisfy the Rep that they "will continue to identify sufficiently with the United States to enable him or her to continue to serve effectively in that country" and, in the case of a female volunteer, demonstrate they were "fully aware of the general status of married women in the society she may be joining."[44]

As in other development volunteering programs, women came under additional pressures. Peace Corps policies were significantly gendered on paper and even more so in practice. Partly, this stemmed from the recognition that women's legal and citizenship status was thrown into question by marriage to a foreign national. However, gendered assumptions about women's porousness to foreign influence – encountered already in the Australian context – were also widespread in the United States. As the Sierra Leone Rep wrote to Shriver in 1962,

> in the case of a male Peace Corps Volunteer, there would be some assumption that he intended to retain his US citizenship and probably to return to the United States with his wife when his duty with the Peace Corps was finished. On the other hand, there would also be some assumption that a woman Peace Corps Volunteer married to a non-citizen might not intend to return to the United States. I wonder whether in such a case there might not be some dilution of her loyalties, perhaps a problem of

[43] Interim Policy Directive 3.9, June 19, 1962, JFKL: RG 490, Microfilm NK-14, Roll 2 – Marriage Policy.
[44] Ibid.

> cross-loyalties, which should be carefully considered in determining whether she would retain her ability and willingness to represent the United States as a Peace Corps Volunteer?[45]

The assumption that a woman's views and loyalties mirrored those of her husband blurred the line between the problem of loyalties and the problem of gender.

The idea that a volunteer, either male or female, had to remain visibly American was important for the Peace Corps. As we have seen, the concept of "going native" had a long genealogy in the colonial period that continued into the twentieth century. There was also a Cold War overlay: volunteers had to be identified with their home country if the campaign for "hearts and minds" was to convince host country nationals that capitalism offered a more attractive path than communism.

Having positioned their volunteers as representatives of the American nation and embodiments of Western modernity, the Peace Corps assumed that volunteers were under close observation by host country nationals. The first Peace Corps Rep in Peru wrote that "This fish-bowl or glass-house in which we all must exist for two years puts a special obligation on us all to be aware of appearance, manners and conduct at all times." Essentially, the Peace Corps demanded a renegotiation of the public and private spheres. As Sargent Shriver wrote, "the high visibility of PCVs in a host country makes it necessary for the Volunteer to realize that much of the behavior that might be considered in the private domain in the United States enters the public domain abroad. The reputation of our country and the good name of other Volunteers must always be kept foremost in mind."[46]

Sex was of particular concern: official policy stated that the Peace Corps "expects your sexual behavior to be exemplary at all times."[47] Policing of volunteers' sexual behavior was heavily gendered. The 1967 Peace Corps Training Center guide to the "Social Behavior of Volunteers" set out scenarios of "various types of social misconduct" as part of training for Reps heading into the field. One of the scenarios of "misconduct" involved a female volunteer allowing a local man to put his arm around her while they walked, setting local tongues wagging. In managing this situation, the manual suggested Reps would "tell her she must be sent home" and referred them to policies relating to Transfer, Resignation and Termination. Indeed, every one of the manual's scenarios involved a female volunteer and almost always came back to a smear of her perceived virtue. In effect, female volunteers' bodies were imprinted

45 Letter to Sargent Shriver, November 29, 1961, JFKL: RG 490, Microfilm NK-14, Roll 2 – Marriage Policy.

46 "Social Behavior of Volunteers," Peace Corps Training Center, January 1967. JFKL: RG 490, Box 25.

47 Ibid.

with national significance and the sullying of a woman's reputation – whether real or imputed – was seen as a genuine threat to the reputation of the United States.

In practice, the level of vigilance over women volunteers far exceeded that over men. Peter Lee, a Peace Corps volunteer in a small town near Bangkok in Thailand from 1965, considered visits to the local brothel a routine part of his work assignment as an English teacher at a boys' middle school. Only three days after his arrival, he accompanied several male teachers to the next town, where they drank for several hours before heading to the local brothels. As Lee recounted, at this point he "was so grateful" that this issue had been covered in training back in the United States. At the training session, men had been separated from female trainees and a returned volunteer gave what Lee called "the condom lecture" about prostitution. As he recalled, they were told that "you're gonna make the decision about whether you're going to be a prude about it and not go, in which case you will probably cut yourself off from male companionship, or whether you would just go: alright, alright." Like many male volunteers, Lee decided he was not "going to be a prude about it." However, Lee remembered that, in his cohort, a female trainee had been "terminated" from the Peace Corps because of "her sexual attitudes." Whether this referred to her perceived promiscuity or homosexuality was not clear – Lee had not noticed anything unusual about her – but even the rumor of either was reason enough for a woman to be immediately dropped from the program.[48]

Lee's experiences serve as a reminder that not all intimate encounters between volunteers and locals involved affect or emotion. As Stoler notes, concubinage and prostitution served colonial interests and became a well-known (though often denounced) element of imperial power.[49] The rise of American military bases further stimulated industrial-scale prostitution in Thailand and the Philippines at the same time as development volunteering emerged (Peter Lee's experience suggests that the Peace Corps contributed to this market).[50] Both were firmly premised on unequal power relations between European men and "native" women.[51] The Peace Corps' relative lack of policing of male volunteers' encounters with prostitutes is firmly linked to this longer genealogy of Western power. It also suggests that the Peace Corps wasn't vexed by the fact that volunteers were sexually active, but rather by the

[48] Oral history interview with Peter Lee, August 4, 2004, JFKL: RPCV-MR-2005–103-006.

[49] Stoler, *Carnal Knowledge and Imperial Power.*

[50] Cynthia Enloe, *Bananas, Beaches and Bases: Making Feminist Sense of International Politics* (Berkeley, CA: University of California Press, 1990); Thanh-Dam Truong, *Sex, Money and Morality: Prostitution and Tourism in Southeast Asia* (London: Zed Books, 1990). See also Katharine H. S. Moon, *Sex Among Allies: Military Prostitution in U.S. Korea Relations* (New York: Columbia University Press, 1997).

[51] Stoler, *Carnal Knowledge and Imperial Power*, pp. 47–51.

potential for divided loyalties and, more acutely, the potential for a smear on America's reputation, both of which were perceived disproportionately in women volunteers' conduct.

The gender disparity was also clear in policy on pregnancies resulting from a volunteer's relationship with a Host Country National. There was only one course of action for an unmarried female volunteer who fell pregnant: she must immediately be "terminated" and repatriated to Washington, so that "the Peace Corps can ensure that the Volunteer can consider fully and privately what next to do."[52] The fact that remaining in-country and continuing her relationship with the baby's father was not an option suggests that the Peace Corps was less concerned with the volunteer's wellbeing than with the potential for scandal in the community. This consideration also framed policy for male volunteers who impregnated a local woman but, in this scenario, Reps were encouraged to be far more accommodating to the couple's wishes – after all, the appearance of a volunteer abandoning a pregnant woman might cause a greater scandal than if he stayed. The wider range of options allowed male volunteers to continue in the Peace Corps, either in the same assignment or following transfer to a new country. As Director Jack Hood Vaughn explained to Reps in 1966, the main consideration was that "the Volunteer usually should not leave the host country until he has appropriately fulfilled or made arrangements to fulfill any financial and other responsibilities he may have to the mother and child."[53] Policy relating to pregnancy was formulated primarily to maintain the good reputation of the Peace Corps and the United States. In this, it was openly gendered – as one policy document stated, "it might make a difference if the PCV is male or female" – with the implicit moral judgment that an unwed pregnancy irreparably compromised a woman's reputation, whereas a male volunteer could return to work so long as his financial obligations were met.[54]

The extent of surveillance created a fraught terrain in which volunteers maneuvered in the space between Peace Corps policy and the reality of day-to-day life. Marriages between Peace Corps volunteers and host country nationals did eventuate despite the administrative hurdles, and despite the social barriers to intimate encounters explored in the previous chapter. More common was a kaleidoscopic range of romantic and sexual encounters that fell short of marriage, in which American sexual norms negotiated with local mores and in which volunteers' desire to protect personal reputations and national prestige came into tension with a heady emotional cocktail of loneliness and desire.

52 "Social Behavior," Peace Corps Handbook, July 1, 1966, JFKL: RG 490, Box 25.

53 Jack Vaughn to all Peace Corps Representatives, July 5, 1966, JFKL: RG 490, Box 25.

54 "Social Behavior of Volunteers," Peace Corps Training Center, Washington, January 1967. JFKL: RG 490, Box 25.

We can see this play out in the experience of Elinor Dobbins, known as E. V., who was among the first contingent of Peace Corps volunteers to arrive in the Philippines in 1961. Originally from Champaign, Illinois, Dobbins worked as an educational aide in the small beach town of Mayabon on the south coast of Negros Oriental. Living with three other female volunteers, she soon began to desire male company and confessed that "I'm getting a little horny after only four months in the field."[55] Dobbins' diary, a record of her first eight months in the Philippines, provides an insight into how volunteers balanced their own desires with strict Peace Corps regulations. It also allows us to recognize the crosscultural tensions inherent to volunteers' intimate relationships. For Dobbins, negotiating romance with Filipino men proved a minefield as her expectations – shaped by American norms of dating and low-key sexual experimentation – came into conflict with Filipino customs, by which even a social call could be imbued with greater meaning. She confided in her diary that her first experience of hosting "male callers" resulted in a "talk" from her housekeeper, who warned her that "apparently 1 of last night's visitors is father of illegitimate baby. Whole town knows of his visit & is concerned about us."[56] Undeterred, Dobbins kept up a steady stream of flirtations with several of the town's young men, who took to serenading outside her house most evenings. She went on informal outings and formal "dates" out to the movies, often arranging to meet "on the road past the market so people wouldn't talk." Particular favorites were invited for moonlight walks along the beach.[57]

Dobbins was well aware that gossip could lead to repercussions including termination from the Peace Corps. However, she preferred to think of her affairs as furthering intercultural understanding and therefore in line with the Peace Corps' aims. Her first flirtation ended after she decided it was "not fair of me to encourage him" as "Cultural expectations are so different."[58] A couple of weeks later, Dobbins had a new suitor, Victor Valasco, with whom she "enjoyed flirting but am in a culture conflict because Amer. reactions to me are not Fil. reactions." She found Victor physically attractive, but the relationship ended after he became drunk and "very emotional": as she scribbled in her diary, he was "demanding & told me he loved me & I told him he was crazy." What was just a date for Dobbins had been interpreted as something more by a Filipino suitor unaccustomed to American cultural norms. As she reflected, "To these boys a kiss means so much more than in the States. I think that they think love & physical attraction are the same so when they are attracted they think they are in love."[59] Enraged by Dobbins' rejection, Valasco and some

55 Elinor Dobbins to Alex Veech, undated 1961, in Papers of Elinor Capehart, JFKL: RPCV, Box 102.

56 Diary entry, December 27, 1961, Papers of Elinor Capehart, JFKL: RPCV, Box 102.

57 Diary entry, January 21, 1962, Papers of Elinor Capehart, JFKL: RPCV, Box 102.

58 Ibid.

59 Diary entry, March 3, 1962, Papers of Elinor Capehart, JFKL: RPCV, Box 102.

friends became "cocky & obnoxious & when they left they took their empty gin bottle with them & proceeded to throw it at the policeman as they sped by." As always, this drama played to an eager audience: "the whole town was mad, not at us – they were anxious to protect us, but at the guys actions [*sic*]."[60]

Having gone through twelve weeks of intensive training and always aware that the town was watching, Dobbins was initially careful for her reputation and that of her fellow volunteers. Her first reaction when housemate Arlene told her she had almost ended a date with a kiss was "I can imagine the scandal."[61] But as she became increasingly lonely and plagued by doubts about the value of her posting, Dobbins sought solace in romance. She wrote that she "could use a little loving" and wanted "to get back into social circulation ... with the ultimate desire being marriage."[62] By the time Arlene had her first Filipino kiss, Dobbins reported it as a "Momentous occasion ... one cultural barrier kicked down."[63] Her own momentous occasion wasn't far behind: even though "I fear there was an audience, as usual," she soon shared a kiss with another suitor, Marcial, "my first in 18 weeks."[64] Dobbins' loneliness and sexual frustration kept building and when in June she met twenty-one-year-old Adolfo, their relationship quickly became physical. Her diary entry that night speaks to the satisfaction of romance, but also to the cultural differences encoded in their first kiss:

> It's very nice to be kissed again but I didn't realize how much making love is a cultural thing. Adolfo is 21 and I was the first girl he had kissed. My long nose bothered him a bit and he lacks sophistication in his style, but what got me was that he told me to lie down on the beach – I told him he was crazy – as soon as we arrived and his hands kept going to my breasts & butt: not exactly as I remember my first kiss. And he told me before that he loved me and there was no other girl for him [but] I have to keep explaining – for me it lacks a lot.[65]

By now, Dobbins' dalliances were common knowledge and she wrote nonchalantly that these nocturnal "beach activities were observed by all our body guards."[66]

Dobbins' relationships, recorded in a private diary, never came to the attention of the Peace Corps Rep in the Philippines. Indeed, despite the considerable gossip generated among the denizens of Mayabon, the official record presented a glorious (and glorified) picture of Dobbins' volunteer

60 Diary entry, February 16, 1962, Papers of Elinor Capehart, JFKL: RPCV, Box 102.
61 Diary entry, March 3, 1962, Papers of Elinor Capehart, JFKL: RPCV, Box 102.
62 Diary entries, March 11 and April 7, 1962, Papers of Elinor Capehart, JFKL: RPCV, Box 102.
63 Diary entry, March 13, 1962, Papers of Elinor Capehart, JFKL: RPCV, Box 102.
64 Diary entry, April 14, 1962, Papers of Elinor Capehart, JFKL: RPCV, Box 102.
65 Diary entry, June 24, 1962, Papers of Elinor Capehart, JFKL: RPCV, Box 102.
66 Diary entry, April 20, 1962, Papers of Elinor Capehart, JFKL: RPCV, Box 102.

placement as a symbol of American beneficence. Around the time Dobbins was anticipating her first kiss, her hometown paper reported that she and her housemates had collected 156 books towards a municipal library and were now being feted as "four daughters of Uncle Sam whose deed will never fade from the minds of the people of Zamboanguita."[67] Dobbins' return home also attracted considerable local publicity and she became sought after for talks at local high schools and civic clubs.[68] Far from being punished for her contravention of Peace Corps' expectations of exemplary sexual conduct, Dobbins went on to a prestigious internship at the Eleanor Roosevelt Memorial Foundation.[69]

While heterosexual volunteers such as E. V. Dobbins could inhabit the space between the Peace Corps' insistence on "exemplary" social behavior and their own desires, the options were far more limited for those who were same-sex attracted. Homosexuals could not be hired by the US government under an Eisenhower-era Executive Order, still in force during the 1960s, and the Peace Corps actively adhered to the law. The Peace Corps included an inquiry into "a history of homosexual behavior" as part of the background checks performed on each prospective volunteer and psychiatrists kept an eye out for "homosexual tendencies" during training. In-country, the surveillance was continued by the Peace Corps Rep. The policy was unequivocal: "in any case, a volunteer who attempts to or does participate in even a single act of homosexual behavior should be sent to Washington" and, as the volunteer might become "upset and/or unstable," they "must be accompanied home by the Peace Corps Physician." Most volunteers were given a medical termination, but "if this behavior is part of a life-long pattern, however, the PCV is usually not eligible for Peace Corps-sponsored care; and in this case, he might be given an administrative termination." Even the rumor of homosexuality was enough to get a volunteer terminated. As a 1966 memo noted, whether there was any truth to a report was immaterial as "the rumors are damaging the effectiveness of the Volunteer whether they are true or not." The risk was to America's reputation: "To ignore the problem is impossible; it has the potential of becoming a cause celebre."[70] While those who were same-sex attracted were most severely affected, even heterosexual volunteers were alarmed by the severity of the Peace Corps'

67 "Miss Dobbins Gives Books," *Champaign-Urbana Courier*, May 3, 1962, p. 3.

68 Vern Richey, "Elinor Dobbins, Home from Duty in Peace Corps, Evaluates Work," *Champaign-Urbana Courier*, August 25, 1963; Nancy Allison, "Miss Dobbins, PC Veteran, Aids 2 Former Students," *News-Gazette* (Champaign), undated *c.*1963 in Papers of Elinor Capehart, JFKL: RPCV, Box 102.

69 "Miss Dobbins is awarded Fellowship," undated *c.*1963 in Papers of Elinor Capehart, JFKL: RPCV, Box 102.

70 "Memo to all PCVs from Peace Corps Physician and Peace Corps Director," January 13, 1966; "Social Behavior of Volunteers," Peace Corps Training Center, Washington, January 1967, both in JFKL: RG 490, Box 25. Emphasis in original.

policies. Robert Newman, a Peace Corps volunteer in India from 1964, recalled that "it would really make me sweat" when male Indian friends reached out to hold his hand. After several months in India, "I knew well, damn-well that they weren't homosexuals and I understood mentally that this was just their custom." But "It was so difficult, I was looking around thinking 'If any American sees me I am dead'."[71] Although he may not have been literally dead, Peace Corps policy on homosexuality meant he would almost certainly have been terminated.

A similar fear of scandal led development volunteering agencies to paper over incidences of sexual harassment, sexual assault and rape, resulting in considerable distress for volunteers who were sexually abused in the course of their overseas posting. Nonconsensual sexual activity was a perennial issue for development volunteering programs, but the scale of the problem was not revealed until the 1990s in the case of the Peace Corps and even later for VSO and Australian volunteer programs. Throughout the early decades, agencies preferred to ignore sexual assault altogether; the issue is conspicuously absent in the official records of all three agencies. Female volunteers later recounted that they felt discouraged from reporting sexual harassment or assault; presumably, instances that were reported were quickly dealt with by in-country staff eager to avoid a scandal.[72] Instances of serious sexual assault that were reported in the press could not be ignored; in those cases, they were routinely understated, or even dismissed, by volunteer agencies. In June 1971, the VSO Executive Committee met to discuss the gang rape of VSO nurses in Zambia, which had been brutal enough to attract coverage in the British press. These reports were "very exaggerated," the meeting's minutes declared, as "the nurses concerned were not seriously harmed, and returned to work in three days."[73] The Zambian assault had come just weeks after the rape and murder of another VSO volunteer, Sandra Smith, in Papua New Guinea. In that instance, a full investigation into the case was abandoned after VSO was assured that the perpetrator was "sub-normal and will probably be under long-term protective custody."[74] In both cases, no further action was taken or recommended; comprehensive policies on responding to sexual assault would not be devised

[71] Interview with Robert S. Newman, 1994, JFKL: RPCV Collection, Box 92.

[72] Elizabeth Z. Johnk, "Peace Corps Culture and the Language of Violence: A Feminist Discursive Analysis" (MA thesis, Eastern Michigan University, 2016). See also Sheryl Gay Stolberg, "Peace Corps Volunteers Speak Out on Rape," *New York Times*, May 10, 2011, www.nytimes.com/2011/05/11/us/11corps.html, accessed February 4, 2020; Celeste Hicks, "I was raped and my counsellor asked me what I had been wearing," *The Guardian*, April 1, 2016, www.theguardian.com/global-development-professionals-network/2016/mar/31/i-was-raped-and-my-counsellor-asked-me-what-i-had-been-wearing, accessed February 4, 2020.

[73] Minutes of VSO Executive Committee meeting, June 1, 1971, VSO Archive, Box 31.

[74] Minutes of VSO Executive Committee meeting, May 4, 1971, VSO Archive, Box 31.

for decades to come. The goal of protecting the nation's reputation, by hushing up a potential scandal, was privileged over the physical and psychological needs of women, some of whom were ushered back to work just days after suffering a serious sexual assault, while others were dismissed from posts and sent home with little follow-up care.[75]

The Limits of Affect

This chapter has mapped the affective regimes that accompanied young volunteers to the Global South during the 1950s and 1960s. Despite rhetoric that emphasized crosscultural engagement, volunteer agencies and sponsoring governments were often challenged by the reality of young Australians, Britons and Americans becoming intimately involved – both emotionally and physically – with the people they worked among. From the mid-1950s, policies and regulations attempted to delineate the boundaries of correct emotional relations between volunteers and host communities. The emotional registers of humanitarianism and internationalism – empathy, identification and cooperation – were praised and rewarded, but only to a point. Identification was routinely stymied before it could become "going native," especially when romance was involved and especially for women.

The three volunteer programs and their sponsoring nations responded to the question of intercultural intimacy in slightly different ways. Australia's Volunteer Graduate Scheme was strongly supportive of affective and romantic relationships between Australian volunteers and Indonesians, believing that these were the "best way of showing we mean this identification business." But the Australian government – and particularly the Embassy in Jakarta – disagreed, holding that such relationships lowered Australia's "prestige" in Indonesia and threatened racial miscegenation in the context of the White Australia Policy. Britain's VSO marked a high point of affective rhetoric, but, in reality, relationships that were thought to threaten a volunteer's reputation were strictly policed. British volunteers were also pressured to conform to the norms of the expatriate communities to which they were preferentially posted well into the 1960s, many of which maintained strict social divisions between "Europeans" and "natives." Where VSO preferred to operate on an ad hoc basis, the Peace Corps devoted countless hours to debating and devising policy that appeared consistent with its promise of international friendship, while still discouraging volunteers from entering into relations that could threaten either

[75] Anna Schecter and Brian Ross, "Peace Corps Gang Rape: Volunteer Says U.S. Agency Ignored Warnings," *ABC News*, January 13, 2011, https://abcnews.go.com/Blotter/peace-corps-gang-rape-volunteer-jess-smochek-us/story?id=12599341, accessed January 25, 2020.

their national loyalties or their own – and by extension their nation's – reputations.

However, the similarities between the programs are greater than their differences. Attitudes and responses were strongly gendered, with additional levels of concern raised when a female volunteer became intimately involved with a local man. Imprinted by long genealogies of colonial sexual exploitation of non-European women, male volunteers' sexual and intimate relationships with locals were often treated differently to those of female counterparts. The Australian government, which responded so strongly to Joan Minogue's intention to marry Hardjono, barely raised a whimper when two male volunteers married Indonesian women within a month in 1963. While VSO removed Heather Making from her role at a Malaysian girls' school in 1965 following a rumored romance with a Sikh, it did not even register a response to John Rogers' letter of the same year bragging that "One of the girls, with shapely figure and twinkling eye, has invited me to stay in her longhouse in the holiday" and that "I have accepted with alacrity."[76] And the Peace Corps, which trained Reps to reprimand or even terminate a female volunteer for "misdemeanors" as minor as allowing a local man to put his arm around her, turned a blind eye to male volunteers' regular patronage of brothels. This imbalance was partly justified by the legal implications of women potentially losing their citizenship upon marriage to a local man. However, this policing was tied to a longer history by which women were seen as weak spots allowing the infiltration of foreign power and in need of paternal protection from the Other. It was also linked to deep-seated fears of racial miscegenation, which remained significant during the 1950s and 1960s across all three nations.

The surveillance of volunteers' relationships mirrored the social policing of intimate behavior that attended European colonialism in Asia and Africa. As Ann Laura Stoler has argued, the discursive management of the sexual practices of colonizer and colonized was fundamental to the colonial order of things.[77] In the colonial case, prescribing and proscribing certain sexual and intimate relationships served to clarify the boundaries between the colonizer and the colonized and thus perpetuate the imperial system of rule. Systemic attempts by all three volunteer programs to determine the boundaries of acceptable conduct, and to police the behavior of volunteers who transgressed those boundaries, suggests that a similar process took place even as volunteer programs' rhetoric portrayed them as the vanguard of postcolonial progress.

On the ground, volunteers from all three programs had to negotiate the fraught space between their own desires, their program's policies and the norms of local and expatriate communities. It is hardly surprising that, in

[76] John Rogers to Miss Green, July 22, 1965, VSO Archive, microfiche files.

[77] Ann Laura Stoler, *Race and the Education of Desire: Foucault's History of Sexuality and the Colonial Order of Things* (Durham, NC: Duke University Press, 1995).

this context, many volunteers preferred to socialize together, as described in the previous chapter. Forming intimate relationships with other volunteers limited the potential for crosscultural conflicts such as those experienced by E. V. Dobbins; it also had the additional benefit of bypassing the town's rumor mill (and so limiting the potential of drawing the attention of inquisitive diplomats or the local volunteer Rep). By the mid-1960s, intra- and interprogram relationships became increasingly common as the number of Western volunteers surged across Asia, Africa and Latin America. Yet, intimate relationships with locals, including sincere and loving marriages, point to the fact that some volunteers transcended the affective boundaries set by sending organizations and governments, as well as the social policing of expatriate communities and, often, the judgment of fellow volunteers.

This chapter has begun to tease out the tensions between micro-level interactions, often involving complex emotional landscapes, and the broader frames of international relations. It helps clarify the quotidian operation of the humanitarian-development complex, which was a mixed economy depending on the close cooperation of ordinary people, NGOs and governments. It serves as a reminder that humanitarianism and international development were always enacted through countless micro-interactions across boundaries of nation, culture and race. Some of those interactions were intimate and forged as a result of personal attraction, friendship and romance. Others were not so positive: as the next chapter shows, the volunteer encounter was also fraught with tension and conflict, which had a political as well as a personal edge.

9

Resistance

Although volunteer agencies' rhetoric emphasized international friendship, in reality volunteers often faced a wealth of conflicts in their daily lives. This chapter explores conflict at both interpersonal and international levels. Many volunteers faced suspicion and enmity in communities suffering the legacies of European colonialism and confronting American neoimperialism. Some host communities regarded volunteers as spies or government agents; others merely resented inexperienced foreigners claiming to hold the key to their development or who professed egalitarian ideals whilst living in relative luxury. In numerous cases, volunteers became entangled in broader conflicts between nations, blocs and ideologies, and in the divisions between East and West, First World and Third World. As a result, the day-to-day experience of numerous development volunteers was marked by tense encounters ranging from minor slights to violent conflict.

Resentment and tension also found direct political expression. As we saw in Chapter 6, the news media in many receiving nations was ambivalent about the arrival of development volunteers. The same reservations that motivated negative press coverage found expression in political pamphlets published across the Global South, which circulated within and between nations as diverse as Indonesia, Nigeria and Ceylon (Sri Lanka from 1972). They also stirred popular resistance. Among the first major expressions of popular hostility to development volunteering was the large protest at Ibadan in Nigeria that followed the Margery Michelmore postcard incident described in Chapter 6. In its wake came dozens more protests that grew in number and intensity during the 1960s and into the 1970s. From Bandung to Lagos, from Colombo to La Paz, ordinary people took to the streets to vent their anger at the cultural and economic intervention of Western volunteers. As the largest and most heavily publicized program and one that was part of the United States government, the Peace Corps drew the largest share of the public's hostility. But British and Australian volunteers were not immune from conflict that was simultaneously interpersonal and international.

"Official Propaganda and Minor Humiliations"

Australia's Volunteer Graduate Scheme was the first to venture the development volunteering model and, of all the programs explored in this book, it came closest to reaching the ideal of volunteers living at a "local" standard (volunteers were paid by the Indonesian government at standardized public service remuneration rates). Even so, the warm welcome accorded volunteers in the early 1950s began to wear thin over the course of the decade. By 1960, members of the Volunteer Graduate Scheme were debating the program's continued viability in the face of official and popular opposition. Even before the Peace Corps had been established, Australian volunteers already questioned the value of development volunteering, worn down by unrelenting personal misunderstandings and professional resentments.

As we saw in this book's earlier chapters, the Volunteer Graduate Scheme enjoyed high-level support in Indonesia. President Sukarno expressed his personal enthusiasm for the scheme and in one speech Indonesian Ambassador to Australia Dr. R. H. Tirtawinata enthused that "nothing which has been done to help my country in the eleven years since we gained our independence, has so appealed to the hearts and minds of my countrymen as the graduate employment scheme."[1] As Chapter 6 illustrated, the Indonesian media coverage of the Volunteer Graduate Scheme in the 1950s was limited but positive and, as the previous chapter revealed, some volunteers built meaningful personal relationships with individual Indonesians. Even so, volunteers encountered significant resistance. Some of this resistance stemmed from the close relationship between the Volunteer Graduate Scheme and organized Christianity. Religion aside, volunteers came under increasing scrutiny as Indonesia's relations with Australia deteriorated from the mid-1950s. Public opinion of Australia in Indonesia, and vice versa, plummeted.[2] Nationalism and xenophobia found fertile soil amid Indonesia's ongoing political and economic crises and runaway inflation.[3] In this context, Indonesian support for schemes encouraging international cooperation, including the Volunteer Graduate Scheme, began to wane.

The shifting political climate added to existing tensions in volunteers' day-to-day relations with Indonesian colleagues and neighbors. By 1960, the situation had grown so grave that the Executive Committee instigated an internal review. Every current and former volunteer was asked to report whether it was "possible for Volunteer Graduates to do useful work" in an increasingly hostile environment. Strictly confidential and in-house, the review provided a space for volunteers to discuss the realities of life as a volunteer. The optimistic tone usually cultivated by the Volunteer Graduate Scheme fell away as volunteers traded

1 "Lemonade with the President," *Djembatan*, Vol. 1, no. 1, July 1957; Speech delivered by His Excellency Dr. R. H. Tirtawinata to the Volunteer Graduate Scheme Conference, August 23, 1956, NLA: MS 2601, Box 2, Folder 21.

2 Sobocinska, "Measuring or Creating Attitudes?"

3 Feith and Castles, *Indonesian Political Thinking, 1945–1965*, pp. 154–77, 342–54. See also Taomo Zhou, *Migration in the Time of Revolution: China, Indonesia, and the Cold War* (Ithaca, NY: Cornell University Press, 2019).

stories of the ambivalent reception they had faced. Many reported that it was difficult to convince neighbors and coworkers that they harbored no ulterior motives. Jakarta-based volunteers Hugh O'Neill and John Gare argued that "Such things as Mr. Tirtawinata's heart-warming speech, for example, might be better left out ... Each new recruit should be told that the people he or she works with are almost certain never to have heard of the VGS and will probably take a lot of convincing." Ian Doig, who had volunteered during the so-called "Golden Age" of the mid-1950s, wrote that, even then, Indonesians had been "very skeptical about a European being prepared to accept their standard of living," and even his closest friends had assumed he received additional pay. Writing from Medan in Sumatra, Elaine Wills noted that her boss "doesn't really believe that I am not subsidised in Australia or in some other way." Even Ailsa Zainu'ddin, a member of the Volunteer Graduate Scheme Executive Committee and one of the program's most optimistic advocates, had to admit that "the gesture of equal pay is pointless if nobody at all believes it is being made." Those who were able to be convinced that volunteers received Indonesian rates of pay were not necessarily impressed. Two volunteers recently returned from teaching in South Kalimantan wrote that their superiors had been "under the impression that [volunteers] sought employment under the scheme because they were not good enough to get jobs in their own country" and that this had led to their being treated as "second-rate experts."[4]

The climate of suspicion affected volunteers personally. The best-case scenario, it seems, was being "regarded as a crazy idealist and an oddity." For many, the situation was far worse. Marcus Bull, a chemist working at the Industrial Research Institute in Jakarta, commented that, although not universal, "attitudes of hostility and indifference are hard to take and leave an impression." Teacher Elaine Wills complained that, far from being welcoming, "some officials are unfriendly, uncooperative, ungrateful." Volunteer doctor Ray Mylius confessed that "one often feels uncomfortable under the barrage of official propaganda and minor humiliations and inclined to take the government at its word – and leave." Another doctor, Keith Lethlean, suspected that Indonesia's Department of Health actively sought to sabotage his work; as he phrased it, "if the Indonesian Government ever felt welcoming toward me I was never aware of it." This view was sometimes offset by the belief that, in most fields "there are people ... who are prepared to put up with a few foreigners for the sake of the work they get out of them if not for anything else." As university lecturer Eric Campbell noted, "it is possible that Indonesians only tolerate the scheme – like all foreign aid schemes – because they want cheap experts at their present stage of development and it is difficult diplomatically to refuse such a Scheme."[5]

4 Review of Volunteer Graduate Scheme, 1960, NLA: MS 2601, Box 14.

5 Ibid.

Suspicion of Australian volunteers was folded into a growing opposition to foreigners in postcolonial Indonesia. Sukarno's response to internal crisis was to escalate nationalist rhetoric that pitted indigenous Indonesian *pribumi* against others. In late 1957, Dutch colonists who had remained after independence were expelled and their property was nationalized. Measures targeting the Chinese minority forced long-term residents to flee or to Indonesianize their names and identities. The anti-foreigner sentiment also affected volunteers, who noted "an increasingly reserved attitude towards not only Dutch, but also other foreigners, including Australians, Americans, Europeans and of course Chinese." Doctors Ray Mylius and Ken Bailey admitted that "situations have arisen where our foreignness has appeared to be an embarrassment" and suggested that, in the atmosphere of self-sufficiency enveloping Indonesia, the best thing for Australian volunteers would be "withdrawing from the field."[6]

Deteriorating economic conditions brought new obstacles. From 1958, a shortage of hard currency led the government to impose a hiring freeze in the civil service. The hiring freeze represented an existential problem for the Volunteer Graduate Scheme, as volunteers were employed as public servants and paid by the Indonesian government. The Volunteer Graduate Scheme's Executive Committee held protracted discussions about the program's viability amidst the rising "'anti-foreign' attitude."[7] Finding suitable accommodation also became a problem. Political and economic instability drove hundreds of thousands of internal migrants to Jakarta, resulting in a severe housing shortage as the population tripled in ten years. The government could no longer provide housing for volunteers and private families were often unwilling to accept foreigners as tenants. Ian Doig wrote that, "For one thing, Indonesians usually want all the space they can get, with up to twenty people crowded into an ordinary house."[8] Those who managed to secure lodging struggled to pay for daily necessities. With inflation escalating, civil service salaries were barely enough to keep food on the table. By early 1962, the Volunteer Graduate Scheme reported that commodity shortages and soaring prices had made nutrition a critical issue and recommended that arriving volunteers bring stores of powdered milk, tinned cheese and dried fruit from Australia to supplement their Indonesian diets.[9]

The internal review reached no firm conclusions and over the next five years a handful of Australian volunteers trickled into Indonesia. But Indonesian resentment continued to grow and volunteers became increasingly disheartened. In 1960, the Melbourne University student magazine *Farrago* wrote an

[6] Ibid.
[7] Ibid.
[8] Ian Doig to Donald Hindley, April 28, 1959, NLA: MS 2601, Box 1, Folder 4.
[9] Jim Webb, "Report: Volunteer Graduate Association for Indonesia – Visit to Indonesia, 12 December 1961 to 4 January 1962," NLA: MS 2601, Box 3, Folder 31.

exposé on the Volunteer Graduate Scheme. "The name has an aura of adventure, good will, sacrificial giving; of friendship with Australia's near neighbour Indonesia," the article began, but "now conditions have changed and some of the volunteer graduates I met were disillusioned and underfed." Rather than devoting their energy to Indonesia's development and cross-cultural friendship, "They were preoccupied with their day-to-day needs and making the best of a bad situation until it is time to return to Australia."[10] Tough conditions and growing opposition, at both official and grassroots levels, squeezed the Volunteer Graduate Scheme out of existence. The trickle of volunteers to Indonesia slowed from the early 1960s and the Volunteer Graduate Scheme was finally folded into larger Australian programs, modeled on the Peace Corps, in 1969.

Blackboard Jungles

Many of the pressures experienced by Australian volunteers in Indonesia during the 1950s were replicated across the Global South following the launch of VSO and the Peace Corps. Although pervasive in the West, the rhetoric of volunteering as an apolitical expression of youthful altruism was not always persuasive in the Global South. During the peak years of decolonization in the 1960s, British volunteers were sometimes regarded as latter-day manifestations of colonialism and American volunteers were viewed as the vanguard of a new form of imperialism that was less concerned with political and territorial sovereignty than with economic and cultural domination.

Both VSO and the Peace Corps placed the largest number of volunteers as teachers and schools became key sites of conflict between Western volunteers and host communities. Students and youth had long been active in African anticolonial politics. In Ghana, for instance, school strikes and organized forms of disciplinary breakdown were favored forms of anticolonial resistance and this continued into the early postcolonial years.[11] Britain's VSO was the first Western development volunteering program to discover that volunteer teachers were not always welcome in African schools and that students did not always see a distinction between well-meaning volunteers and the contract teachers of colonial education systems. In 1960, Governor of Northern Rhodesia Evelyn Hone demanded VSO stop sending teenage school-leavers as volunteer teachers. Volunteers without teaching qualifications were useless, he wrote, "as African pupils tend to be rather critical these days of the abilities

[10] Rex McKenzie, "Beware of Volunteer Graduate Schemes," *Farrago*, April 8, 1960.

[11] Jeremy Pool, "Now Is the Time of Youth: Youth, Nationalism and Cultural Change in Ghana, 1940–1966" (PhD thesis, Emory University, 2009); Emmanuel Asiedu-Acquah, "'We Shall Be Outspoken': Student Political Activism in Post-Independence Ghana, c.1957–1966," *Journal of Asian and African Studies* 54, no. 2 (2019): 169–88.

of their teachers" and volunteers without teaching qualifications and experience "could be used only in sporting and extramural activities."[12] This directly contradicted VSO's founding philosophy, which held that youth and inexperience were more useful to developing nations than trained experts. Although Hone's request was respected in Northern Rhodesia, VSO continued to post untrained school-leaver volunteers to teaching positions in other parts of Africa, as well as Asia, the Middle East and the Caribbean, throughout the 1960s.

The tensions that flowed from VSO's decision to send young and unqualified teachers can be read in letters that arrived at VSO's London office from Nigeria in the mid-1960s. From a girls' school in Abeokuta in Western Nigeria, eighteen-year-old Helen Rosenberg wrote, "You can't imagine how low the discipline & general behaviour of the girls here is and I simply don't know where to begin to improve it." The discipline had become so bad that she came to think they were "little monsters," although "in each class there are 1 or 2 who make up for all the rest."[13] Philip Taylor, teaching in the same town, reported that "all that talk about the phenomenal lust for knowledge of all African children is so much phooey … One has to spend half one's time [in] blind rages, & lashing out punishments."[14] Evelyn Ross, who taught some 200 miles away in Ifaki, reported that "It is a myth that African children are easy to discipline; many of the girls do not know the meaning of the word 'discipline'."[15] Partly this came from Ross' youth and inexperience: among other subjects, Ross taught French and History – even though she had never taken History herself and had an uneasy command of French.[16] As she wrote after the first week of work, "[I] feel an absolute fraud. I haven't the foggiest notion what I'm doing!"

Other volunteers faced conflicts with their fellow-teachers or headmasters. At the boys' school in Abeokuta, Philip Taylor experienced a "violent clash … with a revered member of staff" that Taylor dubbed the "Rasputin of the Western Region." It appears that the teacher's objections were not personal; rather, he resented the steady stream of volunteers arriving at his school each year, each of whom was young and inexperienced and yet simultaneously overconfident. The previous year, the school's principal had threatened to take another VSO, Keith Archer, to court for libel; Archer "left in a cloud of disgrace." A Peace Corps volunteer was also dismissed around the same time.[17] Philip Taylor objected to the teacher's attitude to volunteers and "declared a kind of jihad against

12 Sir Evelyn Hone to Carstairs, October 8, 1960, TNA: CO 859/1445.
13 Helen Rosenberg to Mr. Haig, December 15, 1964, VSO Archive, microfiche files.
14 Philip Taylor to Mr. Thomas, September 30, 1963, VSO Archive, microfiche files.
15 Evelyn Ross, Final Report, 1965, VSO Archive, microfiche files.
16 Evelyn Ross to Mr. Shaw, September 26, 1964, VSO Archive, microfiche files.
17 Philip Taylor to Mr. Hollis, April 18, 1965, VSO Archive, microfiche files.

him."[18] Resentment and conflict simmered for the remainder of Taylor's posting. Some 400 miles to the north, at Maru Teachers Training College, VSO Anthony Thorndike also experienced conflict with his school's principal. As he reported to London, "The Principal ... leaves much to be desired" and Thorndike confessed that "Sometimes I could scream as educational etiquette forbids (and very rightly so in the normal course of events) telling people their jobs." Thorndike was not alone. As he continued, "I was pleased to hear from other GVSOs, PCVs and CUSOs in the course of my travels that many of them had had similar experiences. That made me feel better! Perhaps it is our fault – there must be, somewhere, a reason for everything but I'm darned if I can see it."[19] It is likely that one of the other volunteers Thorndike talked to was VSO Nigel Turner, who worked nearby at the Comprehensive High School, a "prestige" institution staffed by a large number of American teachers. Turner's posting was one of "luxury and kudos," but also of ongoing antagonism between the school's "large American contingent and the Nigerians."[20] The cultural chauvinism that drove inexperienced young volunteers to be "telling people their jobs" rankled with African counterparts and superiors and resulted in chronic tension and occasional conflict.

Tensions were particularly acute in Ghana. Kwame Nkrumah's Convention People's Party paid particular attention to cultivating anticolonial sympathies in children and youth.[21] Young people in Nkrumah's Ghana formed a significant political cohort; as Emmanuel Asiedu-Acquah notes, "student activism established itself as a fulcrum of the country's evolving postcolonial political order."[22] The arrival of hundreds of Peace Corps and VSO teachers provided a new site for the expression of anticolonial politics. We can see this play out in the experiences of Alice O'Grady, a member of the first Peace Corps contingent in Ghana, who taught at a secondary school in the nation's far west from 1961. Over the course of her two-year posting, O'Grady faced constant and growing hostility from students who considered defiance of "European" teachers to be a matter of Nkrumahist principle. The Peace Corps recruited social scientists to conduct in-depth interviews with each member of the Ghana I contingent on a yearly basis. In the course of these interviews, O'Grady revealed the difficulty of her situation. Her students "treated me with a lot of disrespect. And made life miserable for me." On one occasion, a group of boys threw stones and hissed at her until O'Grady fled in tears. As she recounted, "they knew I was crying, and the ones that I left cheered as

18 Philip Taylor to Mr. Hollis, September 4, 1965, VSO Archive, microfiche files.

19 Anthony Thorndike to Mrs. Hooper, July 20, 1965, VSO Archive, microfiche files. GVSO = Graduate VSOs; PCVs = Peace Corps Volunteers; CUSOs = Canadian volunteers.

20 Confidential report on Nigel Turner, November 23, 1965, VSO Archive, microfiche files.

21 Pool, "Now Is the Time of Youth," pp. 83–130.

22 Asiedu-Acquah, "'We Shall Be Outspoken'," p. 169.

I walked away . . . they were happy that they had gotten rid of me . . . that they'd won."[23] The situation became so bad that O'Grady seriously considered leaving Ghana, and the Peace Corps, altogether.

The students' animosity was tied to national and international politics. As we saw in Chapter 6, Nkrumah's decision to welcome American volunteers to Ghana was out of step with his political ideology of anticolonialism, modernism and African self-sufficiency, and the first Peace Corps volunteers faced significant resistance from the national media on their arrival in Ghana. Resistance continued at a grassroots level and many volunteers reported rising popular anti-Americanism. O'Grady's school hosted a large contingent of Young Pioneers, a youth organization aiming to inculcate young Ghanaians with Nkrumahist principles, with a particular stress on social cohesion and anticolonial rhetoric.[24] O'Grady had fallen foul of the Young Pioneers when she tried to ban meetings during her class times; even though she ultimately apologized and reversed her decision (having been told that "it's a dangerous thing to do and I had really not thought about what I was doing"), the Young Pioneers continued to target her as a representative of American neocolonialism.

The resistance of O'Grady's students must be read in light of broader political significance. And yet, political resentment was amplified by personal aversion; as O'Grady admitted, the worst of the students' misbehavior began after she introduced a strict new disciplinary code that subjected students to formal punishment for even minor infractions. Moreover, she struggled to remember African pupils' names, had a short temper and regularly called students who struggled to understand her English "stupid." As she reflected, "I'm aware that when I say it I perhaps should be more careful. This is a very, really a bad thing to say . . . and to be called 'stupid' is really an insult"; an insult that was exacerbated by her white skin. Just as significantly, O'Grady refused to learn the local Twi language, which caused conflict with fellow teachers as well as students; all agreed that "I'm in Ghana and I must learn [their] language."[25] Even though English was Ghana's official language, the vernacular held particular significance in numerous postcolonial societies. Many Peace Corps volunteers reported friction arising from an unwillingness or inability to learn national languages or local dialects. O'Grady considered her failings – short-temperedness, irritability, poor memory – as personal failings, but her students interpreted them within a broader political context. Her perceived haughtiness, inability to remember African names and unwillingness to learn Twi resonated with a long history of colonialism and rising American

23 Interview with Alice O'Grady, June 15, 1962, JFKL: RPCV, Box 65.

24 Ahlman, *Living with Nkrumahism*, pp. 84–114; Pool, "Now Is the Time of Youth," pp. 80–130.

25 Interview with Alice O'Grady, June 15, 1962, JFKL: RPCV, Box 65.

hegemony. In O'Grady's case, conflict arose from the intersection of personal and political tension, reflecting the ambiguous position occupied by Western volunteers abroad.

Volunteers with teaching qualifications and experience often managed to sidestep such conflict. Robert Klein had arrived alongside Alice O'Grady in the first Peace Corps contingent to Ghana and his progress was similarly documented in extensive yearly interviews. But where O'Grady had arrived straight from college, where she had taken a biology degree, Klein came to the Peace Corps with five years' teaching experience in a "problem" school in Harlem. He taught some 100 miles from Alice O'Grady, but his experience could not have been more different. Where O'Grady was one of twelve "European" teachers, who outnumbered the Ghanaian staff almost two to one, Klein was the only non-Ghanaian teacher at his school. Klein was also a confident educator; as a result, he felt that classroom discipline was "No problem at all . . . the kids are just extremely well-behaved," so much so that "At times I wish they weren't so well behaved. They would be more willing to open up, relax a little, and not be afraid of getting up and making a wrong answer."[26] Klein's prior experience armed him with the skills to manage his classroom, but, just as importantly, a qualified teacher sent a very different message than unskilled volunteers who had been placed in positions of authority simply because they came from the "developed" West.

Although Klein was not the only volunteer to experience a relatively smooth teaching experience in Africa, he was exceptional – the majority of VSO and Peace Corps teachers were neither qualified nor experienced. And yet, Western media reports erased the tense day-to-day experiences of volunteers like Alice O'Grady, Helen Rosenberg or Philip Taylor. The May 1962 issue of *This Month* magazine ran a special feature on the first contingent of Peace Corps volunteers in Ghana. The story claimed that the Peace Corps was "paying dividends in Ghana," where "from the very beginning, the Corps men and women have found their students extraordinarily receptive, and the school officials extremely cooperative."[27] While this was certainly true for Robert Klein, it elided the experiences of the many volunteer teachers who found their daily lives marred by tension and conflict. Tensions were further papered over, or even forgotten, by Peace Corps volunteers in subsequent years. After completing her Ghanaian posting in 1962, Alice O'Grady became Deputy Director of the Peace Corps in Ibadan, Nigeria, and in 1968 she returned to Ghana to teach for a further four years. By the time researcher Molly Geidel interviewed O'Grady in 2010, her memories had reconfigured; based on oral history interviews, Geidel characterized O'Grady as "a teacher from the first Ghana

26 Interview with Robert Klein, June 5, 1962, JFKL: RPCV, Box 64.

27 "The Peace Corps in Ghana: America's Bold Experiment," *This Month*, May 1962, pp. 32–3.

group who developed close and lasting connections with her former students."[28] The memory work performed by O'Grady over the course of decades largely erased tension and conflict from her Peace Corps experience, even though it dominated the interviews she undertook with researchers at the time. Contemporary media coverage and volunteers' personal reminiscences marginalized criticism and opposition and helped entrench the humanitarian-development complex by eliding the widespread resistance of volunteer-receiving communities.

The Don Quixotes of Development

Schools were not the only sites of intercultural tension and conflict. Volunteers assigned to community development roles faced a difficult task: to cajole "traditional" communities into adopting various forms of Western modernity.[29] Unsurprisingly, many volunteers faced local resistance and community development projects often became mired in conflict. Much of the resistance sprang from the speed and ambition with which volunteers sought to upend communities' lives. The heroic image cultivated by development volunteering, of hardy volunteers transforming "backward" communities through charismatic intervention, could appear arrogant and condescending to non-Western audiences, especially those with histories of colonial interference. Well-meaning volunteers sought to make maximum impact and those in community development roles devised ambitious schemes that often proved untenable. Volunteers were relatively unaffected when their community development schemes failed, but the cost to local communities was typically greater. All these factors created a recipe for resentment, tension and conflict that again combined both personal and political factors.

We can see this in Vicos, a small rural community in the Northern Andes of Peru. Since 1952, Vicos had been part of a Cornell University community development program intended to privatize land and integrate local potato farmers into the regional and global market. (The project's website still boasts that it was "a paradigm for international development in the third world."[30]) When the Peace Corps arrived in October 1962, therefore, they found a community that was already accustomed to foreign development intervention. However, they were not used to the quixotic pace with which Peace Corps volunteers devised, commenced and abandoned new schemes. The Peace Corps arrived in a large contingent of thirteen volunteers who competed with each other to personify the ideal volunteer, one who was innovative and

[28] Geidel, *Peace Corps Fantasies*, p. 105.

[29] See Immerwahr, *Thinking Small*, especially pp. 140–4.

[30] Cornell-Peru Project, "Vicos: A Virtual Tour," vicosperu.cornell.edu/vicos-site/cornell peru_page_1.htm, accessed November 18, 2019.

prolific. One volunteer, Robert Roberts, hit on a scheme that was both big and imaginative: to purchase a tract of land adjoining the village, renovate it and reopen a failed tourist hotel at its edges. The project seemed attractive, but, as a later report concluded, it would "require capital outlays of a magnitude hardly to be contemplated by a community with its own capital-hungry agricultural co-operative ventures."[31] Peruvian banks refused to loan money, citing the hotel's proven inability to turn a profit; undeterred, Roberts secured a $10,000 loan from an American bank, which he personally guaranteed. In his haste, Roberts failed to seek the community's permission before taking out the loan, causing widespread anxiety over the rate of repayments and consequences of defaulting. Some villagers began to speculate that the Peace Corps had intended to defraud Vicos all along; rumors began to spread that the Americans were even stockpiling weapons at the hotel. A public meeting was called and recriminations began to fly. The atmosphere, already tense, turned violent after one Vicosino threatened to "slit open the gringos." The police were summoned and the villagers demanded that all Peace Corps volunteers immediately depart Vicos.[32] As they had not learned the local Chechua dialect, the Peace Corps volunteers were unable to defend themselves. As the local newspaper noted, the Peace Corps left "Under Threat of Violence" in March 1964, seventeen months after its arrival.[33]

The Peace Corps commissioned two reports into the Vicos project and its spectacular demise. One report, prepared by the American Universities Field Staff, attempted to minimize the magnitude of the event, claiming it was "more a farce than an incident." It reported that "a community is seldom grateful for being 'developed'" and that community development projects upended traditional power structures, typically elevating younger men who "place a high value on Western ideas and techniques" at the expense of traditional leaders. In this account, "Discontent and conflict were built into the community by the very process of the attempt to change it." Far from attributing blame to individual Peace Corps volunteers, the report claimed that "A successful development project, whatever else it may do, infinitely increases the capacity of the community to bite the hand that develops it."[34]

The second report, written by Cornell academics familiar with the Vicos program, advanced a more complicated explanation. Locals had enthusiastically participated in some development projects, the report claimed, but were repeatedly disappointed by Peace Corps volunteers who proved unskilled and unreliable. Ultimately, it blamed "the psychology of the Peace Corps volunteer

[31] Richard W. Patch, "Vicos and the Peace Corps: A Failure in Intercultural Communication," March 1964 report to the Peace Corps, JFKL: RG 490, Box 7.

[32] Ibid.

[33] "Volunteers of the Peace Corps Leave Vicos Under Threat of Violence," *La Prensa*, March 13, 1964, p. 1.

[34] Patch, "Vicos and the Peace Corps," JFKL: RG 490, Box 7.

who wishes to leave behind him or her a tangible, physical monument of his foreign assignment." The report cataloged numerous quixotic projects trialed in Vicos, many of which required locals' investment of time and money and all of which eventually failed. One Peace Corps volunteer initially set out to train a new breed of work horse, but abandoned the project after a pony shied, destroying costly local-owned agricultural equipment. He then developed an interest in afforestation and introduced a eucalyptus plantation to Vicos; after feverishly planting 10,000 seedlings, he went on vacation and returned to find them dead for lack of irrigation. His next plan was to install hot showers at the Vicos school. After extracting money from the community council for the cost of timber, bricks and cement and dragooning villagers for some of the heavy labor involved, the volunteer simply "tired of the activity and abandoned the project." The timber warped, the cement turned to stone and some expensive tools disappeared. The volunteer then turned his enthusiasm to forming a local band. A talented musician himself, he encouraged several villagers to purchase expensive brass instruments, representing a considerable cash investment for rural Peruvians. However, again the volunteer's "interest in the project vanished" and, again, the project foundered.[35]

Other Vicos volunteers had similar records. A second male volunteer had attempted to castrate a valuable donkey stud by using a new method he called "the American style." The animal promptly died and although the volunteer had promised to reimburse the owner half the value of the donkey, the payment was never made. (The owner's son, who had entrusted the procedure to the volunteer, ran away after this incident and did not return for years.) The same volunteer then developed an interest in horses and commandeered a room used by local teachers to store his horse-riding equipment. Furious, the teachers dumped his equipment out on the patio; two male Peace Corps volunteers responded aggressively and open conflict ensued. The volunteer's next project involved vehicle maintenance and driving lessons for local townspeople, which came to a sudden halt after the volunteer knocked down a pedestrian and attempted to "arrange" the consequences himself. The police became involved, a minor scandal erupted and the volunteer was transferred to another town.

Peace Corps volunteers' lifestyles also eroded locals' trust. As the Cornell University report noted, "early during their period of residence in Vicos . . . the Peace Corps volunteers began to isolate themselves from their Peruvian counterparts." In an echo of the privileged and isolated lifestyles explored in Chapter 7 of this book, the Peace Corps volunteers in Vicos refused to eat alongside their Peruvian colleagues, preferring to pool their cash to buy higher

[35] Henry F. Dobbins, Paul L. Doughty and Allan R. Holmberg, "Peace Corps Program Impact in the Peruvian Andes: Final Report," Cornell University Department of Anthropology, 1966, pp. 74–7, JFKL: RG 490, Box 19.

quality food that they ate together at home. Relations between volunteers and coworkers quickly deteriorated "to the point where there was no effective communication between them after the first three months." Although the Peace Corps had arrived with good intentions, conflict with the local community erupted over seemingly trivial matters. The volunteers increasingly kept to themselves, their distance from the local community symbolized by a sign hanging over their door: "The Vicos Hilton."[36] The land purchase and foreign loan that triggered the Peace Corps' expulsion was, therefore, less a "farce" and more "a crisis that had long been building" as "numerous accidents, blunders, and misunderstandings ... were compounded by some strong personal grudges and enmities."[37]

The situation at Vicos was extreme but not unique. Numerous young and inexperienced volunteers rushed into quick-fix solutions to local underdevelopment. In their quixotic enthusiasm, many failed to consult the locals who knew the region best and whose interests were most at stake. To communities with long histories of colonial or neocolonial subjugation, a volunteer's determination to effect change could appear just as supercilious as previous generations of colonizers. Their tendency to club together further exacerbated tensions and led to interpersonal conflicts with local residents. In the mid-1960s, the Peace Corps commissioned a study of relations between volunteers and local communities, in recognition that many volunteers found these relationships "often difficult and trying, sometimes downright exasperating." Although the report sympathized with volunteers who wanted to move faster than their communities, it warned volunteers to "Beware" as "Peace Corps popularity is often founded on sandy ground." Ultimately, the Peace Corps warned, many projects failed because "good as may be the Volunteer's plans judged by criteria familiar to us, PCVs just do not know the human backdrop in this country well enough to tailor projects to local needs and local possibilities all on their own."[38] The space between volunteers' and host communities' notions of development, and the best way to achieve it, was a fertile breeding ground for conflict.

Neocolonial Running Dogs

The tensions faced by individual volunteers played out on a larger canvas. From the mid-1960s, organized political opposition to Western influence became increasingly common in Asia, Africa and Latin America. Volunteers were among the most visible and accessible manifestations of Western political

36 Ibid, p. 66.
37 Ibid, p. 83.
38 "The Peace Corps Volunteer's Relationship with Co-Workers: By a Peace Corps Volunteer in Africa," JFKL: RG 490, Box 24.

and cultural intervention in the Global South during the 1960s. Opposition to VSO or Peace Corps volunteers therefore represented a means through which broader hostility to development intervention, British colonialism or American hegemony could be expressed.

As we have seen, in Indonesia the most vocal early opposition to Western volunteers came from the Indonesian Communist Party (PKI) and its newspaper, *Harian Rakjat*. But pamphlets and books opposing Western influence were also published by nominally independent publishing houses. One book, titled *Peace Corps* and published in Indonesian in 1964 by the (possibly pseudonymous) author Sumarga, put forward a sophisticated and highly critical analysis that situated the Peace Corps within broader American intervention in the Global South. Quoting American sources and providing a sophisticated overview of tied aid and dollar diplomacy, Sumarga argued that the entire US foreign aid program was simply a tool to expand American power abroad. Accepting Peace Corps volunteers was, therefore, "encouraging the octopus of imperialism, colonialism and neo-colonialism."[39] Illustrating Sumarga's argument was a cartoon depicting the Peace Corps in Africa as a market hawker holding shackles while shouting: "Selling at a cheap price! Bracelets for brothers" (Figure 9.1).

Rather than situating the origins of development volunteering with the Australian Volunteer Graduate Scheme, Sumarga's *Peace Corps* pointed to US Senators Henry S. Reuss and Hubert Humphrey as the program's originators.[40] This followed the script favored in Washington but, in this context, it also served to confirm suspicions that the Peace Corps was a tool of US foreign policy, initiated by politicians for political purposes. "This Peace Corps program does not stand alone," wrote Sumarga, "but is accompanied by all Pentagon activities, all CIA activities, the activities of monopolists in banks, and the activities of various international funding agencies."[41] As we saw in Chapter 6 of this book, newspapers across the Global South, including Indonesia, seized on the image of the wolf in sheep's clothing as a symbol of the Peace Corps' ulterior motives. Sumarga further advanced the metaphor of the *Kuda Troja* or Trojan Horse. This image performed similar work, suggesting that the aid and international friendship publicized by the Peace Corps were merely cover for US domination. Arguing that the Peace Corps was intended to "obtain maximum psychological benefits for the US," he asked, "Can the American acts of subversion, aggression and intervention, which are known around the world, be rectified with this search for 'peace'?"[42]

Sumarga's book further maintained that the Peace Corps was a cover for SEATO and the military expansion of American power. The name "Peace

[39] Sumarga, *Peace Corps* (Jakarta: Penerbit Djasa, 1964), p. 47. All translations are my own.
[40] Ibid., pp. 33–4.
[41] Ibid., p. 55.
[42] Ibid., p. 32.

Figure 9.1 "Peace Corps in Africa: 'Hey, selling at a cheap price! Bracelets for Brothers!'" in Sumarga, *Peace Corps* (Jakarta: Penerbit Djasa), 1964, p. 48.

Corps," he argued, made it "safe [for US influence] to move to areas that do not have US military bases, do not have diplomatic relations, or other US officials."[43] This argument had roots in Indonesia's *Konfrontasi* with Malaysia (based on Sukarno's claim that Malaysia was a neocolonial puppet state of the British and American alliance). Sumarga claimed that Peace Corps volunteers in Malaysian Borneo had "involved themselves in battles against the North Kalimantan People's Freedom fighters," which served to "prove that in a grave situation the Peace Corps can be transformed into a War Corps"[44] (Figure 9.2).

[43] Ibid., p. 59.
[44] Ibid., p. 88.

Figure 9.2 "The late President Kennedy: 'Peace Corps' = 'War Corps'" in Sumarga, *Peace Corps* (Jakarta: Penerbit Djasa), 1964, p. 61.

Opposition to the Peace Corps was grounded in geopolitics, but it also sprang from direct contact with individual volunteers. Sumarga's book recounted an encounter between an Indonesian member of the Communist-affiliated Institute for People's Culture, Roemandung, and an individual Peace Corps volunteer, R. William Liddle. Liddle had reportedly told Roemandung that volunteers were "obligated to 'save the communities from the threat of Communism'." Sumarga further noted that "Liddle worked hard to influence

Roemandung to agree with his opinions on 'Malaysia,' and we believe this kind of propaganda will continue to be carried out where there is an opportunity to meet young people and the Indonesian people in general."[45] In a charged political atmosphere, the broader slippage between volunteers as individuals and as national representatives took a political slant and the views of an individual volunteer regarding Indonesia's conflict with Malaysia was taken as evidence of the Peace Corps' institutional antagonism to Sukarno's Indonesia.

Alongside political critiques sat resentment that development volunteering extended colonial-era divisions between "Europeans" and "natives" into the postcolonial period. Sumarga contrasted the meager median salaries of host nations with the generous allowances received by Peace Corps volunteers. He quoted from a 1961 *Newsweek* article in which Ghana volunteer Arnold Zeitlin boasted of his substantial stipend, large house and multiple servants.[46] The relatively high standard of living enjoyed by volunteers was compounded by their social distance from local communities. Sumarga cited cases in which the Peace Corps "terminated" volunteers who had established romantic relationships with Host Country Nationals as evidence that Western volunteering agencies sought to perpetuate race-based social apartheid. Like Ghanaian school students and the community at Vicos, Sumarga's political tract fused the political with the personal, drawing together critiques of volunteers' lifestyles and personal opinions with ideological opposition to Western expansion.

Although Sumarga's *Peace Corps* was deeply enmeshed in the Indonesian context, it was remarkably outward-facing. Recent scholarship has drawn out the extent to which the "Third World project" of the 1960s and 1970s arose from a shared political imaginary with nodes in Africa, Asia, the Middle East and Latin America.[47] This shared intellectual and political space was rooted in anticolonial thought of the nineteenth century and strengthened by postwar meetings of Afro-Asian and non-aligned nations and activists.[48] By the 1960s,

[45] Ibid., p. 59.

[46] Ibid., p. 59. See also Arnold Zeitlin, *To the Peace Corps, with Love* (New York: Doubleday, 1965), pp. 79–80.

[47] Prashad, *The Darker Nations*; Christoph Kalter, "A Shared Space of Imagination, Communication and Action: Perspectives on the History of the 'Third World'." In *The Third World in the Global 1960s*, edited by Samantha Christiansen and Zachary A. Scarlett, pp. 23–38 (New York: Berghahn Books, 2012); Adom Getachew, *Worldmaking After Empire: The Rise and Fall of Self-Determination* (Princeton, NJ: Princeton University Press, 2019).

[48] Mishra, *From the Ruins of Empire*; Daniel Brückenhaus, *Policing Transnational Protest: Liberal Imperialism and the Surveillance of Anticolonialists in Europe, 1905–1945* (Oxford: Oxford University Press, 2017); Su Lin Lewis and Carolien Stolte, "Other Bandungs: Afro-Asian Internationalisms in the Early Cold War," *Journal of World History* 30, no. 1/2 (2019): 1–19; See Seng Tan and Amitav Acharya, eds., *Bandung Revisited: The Legacy of*

the Third World project was fueled by networks of people, texts and ideas circulating within and between nations and continents across the Global South.

Sumarga's *Peace Corps* provides a striking example of how antivolunteer opinion and action circulated across the Third World during the 1960s. Although his main concern was always Indonesia, Sumarga wove in critiques from Nigeria, Ghana, Egypt, India, Burma and Ceylon to depict a broad tableau of anti-Peace Corps sentiment. Once published, Sumarga's text also circulated and was reproduced by transnational networks opposed to maximalist development intervention. In 1967, an anonymous booklet heavily based on Sumarga's was published in Ceylon. Titled *The Peace Corps Again: A New Invasion of Ceylon*, it was targeted at a South Asian audience, but its argument was built on the same themes, images and even the same phrases as Sumarga. It, too, relied on the metaphor of the Trojan Horse, declaring that "the wooden horse in this case is the Peace Corps – a totally innocent looking and altruistic institution designed to educate the millions of people of Asia, Africa, and Latin America . . . But cunningly hidden within the Peace Corps are the dangerous spies from the Central Intelligence Agency and other American Agencies."[49] The Ceylonese and Indonesian tracts cited many of the same sources. Both featured a chapter titled "Peace Corps or War Corps?" that exposed the perceived intersection between Peace Corps volunteers and the US Army. The Ceylonese text, published three years after Sumarga's, updated the material to cover Jack Hood Vaughn's assumption of the role of Peace Corps Director and claimed that the Peace Corps was directly involved in the unfolding war in Vietnam. Like Sumarga, it drew on media and political opposition to Peace Corps deployments in Tanzania, Nigeria, Kenya, Ghana and India, among others. But its purpose was always local: to oppose the Peace Corps reentering Ceylon, as proposed in 1967 by the incoming National Government led by Dudley Senanayake. The purpose of the pamphlet, the author stated, was to allow Ceylonese "to see the true image of the Peace Corps in the light of their doings in the developing countries of Afroasia and Latin America."[50] Opposition to development volunteering was simultaneously local and transnational. It was rooted in specific movements opposing volunteers in their nations, but rested upon a circulating corpus of information and grievances that together built the case that the Peace Corps represented American neoimperialism.

the 1955 Asian-African Conference for International Order (Singapore: NUS Press, 2008); J. A. C. Mackie, *Bandung 1955: Non-Alignment and Afro-Asian Solidarity* (Singapore: Editions Didier Millet, 2005); Bose, "Frantz Fanon and the Politicization of the Third World as a Collective Subject."

49 *The Peace Corps Again: A New Invasion of Ceylon* (Colombo: Tribune Publication, 1967), p. 55.

50 Ibid., p. 3.

The anonymous Ceylonese tract in turn inspired a Nigerian pamphlet, *The Ugly American: A Study of the Peace Corps*, published by the Lagos Study Group in 1969. *The Ugly American* again borrowed the imagery of the Trojan Horse and again featured a chapter titled "Peace Corps or War Corps?"[51] In addition to republishing long extracts from the Ceylonese pamphlet, the Nigerian publication added updated sections linking the latest Peace Corps Director, Joe Blatchford, to the CIA. It featured recent reports from Africa reporting the Peace Corps' diminished popularity across the continent. It also profiled volunteers who had come to oppose the Peace Corps' increasingly strict policies on personal behavior and the expression of political views. (As the following chapter shows, domestic opposition to development volunteering arose in the United States and Britain from the mid-1960s.)[52] Sumarga's book had been published in Indonesian and the Ceylonese and Nigerian booklets were in English. Yet, the overlap in themes, metaphors and phrases points to a significant circulation of opinion in opposition to development volunteering across the Global South from the mid-1960s.

Expelling the Peace Corps

The simmering tensions that accompanied Western volunteers in their day-to-day lives increasingly bubbled over into organized opposition movements. Until the mid-1960s, opposition was largely overshadowed by the vast outpouring of support and enthusiasm for development volunteering in the West and by the pragmatic approach of Global South elites who were content to wait and see what benefits volunteers might bring. But this underwent a gradual shift during the late 1960s and into the 1970s, as development volunteering programs came under increasing pressure and nation after nation took the drastic step of expelling volunteers. Most organized opposition groups focused on the Peace Corps. As the largest development volunteering program, as the program attracting the greatest publicity and as an American export the Peace Corps functioned as a symbol of both US political hegemony and cultural Westernization. Protests opposing the Peace Corps took place in towns and cities across the Global South. The rising tide of popular opposition in turn influenced national governments and leaders to reassess the value of development volunteering.

Attitudes to Western volunteers were related to broader trends in foreign aid and international development. Enthusiasm for development rhetoric and projects peaked during the early to mid-1960s. After this time, recipients and donors alike began to question the efficacy of development. After fifteen or

51 Lagos Study Group, *The Ugly American: A Study of the Peace Corps* (Lagos: Lagos Study Group, 1969), p. 20.

52 Ibid., p. 22.

more years of intensive development projects, many Global South nations had yet to reach the projected "take off" stage; in some nations, poverty only seemed to be getting worse.[53] The technological optimism underpinning modernization and developmentalism was dented by recognition of environmental damage.[54] Support for development was also checked by political, philosophical and cultural critiques of Western modernity. In the Global North, countercultural movements critiqued late capitalist modernity, arguing that cultural "authenticity" had been replaced by monotony, mechanization and social control.[55] In the Global South, too, activists questioned the value of Westernization, drawing on indigenous political and social models to propose paths toward African or Asian modernity that sidestepped Western templates.[56]

Resistance to development volunteering was further related to growing opposition to American political and military intervention across the Third World. The postcolonial governments of new nations in Africa, Asia and Latin America took many forms, but they were united by a jealous determination to safeguard domestic affairs from outside interference. At the same time, the 1960s and 1970s saw a startling escalation of US government intervention in the domestic politics of sovereign nations. Some of these intrusions were overt and included military action. But the US also ran multiple covert operations to counter communist and left-wing influence that installed and propped up compliant regimes across the globe.[57] Although the Peace Corps claimed to be a non-political organization, many Third World leaders and grassroots movements regarded it as a tool of US statecraft. In several key nations, Peace Corps volunteers were expelled after diplomatic relations with the United States soured amid accusations of American interference in domestic politics.

Ceylon was the first nation to expel the Peace Corps. In 1964, President Sirivamo Bandaranaike declined to accept any more Peace Corps volunteers after the first tranche of thirty-six volunteer teachers completed their postings in the nation's schools. The volunteers had arrived in 1962 to "improve the educational system and extend the curriculum into scientific and technological

[53] Jeremy Adelman, "Epilogue: Development Dreams." In *The Development Century: A Global History*, edited by Stephen Macekura and Erez Manela (New York: Cambridge University Press, 2018), pp. 326–38.

[54] Stephen Macekura, *Of Limits and Growth: The Rise of Global Sustainable Development in the Twentieth Century* (New York: Cambridge University Press, 2015); Lorenzini, *Global Development*, pp. 124–7.

[55] Julie Stephens, *Anti-Disciplinary Protest: Sixties Radicalism and Postmodernism* (Cambridge: Cambridge University Press, 1998). See also Sobocinska, "Following the 'Hippie Sahibs'."

[56] Julius K. Nyerere, *Freedom and Socialism/ Uhuru Na Ujamaa: A Selection from Writings and Speeches, 1965–1967* (Oxford: Oxford University Press, 1968); Feith and Castles, *Indonesian Political Thinking, 1945–1965*, pp. 377–410.

[57] Westad, *The Global Cold War*, pp. 8–38.

fields."[58] Colombo's left-wing parties organized mass meetings and street protests opposing the Peace Corps' arrival, which continued sporadically over the next two years. In the town of Bandarawela, deep in the highlands of southern Ceylon, one Peace Corps volunteer teacher arrived to find his school and town plastered with anti-Peace Corps posters in English and Sinhalese.[59] While grassroots opposition simmered on, the ultimate expulsion of the Peace Corps was related to a broader crisis. Ceylon–US relations soured following the Bandaranaike government's nationalization of the assets of two American oil companies, ESSO and Caltex (it also nationalized assets of British-owned Shell). The United States suspended aid to Ceylon in retaliation, although the Peace Corps was allowed to remain. Volunteers already in-country served out the remainder of their two-year terms, but the Ceylon government refused further Peace Corps volunteers amid rising anti-Americanism and increasingly trenchant demands that the government remove "subversive U.S. agencies."[60] As the *Times of India* warned, "Ceylon's experiences in this instance shows that reliance on foreign aid could entail some measure of surrender of the country's freedom."[61]

The Ceylonese expulsion was a blot on the Peace Corps' record at a stage when officials proudly claimed that volunteers were eagerly desired across the Global South. The Peace Corps barely acknowledged the Ceylonese withdrawal; a 1964 promotional pamphlet, *Peace Corps Facts*, was revised and reissued with all references to Ceylon quietly removed.[62] Similarly, the Peace Corps Annual Report for 1964 made no mention of Ceylon's disappearance from its list of recipient nations, preferring a narrative of "steady and rapid expansion of overseas programs . . . as requests for Volunteers burgeoned."[63]

Indonesia was the next major nation to expel the Peace Corps. After years of pressure from the PKI and its allied trade unions and cultural groups, President Sukarno announced in April 1965 that the Peace Corps would cease operations after the first contingent of seventeen volunteers completed their terms later that year. Sukarno's decision came amid a broader breakdown in US–Indonesian relations caused by rising US concern about Communist influence and Indonesia's *Konfrontasi* with neighboring Malaysia. As historian Brad Simpson has argued, US foreign aid policy was heavily politicized in Cold

58 Peace Corps, 2nd Annual Peace Corps Report (Washington, DC: Peace Corps, 1963), p. 21.

59 Peace Corps Memorandum for the President, February 19, 1963, JFKL: RG 490, Box 30.

60 "Leftist Anti-U.S. Morcha in Colombo," *Times of India*, February 17, 1963, p. 1.

61 "'Rely on own endeavours', Ceylon Govt. Call to People," *Times of India*, February 11, 1963, p. 8.

62 *Peace Corps Facts*, March 5, 1964; *Peace Corps Facts*, revised May 1, 1964, both in NACP: RG 490, Public Relations Publications, Box 2.

63 Peace Corps, "3rd Annual Peace Corps Report" (Washington, DC: Peace Corps, 1964), p. 11.

War Indonesia.[64] Sukarno's expulsion of the Peace Corps in early 1965 shows that the game could be played both ways as Third World leaders symbolically cut ties with the Peace Corps to demonstrate their opposition to American policies. This could be a dangerous game, however; Sukarno was toppled in a CIA-backed coup later the same year.

Peace Corps expulsions were especially frequent in Africa. In November 1966, Guinea expelled its sixty-two Peace Corps volunteers following a dispute over the arrest of Guinean diplomats in Ghana, for which President Sékou Touré blamed the United States.[65] Anti-American protests swept Guinea's capital, Conakry, and Peace Corps volunteers across the country were placed under house arrest, ostensibly for their own safety. The charge that the United States exerted undue influence on international relations was disputed by the Peace Corps, which claimed Guinea's expulsion of its volunteers as "one of the most bizarre episodes in its brief history."[66] Yet, it was by no means an isolated accusation. In June 1967, Mauritania expelled its twelve Peace Corps volunteers after it broke diplomatic relations with the United States over accusations of US intervention in the Arab-Israeli War.[67] In December the same year, Gabon dismissed its fifty-seven volunteers.

Most significantly, Tanzania's President Julius Nyerere announced that the number of Peace Corps volunteers in Tanzania would be slashed from 394 to just eight by the end of 1967 and would be phased out altogether in 1970. The expulsion of volunteers from Tanzania was a bitter blow to the Peace Corps. In 1966, a British diplomatic memo had listed Tanzania among a handful of "Places where the Peace Corps feels that it has done particularly well."[68] The 1967 expulsion was unexpected and a setback to the Peace Corps' image. The official reason was the Peace Corps' administrative consolidation with other agencies of the US government, including the Embassy, State Department and CIA in Tanzania. But, according to a confidential Australian assessment, the "decision was in fact political, based on needs to eradicate alien influences ... [and the] alleged involvement of CIA in Peace Corps."[69] The expulsion of the Peace Corps was also a criticism of American foreign policy across the globe. Although formally unaligned, Nyerere strongly opposed the Vietnam War. Peace Corps

[64] Simpson, *Economists with Guns*. See also Timothy P. Maga, "The New Frontier Vs. Guided Democracy: JFK, Sukarno, and Indonesia, 1961–1963," *Presidential Studies Quarterly* 20, no. 1 (1990): 91–102.

[65] W. A. E. Skurnik, "Ghana and Guinea, 1966 – a Case Study in Inter-African Relations," *Journal of Modern African Studies* 5, no. 3 (1967): 369–84.

[66] Peace Corps, 6th Annual Report (Washington DC: Peace Corps, 1967), p. 1.

[67] Stanley Meisler, "Peace Corps in Africa," *Herald Tribune*, July 4, 1969.

[68] Patrick Dean and Bill Drewer, "Report: Peace Corps in Guatemala," July 18, 1966, TNA: FO 371/185049.

[69] Australian High Commission, Dar es Salaam, Confidential Memo 129, June 7, 1967, NAA: A1838, 936/20/3 Part 1.

volunteers noted that "no other issue produced a greater solidarity of anti-American sentiment . . . than the escalation of the war in Vietnam. To almost all Tanzanians – from house servants to intellectuals – this seemed clear evidence of a predominantly white belligerent, capitalist America." Anti-Americanism flourished, most obviously in street protests and rallies outside the American Embassy, but also, as one volunteer noted, in the cheering that accompanied "the killing of Americans . . . in war films."[70] As one journalist reported, "Tanzanians have the feeling that the United States is not on their side – that it kills brown people in Vietnam, that it supports South Africa and Portugal."[71] Nyerere summed up that "the Peace Corps has changed its character" and "some of its idealism has gone out."[72] At a time of escalating global tension, the growing divide between an increasingly interventionist United States and the Third World was expressed by the expulsion of Peace Corps volunteers.

Beneath the politics, Nyerere had also become increasingly dissatisfied with the type and quality of Peace Corps volunteers. Initially, Peace Corps volunteers in Tanzania had diverse skills and worked as nurses, surveyors and engineers. But by the mid-1960s, some 75 percent were posted as school teachers. The BA generalists supplied by the Peace Corps ran counter to Tanzania's demands for technical experts; the ideology of self-sufficiency embedded in Tanzania's *Ujamaa*, or African socialism, held that non-technical roles, including teaching, were to be tackled in a cooperative spirit by Tanzanians themselves. Moreover, both volunteers and the extensive Peace Corps bureaucracy in Tanzania had a tendency to remain separate from the community. As a result, as a former volunteer recounted, "when government leaders stepped up their denunciations of the Peace Corps, hardly anyone in the Tanzanian community defended it – because the Peace Corps had virtually no ties with the community." Rather, volunteers bore the brunt of grassroots opposition to American influence and encountered "harsh sentiments from their superiors, peers and sometimes even from students."[73]

The Tanzanian expulsion was particularly bruising for the Peace Corps. In its wake, an Executive Order was signed prohibiting the CIA from approaching any members of the Peace Corps. (This was also motivated by domestic US pressure following the revelation of widespread CIA infiltration of the National Student Association in early 1967.[74]) But accusations that the Peace

70 Ron Hert, "No room for PC in Tanzania's Policy of Self-Reliance," *Peace Corps Volunteer*, Vol. 7, no. 10, September 1969, pp. 2–8.

71 Stanley Meisler, "Peace Corps in Africa," *Herald Tribune*, July 4, 1969.

72 Stanley Meisler, "Peace Corps in Trouble in Africa," *Washington Post*, July 10, 1969.

73 Ron Hert, "No room for PC in Tanzania's Policy of Self-Reliance," *Peace Corps Volunteer*, Vol. 7, no. 10, September 1969, p. 8.

74 See Karen M. Paget, *Patriotic Betrayal: The Inside Story of the CIA's Secret Campaign to Enroll American Students in the Crusade Against Communism* (New Haven, CT: Yale University Press, 2015).

Corps was aligned with the CIA were revived following the appointment of Joe Blatchford as Peace Corps Director in 1969. Blatchford had formerly been Executive Director of *Accion*, a US volunteer organization in Latin America that was partly funded by CIA front organizations.[75] Blatchford's appointment contributed to a growing sense that the distance between the Peace Corps, the State Department and the CIA had been eroded. As the *Times of India* reported in 1972, "During JFK's Camelot days, the CIA was not permitted to infiltrate the Peace Corps; but during the more pragmatic reign of a Texan President these unhealthy inhibitions and taboos were removed." Now, the report continued, "in many a developing country the CIA operatives indulge in do-gooding jobs," a process it dubbed "Development through CIA."[76] President Nixon's promotion of Blatchford to Director only strengthened the perceived links between the Peace Corps and other instruments of American state power, including military and intelligence agencies that increasingly dictated terms to the Third World.

In this context, the Peace Corps was forced to take note of the grassroots tensions that had long plagued American volunteers. In Ethiopia, student strikes ground the education system to a virtual halt by 1969. One of the key student demands was for the removal of the Peace Corps, who made up more than a third of all teachers in the school system. As historian Beatrice Wayne notes, Peace Corps volunteers across Ethiopia became accustomed to cries of "Yankee, Go Home!"[77] Volunteers also faced direct attacks resulting from "violent anti-Americanism on the part of the university and school students."[78] Ethiopian protestors smashed windows and threw Molotov cocktails at Peace Corps headquarters in Addis Ababa and assaults on Peace Corps volunteers became increasingly common.[79] This anti-Americanism was based not only on politics but, by this stage, on extensive experience: a 1968 report found that students in Ethiopia had, on average, experienced four years of teaching by Peace Corps volunteers.[80] In Ethiopia, as in other Third World nations, the rejection of the Peace Corps was based both on global geopolitics and on personal and intimate knowledge of individual volunteers. But in

75 For example, see "New Peace Corps chief has CIA ties," *Times of India*, May 25, 1969, p. 7.

76 A Special Correspondent, "These magnificent men with their dollar accounts," *Times of India*, October 29, 1972, p. A4.

77 Beatrice Tychsen Wayne, "Restless Youth: Education, Activism and the Peace Corps in Ethiopia, 1962–1976" (PhD thesis, New York University, 2017), pp. 210–84.

78 "U.S. turns down Ethiopian plea for more arms," *Times of India*, February 15, 1970, p. 15.

79 Wayne, "Restless Youth: Education, Activism and the Peace Corps in Ethiopia, 1962–1976, " pp. 280–1.

80 Gary D. Berthold and David C. McLelland, "The Impact of Peace Corps teachers on students in Ethiopia," Human Development Foundation, unpublished report to the Peace Corps, 1968, p. 26.

Ethiopia, grassroots conflict was so overt that the Peace Corps could no longer deny its existence or blame it on a small coterie of communists.

Expulsions multiplied during the late 1960s as the US pursued an increasingly aggressive global Cold War strategy. National leaders assessed Peace Corps deployments in a newly critical light. This was true of anticolonial leaders who veered left, such as Tanzania's Julius Nyerere and Indonesia's Sukarno. But it was also true of less radical leaders such as Pakistan's General Ayub Khan. Ayub Khan's expulsion of the Peace Corps as part of the breakdown in US–Pakistan relations that followed the Indo-Pakistani War of 1965 reveals that non-aligned or Communist-aligned nations were not the only ones to regard the Peace Corps as a constituent part of American foreign policy rather than a disinterested humanitarian enterprise. In a confidential memo, the Australian High Commission in Rawalpindi noted that "One reason for termination is official shift away from US, and phobia about CIA activities."[81] As in Ceylon and Indonesia, the expulsion of the Peace Corps from Pakistan was related to growing suspicions of American political interference across the Global South.

Even nations that typically cooperated with the Western bloc came to reevaluate the benefits of development volunteering by the late 1960s. In Malaysia, the large Peace Corps program came under scrutiny after Malaysia's dominant UMNO party claimed that several Peace Corps volunteers had interfered with local elections in Sabah.[82] In light of the scandal, growing scrutiny of volunteers' activities extended to VSO, which had been in Malaysia since its origins in 1958, and also to Australian volunteers.[83] Volunteers in India also confronted rising suspicion. Coverage in the *Times of India* had been positive during the Peace Corps' first five years, but from the mid-1960s, the tone soured. Complaints about Peace Corps volunteers' inexperience and poor personal conduct were published with increasing frequency.[84] The *Times of India* also ran reports claiming that the Peace Corps were in fact attempting to "indoctrinate Indian students" and were "nothing but U.S. Central Intelligence agents."[85] The Communist government in the South Indian state of Kerala expelled the Peace Corps in 1967, claiming

[81] Australian High Commission Rawalpindi, Confidential Memo #385, June 16, 1967, NAA: A1838, 936/20/3 Part 1.

[82] Australian High Commission Kuala Lumpur, Confidential 1461, June 6, 1967, NAA: A1838, 936/20/3 Part 1.

[83] Australian High Commission Kuala Lumpur, Confidential Savingram 21, June 9, 1967, NAA: A1838, 936/20/3 Part 1.

[84] "Complaints to Govt. Work of Peace Corps Volunteers," *Times of India*, October 19, 1966, p 7; "Charges against Peace Corps," *Times of India*, April 27, 1967, p. 10.

[85] "Charges against Peace Corps," *Times of India*, April 27, 1967, p. 10; "Plea for expulsion of Peace Corps men," *Times of India*, May 10, 1967, p. 10; "MPs allege Indoctrination of Students," *Times of India*, October 20, 1966, p. 1. "AP Govt. vigilant over CIA activities: Reddy," *Times of India*, July 28, 1967, p. 9; "No improper activities by US citizens," *Times*

that, far from a political decision, the expulsion was simply because they were "not very useful."[86] The populous state of West Bengal, which at one time had hosted over 200 volunteers, followed suit in 1969.[87] In 1972, the Indian government put a freeze on Western volunteers in protest at US involvement in the Bangladesh War. The Peace Corps program in India, which, at nearly 500 volunteers, was one of its largest, was progressively wound down; so too was VSO, which had eighty volunteers in India, as well as a smaller contingent of Australian volunteers. Voluntary Service Overseas volunteers were not readmitted to India until 1994; at the time of writing, the Peace Corps has yet to return.

By 1971, as the Peace Corps celebrated its first decade in operation, volunteers had been expelled from Ceylon twice, as well as from Cyprus, Indonesia, Guinea, Gabon, Pakistan, Mauritania, Libya, Tanzania, Somali Republic, Bolivia, Panama, Guyana, Guinea and Nigeria. By the end of the 1970s this number had further grown to include Malawi, Uganda, Malta, Uruguay, Peru, Mauritius, India, Iran, Ethiopia, Venezuela, Nicaragua, Chad, Afghanistan and Bahrain. Although each nation operated under a particular set of circumstances, together the mass expulsion of Peace Corps volunteers in the 1960s and 1970s represents an overlooked corpus of Third World resistance to the humanitarian-development complex.

Conclusion

The high hopes for international friendship fostered by development volunteering agencies did not always translate into reality. On the ground, Western volunteers navigated a tense landscape. The earliest Australian volunteers in Indonesia found rhetorical support from political elites but their daily lives were marred by chronic and ongoing tension. By 1960, the Volunteer Graduate Scheme was on the verge of collapse, squeezed out by a tense political and social climate that looked upon volunteers as potential sources of discord. Tensions only grew worse as Britain's VSO and the United States Peace Corps sent thousands of volunteers to every corner of the Global South during the 1960s. A small proportion of volunteers were disliked for their personalities. Many more aroused frustration through their lack of skills and inexperience or because their community development schemes failed, often at significant cost to the local community. Others still became unpopular because of their luxurious lifestyles and racially exclusive social worlds. However, dislike for

of India, September 28, 1967, p. 6; "Flow of foreign money: M.P.'s allegation," *Times of India*, March 12, 1968, p. 11.

[86] "Kerala request," *Times of India*, June 2, 1967, p. 12.

[87] "Peace Corps men not needed, says Ajoy Govt.," *Times of India*, March 28, 1969, p. 1; "Bengal ban on Peace Corps volunteers," *Times of India*, July 10, 1969, p. 10.

volunteers was underpinned by political sentiments. Snubs and slights directed at volunteers could be understood as acts of resistance towards the legacies of European colonization or the coming threat of American neocolonialism. At certain points, community tensions reached boiling point, resulting in violence or decisions to expel volunteers. In these cases, personal enmity often converged with political resistance, resulting in crises that were both intensely personal and a potential diplomatic incident.

Resistance to development volunteering was overtly political too. Communists and left-leaning parties were the first to advance an ideological critique of development volunteering. From the mid-1960s, their arguments were picked up across the political spectrum as Global South communities and leaders became increasingly skeptical of the benefits brought by Western volunteers and suspicious of the relationship between volunteers and other levers of state power. As a government agency and as the representative of the rising global hegemon, the United States Peace Corps bore the brunt of resistance. As US foreign policy became increasingly interventionist, the image of the Peace Corps as a Trojan Horse for CIA or military infiltration circulated within and between newly independent nations jealous of their sovereignty. The circulation of anti-Peace Corps texts and opinion across Asia and Africa was a significant, but previously unrecognized, component of Third World internationalism in the 1960s.

From the mid-1960s, the cautious optimism of many Third World leaders soured and expulsions of volunteers accelerated. In her influential account, Elizabeth Cobbs depicted the Peace Corps as a moral triumph for the United States, claiming that the ideals embodied by the Peace Corps were "something to which no one could object and which touched core beliefs in many countries."[88] The long list of nations that took steps to expel Peace Corps volunteers suggests otherwise. The Peace Corps marginalized criticism by claiming that resistance was limited and confined to communists and radicals. Individual volunteers, who preferred to paper over or even forget instances of tension and conflict, also contributed to the marginalization of Third World critique. This has obscured the fact that the enthusiasm aroused by the Peace Corps in the early 1960s quickly turned to suspicion across the Global South and that this was true across the political spectrum, from Sukarno's Indonesia to Khan's Pakistan. The VSO and Australian volunteer programs largely avoided overt political clashes, except in the limited regions over which they exercised colonial influence. But as visible representatives of Western influence, they too felt the resistance of host communities, neighbors and co-workers.

Widespread criticism of Western volunteers destabilized the positive image cultivated by development volunteering agencies. In March 1967, a conference

[88] Cobbs Hoffman, *All You Need Is Love*, p. 108.

of the International Secretariat for Volunteer Service was held in New Delhi. As the Australian diplomatic delegation reported, the atmosphere was decidedly downcast, even gloomy. The disenchantment of Third World delegates provided a foil to the enthusiasm of similar meetings earlier in the decade; delegations dismissed "any starry-eyed ideas about volunteers by noting that the days when volunteers were popular and highly regarded as representatives of foreign nations are 'coming to an end'." They reported that "quite a number of volunteers have made little direct contribution in their regular assignments" and a "small minority have even made a negative contribution by leaving unfavourable impressions and disturbing or tying-up organisations and individuals who were actively engaged in useful and productive tasks."[89] Chronic resistance in the Third World, they noted, was joined by growing disillusionment with development volunteering in donor nations, which is the subject of the final chapter to this book. After years of tension, conflict and overt political opposition, delegates at the 1967 conference began to predict the imminent demise of development volunteering.

[89] Australian Embassy Bangkok, Memorandum no. 800, June 2, 1967, NAA: A1838, 936/20/3 Part 1.

10

To Hell with Good Intentions

Young and pretty with a blonde ponytail and a wide smile, Anita Fecht looked "like the public's idea of a Peace Corps volunteer." Until recently a college student and a member of the New Left, Fecht anticipated "the easiest and most natural identification" with Chilean students as she set off for Santiago in 1966. She was in for a rude shock. Far from offering friendship, "As a Peace Corps volunteer . . . the radical progressive students literally spit on me." Following this experience and after working in community development, Fecht began to reassess her presence in Chile. Before long, she began attending the regular anti-Peace-Corps demonstrations taking place across Santiago – even though she was still a Peace Corps volunteer. This "of course made me feel very uncomfortable and very ambivalent about what I was doing in Chile." Having arrived with good intentions, she now thought that "I should not have been in Chile, period." Fecht returned to the United States radicalized. Instead of a vehicle for goodwill, Fecht came to regard the Peace Corps as "really another means of imperialism." She was not alone. Thousands of Western volunteers returned home questioning the value of their postings and many began to demand that development volunteering should be drastically altered or abolished altogether.[1]

By the 1970s, development volunteering was in crisis. Antivolunteer sentiments escalated across the Global South and also spread back to the metropoles of London, Washington and Melbourne. This chapter unearths a largely overlooked cast of Western actors who disputed the value of the humanitarian-development complex and traces their impact on volunteering agencies. Returned volunteers like Anita Fecht were a major locus of antivolunteer critique. They were joined by a growing number of development experts and activists and, in a reversal of the tide of support documented in this book's early chapters, civic organizations and members of the public also began to reassess their support for development volunteering. Just as significantly, recruitment figures plummeted as Western youth increasingly turned to political and popular cultures that questioned the benefits of modernization.

[1] "How to win friends and stop revolution," radio broadcast by CRV members, 1969, Yale University Divinity Library (henceforth YDL): Alice L. Hageman Papers, Box 8, Folder 15.

In response, the United States Peace Corps, Britain's VSO and Australian Volunteers Abroad (the Volunteer Graduate Scheme's successor organization) underwent a decade of reevaluation that verged on identity crisis. All three agencies confronted enduring questions about volunteers' effectiveness, lifestyles and the long-term impacts of their work. They also confronted the ambiguities and tensions that had plagued development volunteering since its origins and instigated extensive reforms. Their success was limited. But development volunteering rose from the ashes regardless, underscoring the resilience and durability of the humanitarian-development complex into the 1980s and beyond.

Reassessments

Anita Fecht's radicalization came about partly because of direct experience with Third World opposition to the Peace Corps. But it was also tied to broader reassessments of international development taking place from the mid-1960s. Although Raúl Prebisch and Hans Singer had argued that the terms of trade for underdeveloped countries were prejudicial and deteriorating from 1949, dependency theory found a wider audience after Prebisch became Secretary-General of the United Nations Conference on Trade and Development (UNCTAD) in 1964. The critique of development was further bolstered by the 1967 publication of Andre Gunder Frank's *Capitalism and Underdevelopment in Latin America* and, later, of Walter Rodney's *How Europe Underdeveloped Africa* in 1972. Concern relating to the ecological destruction wrought by capitalist development also grew as part of the environmental movement arising in the 1960s.[2] These critiques inspired a new wave of development advocacy and activism. In January 1968, a group of British activists produced the Haslemere Declaration, stating that "'Overseas aid' is largely a myth; at best, a wholly inadequate payment for goods received, at worst another name for the continued exploitation of the poor countries by the rich."[3] Influenced by dependency theory, the Haslemere Group called for a restructure of global trade and tariffs and a revolution in foreign aid regimes, as "we cannot continue to be merely polite, respectable and ineffective lobbyists for 'more and better aid' when we have lost all faith in the ability of our governments to respond realistically to the desperate human need of the poor world."[4]

The maximalist development model advanced by development volunteering, combined with volunteer agencies' chronic inability to demonstrate

[2] Macekura, *Of Limits and Growth.*

[3] Haslemere Declaration Group, *The Haslemere Declaration: A Radical Analysis of the Relationships between the Rich World and the Poor World* (London: Battley Brothers Printers, 1968), p. 1. See also O'Sullivan, "The Search for Justice," p. 176.

[4] Haslemere Declaration Group, *The Haslemere Declaration*, p. 2.

benefits brought to host communities, rendered it into a particular site for critique. Among the most influential critics was radical Catholic priest Ivan Illich, who campaigned for the "withdrawal of all North American 'do-gooders'" from his base in Ceurnavaca, south of Mexico City. In 1968, Illich confronted a group of newly arrived volunteers with a speech titled "To Hell with Good Intentions." Far from helping the world's poor, he contended that volunteers were merely vectors for "the US way of life," which had "become a religion which must be accepted by all those who do not want to die by the sword – or napalm."[5] Altruism was not enough, stated Illich, and "you will not help anybody by your good intentions." Lacking technical expertise and dripping with unconscious cultural imperialism, volunteers could only be "irrelevant, misleading and even offensive."[6] Far from aid, development volunteering was an imposition on poorer peoples; if any benefit was to be gained, it accrued to the volunteer and "the damage that volunteers do willy-nilly is too high a price to pay for the belated insight that they shouldn't have been volunteers in the first place."[7]

In the United States, academics and other influential figures who had initially supported the Peace Corps reassessed their views as part of a broader reevaluation of America's role in the world. The liberal idealism of the early 1960s had been tarnished by military involvement in Vietnam and by American intervention in the domestic politics of postcolonial states across Latin America, Africa and Southeast Asia. In 1965, Gerald Berreman, Professor of Anthropology at the University of California, Berkeley, argued that opponents of the war in Vietnam should withhold all support and services from the US government. Berreman acknowledged the temptation to "make an exception of the Peace Corps ... [as] the one agency that seemed to promise something new and different," but he doubled down and encouraged young Americans to boycott the Peace Corps because of its direct involvement in US foreign policy.[8] He was backed by Professor of International Relations at San Francisco State College Marshall Windmiller, who argued that the Peace Corps had revealed itself to be "not an instrument of change ... but a counter-revolutionary organization" and so "Young people who sincerely want to see progressive change in the world would be best advised to stay out of it."[9] Windmiller's stance hardened as the Vietnam War dragged on. In 1970, he

5 Ivan Illich, "To Hell with Good Intentions," www.uvm.edu/~jashman/CDAE195_ESCI375/To%20Hell%20with%20Good%20Intentions.pdf, accessed February 5, 2020.

6 Todd Hartch, *The Prophet of Cuernavaca: Ivan Illich and the Crisis of the West* (Oxford: Oxford University Press, 2015), p. 41.

7 Ivan Illich, "To Hell with Good Intentions."

8 Marshall Windmiller, *The Peace Corps and Pax Americana* (Washington, DC: Public Affairs Press, 1970), p. v.

9 Marshall Windmiller, "Second Thoughts about the Peace Corps," KPFA Radio, November 16, 1967, YDL: Hageman papers, Box 8, Folder 15.

published *The Peace Corps and Pax Americana*, arguing that "The United States was attempting to police the world to protect its interests" and that the Peace Corps was "one of its most effective instruments." Far from an expression of American benevolence, Windmiller claimed the Peace Corps was "counterinsurgency in a velvet glove," which helped to "aid and abet [US] expansionism."[10]

The rise of the counterculture also took a toll on development volunteering. Prominent artists and cultural critics had become newly disenchanted with the artifice and monotony of late capitalist modernity in the 1950s. Their critiques were incorporated into the youth counterculture of the 1960s and 1970s.[11] Among other aspects, the counterculture looked to "traditional" cultures in Asia and North Africa as sites of an authenticity that had been lost in the West. Where the West was decried as a mechanized culture of "cold conformity" and "nine-to-five living," Asia, Africa and Latin America were imagined as its opposite: "a world that had not yet turned plastic" and which gnawed "away at reason and common sense."[12] This view subverted the logic of development: where development agencies sought to lift the Global South out of tradition and into modernity, the counterculture regarded modernity as a straitjacket and looked to developing nations for inspiration.

The alliance between young volunteers and state-led modernization also sat at odds with the nonconformism prized by the counterculture. More radical youth began to regard development volunteers as a throwback to more conservative times. In 1968, young Australian writer Frances Letters published an account of her travels through Southeast Asia. In Malaysia, Letters described an encounter with "a couple of twitty English girls ... whose height-of-the-Empire comments about 'natives' almost drove us to distraction." As Letters noted, the most "appalling thing was that they were with Voluntary Service Overseas, the British equivalent of the US Peace Corps."[13] Development volunteering lost more of its appeal as popular culture "tuned in" to Asia and Africa. Richard Neville's 1971 countercultural manifesto, *Play Power*, dramatized an encounter in Nepal in which a Peace Corps volunteer came face to face with a group of "flower people" travelling on the hippie trail. The Peace Corps had arrived in Nepal with plans to introduce local people to development; the hippies had arrived because they sought to escape the developed West and experience a more "authentic" way of life. In Neville's

10 Windmiller, *The Peace Corps and Pax Americana*, pp. v–vi, 2.

11 Bradford D. Martin, *The Theater Is in the Street: Politics and Performance in Sixties America* (Boston, MA: University of Massachusetts Press, 2004); Stephens, *Anti-Disciplinary Protest*. See also Theodore Roszak, *The Making of a Counter Culture* (London: Faber and Faber, 1969).

12 David Jenkins cited in Sobocinska, "Following the 'Hippie Sahibs'."

13 Frances Letters, *The Surprising Asians: A Hitch-Hike through Malaya, Thailand, Laos, Cambodia and South Vietnam* (Sydney: Angus & Robertson, 1968), pp. 92–3.

book, the counterculture won: the Peace Corps volunteer rebelled against the "culture of rank Xerox" and became "more native than the natives."[14] Development volunteering's maximalist vision of development sat awkwardly with the counterculture's Romantic discovery of "authenticity" in non-Western lifestyles. In Neville's book, the Peace Corps volunteer's conversion to "native" life was recounted with approval; development volunteering was no longer "In."

Others became disenchanted after witnessing the vast gap between volunteers' good intentions and the reality of their day-to-day lives. Glyn Roberts was a young Welshman who had been involved in the international work camp movement before turning his attention to development volunteering. In 1965, Roberts published *Volunteers in Africa and Asia: A Field Study*, based on an eighteen-month, UNESCO-funded tour of eighteen countries where he closely observed VSO, Peace Corps and other volunteers. Although most volunteers had come to Asia and Africa with the best of intentions, Roberts found that "many tend to 'give up trying' after two or three months." As he wrote, "International voluntary service reflects, to some, a heroic image. They see a lone eighteen-year-old in a grass hut: he eats roots and honey, speaks fluent Swahili and builds in one short year a pipeline, three bridges and the village school."[15] Yet, on the ground, the reality was very different: "many volunteers tend to gravitate towards European circles enjoying the food, music and common interests."[16] This was compounded by what Roberts called "The Servant Problem," warning that "it is dangerously easy for inexperienced youth, fresh to Africa (or Asia) to develop master–servant attitudes."[17] Although Roberts called on volunteer agencies to "take a much stronger line" on volunteers' generous stipends, social enclavism and use of servants, at this stage he continued to support development volunteering.[18] In 1965, he thought the abstract potential for volunteering to "form the basis to a new, international morality" overcame the contradictions and tensions encountered at ground level.[19]

This had changed by 1968, when Roberts published his next book, *Volunteers and Neo-Colonialism*, based on subsequent experience as a supervisor of Western volunteers in Ethiopia. By now, Roberts' faith in volunteers' good intentions had melted away. He now thought "there is nothing very remarkable about the volunteer's ideals" and, what is more, "conflict begins the moment he starts to live by them."[20] In Ethiopia, Roberts had borne "special witness" to volunteers enjoying "a standard of living which,

[14] Richard Neville, *Play Power* (London: Jonathan Cape, 1970), p. 220.
[15] Roberts, *Volunteers in Africa and Asia: A Field Study*, p. 7.
[16] Ibid., p. 11.
[17] Ibid., p. 39.
[18] Ibid., p. 40.
[19] Ibid., p. 54.
[20] *Volunteers and Neo-Colonialism*, p. 5.

even by European standards is comfortable middle-class, and by current African standards puts them in the same class as the ruling elite."[21] As a result, he now believed that "no Peace Corps, sponsored and controlled by a rich-country government, can be other than neo-colonialist."[22] Investigating volunteers had led Glyn Roberts to become more critical about development as "a world-wide system for preserving privilege and power," so that he now declared that "Foreign Aid is largely an international deception."[23] From his focus on development volunteering, Roberts moved to a radical critique of the broader international development system in his third and most influential book, Questioning Development, first published in 1974 and reprinted into the 1980s. Building on socialist analyses and social justice theory, Roberts questioned the social value of economic growth, pointed to modernization's dependence on fossil fuels and unearthed its "nasty tendency to concentrate power in the hands of the strong."[24] Roberts' initial distaste at the comfortable lifestyles and racially exclusive social circles of volunteers in Africa and Asia had matured into a structural critique of development volunteering as a form of neocolonialism, before expanding into a critique of foreign aid more generally. The extent of Roberts' personal experience with Western volunteers was unusual, but his growing disenchantment with development volunteering over the course of the 1960s and 1970s was not.

Returned Volunteer Action

From the late 1960s, returned volunteers formed a locus of opposition to development volunteering. Like Anita Fecht, some had begun to reevaluate the value of development volunteering after meeting resistance in the Global South. Others folded opposition to development volunteering within broader critiques that had developed over the course of the 1960s. As one former Peace Corps volunteer recounted, in 1961, "many thought that [the Peace Corps] was a symbol of the generous United States ... Now, in 1969, it is important to recall that the Peace Corps was conceived by the same people who, at the same time, conceived the Green Berets, the war in Viet Nam, and the invasion of the Bay of Pigs."[25]

Radicalized volunteers began to subvert networks of returned VSOs and Peace Corps volunteers. In Britain, Returned Volunteer Action (initially called the Voluntary Overseas Service Association) was established in 1962 to translate the spirit of voluntary service into the domestic sphere and particularly to

21 Ibid., pp. 32–3.
22 Ibid., p. 35.
23 Ibid., pp. 5–6.
24 Glyn Roberts, *Questioning Development* (Hampshire: The Alver Press, 1981), p. 7.
25 "How to win friends and stop revolution," radio broadcast by CRV members, 1969, YDL: Hageman Papers, Box 8, Folder 15.

enable ex-volunteers to "play an active part in the field of race relations in this country."[26] In the United States, the Committee of Returned Volunteers was formed in 1966 to lobby the government on foreign policy.[27] In a statement signed by over 2,000 former Peace Corps and other volunteers, which was forwarded to the White House, the Committee of Returned Volunteers noted that "It has often been said that those who serve abroad will make their most important contribution when they return, by helping the United States understand other nations. It is on the basis of our experience overseas ... that we now speak."[28]

Although established for other purposes, both organizations soon began to question the value of development volunteering. In the United States, the Committee of Returned Volunteers was quickly radicalized. A 1968 position paper held that "Our illusions about the United States lie in shambles, buried beneath the ashes of the Vietnamese and other peoples the world over." It continued: "We have had to face the hard truth that the United States' government, far from being the chief defender of weak and oppressed peoples, is in fact a powerful opponent of freedom, justice and well-being in nearly every country of the world."[29] Having faced this "hard truth," the Committee of Returned Volunteers adopted increasingly radical platforms including "revolutionary armed struggle" and "an international struggle against (US) imperialism."[30] Opposition to the Peace Corps was folded into this broader agenda. For the Committee of Returned Volunteers, the question was no longer how to improve the Peace Corps, but rather "Does Volunteer Service Hinder Development?" Building on members' personal experiences, the Committee of Returned Volunteers criticized Western volunteers' comfortable lifestyles, racially-exclusive social circles and their tendency to devise community development projects that were irrelevant or even harmful to local communities. It also critiqued the Peace Corps' haphazard monitoring and evaluation measures, which neglected to track impacts on recipient communities and kept volunteers in the field "as long as it feels they are doing no damage either to themselves or to their agency." Most broadly, the Committee of Returned Volunteers challenged the maximalist model of development intervention, by which "volunteers see their task as one of changing individuals so

[26] For clarity, this chapter refers to the organization by its later name of Returned Volunteer Action, which was adopted in 1974. The quote is from Elizabeth Bissett-Robinson, *VOSA News*, June/July 1969, p. 5.

[27] "A CRV Chronology," YDL: Hageman Papers, Box 8, Folder 1.

[28] Committee of Returned Volunteers, "Position Paper on Vietnam," September 1967, YDL: Hageman Papers, Box 8, Folder 1.

[29] "Political Position Paper accepted by acclamation at the Assembly and proposed as a new statement of purpose for CRV," 1968, YDL: Hageman Papers, Box 8, Folder 1.

[30] "Some Salient Characteristics of CRV," undated, *c.*1969, YDL: Hageman Papers, Box 8, Folder 1.

they can survive and advance within their society," as this "perpetuates neo-colonialist values and mentalities." They posed "the real question of whether the presence of volunteers only perpetuates existing exploitative patterns … whether volunteers, especially if only B.A. generalists, can be of assistance … [or] whether their own cultural training and biases make them so dysfunctional that their presence is more a liability than an asset."[31]

In Britain, Returned Volunteer Action followed a similar trajectory, albeit a few years later. In February 1970, a letter to the organization's newsletter implored members to "Throw off your neo-colonial attitudes … [and] change the society in your own country first, before you go meddling in others trying to hide from them the true nature of their own oppression."[32] The following year, Returned Volunteer Action published a critique of volunteer teachers in Africa, arguing that their "efforts could easily be counter-productive with the horrifying thought that the volunteer agency is … pushing a developing country further towards economic and social destruction."[33] As Returned Volunteer Action member Tom Reed explained, the jobs performed by volunteers were irrelevant at best and VSO was "simply keeping up a British public relations exercise, perpetuating the idea that a white man is by definition able to do better than blacks."[34] Returned Volunteer Action demanded, and was eventually granted, a seat on the VSO Council and on the Executive Committee. But its power was strictly limited and representatives complained that they were not taken seriously by the old colonial hands who still dominated VSO's staff. Even so, meetings began to take on a new tone as returned volunteers introduced discussion sessions at which "the words 'elitist' and 'cultural imperialist' flowed freely."[35] But reform did not follow and, in 1972, the Returned Volunteer Action National Conference opened with a speech suggesting that "the best sort of volunteer programme was no volunteer programme at all."[36]

The Committee of Returned Volunteers was more strident. From September 1969, it explicitly called for the liquidation of the Peace Corps. A "Position Paper" declared that volunteers had originally been motivated by a desire to "help people improve their lives." However, it continued, "our

[31] "Draft: Preliminary Statement – Volunteer Service and Development: Does Volunteer Service Hinder Development?" undated *c.*1968, YDL: Hageman Papers, Box 8, Folder 1.

[32] "An International Socialist," *VOSA News*, February 1970, p. 3, LSE: RVA records, Box 30.

[33] Dave Brown, "A new kind of thinking about the volunteer movement," *VOSA News*, March 1971, LSE: RVA records, Box 30.

[34] Angela Neustatter, "Many Unhappy Returns," *The Guardian*, July 24, 1975, p. B2.

[35] Peter Collecott, "VSO Returned Volunteers Advisory Committee," *VOSA News*, May 1972, LSE: RVA records, Box 30. See also Minutes of VSO Executive Committee, April 4, 1972, VSO Archive, Box 31.

[36] Josie Hooper, "VOSA National Conference 1972 – Volunteer Programmes," *VOSA News*, May 1972, LSE: RVA records, Box 30.

original idealistic concern did not include an understanding of the underlying causes – social, economic and political – of the underdevelopment we sought to combat." Now, returned volunteers had "come to a new realization that present day underdevelopment is in many cases perpetuated by the negative and destructive policies of the United States."[37] Rather than regarding the Peace Corps as an outlet for goodwill, the Committee of Returned Volunteers deemed it "a graduate school for imperialists" that aimed for the "Americanization of the entire world."[38] The Committee of Returned Volunteers was now "convinced that real development is often impossible without a revolution which carries out an equitable redistribution of economic and political power, including nationalization of all resources; one which makes education, employment, housing and medical care available to all the people."[39]

From early 1969, the Committee of Returned Volunteers sought a public platform for their anti-Peace-Corps campaign, "to make it clear that it is imperialistic, and that people should not go into it with the illusion that they are fostering change."[40] On the morning of May 9, 1970, sixteen members of the Committee of Returned Volunteers occupied the Southeast Asia wing of the Peace Corps building in Washington DC (Figure 10.1). Chanting "Ho Ho Ho Chi Minh, the NLF is gonna win," they used office furniture to create a barricade, declared the site a "Liberated Zone" and draped a large banner reading "Liberation not Pacification" from the windows, alongside the flag of the Provisional Revolutionary Government of South Vietnam, a Ho Chi Minh banner, a Yippie flag and a "Free the Panthers" poster.[41] The Committee of Returned Volunteers released a statement explaining that "our occupation was an attempt to liberate the Peace Corps and to put an end to its role in the exploitation and domination of the Third World." As volunteers, they continued,

> we went abroad to help Asians, Africans and Latin Americans develop their resources and become free people. Once abroad we discovered that we were part of the U.S. worldwide pacification process. We found that U.S. projects in these countries are designed to achieve political control and economic exploitation: to build an Empire for the United States. As volunteers we were part of that strategy; we were the Marines in velvet gloves.[42]

37 "Position Paper on the Peace Corps," September 15, 1969, YDL: Hageman Papers, Box 8, Folder 1.

38 Paul Cowan and Nick Zydycrn, "Let's make the Peace Corps a Graduate School for Revolutionaries," YDL: Hageman Papers, Box 8, Folder 15.

39 "Position Paper on the Peace Corps," September 15, 1969, YDL: Hageman Papers, Box 8, Folder 1.

40 Transcript of CRV National Board Discussion on the Peace Corps, March 28, 1969, YDL: Hageman Papers, Box 8, Folder 15.

41 "Final Statement on the Liberation of the Peace Corps," YDL: Hageman Papers, Box 8, Folder 15.

42 "Liberation, not Pacification," YDL: Hageman Papers, Box 8, Folder 15.

Figure 10.1 Committee of Returned Volunteers members occupying Peace Corps Headquarters in Washington, DC on May 9, 1970. Garth Eliassen/Getty Images.

The Occupation drew national media coverage and featured in global newspapers including the *Times of India.*[43] It continued until the evening of May 10, when protestors were allowed to depart unmolested (as one participant wrote, "it is no longer necessary to prove one's sincerity by going to jail"[44]). The

[43] Karl Bernstein and Peter Osnos, "Officials Meet with Students on Grievances," *Washington Post*, May 9, 1970; Peter Grose, "250 in State Dept. Sign a War Protest," *New York Times*, May 9, 1970, p. 1; "Demonstrators occupy Peace Corps HQ," *Times of India*, May 10, 1970, p. 1.

[44] Tom Newman, "Rationale for Liberating Zones," *CRV Newsletter: Repression, Rebellion, Revolution*, May 1970, no. 4, issue 4, p. 18.

following day, a smaller group of returned volunteers declared their solidarity by entering the San Francisco office of the Peace Corps for a similarly short-lived occupation.

The Occupation was the Committee of Returned Volunteers' most dramatic attempt to destabilize the Peace Corps, but it was buttressed by a range of day-to-day activities. Members tried to convince serving volunteers to terminate from the Peace Corps, thus undermining the organization's major resource. They encouraged dissent by claiming that, in hindsight, volunteers would find that "The important question is not whether we were well-intentioned, but rather were we serving imperialism."[45] Although the Committee of Returned Volunteers built contacts with volunteers working in Africa, Asia and Latin America, there is little evidence they succeeded in converting significant numbers to their cause. More commonly, former volunteers joined the Committee of Returned Volunteers after a period of reflection following their return to the United States.

In the end, the Committee of Returned Volunteers imploded under the weight of its revolutionary culture. In July 1970, a "women's liberation wing" occupied the national office and "liberated" it of what it claimed was an elitist and male-dominated leadership.[46] Subsequent experiments with collective leadership were not successful and contributed to a broader loss of organizational momentum. In mid-1971, both the founding New York chapter and the National Office of the Committee of Returned Volunteers disbanded, claiming that "it is now time to cease defining ourselves politically primarily as returned volunteers."[47] The liquidation of the Committee of Returned Volunteers left a vacuum in American political culture. In the short term, no dedicated North American organization stepped up to provide a sustained critique of the Peace Corps or development volunteering.

Britain's Returned Volunteer Action outlasted the US Committee of Returned Volunteers. Its activism peaked in the mid-1970s as it sought to end "neo-colonialism in the practices of many development aid organisations."[48] Secretary Sue Bullock argued that former volunteers needed to radicalize, "to see the system clearly and one's own place in it" and "not to be hoodwinked into patching up the holes when we're part of the machine that

[45] Bob Pearlman, "The Peace Corps: Servant of U.S. Imperialism," undated, *c.*1969, YDL: Hageman Papers, Box 8, Folder 15.

[46] Memo to CRV Membership, July 30, 1970, YDL: Hageman Papers, Box 8, Folder 1.

[47] Barbara Barnes to CRV/NY members, May 31, 1971, YDL: Hageman Papers, Box 8, Folder 1.

[48] Stephen Butters, "Returned Volunteer Action from 1966 to 2006: an assessment of the life cycle of the fly in the ointment of the British Volunteer Programme," www.history.ac.uk/podcasts/voluntary-action-history/returned-volunteer-action-1966–2006-assessment-life-cycle-fly, accessed July 10, 2019.

makes them."[49] Bullock also sought greater exposure. Returned Volunteer Action's pamphlets were distributed to universities across Britain and former volunteers attacked VSO on national television.[50] In 1974, Bullock featured in a *Guardian* report criticizing VSO's "colonial image." She argued that "VSO is becoming an anachronism" that tried to revive Britain's colonial past rather than advancing developing nations. By working with VSO, Bullock argued, volunteers were "doing more harm than good."[51] Yet, Returned Volunteer Action never went as far as its American counterpart. It did not demand that VSO shut down its operations, but rather called for reform from within. The moderate line came under sustained attack from more radical members, who encouraged returned volunteers to "continually assess and re-assess the potential of a reformist approach towards, as opposed to an explicit attack on, VSO."[52] Their views were represented in the anti-development tract *Power and Poverty*, authored by former VSO volunteer Rachel Heatley and published in 1979. Based on personal experience and academic research, Heatley argued that VSO did little to benefit developing nations, but in fact helped prop up repressive regimes across the Global South. She proposed that, rather than volunteering in distant nations, well-meaning young Britons should become involved in political campaigns to overthrow global capitalism. Although political activism lacked the glamor and adventure of overseas work, she argued, ultimately it was the only way in which young Britons' good intentions could possibly contribute to genuine change in the Global South.[53]

Identity Crisis

The 1970s were a low point for Western development volunteering agencies. The Peace Corps, VSO and the Australian agencies registered critiques voiced by returned volunteers and development activists and each agency also faced a sharp decline in applications. Internally, they began to raise questions about the benefits brought by Western volunteers. As one 1969 inquiry into the Peace Corps noted, "After two decades of technical and financial assistance to the Third World, the major problems of development remain, seemingly as intractable as ever."[54]

49 Sue Bullock, "Checkpoints for Action," *VOSA News*, May 1974, p. 8, LSE: RVA Records, Box 30.

50 "RVA Relations with VSO – Agenda Item 7," RVA Executive Committee, January 26, 1980, LSE: RVA Records, Box 2.

51 "Colonial image must go, overseas volunteers say," *The Guardian*, April 24, 1974, p. 10.

52 Rachel Heatley, *Poverty and Power: The Case for a Political Approach to Development and Its Implications for Action in the West* (London: Zed Press and Returned Volunteer Action, 1979), p. 45.

53 Ibid.

54 Russ Davis, Sol Chafkin, Dave Danielson et al., "Report of the Task Force on Technical Assistance and Peace Corps Programming," presented to the Peace Corps, June 1969, p. 1, JFKL: RG 490, Box 5.

The Peace Corps experienced a substantial crisis over the decade from 1968. The Nixon administration's cuts to aid budgets saw funding for the agency first stagnate, then fall in real terms.[55] This came during a period of national soul searching, as Americans confronted economic stagflation, widespread social discord and a relative decline of US influence around the world.[56] The fall in American morale raised an existential question for the Peace Corps: what did volunteers have to offer the world? Just as importantly, would young people still want to sign up? By the mid-1970s, observers noted that the "cultural revolution" had led to a "tendency of many young people to find expression in groups of their own making, rather than in established institutions like colleges, the military, or even the Peace Corps." Moreover, young people in the 1970s also faced a depressed job market; they no longer asked "the questions only rich men's children used to ask . . . 'If making a living is not going to be that much of a struggle, what are we going to do for adventure?'"[57] Every year from 1966 to 1969 saw a drop of some 15 percent in the number of applicants to the Peace Corps.[58] In 1970, the Peace Corps received fewer than half the number of applications it had at its peak in 1966. The number of volunteers posted abroad also fell. In the mid-1960s, the Peace Corps had more than 15,000 volunteers serving around the world; by mid-1976, that number bottomed out at fewer than 6,000. At the same time, attrition rates rose: by the mid-1970s, almost 50 percent of volunteers were expected to drop out before the end of their two-year terms.[59]

Australian Volunteers Abroad and VSO were much smaller, but they too experienced a steep decline in applications. In 1967, the secretary of Oxford University's Freshman's Association reported that "It's becoming fashionable to join a political society rather than social service groups like the VSO."[60] Those interested in development increasingly supported activist groups such as Oxfam or War on Want rather than the avowedly "apolitical" VSO. As one

[55] In 1966, the Peace Corps had a budget of over $114 million; by 1977 its appropriation had fallen to $67 million. See United States General Accounting Office, "Changes Needed for a Better Peace Corps, Report Presented to Action, Washington, D.C." (1979), pp. i–ii; "Hearings before a subcommittee of the Committee on Appropriations," House of Representatives, March 18, 1976.

[56] Michele Di Donato, "Landslides, Shocks and New Global Rules: The US and Western Europe in the New International History of the 1970s," *Journal of Contemporary History* 55, no. 1 (2020): 182–205; Stephen Tuck, "Introduction: Reconsidering the 1970s – the 1960s to a Disco Beat?" *Journal of Contemporary History* 43, no. 4 (2008): 617–20.

[57] Harlan Cleveland, "'The Future of the Peace Corps', Report Presented to ACTION, Washington, D.C." (1977), p. 27.

[58] Davis et al., "Report of the Task Force on Technical Assistance and Peace Corps Programming," p. 2.

[59] Cleveland, "The Future of the Peace Corps," pp. 4–5.

[60] Violet Johnstone and Michael Srutt, "Today, up at Oxford, the big theme is 'togetherness'," the *Telegraph*, October 14, 1967, p. 9.

young Briton working for Oxfam declared, "I didn't want to go on the VSO programme. I had no interest in teaching the rich to speak English or to mend cars."[61] In this context, the London *Daily Telegraph* speculated that youth had "had its Peace Corps fling."[62] In the decade from 1970, the VSO program halved from 1,483 volunteers to 726.[63] The Australian program was always tiny in comparison with VSO and the Peace Corps. Its high point came in 1968, when ninety-seven volunteers were selected and deployed in a single year. This number ebbed over the following decade, finally reaching a low of fifty-seven in 1980.[64] This drop is significant, however, as government funding remained stable. The falling number of volunteers fielded by Australian Volunteers Abroad reflected a lack of applications and internal discord alone.

All three agencies commissioned multiple reports and enacted new strategies to clarify their purpose and set a path for the future. One influential 1969 report encouraged the Peace Corps to reverse its reliance on BA generalists and instead recruit skilled volunteers to fill identified gaps in host countries' manpower development plans.[65] The BA generalist – Shriver's hero of the 1960s – had become a liability in the 1970s. The report also recommended a shift away from community development and teaching, the core planks of the 1960s Peace Corps. It found that "sending a few dozen teachers . . . is a waste of resources and provides little leverage for system change or development."[66] Incoming Director of the Peace Corps Joe Blatchford adopted many of the report's recommendations. In 1969, in a widely touted "New Directions" policy, Blatchford sought to replace BA generalists with technical specialists. Over the following years, community development fell away as a key focus area for the Peace Corps and the proportion of volunteers working in specialist and technical sectors, especially agriculture and health, grew correspondingly. But education retained its relative importance: in 1976, more than 51 percent of Peace Corps volunteers were still assigned to educational projects.[67] The Peace Corps also tried to present falling recruitments as a strength: Deputy Director Thomas J. Houser announced in 1970 that "we have abandoned the numbers game, which contends that a large number of volunteers indicates success."[68] The 1971 Annual Report claimed that "quantifying the Peace Corps effort is virtually impossible. The difference its Volunteers have made in thousands of

[61] Gill, *Drops in the Ocean: The Work of Oxfam, 1960–1970*, p. 25.
[62] "Students deserting aid work," *Sunday Telegraph*, May 23, 1971, p. 4; "Has youth had its Peace Corps fling?" *Daily Telegraph*, November 12, 1970, p. 11.
[63] Bird, *Never the Same Again*, p. 97.
[64] Britton, *Working for the World*, pp. 64–98. See also NAA: A4250, 1977/1252.
[65] Davis et al., "Report of the Task Force on Technical Assistance and Peace Corps Programming," p. 7.
[66] Ibid., p. 15.
[67] Cleveland, "The Future of the Peace Corps," p. 5.
[68] William Borders, "New Course for Peace Corps," *Times of India*, December 2, 1970, p. 10.

people's lives is not a matter of dollars and cents or facts and figures."[69] After fifteen years of pointing to the agency's growth as a sign of success, the Peace Corps reversed tack to argue for quality over quantity.

"New Directions" proved unable to reinvigorate the Peace Corps. In 1971, Nixon folded the Peace Corps into a new agency, ACTION, alongside the domestic service program Volunteers in Service to America (VISTA) and minor schemes such as the Foster Grandparents program. Nixon's move struck a deep blow to the Peace Corps, long proud of its independence from other agencies of State. It also affected the agency's visibility, setting back its public relations and information campaigns. At the same time, the Peace Corps bureaucracy ballooned. By 1976, the cost of maintaining a volunteer abroad was $14–15,000 per year, which was not much less than the average family income in the United States.[70] "New Directions" was also unable to reverse the Peace Corps' reliance on BA generalists and recent college graduates. Despite its best efforts, the agency was simply unable to recruit significant numbers of skilled workers. As a result, the profile of Peace Corps volunteers in the 1970s was not far removed from those of Shriver's day: the vast majority were white, college-educated, middle class and aged between twenty-one and thirty.[71]

The Peace Corps floundered. Joe Blatchford resigned as Peace Corps Director in 1971; over the next decade, six successors proved unable to hold the job for more than a year or two.[72] Congressional and Senate Committees expressed concern; as Democratic Congressman Lee H. Hamilton of Indiana noted in 1976, even supporters had come to believe that "the novelty of the Peace Corps has worn off" and the agency had begun to veer "in the wrong direction."[73] Detractors were more rancorous. Louisiana Democrat Otto Passman declared that "If there is anything that ever was mythical in the main, it is the Peace Corps," which "caused us nothing but trouble" and must now be brought under control.[74] A 1977 *New York Times* report declared the Peace Corps "Alive But Not So Well" and "a pale, bureaucratic shadow of

69 Peace Corps, *Tenth Annual Report*, p. 6.

70 Cleveland, "The Future of the Peace Corps," p. 5.

71 Ibid., p. 57.

72 Between 1971 and 1981, the position of Peace Corps Director was filled by Kevin O'Donnell (1971–2), Donald Hess (1972–3), Nick Craw (1973–4), John Dellenback (1975–7), Carolyn R. Payton (1977–8) and Richard F. Celeste (1979–81). Between 1971 and 1982, the Peace Corps Director was subordinate to the Director of ACTION.

73 "Statements by Members of Congress on Peace Corps, 15 August 1976," JFKL: RG 490, Box 11. Quote is from "Hearing before the Committee on International Relations: To Amend Further the Peace Corps Act," House of Representatives, February 26, 1976. See also John Chapman Chester and John H. Sullivan, "The Peace Corps in the 1970s," Report Presented to Committee of Foreign Affairs, US House of Representatives, February 1973.

74 "Hearings before a Subcommittee on Appropriations," House of Representatives, March 18, 1976.

one of the most original ideas to come out of the turbulent 1960s."[75] That same year, a further report was commissioned on the future of the Peace Corps from political scientist and former US Ambassador to NATO Harlan Cleveland. Cleveland found the agency "alive but invisible" and declared that "For many reasons the Peace Corps needs a fresh start."[76] He recommended the Peace Corps align itself with the latest trends in development – basic human needs and "appropriate technology" – and that it withdraw from a number of nations. This scaled-down Peace Corps demanded an adjustment of objectives: it was "not out to save the world or even to solve the world poverty problem, but rather to provide a growing experience for some Americans for the mutual benefit of the host country and America's future to cope in an interdependent world."[77] The change in focus was more tolerant of BA generalists: "if the criterion for project selection is that basic human needs are served, there is no reason why the distinction between experts and non-experts should create a doctrinal dilemma." In this context, the Peace Corps wheeled back around, replicating the language of VSO in the late 1950s. The increased focus on basic needs in the 1970s meant "there is plenty of room in this scheme of things for a relevant adventure, available to the young at heart of all ages, who want to express in action American values."[78]

Cleveland's reduced vision for the future of the Peace Corps did not turn around its fortunes. In 1979, the United States General Accounting Office was called in to report on Peace Corps operations. It found that, although volunteer programming was now focused on basic human needs, many projects were still of "questionable value."[79] Volunteers in Afghanistan, for example, were at best "marginally effective" because they were focused on teaching English to a small elite, were limited to urban Kabul and were disdained by local authorities.[80] Audits of volunteer positions in several other countries, from Malaysia and Thailand to Tunisia and Gabon, also suggested that volunteers weren't contributing in any significant way either to the nation's development or to meeting the basic human needs of its poorest citizens.[81] Just as significantly, it found that host countries were largely ambivalent about Peace Corps volunteers.

Britain's VSO also entered the 1970s with an identity crisis. As the Executive Committee noted, "there was an air of uncertainty regarding VSO's role in the

75 Terence Smith, "Peace Corps: Alive But Not So Well," *New York Times*, December 25, 1977, pp. 126–8.

76 Cleveland, "The Future of the Peace Corps," p. iii.

77 Ibid., p. ii.

78 Ibid., pp. 34–5.

79 United States General Accounting Office, "Changes Needed for a Better Peace Corps," pp. i–ii.

80 Ibid., pp. 5, 19.

81 Ibid., pp. 7–12.

1970s," which was "reflected in some criticism from returned volunteers and such organisations as Christian Aid and Oxfam."[82] In 1970, the volunteers' newsletter *VSO News* published a missive from a volunteer in Tunisia, asking "What are we doing here? Are we really necessary? Is there any useful purpose which we can fulfil?"[83] The dissatisfaction extended to younger members of VSO's staff, who differed from their senior colleagues in having no colonial experience. One so-called young turk on the staff noted that "Hundreds of volunteers are in plush secondary schools in relatively wealthy countries, designed to cater for social elites passing on middle-class values and often dealing with a given body of knowledge that is questionable in its irrelevance ... Do we honestly believe that this is right?"[84] Like the Peace Corps, VSO faced the additional problem of being unable to demonstrate its effectiveness. In 1972, VSO's Executive Committee attempted to measure the organization's success over the past ten years, but soon gave up, concluding that "It was almost impossible to give any real assessment of the value of the work done and it was hard to give an account of the work carried out." Even so, it continued, "It was generally felt that the large quantity of money that had been spent over the 10 years had been well used." This vague feeling was enough and the Executive Committee concluded that "it seemed pointless to spend large sums of money in making an appraisal."[85]

The same fundamental ambiguities that had attended VSO's launch in 1958 underpinned the identity crisis of the 1970s. As incoming Director David Collett mused in 1973, "The fundamental question was the philosophy of VSO." Essentially, he asked, "Is VSO to be about volunteers, and the element of altruism which should normally be implicit in volunteering? Or should VSO simply respond to the junior manpower requests of the Third World, whether or not these requests match up to the volunteer ethos?"[86] After years of resolute expansion, VSO was no closer to resolving the ambiguity of its aims than it had been in 1958. Discussions at VSO's London offices floundered on the problem of definitions: several members of the Executive Committee complained that "Motives for volunteering differed from individual to individual" and so "it was virtually impossible to define a volunteer." Some were eager to help the disadvantaged, whereas others "were not afraid of admitting that they wished to see the world."[87] Collett decided to resolve the matter once and for all. In 1974, he declared that VSO was to be a poverty-focused development agency and not a form of adventure training for British youth. The "concept of VSO as junior contract service on junior professional salaries"

[82] Minutes of VSO Executive Committee meeting, October 2, 1973, VSO Archive, Box 31.
[83] Cited in Bird, *Never the Same Again*, p. 87.
[84] Cited in ibid., p. 88.
[85] Minutes of VSO Executive Committee meeting, July 4, 1972, VSO Archive, Box 31.
[86] Minutes of VSO Executive Committee meeting, October 2, 1973, VSO Archive, Box 31.
[87] Minutes of VSO Executive Committee meeting, January 7, 1974, VSO Archive, Box 31.

was unacceptable, he said, "but we must face the fact that to a marked degree this was what we had become."[88] Collett proposed stricter criteria for project selection to ensure volunteers brought discernible benefits to local communities – even if this policy led to a reduction in the overall number of volunteers and the closure of some national programs. From the mid-1970s, VSO aimed to place all volunteers in jobs that would directly contribute to poverty alleviation.[89]

Collett's restructure was in accordance with broader patterns. The 1970s were transformative for the nation's development agencies. In the wake of the Haslemere Declaration, British NGOs and development agencies became resolutely focused on the needs of developing nations.[90] In 1975, Minister for Overseas Development Judith Hart announced the new policy focus of "More Help for the Poorest."[91] In line with the global shift to basic human needs, Hart directed that agencies and NGOs receiving government grants (including VSO) should focus on targeting the poorest people in the poorest nations, with a particular focus on rural development. Well-paid volunteers filling vacancies in elite institutions carried over from the colonial period no longer fitted with Britain's development strategy and VSO looked increasingly like an anachronism. In response, VSO shifted to prioritize development outcomes over adventure training for British youth. The major outcomes of this shift were the abandonment of the school-leaver "cadet" program, the extension of all VSO postings to a minimum of two years and the termination of VSO's relationship with the British Council as its "overseas arm." The shift was difficult – the old guard believed that the cadet program was the heart and soul of VSO – but it became increasingly unavoidable in the changing context of the 1970s. The British government refused to fund untrained school-leavers from the mid-1960s. For several years, VSO scrambled to find alternative sources of funding, but dwindling applicant numbers combined with a lack of requests from host countries finally forced the cadet program's closure in 1974. The relationship with the British Council was also a difficult one to break. Outsourcing the time-intensive tasks of project procurement and in-country oversight of volunteers had been both financially prudent and administratively convenient. But the British Council was focused on British soft power rather than development and Collett thought the two organizations'

88 Ibid.

89 Bird, *Never the Same Again*, p. 94. See also Robert Chambers and Alan Leather, *Volunteers and the Future of Britain's Development Cadre: Two Papers* (Brighton: Institute of Development Studies, University of Sussex, 1977).

90 Hilton et al., *The Politics of Expertise*; Hilton, "International Aid and Development NGOs in Britain and Human Rights since 1945"; O'Sullivan, "The Search for Justice"; Jones, "British Humanitarian NGOs and the Disaster Relief Industry, 1942–1985."

91 "More Help for the Poorest," Ministry for Overseas Development White Paper, October 1975.

paths had diverged. By 1980, some 80 percent of volunteers were managed by VSO's own staff (many of whom were former volunteers) and the relationship with the British Council was finally terminated in 1982.[92]

Voluntary Service Overseas also sought to distance itself from Britain's established elite and from its colonial past. By the mid-1970s, VSO's Council counted fewer lords and ladies and more development experts among its ranks. Even an organization as committed to amateurism as VSO could not escape the professionalization of international development in the 1970s.[93] The shift extended to volunteer recruitment. Rather than relying on recommendations from the headmasters of Britain's elite schools, VSO trialed new forms of recruitment, even extending to "the experiment of advertising in a popular daily paper, namely the *Sun*, for technicians," an initiative that resulted in over 1,000 enquiries.[94] A comparison of volunteer placements reveals that fewer volunteers were sent to elite schools or expatriate institutions in the 1970s than a decade prior and many more volunteers were deployed to hospitals, land cooperatives, irrigation schemes and livestock breeding projects.[95]

Yet, VSO's links with the old guard were not cut wholesale. Director David Collett may have increasingly focused on recipient communities' needs, but VSO's complex administrative structure meant that Collett's power was shared with the Chair of the Executive Committee and the Chairman of VSO's Council. Both these roles were held by old colonial hands through the 1970s. Freda Gwilliam, a member of VSO's Executive Committee from 1963 and later its Chair, was a retired civil servant who had entered the Colonial Office as an expert on women's education in 1946. She was a staunch member of the old guard and even as she took up her role at VSO she was conscious of being "more and more out of touch with the shape of things to come."[96] When she finally stepped down as Chair of the Executive Committee at the age of 71 in 1978, she still declared herself an "unashamed imperialist."[97] In 1975, the Chairmanship of VSO's Council passed from former Chancellor of the Exchequer Lord Amory to Malcolm Macdonald, son of Prime Minister Ramsay Macdonald and formerly Governor-General of British territories in Southeast Asia and colonial Kenya. Macdonald died in the role in 1981, just ahead of his eightieth birthday. While supportive of VSO's efforts in development, Macdonald was unwilling to relinquish the idea that volunteers primarily served to boost Britain's image following decolonization. As he remarked in

92 Bird, *Never the Same Again*, p. 95.

93 Hilton et al., *The Politics of Expertise*, pp. 54–79.

94 Minutes of Thirteenth Annual General Meeting, April 23, 1974, VSO Archive, Box 31.

95 Volunteer Placements, VSO Archive, Box 698.

96 Clive Whitehead, "Miss Freda Gwilliam (1907–1987): A Portrait of the 'Great Aunt' of British Colonial Education," *Journal of Educational Administration and History* 24, no. 2 (1992), p. 160.

97 Ibid., p. 156.

1979, Britain was ably represented by its foreign service, but "Volunteers are the real ambassadors."[98]

The problems and contradictions of volunteers living in comfort, often in quasi-colonial conditions, also proved impossible to resolve for VSO. As a result of lobbying by Returned Volunteer Action, from 1968 VSO's pre-departure training included a session on the "Ethos of Volunteering," with discussion of questions including "Are there 'right' motives for volunteers?", "How much should a volunteer be paid?" and "Should a volunteer employ a servant?" The accompanying material drew heavily upon Glyn Roberts' critiques and recommended *Volunteers and Neo-Colonialism* as preparatory reading for discussion groups. Yet, VSO did not make direct recommendations. Instead, individual discussion groups and volunteers were left to decide for themselves whether it was acceptable for volunteers to be "far richer than you ever expected to be" or whether it was better for them to seek out locals who could "[turn] us on to the poverty" and spend their generous stipends "buying irrigating equipment for local schools."[99] The VSO shift towards development may have been sincere but its ties to the colonial past proved difficult to sever.

Although it was the smallest agency, the Australian volunteer program suffered perhaps the greatest internal crisis. Initial enthusiasm surrounding development volunteering had dampened by the late 1960s. Australian volunteers' work in the colony of Papua New Guinea came under scrutiny amidst Indigenous opposition to white Australians' dominance of the territory's public service. Volunteers' effectiveness in Asia and Africa was also questioned, with critics arguing that the small number of volunteers sent by Australia meant that their contribution to development could hardly be more than tokenistic. The indefatigable Jim Webb had devoted more than a decade of unpaid work to the Volunteer Graduate Scheme from 1951; he then founded its successor organizations, Overseas Service Bureau and Australian Volunteers Abroad, and worked as Director of both. By the late 1960s, however, even a true believer like Webb had begun to ask critical questions. While volunteers certainly "demonstrate a commitment to the highest ideals," he now thought that "the goodwill, idealism and enthusiasm of those who offer their services in this way are only parts of the story." Webb took stock of critiques that volunteering agencies were often "guided more by the emotional desire on a young person's part to do voluntary service abroad" than by their capacity to contribute to host communities. He also registered receiving nations' disapproval.[100] Webb resigned from

[98] Bird, *Never the Same Again*, p. 97.

[99] "The Ethos of Volunteering – some suggested quotes for discussion," undated, *c.*1968, VSO Archive, Box 699.

[100] Jim Webb, "Volunteers and Overseas Aid," address to the Constitutional Association, Sydney, 1967, in James B. Webb, *Towards Survival: A Programme for Australia's Overseas Aid* (Melbourne: Community Aid Abroad, 1971), pp. 43–4.

all three Australian volunteer programs in 1969. Two years later, he published *Towards Survival: A Programme for Australia's Overseas Aid*, an overview of Australian development programs that included an analysis of development volunteering. By this time, Webb had come to believe that "foreign volunteers who stay for one or two years can not provide an adequate answer or even make a very crucial contribution to the profound and long-term problems of economic development and social change in Asia, Africa and elsewhere." Reversing nearly two decades of commitment to development volunteering, he now advised that "rather than developing a huge export volunteer scheme, it may be more appropriate for Australia to find ways to assist developing countries to tackle their internal problem of human skill and motivation."[101]

Following Webb's resignation, the three volunteering organizations were rolled into one program, Australian Volunteers Abroad. The new Director, Allan Martin, proved to be less successful than his predecessor. But the organization's woes extended beyond any one individual, reflecting broader ambiguities in Australian attitudes to development. In the 1970s, VSO and the Peace Corps gradually adopted development-focused policies, albeit with limited success. The Australian volunteer program's priorities skewed in a different direction, emphasizing diplomatic aims in the recognition that its limited resources could have little impact on developmental goals. This reflected government policy. In the 1970s, the vast majority of Australian aid budgets were expended in its colony of Papua New Guinea (which gained independence in 1975) and the neighboring nation of Indonesia, with aid expenditure pegged to political goals.[102] Australian volunteers were situated within a broader framework that regarded development as a significant form of soft power: as Prime Minister Gough Whitlam noted in 1973, "the work of Australian Volunteers Abroad is a personal communication between Australians and the people of developing countries."[103]

Although returned volunteers did not establish a formal association until the 1980s, a small but vocal group became increasingly trenchant in their disapproval of the direction taken by Australian Volunteers Abroad. Elizabeth Britten, a volunteer in Papua New Guinea in 1965–6, and Roger King, who had returned from Malaysia in 1972, became key critics of the agency's philosophical and managerial drift. Britten was elected to the Australian Volunteers Abroad Committee in 1975; over the next five years she led a campaign of opposition to Allan Martin's policies, ultimately provoking a vote of no confidence in his leadership. The Australian volunteer

[101] Ibid., pp. 46–7.

[102] Nicholas Ferns, *Australian Colonial and Foreign Policy in the Age of International Development* (Basingstoke, UK: Palgrave Macmillan, 2020); Philip Eldridge, "Australian Aid to Indonesia: Diplomacy or Development?" *Australian Outlook* 25, no. 2 (1971): 141–58; Frank Jarrett, *The Evolution of Australia's Aid Program* (Canberra: Australian Development Studies Network, 1994).

[103] Cited in Britton, *Working for the World*, p. 66.

program floundered, seemingly directionless, during this period of internal crisis. The future of Australian Volunteers Abroad seemed so uncertain that the Foreign Minister stepped in, commissioning a formal governmental review in 1981. The review determined that the agency could "no longer rely upon general tradition and brief statements of goals but now should explicitly determine and publish the objectives of the AVA program." These objectives should give "first priority to development cooperation which contributes to the advancement of the social and economic well-being of people in developing countries," while still including "other valuable goals" including cultural exchange, personal enrichment and professional experience in a new environment.[104] The multiple, and often conflicting, aims remained. After thirty years, the Australian program was no closer to resolving the essential ambiguity of purpose that lay at the heart of development volunteering.

The Developmental Phoenix

In 1972, delegates to a development volunteering conference in Ghana predicted that, due to their many contradictions, "this would be the last decade for such programmes to exist on a large scale."[105] The crises sustained by the Peace Corps, VSO and Australian Volunteers Abroad over the 1970s seemed to bear their predictions out; and yet, the development volunteering model did not collapse. Rather, the humanitarian-development complex endured its nadir and went on to reach new heights in the 1980s and beyond.

The Peace Corps bottomed out in 1976, after which volunteer numbers and political support again began to rise. Even at its lowest point, Peace Corps volunteers served in sixty-eight nations or, as Harlan Cleveland put it, "roughly half the UN's membership".[106] Britain's VSO also experienced a slow but steady resurgence; by 1978, a review of the British Volunteer Programme was optimistic about the organization's prospects for the 1980s.[107] In Australia, too, the 1981 government review of Australian Volunteers Abroad, instigated after a decade of stagnation, resulted in increased government support and investment, leading to organizational renewal and a resurgence in volunteer numbers during the 1980s.[108]

104 "Report to the Minister for Foreign Affairs by the Committee of Review into the Australian Volunteers Abroad Program" (Canberra: The Committee, 1981), p. vii.

105 Paul Osborn, "Domestic Volunteer Programs," *VOSA News*, May 1973, p. 14, LSE: RVA Records, Box 30.

106 Cleveland, "The Future of the Peace Corps," p. 5.

107 Overseas Development Group at the University of East Anglia, "The British Volunteer Programme: An Evaluation – Report Submitted to the British Volunteer Programme, April 1978" (University of East Anglia: Overseas Development Group, 1978), p. 2.

108 "Report to the Minister for Foreign Affairs by the Committee of Review into the Australian Volunteers Abroad Program." See also Britton, *Working for the World*, pp. 99–129.

The revitalization of development volunteering was aided by the broader shift to basic human needs. From the mid-1970s, the World Bank, United Nations agencies and bilateral aid programs shifted from large-scale modernization schemes to grassroots projects that targeted poverty and living conditions for the world's poorest people. Development volunteering agencies were ahead of the curve; as Cleveland noted, "'Basic human needs' is what overseas volunteer programs, both public and private, have always considered they were helping to meet."[109] Basic human needs also provided development volunteering organizations with a ready answer to questions about their effectiveness, which had plagued the Australian, British and American programs from the start. Volunteer agencies could never prove that volunteers made a marked difference to a nation's GDP or even a community's standard of living; the basic human needs paradigm discarded these development metrics, preferring the sort of qualitative stories about individual progress that volunteer agencies had been telling since the 1950s.

The turning tide of development volunteering's fortunes was also assisted by the launch of United Nations Volunteers (UNV). After years of assiduous lobbying by the United States, United Nations Secretary General U Thant established UNV in January 1971. Closely linked to the UN Development Programme, UNV removed some of the contradictions of bilateral development volunteering; in the absence of a national diplomatic role, volunteers were to be selected and placed in accordance to the needs of recipient nations.[110] As a multilateral agency, UNV also promised to solve the problem of political opposition faced by the Peace Corps and VSO; even the US Committee of Returned Volunteers supported the formation of UNV at the same time as it called for the abolition of the Peace Corps.[111] While the reality proved more complicated, with UNV quickly becoming an elite organization that shored up systems of privilege in both the Global North and Global South, the establishment of United Nations Volunteers helped rehabilitate the image of development volunteering and recover it as a site for idealism and hope.

Some volunteers continued to critique development volunteering throughout the 1970s, both through Returned Volunteer Action and individually. But the number of critics decreased and surveys of returned volunteers captured increasing rates of satisfaction from the late 1970s. The shift in development rhetoric towards basic human needs played a part, but the primary reason for the resurgence in volunteer satisfaction was the increased rate of unemployment experienced in the West during the 1970s. Many returned volunteers in

[109] Cleveland, "The Future of the Peace Corps," pp. 23–4.

[110] "United Nations Volunteers," April 5, 1972–December 12, 1973, United Nations Archive, AAG-006, S-0988-0001-03.

[111] "Preliminary Statement – Volunteer Service and Development: Does Volunteer Service Hinder Development?" 1968, YDL: Hageman Papers, Box 8, Folder 1.

the late 1960s had denounced volunteer agencies as harbingers of neocolonialism. A decade later, their successors were more interested in boosting their job prospects. A 1977 study found that few VSO volunteers had any regrets and that they were particularly satisfied with the benefits volunteering had brought to their careers. Notably, it found that a significant number of volunteers had gone on to work for development agencies including the British Ministry of Overseas Development or multilateral organizations like UNHCR, or else were employed with the British Council or in Christian missions.[112]

On balance, the opposition of radicalized former volunteers was outweighed by those who went on to become part of the humanitarian-development complex. By the mid-1970s, returned volunteers represented a growing proportion of permanent staff at the Peace Corps, VSO and Australian Volunteers Abroad. Former volunteers were also well represented among the professional "development cadres" entering NGOs and aid agencies from the 1970s.[113] Former volunteers were common among staff of official aid agencies including USAID, Britain's Ministry of Overseas Development and Australia's Development Assistance Bureau. They also formed a core cohort in development NGOs as they expanded and professionalized from the 1970s. Returned Australian volunteers, for instance, had an influence that belied their small number. Before Jim Webb resigned from development volunteering, he played a central role in the 1965 formation of the Australian Council for Overseas Aid (now ACFID), the peak body for development NGOs. Subsequently, he became Director of Community Aid Abroad, a major Australian NGO that later amalgamated with Oxfam Australia. Gwenda Rodda, the first female volunteer to Indonesia, went on to work on Colombo Plan projects in Singapore and South Asia. Vern Bailey, a doctor and two-time volunteer with the Volunteer Graduate Scheme, went on to develop a high-protein peanut paste to rehabilitate malnourished children, leading to a position at the World Health Organization and postings in Asia, the Pacific and Africa over more than three decades.[114] Other returned volunteers embarked on careers in academia. Herb Feith, the Volunteer Graduate Scheme's first volunteer, became a leading political scientist and Indonesianist in a career spanning four decades at Melbourne's Monash University. Ailsa Zainu'ddin, a former volunteer and editor of the Volunteer Graduate Scheme's magazine *Djembatan*, specialized in education and Australian–Indonesian relations at the same institution. This trajectory was not limited to Australian volunteers. The number of returned Peace Corps volunteers in academic area studies, for

112 Tim Albert, "Where the volunteer benefits," the *Observer*, June 12, 1977, p. 16.

113 Chambers and Leather, *Volunteers and the Future of Britain's Development Cadre: Two Papers*.

114 "Kenneth Vernon Bailey (World Health Organization 1964–1990)," www.who.int/formerstaff/history/bailey_kv.pdf, accessed February 20, 2017.

instance, remains remarkably high even today. Others still leveraged their volunteering experience into political influence. One 1977 report found that two congressmen and an estimated 100 congressional staffers were former Peace Corps volunteers.[115] It also reported that returned Peace Corps volunteers had a great "emotional commitment to doing something to enable other Americans to volunteer for an equally frustrating and exhilarating time of their lives."[116] Far from critiquing the experience of development volunteering as a form of neocolonialism, in the long term returned volunteers became its greatest boosters.

By the end of the 1970s, development volunteering had restored its legitimacy as an outlet for well-meaning Westerners who wished to assist development in the Global South. Over the following decades, the attractive image of development volunteering was monetized. From the late 1980s, development volunteering merged with the tourist industry to produce for-profit volunteer tourism, or voluntourism, which quickly grew into one of the fastest-growing segments of the tourism industry.[117] Far from resolving development volunteering's tensions between altruism and neocolonialism, for-profit voluntourism exacerbated them: voluntourists typically worked for far shorter periods than development volunteers (typically a few days or weeks) and were often involved in projects of questionable value to host communities.[118] Voluntourism also multiplied the number of volunteers setting off to save the world: by 2010, an estimated 3.3 million people per year volunteered abroad within a global industry valued in the billions of dollars.[119] The commercial success of voluntourism exposed the full appeal of the image of the volunteer, as established by the Volunteer Graduate Scheme, VSO and the Peace Corps in the 1950s and 1960s. By the twenty-first century, millions of

115 Cleveland, "The Future of the Peace Corps," p. 4.

116 Ibid., p. 9.

117 Wearing, *Volunteer Tourism*; Mostafanezhad, *Volunteer Tourism: Popular Humanitarianism in Neoliberal Times*; Mostafanezhad, "Volunteer Tourism and the Popular Humanitarian Gaze."

118 Kevin Lyons and Stephen Wearing, "All for a Good Cause? The Blurred Boundaries of Volunteering and Tourism." In *Journeys of Discovery in Volunteer Tourism*, edited by Kevin Lyons and Stephen Wearing (Wallingford, UK: CAB International, 2008), pp. 147–54; Daniel A. Guttentag, "The Possible Negative Impacts of Volunteer Tourism," *International Journal of Tourism Research* 11, no. 6 (2009): 537–51; Eliza Marguerite Raymond and C. Michael Hall, "The Development of Cross-Cultural (Mis) Understanding through Volunteer Tourism," *Journal of Sustainable Tourism* 6, no. 5 (2008): 530–43; Harng Luh Sin, "Volunteer Tourism: 'Involve Me and I Will Learn'?" *Annals of Tourism Research* 36, no. 3 (2009): 480–501.

119 Mostafanezhad, *Volunteer Tourism: Popular Humanitarianism in Neoliberal Times*, p. 6; Stephen Wearing and Nancy Gard McGehee, "Volunteer Tourism: A Review," *Tourism Management* 38 (2013): 120–30.

Westerners were willing to pay for the opportunity to play a part in the humanitarian-development complex.

Conclusion

Development volunteering faced a crisis of identity and appeal during the 1970s. Resistance to development volunteering, already commonplace across the Global South, now spread back home. Inherent tensions – between altruism and neocolonialism, between volunteers and host communities and between the Global North and the Global South – were drawn out by returned volunteers, activists and a popular culture that increasingly questioned the value of modernization and international development. Organized resistance movements demanded the cessation of development volunteering and the shuttering of VSO and the Peace Corps. In response, all three agencies explored in this book underwent a decade of internal reform in an attempt to turn the tide of expert opinion and diminishing popular interest. Although each agency took a slightly different course, they all confronted the overlapping and oftentimes contradictory motives that lay at their heart. Was development volunteering intended primarily to assist developing nations, to provide experience and adventure for Western youth or to project a positive national image? All three organizations failed to resolve this fundamental problem but, again, the essential ambiguity of development volunteering helped extend its appeal. By the end of the 1970s, the outlook for development volunteering had improved. The turn to basic human needs and establishment of United Nations Volunteers restored the injured legitimacy of the development volunteering model and the worsening economic conditions of the decade revived its appeal to Western youth.

And so, perhaps unexpectedly, the tide turned again. Far from collapsing under the weight of its own contradictions, development volunteering expanded over following decades. Entering the neoliberal market as voluntourism, by the twenty-first century development volunteering attracted millions of new recruits eager to save the world, whether it wanted saving or not. Their presence helped sustain the humanitarian-development complex. Development volunteering depoliticized the question of global inequality by suggesting that it could – and should – be solved by well-meaning individuals bringing economic, social and psychological models to the Global South. This diverted public attention and political will away from demands for structural change. Redistributive projects including UNCTAD and the New International Economic Order failed for a number of reasons, but significant among them was a lack of political support from Western publics preoccupied with popular humanitarianism and development volunteering.[120] The appeal

[120] See O'Sullivan, "The Search for Justice"; Vanessa Ogle, "State Rights Against Private Capital: The 'New International Economic Order' and the Struggle over Aid, Trade, and

of structural solutions was dampened by the recognition that they might negatively impact on Western lifestyles. But it was also drowned out by the established attraction of the humanitarian-development complex, which suggested that Western good intentions were enough to save the world. Internal contradictions of the development volunteering model, alongside its darker political and discursive undercurrents, had threatened the Peace Corps, VSO and Australian volunteer programs in the 1970s. But over subsequent decades, the apparent permanence of the humanitarian-development complex – both as a transnational cultural logic and as a tangible system of Western development intervention – was confirmed.

Foreign Investment, 1962–1981," *Humanity* 5, no. 2 (2014): 211–34; Nils Gilman, "The New International Economic Order: A Reintroduction," *Humanity* 6, no. 1 (2015): 1–16; Daniel J. Whelan, "'Under the Aegis of Man': The Right to Development and the Origins of the New International Economic Order," *Humanity* 6, no. 1 (2015): 93–108.

BIBLIOGRAPHY

Manuscript and Archival Sources

John F. Kennedy Presidential Library (JFKL)

Max Millikan, "Proposal on International Youth Service," MMPP-001–004.
Papers of Sargent Shriver.
Returned Peace Corps Volunteers Collection (RPCV).
RG 490: Records of the Peace Corps.

London School of Economics Women's Library (LSE)

Returned Volunteer Action Records.

National Archives of Australia (NAA)

A433, 1949/2/4823: Australian wives of Indonesians – Question of assistance.
A452, 1965/7235: Voluntary Overseas Service – Programme for 1966 AVA.
A452, 1965/8420: Australian Volunteers Abroad – Program for 1967 departures.
A452, 1966/6041: Policy aspects of government supported Australian Volunteers Abroad scheme of Overseas Service Bureau.
A452, 1971/1497: AVA, 1971.
A452, 1972/2549: AVA, 1972.
A463, 1965/4970: Parliamentary Question regarding government assistance to Australian Volunteers Abroad.
A1838, 250/7/20 Part 1: USA – External Relations – The Peace Corps.
A1838, 250/7/20 Part 2: USA – External Relations – The Peace Corps.
A1838, 936/20/3 Part 1: Papua and New Guinea – Foreign aid – Peace Corps proposals.
A1838, 2020/1/24/23: Review of Australian Aid Program.
A1838, 2032/1/31: Colombo Plan – Experts – Peace Corps.

A1893, 2032/5/4 Part 1: Recruitment of Experts – Indonesia – Volunteer Graduate Scheme.
A1838, 3034/10/20: Indonesia – Relations with Australia – Volunteer Graduate Association for Indonesia – Publications.
A4250, 1977/1252: Overseas Service Bureau – Annual Reports and Meetings.
A4250, 1977/1274: Overseas Service Bureau – Australian Volunteers Abroad – General.
A4359, 221/4/28A: Jakarta – United States Peace Corps.

National Library of Australia (NLA)

Ephemera, Overseas Service Bureau.
MP 377: US Embassy, Jakarta, Djakarta Press Summary, 1961–1965.
MS 980: Records of the Australian Student Christian Movement.
MS 2601: Records of Australian Scheme for Graduate Employment in Indonesia, 1950–1968.
MS 9073: Papers of Rev. Frank Engel.
MS 9347: Records of the Australian Council for International Development, 1960–2003.
MS 9926: Papers of Herb Feith.

New York Public Library, Performing Arts Research Collection

The Patty Duke Show: "Patty and the Peace Corps" typescript, CTR 366E.

The National Archives at Kew (TNA)

BW 93/24: British Council volunteer program, including VSO tour reports.
BW 167/5: Non-council posts – British volunteer program.
CO 859/1445: VSO policy.
CO 859/1446: VSO policy.
DO 162/23: VSO policy.
DO 163/22: VSO movement, 1960–1962.
DO 163/23: VSO policy.
DO 183/647: Future of VSO, 1965.
FCO 45/767: VSO in Malawi.
FO 371/185049: US Peace Corps – despatch and comparisons with VSO.
FO 371/185050: US Peace Corps – despatch and comparisons with VSO.
OD 8/465: VSO – Council Membership.
OD 8/466: VSO – Conditions of Service.
OD 8/467: VSO – Conditions of Service.

OD 10/3: VSO Policy, 1961–1962.
OD 10/4: VSO Policy.
OD 10/5: VSO Policy, 1963.
OD 10/6: VSO - Overseas administration.
OD 10/39: Voluntary Societies Committee for Service Overseas.
OD 10/40: Voluntary Societies Committee for Service Overseas.
OD 122/1: Policy of VSO.

United Nations Archives

UN Volunteer Program, S-0855–0012-16.
United Nations Volunteers, AAG-006, S-0988–0001-03.
United Nations Volunteers, S-0858–0005-08.

United States National Archives and Records Administration: The National Archives at College Park (NACP)

RG 490: Records of the Peace Corps.

Yale University Divinity Library (YDL)

Alice L. Hageman Papers.

Private Collections

VSO Archives.
Papers of Ailsa Zainu'ddin.
Papers of Frank Heffron relating to Margery Michelmore.
Photographs of Lindsey and Sylvia Cleland.

Periodicals (Place of Publication Unless Stated in Title)

The Age (Melbourne).
The Argus (Melbourne).
Antara News Service (Jakarta).
Ashanti Pioneer (Kumasi).
Atlantic Monthly (Boston).
Berita Harian (Kuala Lumpur).
Canberra Times.

Champaign-Urbana Courier.
Christian Comment (London).
Commonwealth Today (London).
CRV Newsletter: Repression, Rebellion, Revolution (New York).
Daily Express (Lagos).
Daily Graphic (Accra).
Daily Mail (London).
Djembatan (Melbourne).
Duta Masyarakat (Jakarta).
Farrago (Melbourne).
Ghanaian Times (Accra).
Guardian (Manchester).
Harian Rakyat (Jakarta).
Harian Umum (Yogyakarta).
Herald Tribune (New York).
The Hindu (Chennai).
In Unity (Melbourne).
La Prensa (Lima).
Malay Mail (Kuala Lumpur).
Merdeka (Jakarta).
News-Gazette (Champaign).
New York Times.
Observer (London).
Peace Corps Volunteer (Washington, DC).
Pedoman Minggu (Jakarta).
Singapore Free Press.
Straits Times (Singapore and Kuala Lumpur).
Sunday Express (Lagos).
Sunday Post (Lagos).
Sunday Telegraph (London).
Sydney Morning Herald.
Telegraph (London).
The Economist (London).
The National Observer (Washington, DC).
The New Yorker.
The Times (London).
This Month (USA).
Time (New York).
Times of India (Delhi).
Variety (Los Angeles).
Vogue (New York).
VOSA News (London).
Warta Berita (Jakarta).
Washington Post.

Interviews

Author's interview with Don Anderson, Canberra, May 2, 2016.
Author's interview with Lindsey and Sylvia Cleland, Canberra, May 5, 2016.
Author's interview with Jeff Miles, Canberra, May 3, 2016.
Author's interview with Ailsa Zainu'ddin, Melbourne, November 5, 2014 and May 14, 2015.

Official and Statistical Publications

Australian Bureau of Statistics, *Year Book Australia,* 1977–8.
Commonwealth of Australia, *Official Year Book of the Commonwealth of Australia,* No. 37 (1946–7).
Ministry for Overseas Development (UK), White Paper, *More Help for the Poorest,* October 1975.
Report of the Chairman of the United States Delegation to the 32nd Session of the UN Economic and Social Council, July 5–August 4, 1961.
United Nations World Tourism Organization. *Yearbook of Tourism Statistics,* 1988.

US Congressional and Senate Hearings

United States Senate, Committee on Foreign Relations, "Nomination of Robert Sargent Shriver to be Director of the Peace Corps," March 21, 1961.
Hearings before the Committee on Foreign Relations, United States Senate, on the Peace Corps, June 22 and 23, 1961.
Hearings before the Committee on Foreign Affairs, House of Representatives, August 11 and 15, 1961.
Hearings before the Committee on International Relations, House of Representatives, February 26, 1976.
Hearings before a Subcommittee of the Committee on Appropriations, House of Representatives, March 18, 1976.
Statements by Members of Congress on the Peace Corps, August 15, 1976.

United Kingdom Hansard

House of Commons Debates, March 9, 1961, Vol. 636, cc679–82.
House of Commons Debates, December 12, 1962, Vol. 669, cc423–81.

Unpublished Reports

Berthold, Gary D. and David C. McLelland. "The Impact of Peace Corps teachers on students in Ethiopia," Human Development Foundation, unpublished report to the Peace Corps, 1968.

Chambers, Robert and Alan Leather. Volunteers and the Future of Britain's Development Cadre: Two Papers. Brighton: Institute of Development Studies, University of Sussex, 1977.

Chester, John Chapman and John H. Sullivan. "The Peace Corps in the 1970s," Report Presented to the Committee of Foreign Affairs, US House of Representatives, February 1973.

Cleveland, Harlan. "The Future of the Peace Corps," Report Presented to ACTION, Washington, DC, 1977.

Davis, Russ, Sol Chafkin, Dave Danielson, Glenn Ferguson, Harry Petrequin and Irv Tragen. "Report of the Task Force on Technical Assistance and Peace Corps Programming," Report Presented to the Peace Corps, June 1969.

Dobbins, Henry F., Paul L. Doughty and Allan R. Holmberg. "Peace Corps Program Impact in the Peruvian Andes: Final Report," Cornell University Department of Anthropology, 1966.

Overseas Development Group at the University of East Anglia. "The British Volunteer Programme: An Evaluation," Report Submitted to the British Volunteer Programme, April 1978.

Peace Corps. *Peace Corps Fact Book*. Washington, DC: Peace Corps, 1961.

1st Annual Peace Corps Report. Washington, DC: Peace Corps, 1962.

2nd Annual Peace Corps Report. Washington, DC: Peace Corps, 1963.

3rd Annual Peace Corps Report. Washington, DC: Peace Corps, 1964.

5th Annual Report to Congress. Washington, DC: Peace Corps, 1966.

6th Annual Report. Washington, DC: Peace Corps, 1967.

Tenth Annual Report. Washington, DC: Peace Corps, 1971.

Report to the Minister for Foreign Affairs by the Committee of Review into the Australian Volunteers Abroad Program. Canberra, 1981.

United States General Accounting Office. "Changes Needed for a Better Peace Corps," Report Presented to ACTION, Washington, DC, 1979.

Volunteer Graduate Scheme. "Living and Working in Indonesia". Melbourne: Volunteer Graduate Association for Indonesia, 1962.

Internet Resources

Butters, Stephen. "Returned Volunteer Action from 1966 to 2006: An Assessment of the Life Cycle of the Fly in the Ointment of the British Volunteer Programme," www.history.ac.uk/podcasts/voluntary-action-history/returned-volunteer-action-1966–2006-assessment-life-cycle-fly, accessed July 10, 2019.

Cornell-Peru Project. "Vicos: A Virtual Tour," vicosperu.cornell.edu/vicos-site/cornellperu_page_1.htm, accessed November 18, 2019.

"Eton of the East," http://mayocollege.com/Eton.html, accessed July 18, 2019.

Hicks, Celeste. "I Was Raped and My Counsellor Asked Me What I Had Been Wearing," *The Guardian*, April 1, 2016, www.theguardian.com/global-development-professionals-network/2016/mar/31/i-was-raped-and-my-counsellor-asked-me-what-i-had-been-wearing, accessed February 4, 2020.

Kennedy, John F. Inaugural Address, January 20, 1961, www.jfklibrary.org/Research/Research-Aids/Ready-Reference/JFK-Quotations/Inaugural-Address.aspx, accessed October 21, 2016.

"Kenneth Vernon Bailey (World Health Organization 1964–1990)," www.who.int/formerstaff/history/bailey_kv.pdf, accessed February 20, 2017.

Illich, Ivan. "To Hell With Good Intentions," www.uvm.edu/~jashman/CDAE195_ESCI375/To%20Hell%20with%20Good%20Intentions.pdf, accessed February 5, 2020.

"Measuring Worth: Relative Worth Comparators and Data Sets," www.measuringworth.com, accessed May 30, 2020.

Schecter, Anna and Brian Ross. "Peace Corps Gang Rape: Volunteer Says U.S. Agency Ignored Warnings," *ABC News*, January 13, 2011, https://abcnews.go.com/Blotter/peace-corps-gang-rape-volunteer-jess-smochek-us/story?id=12599341, accessed January 25, 2020.

Stolberg, Sheryl Gay. "Peace Corps Volunteers Speak Out on Rape," *New York Times*, May 10, 2011, www.nytimes.com/2011/05/11/us/11corps.html, accessed February 4, 2020.

United Nations. Preamble to the UN Charter, signed June 26, 1945, www.un.org/en/sections/un-charter/preamble/index.html, accessed April 1, 2020.

Theses and Unpublished Secondary Sources

Bocking-Welch, Anna. "The British Public in a Shrinking World: Civic Engagement with the Declining Empire, 1960–1970." PhD thesis, University of York, 2012.

Feith, Betty. "Putting in a Stitch or Two: An Episode in Education for International Understanding – The Volunteer Graduate Scheme in Indonesia, 1950–63." M. Ed. Thesis, Monash University, 1984.

Jahanbani, Sheyda. "'A Different Kind of People': The Poor at Home and Abroad, 1935–1968." PhD thesis, Brown University, 2009.

Johnk, Elizabeth Z. "Peace Corps Culture and the Language of Violence: A Feminist Discursive Analysis." MA thesis, Eastern Michigan University, 2016.

Jones, Andrew. "British Humanitarian NGOs and the Disaster Relief Industry, 1942–1985." PhD thesis, University of Birmingham, 2014.

Jones, Charles C. "The Peace Corps: An Analysis of the Development, Problems, Preliminary Evaluation, and Future." PhD thesis, West Virginia University, 1967.

Kuhns Jr., Woodrow J. "The German Democratic Republic in the Third World." PhD thesis, University of Pennsylvania, 1985.

Penders, Christiaan Lambert. "Colonial Education Policy and Practice in Indonesia, 1900–1942." PhD thesis, Australian National University, 1968.

Pool, Jeremy. "Now Is the Time of Youth: Youth, Nationalism and Cultural Change in Ghana, 1940–1966." PhD thesis, Emory University, 2009.

Powell, Edward John. "Postcolonial Critical Perspectives on 'the West': Social Hegemony and Political Participation." PhD thesis, University of Leeds, 2014.

Riley, Charlotte Lydia. "Monstrous Predatory Vampires and Beneficent Fairy-Godmothers: British Post-War Colonial Development in Africa." PhD thesis, University College London, 2013.

Sasson, Tehila. "In the Name of Humanity: Britain and the Rise of Global Humanitarianism." PhD thesis, University of California, Berkeley, 2015.

Schein, Rebecca. "Landscape for a Good Citizen: The Peace Corps and the Cultural Logics of American Cosmopolitanism." PhD thesis, University of California, Santa Cruz, 2008.

Wayne, Beatrice Tychsen. "Restless Youth: Education, Activism and the Peace Corps in Ethiopia, 1962–1976." PhD thesis, New York University, 2017.

Published Sources

Abruzzo, Margaret. *Polemical Pain: Slavery, Cruelty and the Rise of Humanitarianism*. Baltimore, MD: The Johns Hopkins University Press, 2011.

Abu-Lughod, Lila and Catherine A. Lutz, eds. *Language and the Politics of Emotion*. Cambridge: Cambridge University Press, 1990.

Adams, Michael. *Voluntary Service Overseas: The Story of the First Ten Years*. London: Faber and Faber, 1968.

Adelman, Jeremy. "Epilogue: Development Dreams." In *The Development Century: A Global History*, edited by Stephen Macekura and Erez Manela, pp. 326–38. Cambridge: Cambridge University Press, 2018.

Ahlman, Jeffrey S. *Living with Nkrumahism: Nation, State and Pan-Africanism in Ghana*. Athens, OH: Ohio University Press, 2017.

Ahmed, Sara. *The Cultural Politics of Emotion*. Edinburgh: Edinburgh University Press, 2004.

Alanamu, Temilola. "Church Missionary Society Evangelists and Women's Labour in Nineteenth-Century Abẹ́òkúta." *Africa* 88, no. 2 (2018): 291–311.

Albertson, Maurice L., Andrew E. Rice and Pauline E. Birky. *New Frontiers for American Youth: Perspective on the Peace Corps*. Washington, DC: Public Affairs Press, 1961.

Allman, Jean Marie. *The Quills of the Porcupine: Asante Nationalism in an Emergent Ghana*. Madison, WI: University of Wisconsin Press, 1993.

Amin, Julius A. "The Perils of Missionary Diplomacy: The United States Peace Corps in Ghana." *Western Journal of Black Studies* 23, no. 1 (1999): 35–48.

Anderson, Benedict. *Imagined Communities: Reflections on the Origin and Spread of Nationalism*. London: Verso, 1991.

Anon. *The Peace Corps Again: A New Invasion of Ceylon*. Colombo: Tribune Publication, 1967.

Armstrong, Roger D. *Peace Corps and Christian Mission*. New York: Friendship Press, 1965.

Ashworth, John. "The Relationship Between Capitalism and Humanitarianism." *American Historical Review* 92, no. 4 (1987): 813–28.

Asiedu-Acquah, Emmanuel. "'We Shall Be Outspoken': Student Political Activism in Post-Independence Ghana, *c*.1957–1966." *Journal of Asian and African Studies* 54, no. 2 (2019): 169–88.

Azoulay, Ariella. *The Civil Contract of Photography*. New York: Zone Books, 2008.

Bailey, Beth. *Sex in the Heartland*. Cambridge, MA: Harvard University Press, 1999.

From Front Porch to Back Seat: Courtship in Twentieth-Century America. Baltimore, MD: Johns Hopkins University Press, 1988.

Bailkin, Jordanna. *The Afterlife of Empire*. Berkeley, CA: University of California Press, 2012.

Baillie Smith, Matt, Nina Laurie and Mark Griffiths. "South–South Volunteering and Development." *The Geographical Journal* 184, no. 2 (2017) 158–68.

Barnett, Michael. *Empire of Humanity: A History of Humanitarianism*. Ithaca, NY: Cornell University Press, 2011.

Barton, Frank. *The Press of Africa: Persecution and Perseverance*. New York: Africana Publishing Company, 1979.

Baugham, Emily. "'Every Citizen of Empire Implored to Save the Children!' Empire, Internationalism and the Save the Children Fund in Inter-War Britain." *Historical Research* 86, no. 231 (2013): 116–37.

Belmonte, Laura A. *Selling the American Way: U.S. Propaganda and the Cold War*. Philadelphia, PA: University of Pennsylvania Press, 2008.

Berry, Joseph B. *John F. Kennedy and the Media: The First Television President*. Lanham, MD: University Press of America, 1987.

Bially Mattern, Janice. "On Being Convinced: An Emotional Epistemology of International Relations." *International Theory* 6, no. 3 (2014): 589–94.

Biccum, April. "Marketing Development: Celebrity Politics and the 'New' Development Advocacy." *Third World Quarterly* 32, no. 7 (2011): 1331–46.

Bickers, Robert, ed. *Settlers and Expatriates: Britons Over the Seas*. Oxford: Oxford University Press, 2010.

Bird, Dick. *Never the Same Again: A History of VSO*. Cambridge: Lutterworth Press, 1998.

Bocking-Welch, Anna. *British Civic Society at the End of Empire: Decolonisation, Globalisation and International Responsibility*. Manchester, UK: Manchester University Press, 2018.

"Youth Against Hunger: Service, Activism and the Mobilisation of Young Humanitarians in 1960s Britain." *European Review of History* 23, no. 1–2 (2016): 154–70.

"Imperial Legacies and Internationalist Discourses: British Involvement in the United Nations Freedom from Hunger Campaign, 1960–70." *Journal of Imperial and Commonwealth History* 40, no. 5 (2012, December): 879–96.

Bodroghozy, Aniko. "The Media." In *A Companion to John F. Kennedy*, edited by Marc J. Selverstone, pp. 187–206. Chichester, UK: Wiley Blackwell, 2014.

Bose, Anuja. "Frantz Fanon and the Politicization of the Third World as a Collective Subject." *interventions* 21, no. 5 (2019): 671–89.

Brewis, Georgina. *A Social History of Student Volunteering*. New York: Palgrave Macmillan, 2014.

"From Service to Action? Students, Volunteering and Community Action in Mid Twentieth-Century Britain." *British Journal of Education Studies* 58, no. 4 (2010): 439–49.

Britton, Peter. *Working for the World: The Evolution of Australian Volunteers International*. Melbourne: Australian Scholarly Publishing, 2019.

Brouwer, Ruth Compton. *Canada's Global Villagers: CUSO in Development, 1961–86*. Vancouver and Toronto: UBC Press, 2013.

Brückenhaus, Daniel. *Policing Transnational Protest: Liberal Imperialism and the Surveillance of Anticolonialists in Europe, 1905–1945*. Oxford: Oxford University Press, 2017.

Busch, David S. "The Politics of International Volunteerism: The Peace Corps and Volunteers to America in the 1960s." *Diplomatic History* 42, no. 4 (2017): 669–93.

Byfield, Judith A. "Taxation, Women and the Colonial State: Egba Women's Tax Revolt." *Meridians: Feminism, Race, Transnationalism* 3, no. 2 (2003): 250–77.

Cameron, John and Anna Haanstra. "Development Made Sexy: How It Happened and What It Means." *Third World Quarterly* 29, no. 8 (2008): 1475–89.

Carey, Hilary M. *God's Empire: Religion and Colonialism in the British World, c.1801–1908*. Cambridge: Cambridge University Press, 2011.

Chouliaraki, Lilie. *The Spectatorship of Suffering*. London: SAGE, 2006.

Christiansen, Samantha and Zachary A. Scarlett, eds. *The Third World in the Global 1960s*. New York: Berghahn Books, 2013.

Clune, Frank. *Song of India*. Bombay: Thacker & Co. Ltd, 1947.

Cobbs, Elizabeth. "Decolonization, the Cold War, and the Foreign Policy of the Peace Corps." *Diplomatic History* 20, no. 1 (1996): 79–105.

Cobbs Hoffman, Elizabeth. *All You Need Is Love: The Peace Corps and the Spirit of the 1960s*. Cambridge, MA: Harvard University Press, 1998.

Coffey, Kenneth J. "Nurses and the Peace Corps", *American Journal of Nursing* 62, no. 7 (1962): 50–2.

Colley, Linda. "Going Native, Telling Tales: Captivity, Collaborations and Empire." *Past & Present*, 168, no. 1 (2000): 170–93.

Collins, Marcus. "Pride and Prejudice: West Indian Men in Mid-Twentieth-Century Britain." *Journal of British Studies* 40 (2001): 391–418.

Connelly, Chris A. "The Politics of the Games of the New Emerging Forces (GANEFO)." *The International Journal of the History of Sport* 29, no. 9 (2012): 1311–24.

Connelly, Matthew. "Taking Off the Cold War Lens: Visions of North–South Conflict During the Algerian War for Independence." *American Historical Review* 105, no. 3 (2000): 739–69.

Craggs, Ruth. "'The Long and Dusty Road': Comex Travel Cultures and Commonwealth Citizenship on the Asian Highway." *Cultural Geographies* 18, no. 3 (2011): 363–83.

"Situating the Imperial Archive: The Royal Empire Society Library, 1868–1945." *Journal of Historical Geography* 34, no. 1 (2008): 48–67.

Craggs, Ruth and Hannah Neate. "Post-Colonial Careering and Urban Policy Mobility: Between Britain and Nigeria, 1945–1990." *Transactions of the Institute of British Geographers* 42, no. 1 (2017): 44–57.

Craggs, Ruth and Claire Wintle, eds. *Cultures of Decolonisation: Transnational Productions and Practices, 1945–1970*. Manchester, UK: Manchester University Press, 2016.

Crossland, James, Melanie Oppenheimer, and Neville Wylie, eds. *The Red Cross Movement: Re-Evaluating and Re-Imagining the History of Humanitarianism*. Manchester, UK: Manchester University Press, 2020.

Cull, Nicholas J. *The Cold War and the United States Information Agency: American Propaganda and Public Diplomacy, 1945–1989*. Cambridge: Cambridge University Press, 2008.

Cuordileone, Kyle A. "'Politics in an Age of Anxiety': Cold War Political Culture and the Crisis in American Masculinity, 1949–1960." *The Journal of American History* 87, no. 2 (2000): 515–45.

Daly, Samuel Fury Childs. "From Crime to Coercion: Policing Dissent in Abeokuta, Nigeria, 1900–1940." *Journal of Imperial and Commonwealth History* 47, no. 3 (2019): 474–89.

D'Auria, Viviana. "More Than Tropical? Modern Housing, Expatriate Practitioners and the Volta River Project in Decolonising Ghana." In *Cultures of Decolonisation: Transnational Productions and Practices, 1945–70*, edited by Ruth Craggs and Claire Wintle, pp. 196–221. Manchester, UK: Manchester University Press, 2016.

Dickson, Mora ed. *A Chance to Serve*. London: Dennis Dobson, 1976.

A World Elsewhere: Voluntary Service Overseas. London: Dennis Dobson, 1964.

A Season in Sarawak. London: Dennis Dobson, 1962.

Di Donato, Michele. “Landslides, Shocks and New Global Rules: The US and Western Europe in the New International History of the 1970s.” *Journal of Contemporary History* 55, no. 1 (2020): 182–205.

Dimier, Veronique. *The Invention of a European Development Aid Bureaucracy: Recycling Empire*. London: Palgrave Macmillan, 2014.

Dirlik, Arif. “Spectres of the Third World: Global Modernity and the End of the Three Worlds.” *Third World Quarterly* 25, no. 1 (2004): 131–48.

Doran, Stuart. “Toeing the Line: Australia’s Abandonment of ‘Traditional’ West New Guinea Policy.” *Journal of Pacific History* 36, no. 1 (2001): 5–18.

Dudziak, Mary L. “*Brown* as a Cold War Case.” *Journal of American History* 91, no. 1 (2004, June): 32–42.

Easterly, William. *The White Man’s Burden: Why the West’s Efforts to Aid the Rest Have Done So Little Good*. New York: Penguin Press, 2006.

Ekbladh, David. *The Great American Mission: Modernization and the Construction of an American World Order*. Princeton, NJ: Princeton University Press, 2011.

Eldridge, Philip. “Australian Aid to Indonesia: Diplomacy or Development?” *Australian Outlook* 25, no. 2 (1971): 141–58.

Engerman, David C. *The Price of Aid: The Economic Cold War in India*. Cambridge, MA: Harvard University Press, 2018.

“The Romance of Economic Development and New Histories of the Cold War.” *Diplomatic History* 28, no. 1 (2004): 23–54.

Enloe, Cynthia. *Bananas, Beaches and Bases: Making Feminist Sense of International Politics*. Berkeley, CA: University of California Press, 1990.

Erickson, Aaron J., ed. *The Peace Corps: A Pictorial History*. New York: Hill and Wang, 1965.

Escobar, Arturo. *Encountering Development: The Making and Unmaking of the Third World*. Princeton, NJ: Princeton University Press, 1995.

Fassin, Didier. *Humanitarian Reason: A Moral History of the Present*. Berkeley, CA: University of California Press, 2012.

Fechter, Anne-Meike. *Transnational Lives: Expatriates in Indonesia*. Abingdon: Routledge, 2007.

Fechter, Anne-Meike and Katie Walsh. “Examining ‘Expatriate’ Continuities: Postcolonial Approaches to Mobile Professionals.” *Journal of Ethnic and Migration Studies* 36, no. 8 (2010): 1197–210.

Fehrenbach, Heide and Davide Rodogno, eds. *Humanitarian Photography: A History*. Cambridge: Cambridge University Press, 2016.

Feith, Herbert. *The Decline of Constitutional Democracy in Indonesia*. Ithaca, NY: Cornell University Press, 1962.

Feith, Herbert and Lance Castles, eds. *Indonesian Political Thinking, 1945–1965*. Ithaca, NY: Cornell University Press, 1970.

Ferguson, James. *The Anti-Politics Machine: ‘Development’, Depoliticization, and Bureaucratic Power in Lesotho*. Cambridge: Cambridge University Press, 1990.

Ferns, Nicholas. *Australian Colonial and Foreign Policy in the Age of International Development*. Basingstoke, UK: Palgrave Macmillan, 2020.

Fischer, Fritz. *Making Them Like Us: Peace Corps Volunteers in the 1960s*. Washington, DC: Smithsonian Institution Press, 1998.

Frey, Marc. "Control, Legitimacy, and the Securing of Interests: European Development Policy in South-East Asia from the Late Colonial Period to the Early 1960s." *Contemporary European History* 12, no. 4 (2003): 395–412.

Fuchs, Lawrence H. *Those Peculiar Americans: The Peace Corps and American National Character*. New York: Meredith Press, 1967.

Garner, Alice and Diane Kirkby. *Academic Ambassadors, Pacific Allies: Australia, America and the Fulbright Program*. Manchester, UK: Manchester University Press, 2019.

Geidel, Molly. *Peace Corps Fantasies: How Development Shaped the Global Sixties*. Minneapolis, MN: University of Minnesota Press, 2015.

Getachew, Adom. *Worldmaking After Empire: The Rise and Fall of Self-Determination*. Princeton, NJ: Princeton University Press, 2019.

Gill, Peter. *Drops in the Ocean: The Work of Oxfam, 1960–1970*. London: Macdonald Unit 75, 1970.

Gillette, Arthur. *One Million Volunteers: The Story of Volunteer Youth Service*. Harmondsworth, UK: Penguin, 1968.

Gilman, Nils. "The New International Economic Order: A Reintroduction." *Humanity* 6, no. 1 (2015): 1–16.

Mandarins of the Future: Modernization Theory in Cold War America. Baltimore, MD: Johns Hopkins University Press, 2003.

Gilroy, Paul. *After Empire: Melancholia or Convivial Culture*. Abingdon: Routledge, 2004.

Godwin, Francis W., Richard N. Goodwin and William F. Haddad. *The Hidden Force: A Report of the International Conference on Middle Level Manpower, San Juan, Puerto Rico, October 10–12, 1962*. New York: Harper & Row, 1963.

Goenawan, Andrew. "The Indonesian Press, Indonesian Journalism and Guided Democracy." In *The Indonesian Press: Its Past, Its People, Its Problems*, edited by Paul Tickell, pp. 15–19. Melbourne: Monash University Annual Indonesian Lecture Series, 1987.

Goldstein, Alyosha. "On the Internal Border: Colonial Difference, the Cold War, and the Locations of 'Underdevelopment'." *Comparative Studies in Society and History* 50, no. 1 (2008): 26–56.

Goodman, Michael K. and Christine Barnes. "Star/Poverty Space: The Making of the 'Development Celebrity'." *Celebrity Studies* 2, no. 1 (2011): 69–85.

Gordon, Suzanne N. and Nancy K. Sizer. *Why People Join the Peace Corps*. Washington DC: Institute for International Services, 1963.

Grubbs, Larry. *Secular Missionaries: Americans and African Development in the 1960s*. Amherst, MA: University of Massachusetts Press, 2009.

"Bringing 'the Gospel of Modernization' to Nigeria: American Nation Builders and Development Planning in the 1960s." *Peace and Change* 31, no. 3 (2006, July): 279–308.

Guttentag, Daniel A. "The Possible Negative Impacts of Volunteer Tourism." *International Journal of Tourism Research* 11, no. 6 (2009): 537–51.

Hardjono, Joan and Charles Warner, eds. *In Love with a Nation: Molly Bondan and Indonesia.* Picton, NSW: Charles Warner, 1995.

Hardjono, Ratih. *White Tribe of Asia: An Indonesian View of Australia.* Melbourne: Hyland House, 1994.

Harper, Tim. "The British 'Malayans'." In *Settlers and Expatriates: Britons over the Seas*, edited by Robert Bickers, The Oxford History of the British Empire Companion Series, pp. 233–68. Oxford: Oxford University Press, 2010.

Hartch, Todd. *The Prophet of Cuernavaca: Ivan Illich and the Crisis of the West.* Oxford: Oxford University Press, 2015.

Hashim, Azirah. "Not Plain Sailing: Malaysia's Language Choice in Policy and Education." *AILA Review* 22, no. 1 (2009): 36–51.

Haskell, Thomas L. "Capitalism and the Origins of the Humanitarian Sensibility, Part 1." *American Historical Review* 90, no. 2 (1985): 339–61.

"Capitalism and the Origins of the Humanitarian Sensibility, Part 2." *American Historical Review* 90, no. 3 (1985): 547–66.

Haslemere Declaration Group. *The Haslemere Declaration: A Radical Analysis of the Relationships Between the Rich World and the Poor World.* London: Battley Brothers Printers, 1968.

Hayes, Samuel P. *An International Peace Corps: The Promise and Problems.* Washington DC: Public Affairs Institute, 1961.

Heatley, Rachel. *Poverty and Power: The Case for a Political Approach to Development and Its Implications for Action in the West.* London: Zed Press and Returned Volunteer Action, 1979.

Hill, David T. "Press Challenges, Government Responses: Two Campaigns in 'Indonesia Raya'." In *The Indonesian Press: Its Past, Its People, Its Problems*, edited by Paul Tickell, pp. 21–38. Melbourne: Monash University Indonesian Lecture Series, 1987.

Hilton, Matthew. "Charity and the End of Empire: British Non-Governmental Organizations, Africa, and International Development in the 1960s." *American Historical Review* 123, no. 2 (2018): 493–517.

"International Aid and Development NGOs in Britain and Human Rights since 1945." *Humanity: An International Journal of Human Rights, Humanitarianism, and Development* 3, no. 3 (2012): 449–72.

"Politics Is Ordinary: Non-Governmental Organizations and Political Participation in Contemporary Britain." *Twentieth Century British History* 22, no. 2 (2011): 230–68.

Hilton, Matthew, James McKay, Nicholas Crowson and Jean-Francois Mouhot. *The Politics of Expertise: How NGOs Shaped Modern Britain*. Oxford: Oxford University Press, 2013.

Hodge, Joseph Morgan. "Writing the History of Development (Part 2: Longer, Deeper, Wider)." *Humanity: An International Journal of Human Rights, Humanitarianism and Development* 7, no. 1 (2016): 125–74.

"Writing the History of Development (Part 1: The First Wave)." *Humanity: An International Journal of Human Rights, Humanitarianism and Development* 6, no. 3 (2015, Winter): 429–63.

Triumph of the Expert: Agrarian Doctrines of Development and the Legacies of British Colonialism. Athens, OH: Ohio University Press, 2007.

Hong, Young-Sun. *Cold War Germany, the Third World, and the Global Humanitarian Regime*. Cambridge: Cambridge University Press, 2015.

Hoopes, Roy. *The Peace Corps Experience*. New York: Clarkson N. Potter Inc., 1968.

The Complete Peace Corps Guide. New York: The Dial Press, 1961.

Howe, Renate. *A Century of Influence: The Australian Student Christian Movement 1896–1996*. Sydney: UNSW Press, 2009.

"The Australian Student Christian Movement and Women's Activism in the Asia-Pacific Region, 1890s–1920s." *Australian Feminist Studies* 16, no. 36 (2001): 311–23.

Hutchison, Emma and Roland Bleicker. "Theorizing Emotions in World Politics." *International Theory* 6, no. 3 (2014): 491–514.

Immerwahr, Daniel. *Thinking Small: The United States and the Lure of Community Development*. Cambridge, MA: Harvard University Press, 2015.

Iriye, Akira. *Global Community: The Role of International Organizations in the Making of the Contemporary World*. Berkeley, CA: University of California Press, 2002.

Irwin, Julia F. *Making the World Safe: The American Red Cross and a Nation's Humanitarian Awakening*. New York: Oxford University Press, 2013.

Jarrett, Frank. *The Evolution of Australia's Aid Program*. Canberra: Australian Development Studies Network, 1994.

Jobs, Richard Ivan. "Where the Hell Are the People?" *Journal of Social History* 39, no. 2 (2005, Winter): 309–14.

Jones, Andrew. "Band Aid Revisited: Humanitarianism, Consumption and Philanthropy in the 1980s." *Contemporary British History* 31, no. 2 (2017): 189–209.

Kalter, Christoph. "A Shared Space of Imagination, Communication and Action: Perspectives on the History of the 'Third World'." In *The Third World in the Global 1960s*, edited by Samantha Christiansen and Zachary A. Scarlett, pp. 23–38. New York: Berghahn Books, 2012.

Kennedy, Dane. *The Magic Mountains: Hill Stations and the British Raj*. Berkeley, CA: University of California Press, 1996.

Kittler, Glenn D. *The Peace Corps*. New York: Paperback Library, 1963.

Klein, Christina. *Cold War Orientalism: Asia in the Middlebrow Imagination, 1945–1961*. Berkeley, CA: University of California Press, 2003.

Kotchemidova, Christina. "'From Good Cheer to Drive-by Smiling': A Social History of Cheerfulness." *Journal of Social History* 39, no. 1 (2005): 5–37.

Kothari, Uma. "Spatial Practices and Imaginaries: Experiences of Colonial Officers and Development Professionals." *Singapore Journal of Tropical Geography* 27 (2006): 235–53.

"Authority and Expertise: The Professionalisation of International Development and the Ordering of Dissent." *Antipode* 37, no. 3 (2005): 425–46.

Krozewski, Gerold. "Global Britain and the Post-Colonial World: The British Approach to Aid Policies at the 1964 Juncture." *Contemporary British History* 29, no. 2 (2015): 222–40.

Kunkel, Sönke. *Empire of Pictures: Global Media and the 1960s Remaking of American Foreign Policy*. New York: Berghahn Books, 2016.

Kushner, Barak. "Treacherous Allies: The Cold War in East Asia and American Postwar Anxiety." *Journal of Contemporary History* 45, no. 4 (2010): 812–43.

Lagos Study Group. *The Ugly American: A Study of the Peace Corps*. Lagos: Lagos Study Group, 1969.

Lake, Meredith. "Faith in Crisis: Christian University Students in Peace and War." *Australian Journal of Politics and History* 56, no. 3 (2010): 441–54.

Lal, Priya. *African Socialism in Postcolonial Tanzania: Between the Village and the World*. Cambridge: Cambridge University Press, 2015.

Lambert, David and Alan Lester, eds. *Colonial Lives Across the British Empire: Imperial Careering in the Long Nineteenth Century*. Cambridge: Cambridge University Press, 2006.

Latham, Michael E. *The Right Kind of Revolution: Modernization, Development and US Foreign Policy from the Cold War to the Present*. Ithaca, NY: Cornell University Press, 2010.

Modernization as Ideology: American Social Science and 'Nation Building' in the Kennedy Era. Chapel Hill, NC: University of North Carolina Press, 2000.

Lawrence, Michael and Rachel Tavernor, eds. *Global Humanitarianism and Media Culture*. Manchester, UK: Manchester University Press, 2019.

Lebovic, Sam. "From War Junk to Educational Exchange: The World War II Origins of the Fulbright Program and the Foundations of American Cultural Globalism, 1945–1950." *Diplomatic History* 37, no. 2 (2013): 280–312.

Lederer, William J. and Eugene Burdick. *The Ugly American*. New York: W. W. Norton & Company, 1958.

Lemberg, Diana. "The Universal Language of the Future: Decolonization, Development, and the American Embrace of Global English, 1945–1965." *Modern Intellectual History* 15, no. 2 (2018): 561–92.

Leonard, Pauline. *Expatriate Identities in Postcolonial Organizations: Working Whiteness*. Farnham, UK: Ashgate, 2010.

Letters, Frances. *The Surprising Asians: A Hitch-Hike through Malaya, Thailand, Laos, Cambodia and South Vietnam*. Sydney: Angus & Robertson, 1968.

Levine, Alan J. *After Sputnik: America, the World, and Cold War Conflicts*. New York: Routledge, 2018.

Lewis, Su Lin and Carolien Stolte. "Other Bandungs: Afro-Asian Internationalisms in the Early Cold War." *Journal of World History* 30, no. 1/2 (2019): 1–19.

Leys, Ruth. "The Turn to Affect: A Critique." *Critical Inquiry* 37, no. 3 (2011): 434–72.

Lockwood, Rupert. *Black Armada: Australia and the Struggle for Indonesian Independence, 1942–49*. Sydney: Hale & Iremonger, 1982.

Lorenzini, Sara. *Global Development: A Cold War History*. Princeton, NJ: Princeton University Press, 2019.

Lowe, David. "Canberra's Colombo Plan: Public Images of Australia's Relations with Post-Colonial South and Southeast Asia in the 1950s." *South Asia* 25, no. 2 (2010): 183–204.

Lowenhaupt Tsing, Anna. *Friction: An Ethnography of Global Connection*. Princeton, NJ: Princeton University Press, 2005.

Lowrie, Claire. *Masters and Servants: Cultures of Empire in the Tropics*. Manchester, UK: Manchester University Press, 2016.

Lutan, Rusli and Fan Hong. "The Politicization of Sport: GANEFO – a Case Study." *Sport in Society: Cultures, Commerce, Media, Politics* 8, no. 3 (2005): 425–39.

Lydon, Jane. *Imperial Emotions: The Politics of Empathy Across the British Empire*. Cambridge: Cambridge University Press, 2019.

Lyons, Kevin and Stephen Wearing. "All For a Good Cause? The Blurred Boundaries of Volunteering and Tourism." In *Journeys of Discovery in Volunteer Tourism*, edited by Kevin Lyons and Stephen Wearing, pp. 147–54. Wallingford, UK: CAB International, 2008.

MacCannell, Dean. *The Tourist: A New Theory of the Leisure Class*. London: Macmillan, 1976.

MacDonald, J. Fred. *One Nation under Television: The Rise and Decline of Network TV*. New York: Pantheon Books, 1990.

Macekura, Stephen. *Of Limits and Growth: The Rise of Global Sustainable Development in the Twentieth Century*. Cambridge: Cambridge University Press, 2015.

Macekura, Stephen and Erez Manela, eds. *The Development Century: A Global History*. Cambridge: Cambridge University Press, 2018.

Mackie, James Austin Copland. *Bandung 1955: Non-Alignment and Afro-Asian Solidarity*. Singapore: Editions Didier Millet, 2005.

Madow, Pauline, ed. *The Peace Corps*. New York: The H. W. Wilson Company, 1964.

Maga, Timothy P. "The New Frontier vs. Guided Democracy: JFK, Sukarno, and Indonesia, 1961–1963." *Presidential Studies Quarterly* 20, no. 1 (1990): 91–102.

Mansfield, Peter. *The British in Egypt*. New York: Weidenfeld and Nicolson, 1971.

Martin, Bradford D. *The Theater Is in the Street: Politics and Performance in Sixties America*. Boston, MA: University of Massachusetts Press, 2004.

McAlister, Melani. *The Kingdom of God Has No Borders: A Global History of American Evangelicals*. New York: Oxford University Press, 2018.

McKenzie, Beatrice Loftus. "The Problem of Women in the Department: Sex and Gender Discrimination in the 1960s United States Foreign Diplomatic Service." *European Journal of American Studies* 10, no. 1 (2015): 1–21.

McLisky, Claire. "'Due Observance of Justice, and the Protection of Their Rights': Philanthropy, Humanitarianism and Moral Purpose in the Aborigines Protection Society Circa 1837 and Its Portrayal in Australian Historiography, 1883–2003." *Limina* 11 (2005): 57–66.

Ministry of Overseas Development (UK). *Overseas Development: The Work of the New Ministry*. London: Her Majesty's Stationery Office, 1965.

Mishra, Pankaj. *From the Ruins of Empire: The Revolt Against the West and the Remaking of Asia*. London: Allen Lane, 2012.

Modell, John. *Into One's Own: From Youth to Adulthood in the United States, 1920–1975*. Berkeley, CA: University of California Press, 1989.

Moon, Katharine H. S. *Sex Among Allies: Military Prostitution in US–Korea Relations*. New York: Columbia University Press, 1997.

Moon, Suzanne. *Technology and Ethical Idealism: A History of Development in the Netherlands East Indies*. Leiden: CNWS Publications, 2007.

Morris, Robert C. *Overseas Volunteer Programs: Their Evolution and the Role of Governments in Their Support*. Lanham, MD: Lexington Books, 1973.

Mosher, Norman. "Taxes and Forced Savings in Ghana." *West Africa Report* 6, no. 9 (1961, October): 8.

Mosse, David, ed. *Adventures in Aidland: The Anthropology of Professionals in International Development*. New York: Berghahn Books, 2011.

Mostafanezhad, Mary. *Volunteer Tourism: Popular Humanitarianism in Neoliberal Times*. Farnham, UK: Ashgate, 2014.

"Volunteer Tourism and the Popular Humanitarian Gaze." *Geoforum* 54 (2014): 111–18.

Moyes, Adrian. *Volunteers in Development*. London: Overseas Development Institute, 1966.

Moyn, Samuel. *Not Enough: Human Rights in an Unequal World*. Cambridge, MA: Harvard University Press, 2018.

Muschik, Eva-Maria. "The Art of Chameleon Politics: From Colonial Servant to International Development Expert." *Humanity* 9, no. 2 (2018): 219–44.

Neville, Richard. *Play Power*. London: Jonathan Cape, 1970.

Nguyen, Vinh-Kim. "Antiretroviral Globalism, Biopolitics and Therapeutic Citizenship." In *Global Assemblages: Technology, Politics and Ethics as Anthropological Problems*, edited by Aihwa Ong and Stephen Collier, pp. 124–44. Oxford: Blackwell, 2005.

Nunan, Timothy. *Humanitarian Invasion: Global Development in Cold War Afghanistan*. Cambridge: Cambridge University Press, 2016.

Nyerere, Julius K. *Freedom and Socialism/Uhuru Na Ujamaa: A Selection from Writings and Speeches, 1965–1967*. Oxford: Oxford University Press, 1968.

Oakman, Daniel. *Facing Asia: A History of the Colombo Plan*. Canberra: Pandanus Books, 2004.

"The Seed of Freedom: Regional Security and the Colombo Plan." *Australian Journal of Politics and History* 46, no. 1 (2000): 67–85.

O'Brien, Anne. "Humanitarianism and Reparation in Colonial Australia." *Journal of Colonialism and Colonial History* 12, no. 2 (2011).

Ogle, Vanessa. "State Rights Against Private Capital: The 'New International Economic Order' and the Struggle Over Aid, Trade, and Foreign Investment, 1962–1981." *Humanity* 5, no. 2 (2014): 211–34.

O'Sullivan, Kevin. "The Search for Justice: NGOs in Britain and Ireland and the New International Economic Order, 1968–82." *Humanity* 6, no. 1 (2015): 173–87.

"A 'Global Nervous System': The Rise and Rise of European Humanitarian NGOs, 1945–1985." In *International Organizations and Development, 1945–1990*, edited by Sonke Kunkel, Marc Frey and Corinna R. Unger, pp. 196–219. Basingstoke, UK: Palgrave Macmillan, 2014.

"Humanitarian Encounters: Biafra, NGOs and Imaginings of the Third World in Britain and Ireland, 1967–1970." *Journal of Genocide Research* 16, no. 2–3 (2014): 299–315.

Paget, Karen M. *Patriotic Betrayal: The Inside Story of the CIA's Secret Campaign to Enroll American Students in the Crusade Against Communism*. New Haven, CT: Yale University Press, 2015.

Parker, Jason C. *Hearts, Minds, Voices: US Cold War Public Diplomacy and the Formation of the Third World*. New York: Oxford University Press, 2016.

Paulman, Johannes, ed. *Humanitarianism & Media: 1900 to the Present*. New York: Berghahn Books, 2019.

Peters, William. *Passport to Friendship: The Story of the Experiment in International Living*. New York: J. B. Lippincott Company, 1957.

Peterson, Derek R., Emma Hunter and Stephanie Newell, eds. *African Print Cultures: Newspapers and Their Publics in the Twentieth Century*. Ann Arbor, MI: University of Michigan Press, 2016.

Phillips, Anne. "What's Wrong with Essentialism?" *Distinktion: Journal of Social Theory* 11 (2010): 47–60.

Phillipson, Robert. *Linguistic Imperialism*. Oxford: Oxford University Press, 1992.

Philpott, Simon. "Fear of the Dark: Indonesia and the Australian National Imagination." *Australian Journal of International Affairs* 55, no. 3 (2001): 371–88.

Pietsch, Tamson. "Many Rhodes: Travelling Scholarships and Imperial Citizenship in the British Academic World, 1880–1940." *History of Education* 40, no. 6 (2011): 723–39.

Porter, Andrew. *Religion Versus Empire? British Protestant Missionaries and Overseas Expansion, 1700–1914*. Manchester, UK: Manchester University Press, 2004.

Prashad, Vijay. *The Poorer Nations: A Possible History of the Global South*. London: Verso, 2014.

The Darker Nations: A People's History of the Third World. New York: W. W. Norton, 2007.

Pratt, Mary Louise. *Imperial Eyes: Travel Writing and Transculturation*. Abingdon: Routledge, 1992.

Purcell, Fernando. *The Peace Corps in South America: Volunteers and the Global War on Poverty in the 1960s*. London: Palgrave Macmillan, 2019.

Purdey, Jemma. *From Vienna to Yogyakarta: The Life of Herb Feith*. Sydney: UNSW Press, 2011.

Radcliffe, Mathew. *Kampong Australia: The RAAF at Butterworth*. Sydney: NewSouth, 2017.

"In Defence of White Australia: Discouraging 'Asian Marriage' in Postwar South-East Asia." *Australian Historical Studies* 45, no. 2 (2014): 184–201.

Randall, Vicky. "Using and Abusing the Concept of the Third World: Geopolitics and the Comparative Political Study of Development and Underdevelopment." *Third World Quarterly* 25, no. 1 (2004): 41–53.

Rappa, Antonio L. and Lionel Wee. *Language Policy and Modernity in Southeast Asia: Malaysia, the Philippines, Singapore, and Thailand*. New York: Springer, 2006.

Rasiah, Rajah. *Foreign Capital and Industrialization in Malaysia*. Basingstoke, UK: Palgrave Macmillan, 1995.

Raymond, Eliza Marguerite and C. Michael Hall. "The Development of Cross-Cultural (Mis)Understanding through Volunteer Tourism." *Journal of Sustainable Tourism* 6, no. 5 (2008): 530–43.

Rideout, Lisa. "Representations of the 'Third World' in NGO Advertising: Practicalities, Colonial Discourse and Western Understandings of Development." *Journal of African Media Studies* 3, no. 1 (2011): 25–41.

Rist, Gilbert. *The History of Development: From Western Origins to Global Faith*. New York: Zed Books, 2002.

Roberts, Glyn. *Questioning Development*. Alverstoke, UK: The Alver Press, 1981.

Volunteers and Neo-Colonialism: An Inquiry into the Role of Foreign Volunteers in the Third World. Manchester, UK: A. J. Wright & Sons, 1968.

Volunteers in Africa and Asia: A Field Study. London: The Stanhope Press, 1965.

Rodgers, Willard L. and Arland Thornton. "Changing Patterns of First Marriage in the United States." *Demography* 22, no. 2 (1985): 265–79.

Rosenberg, Emily S. *Spreading the American Dream: American Economic and Cultural Expansion, 1890–1945*. New York: Hill and Wang, 1982.

Rostam-Kolayi, Jasamin. "The New Frontier Meets the White Revolution: The Peace Corps in Iran, 1962–76." *Iranian Studies* 51, no. 4 (2018): 587–612.

Roszak, Theodore. *The Making of a Counter Culture*. London: Faber and Faber, 1969.

Rottinghaus, Brandon. "'Dear Mr. President': The Institutionalization and Politicization of Public Opinion Mail in the White House." *Political Science Quarterly* 121, no. 3 (2006): 451–76.

Rozario, Kevin. "'Delicious Horrors': Mass Culture, The Red Cross, and the Appeal of Modern American Humanitarianism." *American Quarterly* 55, no. 3 (2003): 417–55.

Sasson, Tehila. "Milking the Third World? Humanitarianism, Capitalism, and the Moral Economy of the Nestle Boycott." *American Historical Review* 121, no. 4 (2016): 1196–224.

Seng Tan, See and Amitav Acharya, eds. *Bandung Revisited: The Legacy of the 1955 Asian-African Conference for International Order*. Singapore: NUS Press, 2008.

Shriver, R. Sargent. "Introduction." In Roy Hoopes, *The Complete Peace Corps Guide*. New York: The Dial Press, 1961.

Simpson, Bradley R. *Economists with Guns: Authoritarian Development and US-Indonesian Relations, 1960–1968*. Stanford, CA: Stanford University Press, 2008.

Sin, Harng Luh. "Volunteer Tourism: 'Involve Me and I Will Learn'?" *Annals of Tourism Research* 36, no. 3 (2009): 480–501.

Skinner, Rob and Alan Lester. "Humanitarianism and Empire: New Research Agendas." *Journal of Imperial and Commonwealth History* 40, no. 5 (2012): 729–47.

Skurnik, Walter A. E. "Ghana and Guinea, 1966 – a Case Study in Inter-African Relations." *Journal of Modern African Studies* 5, no. 3 (1967): 369–84.

Sluga, Glenda. *Internationalism in the Age of Nationalism*. Philadelphia, PA: University of Pennsylvania Press, 2013.

Smiley, Sarah L. "Expatriate Everyday Life in Dar Es Salaam, Tanzania: Colonial Origins and Contemporary Legacies." *Social & Cultural Geography* 11, no. 4 (2010): 327–42.

Smillie, Ian. *The Land of Lost Content: A History of CUSO*. Toronto: Deneau Publishers, 1985.

Smirl, Lisa. *Spaces of Aid: How Cars, Compounds and Hotels Shape Humanitarianism*. London: Zed Books, 2015.

Smith, Matt and Helen Yanacopoulos. "The Public Faces of Development: An Introduction." *Journal of International Development* 16, no. 5 (2004): 657–64.

Sobocinska, Agnieszka. "Popular Causes: The Volunteer Graduate Scheme, the Freedom from Hunger Campaign and Altruistic Internationalism in Australia." *Journal of Australian Studies* 43, no. 4 (2019): 509–24.

"How to Win Friends and Influence Nations: The International History of Development Volunteering." *Journal of Global History* 12, no. 1 (2017): 49–73.

"Measuring or Creating Attitudes? Seventy Years of Australian Public Opinion Polling About Indonesia." *Asian Studies Review* 41, no. 2 (2017): 371–88.

"A New Kind of Mission: The Volunteer Graduate Scheme and the Cultural History of International Development." *Australian Journal of Politics and History* 61, no. 3 (2016): 369–87.

"The Expedition's Afterlives: Echoes of Empire in Travel to Asia." In *Expedition into Empire: Exploratory Journeys and the Making of the Modern World*, edited by Martin Thomas, pp. 214–32. Abingdon: Routledge, 2015.

"Following the 'Hippie Sahibs': Colonial Cultures of Travel and the Hippie Trail." *Journal of Colonialism and Colonial History* 15, no. 2 (2014, Summer).

Visiting the Neighbours: Australians in Asia. Sydney: University of New South Wales Press/NewSouth, 2014.

"Visiting the Neighbours: The Political Meanings of Australian Travel to Cold War Asia." *Australian Historical Studies* 44, no. 3 (2013): 382–404.

"Hearts of Darkness, Hearts of Gold." In *Australia's Asia: From Yellow Peril to Asian Century*, edited by David Walker and Agnieszka Sobocinska, pp. 173–97. Crawley, Western Australia: UWA Press, 2012.

Sobocinska, Agnieszka and Richard White. "Travel and Connections." In *The Cambridge History of Australia, Volume 2: The Commonwealth of Australia*, edited by Alison Bashford and Stuart Macintyre, pp. 472–93. Melbourne: Cambridge University Press, 2013.

Sontag, Susan. *Regarding the Pain of Others*. London: Penguin, 2004.

Spigel, Lynn. *Welcome to the Dreamhouse: Popular Media and Postwar Suburbs*. Durham, NC: Duke University Press, 2001.

Stephens, Julie. *Anti-Disciplinary Protest: Sixties Radicalism and Postmodernism*. Cambridge: Cambridge University Press, 1998.

Stevenson, Betsey and Justin Wolfers. "Marriage and Divorce: Changes and Their Driving Forces." *Journal of Economic Perspectives* 21, no. 2 (2007): 27–52.

Stoler, Ann Laura. *Duress: Imperial Durabilities in Our Times*. Durham, NC: Duke University Press, 2016.

Carnal Knowledge and Imperial Power: Race and the Intimate in Colonial Rule. Berkeley, CA: University of California Press, 2002.

Race and the Education of Desire: Foucault's History of Sexuality and the Colonial Order of Things. Durham, NC: Duke University Press, 1995.

"Rethinking Colonial Categories: European Communities and the Boundaries of Rule." *Comparative Studies in Society and History* 31, no. 1 (1989, January): 134–61.

Sumarga. *Peace Corps*. Jakarta: Penerbit Djasa, 1964.

Taithe, Bertrand. "Compassion Fatigue: The Changing Nature of Humanitarian Emotions." In *Emotional Bodies: The Historical Performativity of Emotions*, edited by Delores Martin-Moruno and Beatriz Pichel, pp. 242–62. Champaign, IL: University of Illinois Press, 2019.

Tapsell, Ross. *By-Lines, Balibo, Bali Bombings: Australian Journalists in Indonesia*. Melbourne: Australian Scholarly Publishing, 2014.

Tavan, Gwenda. *The Long, Slow Death of White Australia*. Melbourne: Scribe Publications, 2005.

Textor, Robert B., ed. *Cultural Frontiers of the Peace Corps*. Cambridge, MA: MIT Press, 1966.

Thompson, Andrew S. "Unravelling the Relationships Between Humanitarianism, Human Rights and Decolonization: Time for a Radical Rethink?" In *The Oxford Handbook of the Ends of Empire* edited by Martin Thomas and Andrew S. Thompson, pp. 453–74 (Oxford: Oxford University Press, 2018).

Torney-Parlicki, Prue. *Somewhere in Asia: War, Journalism and Australia's Neighbours, 1941–75*. Sydney: University of New South Wales Press, 2000.

Truong, Thanh-Dam. *Sex, Money and Morality: Prostitution and Tourism in Southeast Asia*. London: Zed Books, 1990.

Tuck, Stephen. "Introduction: Reconsidering the 1970s – the 1960s to a Disco Beat?" *Journal of Contemporary History* 43, no. 4 (2008): 617–20.

Twomey, Christina. "Framing Atrocity: Photography and Humanitarianism." *History of Photography* 36, no. 2 (2012): 255–64.

Twomey, Christina, Agnieszka Sobocinska, Mathew Radcliffe and Sean Brawley. "Australia's Asian Garrisons: Decolonisation and the Colonial Dynamics of Expatriate Military Communities in Cold War Asia." *Australian Historical Studies* 51, no. 2 (2020): 184–211.

Tyrrell, Ian. *Reforming the World: The Creation of America's Moral Empire*. Princeton, NJ: Princeton University Press, 2010.

Umetsu, Hiroyuki. "Australia's Action Towards Accepting Indonesian Control of Netherlands New Guinea." *Journal of Pacific History* 41, no. 1 (June 2006): 31–47.

"Australia's Response to the West New Guinea Dispute, 1952–53." *Journal of Pacific History* 39, no. 1 (2004): 59–77.

Unger, Corinna R. *International Development: A Postwar History*. London: Bloomsbury Academic, 2018.

Urry, John. *The Tourist Gaze*, 2nd ed. London: SAGE Publications, 2002.

Van Vleck, Jenifer. *Empire of the Air: Aviation and the American Ascendancy*. Cambridge, MA: Harvard University Press, 2013.

Vickers, Adrian. *Bali: A Paradise Created*. Ringwood, Victoria: Penguin Books, 1989.

Wainwright, David. *The Volunteers: The Story of Overseas Voluntary Service.* London: Macdonald, 1965.

Walker, David. *Stranded Nation: White Australia in an Asian Region.* Crawley, Western Australia: UWA Publishing, 2019.

"General Cariappa Encounters 'White Australia': Australia, India and the Commonwealth in the 1950s." *The Journal of Imperial and Commonwealth History* 34, no. 3 (2006): 389–406.

Anxious Nation: Australia and the Rise of Asia, 1850–1939. St. Lucia, Queensland: University of Queensland Press, 1999.

Walker, David and Agnieszka Sobocinska, eds. *Australia's Asia: From Yellow Peril to Asian Century.* Crawley, Western Australia: UWA Press, 2012.

Ward, Stuart, ed. *British Culture and the End of Empire.* Manchester, UK: Manchester University Press, 2001.

Washbrook, David. "Avatars of Identity: The British Community in India." In *Settlers and Expatriates: Britons over the Seas* edited by Robert Bickers, pp. 178–204. Oxford: Oxford University Press, 2010.

wa Thiong'o, Ngugi. *Decolonising the Mind: The Politics of Language in African Literature.* London: J. Currey, 1986.

Watson Andaya, Barbara and Leonard Andaya. *A History of Malaysia.* Honolulu, HI: University of Hawai'i Press, 2001.

Wearing, Stephen. *Volunteer Tourism: Experiences That Make a Difference.* Wallingford, UK: CABI, 2001.

Wearing, Stephen and Nancy Gard McGehee. "Volunteer Tourism: A Review." *Tourism Management* 38 (2013): 120–30.

Webb, James B. *Towards Survival: A Programme for Australia's Overseas Aid.* Melbourne: Community Aid Abroad, 1971.

Webster, David. "Development Advisors in a Time of Cold War and Decolonization: The United Nations Technical Assistance Administration, 1950–1959." *Journal of Global History*, 6, no. 2 (2011): 249–72.

Westad, Odd Arne. *The Global Cold War: Third World Interventions and the Making of Our Times.* Cambridge: Cambridge University Press, 2007.

Whelan, Daniel J. "'Under the Aegis of Man': The Right to Development and the Origins of the New International Economic Order." *Humanity* 6, no. 1 (2015): 93–108.

Whitehead, Clive. "Miss Freda Gwilliam (1907–1987): A Portrait of the 'Great Aunt' of British Colonial Education." *Journal of Educational Administration and History* 24, no. 2 (1992): 145–63.

Wieters, Heike. "Ever Tried – Ever Failed? The Short Summer of Cooperation between CARE and the Peace Corps." *International Journal* 70, no. 1 (2015): 147–58.

Williams, Peter and Adrian Moyes. *Not by Governments Alone: The Role of British Non-Governmental Organisations in the Development Decade.* London: Overseas Development Institute, 1964.

Windmiller, Marshall. *The Peace Corps and Pax Americana.* Washington, DC: Public Affairs Press, 1970.

Wirth, Christa. "The Creation of a Postcolonial Subject: The Chicago and Ateneo De Manila Schools and the Peace Corps in the Philippines, 1960–1970." *Journal of the History of the Behavioural Sciences* 54, no. 1 (2018): 5–24.

Young, Alden. *Transforming Sudan.* Cambridge: Cambridge University Press, 2017.

Zeitlin, Arnold. *To the Peace Corps, with Love.* New York: Doubleday, 1965.

Zhou, Taomo. *Migration in the Time of Revolution: China, Indonesia, and the Cold War.* Ithaca, NY: Cornell University Press, 2019.

Zimmerman, Jonathan. "Beyond Double Consciousness: Black Peace Corps Volunteers in Africa, 1961–1971." *The Journal of American History* 82, no. 3 (1995): 999–1028.

INDEX

Printed in the USA
CPSIA information can be obtained
at www.ICGtesting.com
LVHW091659201223
766987LV00003B/195

9 781108 746885